THE CHANGING FACE OF
SOUTHEAST ASIA

THE CHANGING FACE OF
Southeast Asia

AMRY VANDENBOSCH
RICHARD BUTWELL

KENTUCKY PAPERBACKS
UNIVERSITY OF KENTUCKY PRESS
Lexington, 1967

COPYRIGHT © 1966 by the University of Kentucky Press, Lexington
Manufactured in the United States of America. Library of Congress Catalog Card No. 66-16234.

PREFACE

TEN YEARS AGO the present authors surveyed the scene in Southeast Asia in the wake of the 1954 Geneva Conference on Indochina and on the eve of Britain's grant of independence to Malaya, the last remaining major European colonial holding in the area. They sought to explain the previous decade of political development in Southeast Asia, the most momentous to date in the region's history. Despite the establishment of a Communist state in North Vietnam as an aspect of the 1954 Geneva settlement, the prospects for the growth and survival of several democratic states in Southeast Asia seemed fairly bright a decade ago. Externally, Southeast Asia was moving toward a position of greater importance in international relations, but man's hopes for peace did not then seem to hang in the balance because of any war taking place at the time in the area.

Ten years later the situation had changed dramatically—or so it seemed. Autocracy was the general type of political system to be found in the area, and Southeast Asia was, at long last, at the very center of world political attention. The state of world peace—or war—could clearly be influenced by what happened in the countries to China's south and east of India.

Preface

When the authors sought to revise their earlier work, *Southeast Asia among the World Powers,* they soon found themselves writing a new book. That book is the present volume, which includes modest excerpts from their 1957 work in its historical sections but is otherwise an altogether new survey.

The need for such a new look at Southeast Asia requires little justification. It is as self-evident as the events of recent years are frightening in the ways in which they seem to threaten the peace not only of Southeast Asia but also of an already more than moderately troubled world. Few, however, fully anticipated ten years ago the developments of the last decade. But, if these events were not wholly predicted, they must still be explained in order that we may better understand where we are and the direction in which we are moving.

The United States in mid-1966 was seeking both to check the Communists militarily in South Vietnam and to negotiate the earliest possible honorable settlement with its adversary. The war in Vietnam seemed to have become almost overnight the most important foreign policy problem the United States had faced since the end of the Second World War. It was a problem for America—not only because it threatened and therefore tested the global leadership of the United States—but also because it could lead to a major war with Communist China and, no less equally important, could have most serious consequences for the rest of increasingly interrelated Southeast Asia. The nations that lay beyond Vietnam in different directions—Laos, Cambodia, Thailand, Burma, the Philippines, Malaysia and Indonesia —stood variously prepared for the possible fall of Vietnam as for other major challenges of the youth of their independence.

This volume seeks to survey the present state of these nations, being concerned not only with their internal and international politics as such but, most importantly, with the

Preface

relationship between the two. The political development of these nations is surveyed in separate chapters, and these are followed by examination of the international relations of the region and American foreign policy toward the area.

Some of the material in these chapters is new, reflecting the research interests of the two authors. Other material is drawn from the rapidly increasing body of literature dealing with the politics and policies of the Southeast Asian countries, and acknowledgment is made here of the influence of such literature upon the writing of this book. One or the other of the authors, in addition, has visited all of the Southeast Asian countries except North Vietnam—in some cases several times—since their initial collaborative effort appeared in 1957. They hope that such greater personal familiarity with the area—and time—have additionally equipped them for the task they have assumed for a second time—largely because of their affection for the peoples of Southeast Asia and their concern for their future development and America's relations with them.

Amry Vandenbosch
Richard Butwell

University of Kentucky
Lexington, Kentucky

CONTENTS

		page
	Preface	v
1.	Southeast Asia: Politics of a New Era	1
2.	Indonesia: Protracted Revolution	21
3.	Malaysia: Crisis of Confrontation	74
4.	The Philippines: Doubting Democracy	107
5.	Vietnam: Cork in the Bottle?	160
6.	Laos: Captive of Conflict	200
7.	Cambodia: Land of Strange Politics	220
8.	Burma: From Buddha to Mars	239
9.	Thailand: Soldiers in the Saddle	279
10.	International Relations of Southeast Asia	319
11.	American Policy in Southeast Asia	360
12.	Change in the Making	410
	Bibliographical Note	421
	Index	429

CHAPTER 1

SOUTHEAST ASIA
Politics of a New Era

MODERN POLITICAL SYSTEMS are the primary means for attempting to solve problems of a public character, with the control of government the chief goal of the competitors for power. The purpose of this pursuit of power is influence over such policies as are formulated by government and subsequently administered by various of its agencies. Those interests which seek to influence public decision-making and policy execution in areas of their concern hope either to obtain or increase advantages for themselves or to prevent undesirable action.

At least two such types of political systems exist side by side in contemporary Southeast Asia. One of these systems embraces all of Southeast Asia. This is by no means a centralized system after the fashion of the more integrated nation-states, but then neither is that of the world as a whole —which few would deny is today an increasingly interdependent political system, the diversity of its constituent parts notwithstanding. A political system Southeast Asia also surely is, with highly developed competing national (and other) interests striving to influence decisions of importance to the whole area, such as the region's commitment (or noncommitment) in worldwide political controversies and the extent of state economic activity in the area at large.

Each of the Southeast Asian lands has at the same time its own national political system—some of these, most conspicuously Laos, far from fully integrated. In Vietnam's case, there are both North and South political systems of clearly distinguishable character as well as the larger Vietnamese political system within which the Communist and non-Communist portions of the divided and wartorn country interact. The difficulties attending a decision on Laotian neutralization in 1961-1962 clearly attest to the frequent autonomy of such national political processes. The great powers, including both the United States and Communist China, had reached a meeting of the political minds, however unpalatable to various of them in different ways. But for more than a year the world waited for the Laotians to reach comparable agreement among themselves. There may not be a real Laotian nation in fact, but there is a Laotian political process identical with the geographical extent of the so-called nation of Laos.

The countries of Southeast Asia, collectively forming a political system, are distinguished by several common characteristics. They are certainly subject to some of the same influences, and there are, of course, "rules of the game," which, though rarely articulated as such, are fairly widely understood (even as they are undergoing change). On the other hand, it should be noted that some extremely important political events within particular countries have failed to influence in any apparent respect the way in which neighboring countries behaved—for example, Burma's army coup of 1962. Singapore's race riots of mid-1964, however, clearly encouraged Indonesian boldness in pursuit of the policy of "confrontation"—even to the point of apparent encouragement by the Djakarta government of a second outbreak between Malays and Chinese after the first seemingly spontaneous clashes.

Southeast Asia

The most conspicuous—and important—characteristic of Southeast Asia as a political system is the interaction, which is increasing in both quantity and intensity, among its parts. A quarter of a century ago, what happened in the Philippines was not of major immediate importance to Indonesia, although of long-range importance more than was generally realized at the time. Indonesian nationalism, for example, was unquestionably stimulated by the greater maturity of Filipino nationalism and the fact that the Americans had set a timetable for Philippine independence. But today Indonesia far more decisively influences the Philippines than either state had previously influenced the other. The most obvious area is foreign policy. But, domestically, such influence is also considerable and of both a positive and a negative sort—that is, the Philippines is encouraged to do some things and not to do others because of Indonesia's nearby presence and its particular behavior. Indonesian economic failures have not moved the Philippines to imitate Djakarta's example in this policy area, but Indonesian emphasis on the results of the change from foreign to indigenous control of government has had an influence on Filipino attitudes toward remaining American economic interests and, even more profoundly, on the style and intensity of Philippine nationalism (with all that this means in terms of domestic and foreign policy-making).

THE INFLUENCE OF GEOGRAPHY

There are many factors which help to make Southeast Asia an internally interacting political system. One of these is geography. Southeast Asia is set off physically from other areas of human habitation. High mountains divide the area from China and India to the north, except for the northeast coastal region of Vietnam, and oceans form natural boundaries to the east, south, and west. This is not to say that Southeast Asia is forced by physical circumstances to be wholly internally oriented. As a matter of fact, the region is much involved in major aspects of worldwide international relations both economically and politically. North Vietnam, for example, is a communist country caught in the controversy between Moscow and Peking. At the same time, however, North Vietnam itself looks to the south and the west—not only in the direction of South Vietnam, against which it has waged a guerrilla-style war since the late 1950s, but also towards Laos and Cambodia and even Thailand (and perhaps beyond). What happens in North Vietnam, not to mention Vietnam as a whole, clearly influences the behavior of the other states of Southeast Asia—in part because the region is a distinct and interrelated geographical whole, making it virtually impossible for any country within the area to isolate itself from the other parts politically.

Location is a major geographical influence on political behavior throughout Southeast Asia, even when that behavior differs dramatically from country to country in response to the same stimuli. Strategically situated on the main sea route between India and China (from which the term "Indochina" stems), Southeast Asia is much influenced by fear of its big and immediate neighbor, China—internally in such areas as freedom of movement and speech as well as in foreign policy decisions involving such alternatives as alignment or nonalignment. The ease of access to Southeast Asia provided by the very waters which separate the region from its neighbors on three sides is a constant threat to the area as witnessed by its recent history of prolonged external subjection.

One consequence of the circumstance of physical fragmentation is the fact that Southeast Asia's several states are the weaker both because of their size and their continuous concern over relations with their neighbors within the area: Malaysia in reply to Indonesia's policy of confrontation, Thailand in response to Cambodia's accommodation to Peking, and South Vietnam concerning supply routes into its territory from North Vietnam through Laos. The largest country in Southeast Asia is Indonesia, which occupies 750,000 square miles and has a population of about 103 million persons. Burma is the second biggest state territorially but with a total land area much smaller than Indonesia's (more than 260,000 square miles), the Philippines the country with the second largest population (30 million). The other countries are even smaller. Although Southeast Asia as a whole exceeds 1.7 million square miles inhabited by more than 225 million persons, there are three times as many people in China as in all the Southeast Asian countries combined. And China's land area is twice as great as that of the eleven lands which are its southern neighbors.

PRE-WESTERN ATTITUDES AND INSTITUTIONS

Southeast Asia also derives some unity from the fact of near regionwide penetration of Indian cultural influences in the era before the coming of the European. The age of Indianization of most of the pre-Western Southeast Asian kingdoms (except Vietnam) is evident in the architectural majesty of Angkor in Cambodia, Borobudur in Indonesia, and Pagan in Burma as well as in religion, language, clothing, and some surviving political attitudes and institutions. Most important among the latter is the continuing impact of the assumed basic nature of politics and the relationship between ruler and ruled in pre-Western times—that is, the status-oriented conception of political roles and the related gap between leaders and led.

The gulf between leaders and led was also a characteristic of colonial times. Although nationalists have alleged that the Europeans interrupted traditionally democratic practices, there is much just plain nonsense in their claims. If anything, the colonial powers seemed more concerned with the lot of their subjects than most of the pre-European monarchs, sultans or chieftains. And they established representative institutions which, however modest and grudgingly offered, exceeded the accomplishments of their indigenous predecessors. The tradition of autocracy has deep roots in Southeast Asia, and these roots have never been killed, although some autocratic political institutions have been replaced or modified. Among the primary social institutions the family, for example, is the source of authoritarian attitudes throughout Southeast Asia, no less in the ostensibly democratic Philippine Republic than in fiercely dictatorial soldier-run Burma.

No less alive is the influence of mysticism in politics, another legacy of the pre-Western period. Long-time Indonesian President Sukarno, Cambodian Chief of State Prince Norodom Sihanouk, and former Burmese Premier U Nu were probably never regarded by most of their countrymen as leaders whose chief function it was to reconcile the competing interests in their societies and to emerge with fairly reasonable answers to public problems—answers that made sense in terms of means-ends relationships. Leaders are regarded throughout most of Southeast Asia as possessing powers that cannot be defined wholly, if even largely, in terms of conventional political skills and support. Exceptions are few, differences in degree many. U Nu was considered by his countrymen to be both a God-king of the traditional Hindu sort and a Buddha-in-the-process-of-becoming (probably in the final cycle of rebirth). Even the Philippines cannot escape description of its politicians in such terms: President Ferdinand E. Marcos, a much decorated World War II hero, was depicted in a popular 1965 campaign biography as possessed of magic powers of survival.

The expressive dimension of politics is clearly more important in all the countries of Southeast Asia than the modern problem-solution or policy aspect. Indonesia's Sukarno and Burma's Nu proclaimed policies for years with only limited attention to their execution. Likewise, in the Philippines it is customary for the Congress to pass laws for which implementing funds are never expected by anyone to be appropriated. It is as if the political leaders were able to accomplish great things only by lifting their hands and saying, "Let it be done!" This is not to ignore the progress registered in many areas by contemporary Southeast Asian governments, particularly Malaysia, Singapore, the Philippines, and Thailand (and Indonesia, to an amazing extent, in the field of education). It is just that there is a widely prevalent attitude, a holdover of the pre-Western era, that does not relate ends to means in problem solution and which gives a singular unity and mutual understanding to the several national parts of the broader Southeast Asian political process.

THE COLONIAL LEGACY

Another major influence shaping the regional political process results from the period of Western colonial domination, which greatly varied in duration and intensity among the countries, even influencing independent Thailand. Both the benefits and the problems of colonialism have survived withdrawal of the former imperial powers. Economically, the West left the Southeast Asian countries with largely "colonial economies"; that is, the economies are based on the production of raw materials and the extraction of minerals for shipment to other countries with price and other circumstances which are difficult to control partly because of differences in the character of agricultural and manufacturing activities.

The growth of cities is an important legacy of the Western era or, in the case of Thailand (and Bangkok), of indigenous adoption of key facets of Western life. The new elites which today govern the several Southeast Asian countries are mainly urban-based, a major consequence born of forces set in motion by the European presence. Since independence the Southeast Asian governments have probably never been more dissimilar than they are today, ranging from the largely successful Filipino and Malaysian experiments with democracy to the communist and military dictatorships respectively of North Vietnam and Burma. But are the real political processes of these lands as different as their governmental structures seem to suggest? Probably not. The urban-based few rule in Southeast Asia—no less in the Philippines than Burma (though in a different fashion).

Such urban elite rule, differing more in form than in the reality of government by the few, is a characteristic of all the Southeast Asian countries. In varying degrees, political decisions are made in not dissimilar ways from country to country. On many issues, indeed, the various elites must consider the response of elites in adjacent countries as much as mass opinion in their own lands. At the same time, however, these elites—as in the case of the colonial elites before them—are sowing the seeds of their own destruction, whether they realize it or not. They are extending education to the many, for example, at a pace unparalleled in the history of Southeast Asia. This, too, is a consequence of the past Western association, none of the Southeast Asian lands having had higher institutions of learning before the European era and some of them hardly any schools at all. It also reflects a continuing self-image of inferiority in comparison with foreigners that can only be corrected by intensive education.

ANTICOLONIALISM AND NATIONALISM

This attitude of inferiority, possibly most pronounced where least acknowledged, cannot be divorced from the ideological premise most accepted by the leaders of all the Southeast Asian countries—whether democratic or communist, soldier or civilian, Moslem or Buddhist—that colonialism was a grave evil and must be ended in all its manifestations. Anticolonialism is the most important ideological common denominator of the outlook of the several Southeast Asian ruling elites, though not probably the only such common denominator. This anticolonialism may express itself in different ways on many occasions, but on others it does not.

There is every reason to believe, accordingly, that the North Vietnamese political leadership wishes to minimize Chinese influence over its country as much as possible—just as Filipinos are growing increasingly restive over persisting American obstacles to development of national economic autonomy. The world has called this urge for independence nationalism, one of the most potent political forces in all the Southeast Asian countries today. Whether it sufficiently unites the peoples of these lands, on the other hand, is another matter. It is also open to question whether what is called nationalism is always nationalism. That is to say, there are interests in Southeast Asia today, conservative as well as communist (and military as much as economic), that seek to use nationalism as a justification for the satisfaction of their more narrow aspirations.

Nationalism came into being, in major measure, in response to the Western colonial presence and to an outside world to which the European imperial powers largely introduced most of Southeast Asia. Whereas European nationalism sought to explain, justify and perpetuate an increasingly well established state of existence, Southeast Asian nationalism represents an attempt to find answers to questions of individual and group identity that are claimed to restrict the countries of the area from fulfilling many of their proclaimed objectives. Hence, there is a "Burmese Way to Socialism"— which is not that basically different from the search for a "true Filipino personality" or for governing arrangements reflective of an "Indonesian soul."

Such nationalism divides. But this may not be its most important characteristic from the vantage point of attempting to understand present-day Southeast Asia. It may well be that national integration is a necessary prerequisite or, at the very least, a required contemporary occurrence of broader regional integration. The fact is that the European colonial powers inadequately integrated the territories over which they ruled in Southeast Asia for varying periods of time. More rabid nationalist elements charge that they held back national integration, which is a false claim. Indonesia is what it is today, territorially and politically, because the Dutch hastened the integration of the Indonesian peoples to a far greater extent than any other single factor in their history. But the task, a gigantic one, was never completed. Such imperfect integration characterizes even the Philippines, perhaps the most unified of the Southeast Asian countries as a result of the length and intensity of the common government and policies of its imperial rulers (both Spanish and American but particularly the former).

The integrative needs of today are not wholly of an ethno-political character, though these are very important (most especially in the case of Burma). Economic integration also is an imperative. Economic development in the still very recent past was not primarily in terms of national needs. Moreover, tasks formerly performed by aliens in the interest of aliens, whether Western or Asian, must now be performed by nationals or in conformity with national goals. Equally important, military establishments have been formed which are designed to defend national needs and goals rather than to protect, for example, a "life-line" from formerly imperial Britain to erstwhile dominion Australia via ex-colony Singapore.

Such nationalism does not mean that there is not a functioning political system among the country-units of contemporary Southeast Asia. A political system is still a political system, even though divided into component parts.

COMMON PROBLEMS

Still another factor linking the several countries of Southeast Asia is the similarity of the problems they face. These are primarily, but not exclusively, of two types: economic

Southeast Asia

and political. Although many of these problems are shared with other developing states, such as those of Africa and the Middle East, others are not—for instance, the presence in all the Southeast Asian countries of sizable Chinese minorities (a major problem in view of the fact that China is the world's most populous country, has traditionally sought to influence its southern neighbors, and can apparently count on the support of large numbers of overseas Chinese who still regard themselves as more Chinese than members of the societies in which they live).

Foremost among the common economic problems is development or modernization. All of the Southeast Asian countries are still underdeveloped economically—some (like Laos) much more so than others (like the Philippines). The proclaimed paths to economic development of the Southeast Asian countries vary, but the problems they seek to solve are similar. Each, for example, wishes to industrialize—meaning to manufacture ultimately more than merely consumer goods or other products of light industry. But each lacks the capital and technical knowledge and sometimes even the market. The size of most of the Southeast Asian countries, moreover—Indonesia is the exception—is such that none can probably expect to produce the full range of goods of the larger industrial powers whom they have sought to imitate (the U.S.S.R., the United States, Britain, or Japan).

A pressing economic problem for the insular countries—the Philippines, Indonesia and Malaysia—is food production. Malaysia indeed must import to survive. Indonesia and the Philippines are somewhat better off; they grow enough to feed their rapidly expanding populations but not of the staple their nationals want most of all (rice). Burma, Thailand, and, in normal times, Vietnam are rice exporters—major suppliers, as a matter of fact, to the importing peninsular-insular lands to their south. But even the former lands do not export as much rice as they once did, partly because of their own growing populations.

There are at least two ways in which common economic problems reinforce an overall Southeast Asian political system. The example of one country's success or failure is not lost on the others. Particularly will this probably be so in the future if a communist Vietnam, whether united or not, registers spectacular accomplishments economically. Even more important, however, may be the general influence which the fact of being economically underdeveloped has on both elite and mass attitudes the region over. Foreign aid and credits (governmental and private) can meet crises and contribute to long-term development, but there is always an element of uncertainty as to how long such assistance will be continued and on what terms. This circumstance is a characteristic of all the countries, including communist North Vietnam.

The political problems of contemporary Southeast Asia indicate even more dramatically the existence of an overall political system. Although all of the states of the area are concerned with their relations with countries external to the region, particularly China, most—not all—are at least as actively engaged in competition or cooperation with other countries of Southeast Asia itself. Particularly is this so with respect to the settlement of boundary problems remaining from the colonial era. The borders of the lands of Southeast Asia are by no means definitively or satisfactorily established, and problems deriving therefrom can be expected to continue for many years to come.

Several of the states of Southeast Asia are today seeking to carve out the largest possible territories for themselves within the region. Thus they cannot avoid interacting. Indonesia has attempted to force Malaya to disgorge Sarawak and Sabah, previously absorbed to form the new state of Malaysia. The Philippines also has laid claim to Sabah. The Communists of North Vietnam have sought control not only of South Vietnam but also of Laos (and probably will seek to dominate Cambodia, too, in the future). Cambodia has frequently expressed its fear of alleged attempts by Thailand and South Vietnam to take some of its territory. The Laotian government feared that Thai intervention in its behalf against the rebel communist Pathet Lao in 1961-1962 might not have been followed by the withdrawal of Thai forces from lowland Laos.

The fact that the boundaries established by the former colonial powers did not coincide with the pattern of settlement of various ethnic groupings adds to the problem. The same peoples live on both sides of the Indonesian-Malaysian border on the island of Borneo. Malays also live in the four southernmost Thai provinces. The inhabitants of Mindanao, largest of the Philippine islands, are Malays (like the Filipinos and Indonesians) but also Moslems (like only the Indonesians). The Shans, currently the most troublesome of Burma's minorities, are more closely related to the neighboring Thai than to the majority Burmans in their own country. It is inconceivable that wholly separated national political systems could be established under such circumstances.

Boundary controversies and overlapping patterns of ethnic group settlement are not the only political problems that draw the Southeast Asian countries together in a single system. Some of these nations are also partners in the common defense of their region, Thailand and the Philippines being members of the Southeast Asian Treaty Organization (SEATO). Others, including the Philippines and Thailand as well as Malaysia, have aided South Vietnam's government in its efforts to put down the insurgency led by the North Vietnamese directed Vietcong. The Philippines, Malaysia, and Indonesia tried—how hard is open to question—to establish channels of political consultation through what they called "Maphilindo." The first two countries and Thailand attempted to cooperate economically within the framework of the Association of Southeast Asia (ASA).

Some of the internal political problems faced by several of the Southeast Asian countries also serve to draw these nations

INDIA
CHINA
E. PAKISTAN
Calcutta
Burma
Laos
Hanoi
BAY OF BENGAL
Vientiane
Thailand
N.Vietnam
Rangoon
ANDAMAN SEA
Bangkok
S.Vietnam
Pnompenh
Cambodia
Saigon
Brunei
Malaysia
Kuala Lumpur
Singapore
SARAWAK
SUMATRA
KALIMANTAN
(Borneo)
INDIAN OCEAN
Djakarta
JAVA

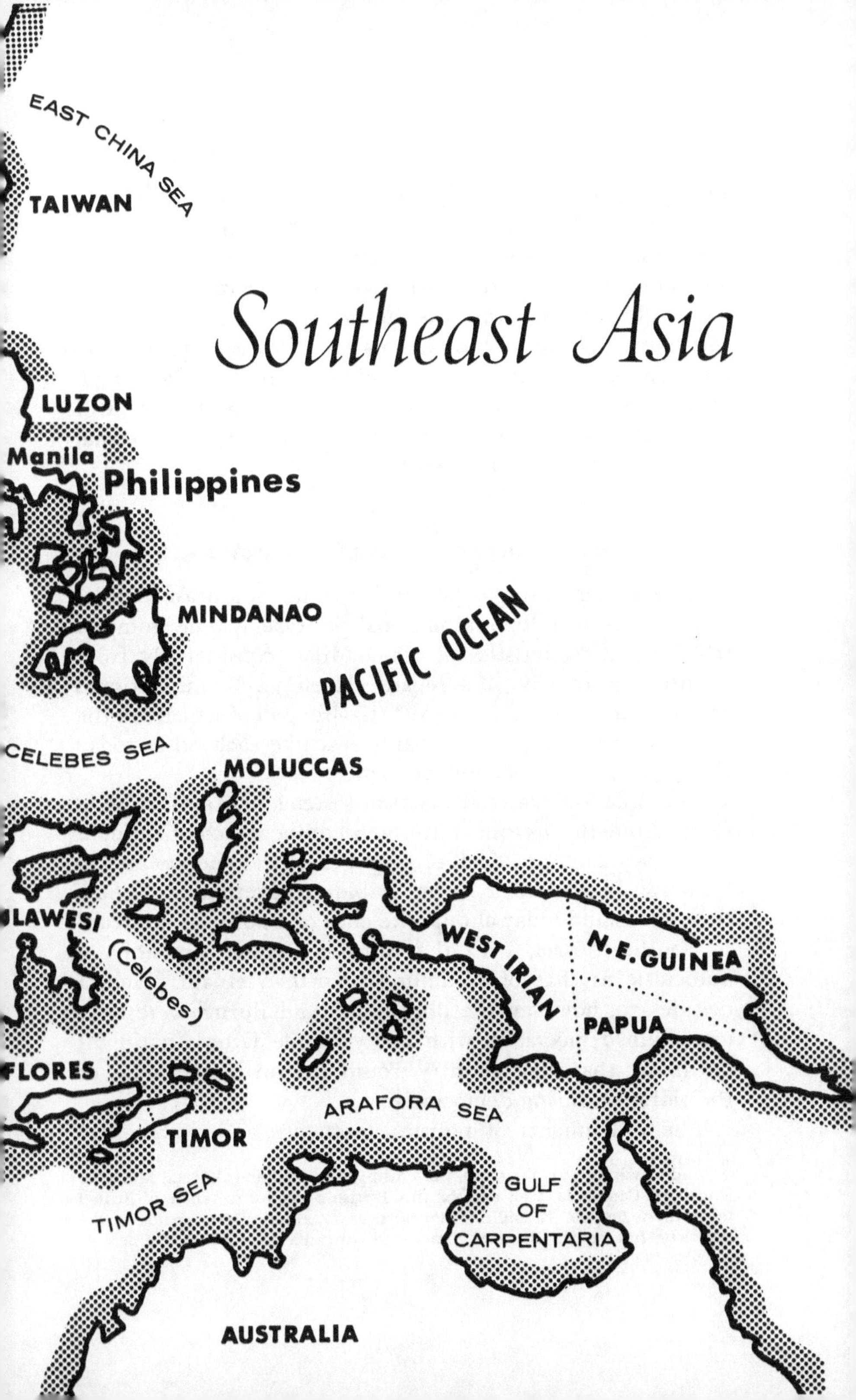

into patterns of persisting interaction. Practically all the governments fear intervention by a neighboring state in support of one or another dissident faction. Democracy's failure —or autocracy's, for that matter—in one country can have discernible effects within the political process of a neighboring state. Failure of efforts at national integration may encourage external intervention; success, on the other hand, may embolden a state to seek to expand to embrace still other peoples. Instability, whatever its cause, makes external subversion the easier to perpetrate.

INDIVIDUAL NATIONAL POLITICAL SYSTEMS

Besides being a single political system, Southeast Asia is also a series of individual national political systems, some of the basic characteristics of which differ considerably from country to country. There are eleven* different national political processes in Southeast Asia—no two of which are the same. In fact, they are probably less like each other today than at any time since independence.

The different national political systems of Southeast Asia range from the unique Filipino wedding of constitutional democracy and practical oligarchy to the xenophobic nationalist absolutism of Burma's soldier government. These two states stand today at opposite ends of a political spectrum in Southeast Asia, with the Burmese regime probably as autocratic as that of communist North Vietnam. Half a decade ago, however, the Philippines and Burma were both ostensible democracies with many of the latter's nationals optimistic that their country would remain in the ranks of the world's aspiring democracies.

The instruments of political influence and power vary

* Indonesia, the two Vietnams, the Philippines, Thailand, Burma, Malaysia, Singapore, Cambodia, Laos and the tiny British-protected sultanate of Brunei in northern Borneo. In addition, Portugal governs the eastern portion of the otherwise Indonesian island of Timor and Australia eastern New Guinea.

from country to country in Southeast Asia today. Political parties, for example, have never been less significant, the Philippines, Malaysia, and Singapore excepted. On the other hand, the chief interests of some of the national societies are beginning to assume new importance as they organize to influence public policy. Such interests are probably as important today as they have ever been—in Indonesia and Thailand, neither of which is a democracy by any stretch of the imagination, as well as in the Philippines and Malaysia. In some countries—Laos would be a good example—the military is one of the chief organized interests as well as an arm of state policy. In other countries, Burma, Thailand, and Vietnam, the army is the government, and there can be little question about its involvement in nonmilitary matters.

Although there have been similarities among the changes that have taken place in some of the countries of Southeast Asia since independence, these lands, on the whole, have experienced quite different patterns of political development in the nearly two decades since the first Southeast Asian country gained its independence from colonial rule. It is not merely that the Southeast Asian countries differ markedly one from the other but that they seem likely to differ even more in the years immediately ahead.

The differing attitudes of the national political elites on a wide range of questions produce variations in the policies proclaimed by such elites. Not only are there differences in patterns of economic development, primarily involving the extent to which the methods of socialism are adopted, but there are also important variations in the ways in which Filipinos, Cambodians, and Vietnamese, for example, view their Chinese minorities, foreigners in general, and other subjects.

There are ingredients of practically every possible point of view present in each of the several Southeast Asian countries. The difference between countries, resultingly, is many times one of emphasis. But this variation in emphasis is nonetheless major. Consider, for example, prevailing elite attitudes on the subject of mass participation in selection of political leaders and public policy formation. The official Filipino and Malaysian political ideologies proclaim the desirability of popular choice. But not so that of Burma. Burmese are to decide questions primarily involving Burma, the Ne Win government states, but which Burmese? Jailed former Premier U Nu? The banned political parties? The dissolved Parliament? Or dictator General Ne Win? Ne Win's answer has been proclaimed. But not all Burmese agree, even if they cannot act to support their beliefs.

The state of instruments of political communication also varies from land to land. Probably no country in the world has a freer press than the Philippines. Burma's last independently owned newspaper, on the other hand, was "nationalized" in 1964. The press in Thailand is privately owned, but editors and reporters know the *de facto* bounds of free speech. There is likewise great variation from country to country in terms of what may be called the tendency to use force for political purposes. Riots take place far less frequently in military-dominated Thailand than in autocratic General Ne Win's Burma—more often in democratic Singapore than in the similarly oriented Philippine Republic.

THE PAST MEETS THE PRESENT

The several states of Southeast Asia had quite different political systems traditionally—whether or not such ancient kingdoms were identical with the present-day nations of this part of the world. In addition, the various peoples of Southeast Asia lived for periods ranging from 45 to 350 years under different former colonial rulers. They also gained their independence from these rulers in different ways. The Indonesians and Vietnamese fought bitter wars,

Southeast Asia

the Burmese threatened to fight, the Filipinos and the Malaysians neither fired nor threatened to fire a single shot to free themselves from their American or British rulers.

Although the colonial rulers differed considerably one from another, they had experienced most of the same historical forces at roughly the same time—nationalism, industrialization, and such. They reflected, moreover, a fairly common ideological heritage—much more so than, say, Burma and the Philippines at the time of the coming of the Englishman and the Spaniard (at quite separated points in history). The colonial embrace made the several Southeast Asian peoples seem more alike than they actually were. They had to play the foreign ruler's game, so to speak, in order to survive. And surely one of the implicit conditions of independence, when granted rather than fought for, was the adoption of a state form consistent with the ideology of the departing colonial power.

Once the colonial embrace was removed, however, the natural impulses, political and otherwise, of the various Southeast Asian countries began to express themselves—whether in Sukarno's "guided democracy," U Nu's "Buddhist state," or Norodom Sihanouk's "Khmer socialism." The fact is that the Southeast Asian nations returned to form—far from completely, of course, but more so than many foreign observers suspected for a long time (or some do even today). The politics of such countries reflect today the long submerged influences of primary social forces—like religion and the pattern of intrafamily relations. They also represent a conscious search for the unique in the historical past—largely in reaction to the prospect of being no more than inferior copies of their former colonial masters ("little brown brothers," as the Filipinos say).

At the same time, the impact of worldwide forces—like the cold war, the industrial revolution, and growing economic interdependence—makes isolation quite impossible. Southeast Asia, once an outpost of world politics, can probably never again enjoy such complete noninvolvement in the main issues of international relations. Likewise, no Southeast Asian country can enjoy full freedom from influence, direct or indirect, from its nearest neighbors—including the other states of Southeast Asia. Hence, the simultaneous existence of both distinct national political systems in Southeast Asia and a broader, equally vital Southeast Asian political system.

CHAPTER 2

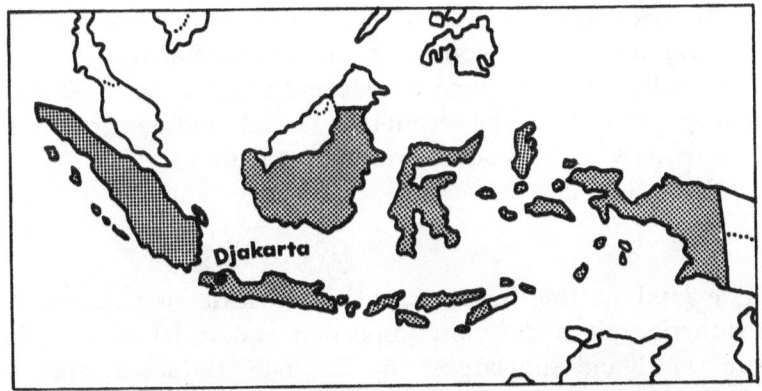

INDONESIA
Protracted Revolution

INDONESIA IN THE two decades following World War II came increasingly to be known throughout the world as "Sukarno's Indonesia." During these years Indonesia moved from a so-called democracy of appointed legislators and other leaders to a freely and fairly elected cabinet government, then to an increasingly pro-Communist dictatorship. Sukarno, as his country's never-elected president, was probably the most important political constant throughout this period of change. The story of Indonesia's political development was in effect an account of Sukarno's amazing adaptability to the various roles allowed him by his evolving and restless nation. As dictator, Sukarno nonetheless mirrored as much as directed Indonesia's political development. Dictators, however, have a tendency to lose their power; few die in office at the peak of their authority—except by the assassin's bullet. And so it was that the start of the third decade of Sukarno's presidency saw a decline in his influence; the Indonesian army, reacting to an abortive coup attempted by Sukarno's Communist allies, appeared to be seeking to reduce him to a figurehead. A new political order was in the process of being established. And the roots of it all were variously located in the bygone Dutch colonial era, the revolutionary years of 1945-1949, the subsequent decade-and-a-half of political mismanagement, and the economic, social and geographical foundations of the modern Indonesian nation.

A KEY NATION

The land of the Indonesians has at least two claims to distinction: it is the most important equatorial country in the world and the largest insular state. Its actual area is about 733,000 square miles—nearly three times the size of France—but, because it is composed of over 3,000 islands, this territory is spread over an area of the earth's surface more than four times as great. In terms of population, Indonesia is the fifth largest country in the world today. In October 1961, when the first census in 30 years was taken, its population stood at 97,085,000. Since its people are increasing at the rate of over two million a year, its total population is now well over 100,000,000. Whether or not this rapid growth is a source of strength, a people who constitute a thirtieth of the human race must play an important role in world politics. And when they occupy a territory strategically located athwart important sea and air routes, their potential role in international politics is greatly enhanced.

Climate has been an important factor in the shaping of present-day Indonesia. Much of the country, for example, has a heavy rainfall, and, where the rains are too abundant, the soil is leached of nutrients and impoverished. This undoubtedly accounts for the sparse population of Borneo. Java, by contrast, supports an extraordinarily dense popula-

Indonesia

tion because its rainfall is considerably less and its soil has been renewed by recent volcanic activity.

Although a rich country, Indonesia's people are poor. It has considerable resources and is an important producer of commodities for the world market. Before World War II (1939) its share of the total world exports of a number of basic commodities was large: cinchona bark (quinine), 91 percent; pepper, 86; kapok, 72; rubber, 37; agave, 33; copra products, 27; oil palm products, 19; tin, 17; petroleum, 17; sugar, 11; and coffee, 4 percent. While the number of people who must share this wealth has increased by half since 1939, production has not kept pace. Indeed, production has declined absolutely; it is below what it was on the eve of the Second World War. Undeveloped or unused natural resources do not raise levels of living. Before World War II nationalist leaders ascribed their poverty to colonial exploitation, but during the fifteen years of political independence economic conditions have grown worse rather than better, and Indonesians have been getting poorer.

Upon emerging from colonial status, Indonesia experienced the typical psychological and other effects and its revolutionary leaders naturally inveighed bitterly against imperialism. In their struggle for independence the Indonesian nationalist leaders stressed the right of self-determination and democratic government, but within a decade they abandoned responsible, parliamentary government for "guided democracy"; national independence has been won but much personal freedom has been lost; compared with the last decade of Dutch rule before World War II, even political rights have diminished. And today the young republic itself ironically seems bent on an imperialistic course.

Young nationalism anxiously examines the past for evidence of a great national history on which to build ardent expectations of an even greater future. Indonesians like to think of their republic as the successor to earlier Indonesian kingdoms of glorious memory. Only a few of these kingdoms, however, extended their rule over considerable areas—and none brought under control anywhere near all of what is now Indonesian territory. Moreover, their great periods were of short duration. The latest of these kingdoms was Majapahit, a state which controlled Java and extended its rule over other islands. Victory over an invading Chinese army inaugurated the history of this empire, which endured from about 1300 to 1500 A.D. or until about the time the first Europeans arrived.

Indonesia would seem to enjoy a high degree of religious homogeneity since about 85 percent of the population adheres to Islam. Yet even here outward appearances are somewhat deceiving. Islam made a powerful impact on society in some areas but much less in others. Moreover, there are conflicting currents in Indonesian Islam. There is an old school which has made considerable concessions to mystical animism, and a new school, relatively more orthodox, which is reformist-modernist. Some Moslems want a secular state, others an Islamic one embracing the whole of Indonesia; the latter have resorted to violence and terrorism to achieve their objective. Moreover, large religious minorities occupy compact areas, such as the nearly two million Hindus on Bali, and the Christians totaling some five million are concentrated in some three or four areas: north central Sumatra, north Sulawesi (the Minahassa), Flores and the Moluccas. There are also about two and a half million Chinese, whose religious and social life is quite different. They are unpopular, not so much because of their religion as because of their business ability.

DUTCH COLONIAL RULE

The Indonesian state is the product of three centuries of Dutch rule, which brought the numerous widely scattered islands under a common dominion.

The first Dutch ships came to Java in 1596. They were

followed by many others. These Netherlanders did not come to establish an empire; they came to trade, but they soon discovered that they could not trade profitably unless they also ruled. Competition by other European powers could only drive up commodity prices in the Indies and reduce prices obtained for them in Europe. The Dutch accordingly sought to obtain a monopoly by expelling the Portuguese, whose arrival had preceded their own. To open markets and to insure subsequent monopolies, alliances with native rulers were made. To prevent ruinous competition among Netherlanders themselves, the United East India Company was formed in 1602; it received from the Dutch government a monopoly of all commerce with Asia. Uncertain relations with the Indonesian sultans—and hostility and wars among the latter—convinced the East India Company that the conditions for profitable trade could be created only by establishing its own rule. Although the company made large profits for a lengthy period, toward the end of the 18th century it was experiencing grave financial trouble, and in 1798 the Dutch government took over its affairs.

The character of Dutch colonial rule helps to explain some of the more important developments since independence. One of Indonesia's most basic problems is its lack of national unity. "Unity in Diversity" is the hopeful motto of Indonesia. There can be no doubt of the diversity, but real unity is more of an aspiration than a reality. Obviously, the geography of the country presents formidable barriers to the unification of its various peoples. Indonesia is composed of several large—and thousands of small—islands scattered over a very large area. East and west it stretches some 3,400 miles and about 1,000 north and south. Furthermore, there is little ethnological unity in Indonesia; according to the 1930 census, there were nearly fifty ethnic groups, most of them with their own language.

Nor was Dutch policy such as actively to promote either social unity or economic integration. The Netherlands claimed sovereignty over the whole of what is now Indonesia, but large areas in the islands outside Java were either indirectly governed through native chieftans or were only slightly penetrated by Dutch administration. Indeed, the primitive inhabitants of the interior of West Irian were not reached by Dutch administration until after World War II. In the islands and areas in which the Dutch concentrated their activities, administration was intense. Thus the penetration of Western influences has been long and intense on Java and in some other areas, such as Ambon, North Celebes and the East Coast of Sumatra, but very superficial in other parts of the outer islands. As a result social and economic development was uneven in the archipelago. The Dutch avoided the introduction of direct rule as much as possible, leaving the inhabitants under their sultans or semi-hereditary regents and allowing them to continue under their traditional law. This policy of protecting and preserving the native customs and institutions slowed down the cultural unification of the scores of ethnic groups which composed the population of the Indies.

Economic integration of the widespread islands had not developed far at the time of the Japanese invasion. Indonesia remained agrarian. Dutch and other foreign capital was invested in the development of large scale plantation agriculture, which produced for the world market. While this development was truly noteworthy and was of tremendous importance for the economy of the country, it did not make for economic integration. However, transportation between the islands made rapid strides in the last years before the war, and inter-island trade, chiefly between Java and the outer islands, was on the increase. In the last decade before Pearl Harbor the Dutch began actively to promote the industrialization of Java, but such economic change was still in its infancy when the war came.

The pattern of population distribution among the islands makes more difficult the problem of national unification.

Indonesia

Java and the adjacent island of Madura account for less than seven percent of the land area of Indonesia but have two-thirds of the country's total population according to the 1961 census. Java with a population of 63,000,000 has an average density per square mile of over 1,200, which is a greater population density than that of either Belgium or Holland. By contrast, the average density per square mile in the other large islands is as follows: Sumatra 85; Borneo 20; Celebes 96; the Moluccas 96; and West Irian under 5. The population pressure on Java depresses its level of living below that of most of the outer islands where conditions have permitted and stimulated native farmers to produce for the export market. Moreover, the outer islands produce the export commodities, such as petroleum, tin, rubber and copra, which earn the bulk of the foreign exchange. Being more prosperous, the inhabitants of the outer islands naturally must pay higher per capita taxes to the central government than do the people on Java. The outer islanders want a greater portion of the foreign exchange which they earn and the taxes which they pay to be used to develop their own areas. They look upon impoverished Java as a burden on the country and a handicap to its development. The inhabitants of Sumatra, Borneo and the Celebes therefore can hardly escape the conclusion that they would be better off without Java.

The main resulting political issue has been that of centralization. The outer islands quite naturally favored federalism, as any highly centralized form of government almost necessarily means rule by Java, with two-thirds of the country's total population, and consequent exploitation of the many islands by one. On the other hand, a strongly decentralized government would mean financial strangulation of the central government and slow but certain economic deterioration for overpopulated Java.

The rebellion which broke out in 1957 was chiefly a revolt against "Javanese centralism" and radicalism. The rebellion was put down but the basic problem remains to plague the Indonesian government. The "confrontation" of the Dutch in the struggle for West Irian (West New Guinea) undoubtedly stirred national sentiments, but the basic differences between Java and the outer islands were not so easily solved. They persist.

The Dutch were reluctant to develop educational facilities for the Indonesians. Closely related to their general policy of respecting native customs and institutions was that of differentiation in accordance with need in education. This led to a great variety of schools to meet the supposedly peculiar requirements of the various population groups—folk and standard schools, Dutch-Indonesian and Dutch-Chinese, and link or connecting schools—while all higher education was Western with Dutch as the medium of instruction. This variety of schools did not help to merge the different ethnic groups into a nation; rather it tended to keep them apart. In all of Indonesia there were fewer than 2,000 college and university students on the eve of Pearl Harbor. The Philippines with about one-fourth of the population of Indonesia had more than four times as many young people pursuing higher education, though the standards were considerably lower. Thus the young Indonesian republic began its independent existence with a dearth of educated persons for positions of leadership.

The situation with respect to government was similar. Standards of public administration were exceptionally high, but few Indonesians were found in the higher positions. Representative bodies had not been granted wide powers, and Europeans held membership in them far out of proportion to their numbers in the population. The Indies Civil Service was composed of a body of highly selected and well-trained persons who until the last two decades could carry on their work free from political interference and the pressure of public opinion. Within the limits of the system they acquitted themselves well, but the sytem did not develop a

Indonesia

democratic society or government. At the time of the fall of the country to Japan no Indonesian had yet been appointed to the governorship of a province and only one to a headship of a department of the central government.

The first representative body for the whole of the Indies, called the Volksraad, was established in 1917. During the first decade of its existence it had only advisory powers. Though the number of Netherlanders in the Indies constituted less than one percent of the population, nearly one-half of the seats of the Volksraad were reserved for them. In the provincial councils the membership was distributed in about the same way, but in the regency councils the Indonesians predominated. The urban councils were dominated by Europeans. The provincial and regency councils had functioned for only about a decade before the Japanese invasion. Thus when the Indonesians upon the capitulation of Japan in 1945 determined to take over the reins of government, they had had little experience in politics and administration.

It is generally assumed that Indonesia received a bitter and meager heritage from the long years of Dutch rule. While the inheritance was poor on the educational, administrative, and political side, it was good in at least three respects. In many other dependencies foreigners acquired ownership of much of the land, which is about the only form of wealth in underdeveloped countries, but Indonesia began its independence with no such handicap. Under the provisions of the Netherlands Indies Government Act only indigenous persons could own land; thus the natives could not sell their land to foreigners. The Indonesian republic took over its national estate without a heavy foreign mortage on it.

Secondly, the Indies government owned and operated most of the public utilities and in addition engaged in a wide range of economic activities. It owned and operated pawnshops, railroads, telephone and telegraph services, tramcars, bus lines, gold, silver and coal mines, teak forests, and large cinchona, rubber, tea and guttapercha plantations. The government was also part-owner of corporations which exploited some of the richest oil fields in the country. The new state of Indonesia fell heir to all of these assets.

Thirdly, the Dutch followed a policy of the open door with respect to the external trade of the Indies. Dutch goods received no tariff preference over goods coming into the Indies from other countries. While the Indies' economy was "colonial" in that it produced chiefly primary commodities, it was not heavily dependent upon the market of a single foreign country, as was its neighbor the Philippines, where an abrupt imposition of the full American tariff would have produced serious economic trouble.

WAR AND REVOLUTION

When the Dutch sought to return to the Indies after the capitulation of Japan in 1945 they were astonished and dismayed at the fierceness of the Indonesian nationalism they encountered. On the eve of World War II the Indonesian nationalist movement was relatively mild and immature and seemingly under control. The social convulsion produced by the war and Japanese occupation had wrought a profound change.

The Netherlands was overrun by the Germans in May 1940, and Queen Wilhelmina and her ministers fled to London, where they set up a government in exile. Thus abruptly cut off from the Netherlands, society in the Indies, Dutch as well as Indonesian, underwent a change. The Indonesians demanded political reforms which would make their country a parliamentary democracy with "dominion" status. These requests were made by moderate nationalists, and had the Dutch government dealt with them constructively in the short time remaining before the Japanese invasion, the postwar story might have been somewhat different.

The West suffered such a loss of prestige from the rapid conquest of the region by the Japanese that European rule

Indonesia

on anything like the old basis could never again be restored. In Indonesia the top Dutch officials were replaced by Japanese, but the latter, being wholly ignorant of the local situation and conditions, had to allow their Indonesian subordinates to run the government offices. When in 1944 the Japanese leaders became alarmed at the American advance in the Pacific, they decided that their position in Southeast Asia had to be strengthened, and to secure the cooperation of the Indonesians, they promised them national independence. From that time on, more Indonesians were admitted to positions in the government, including those in the top ranks. After the capitulation some Japanese officers allowed the nationalists to seize stores of arms.

The Netherlands had been completely liberated only a few months before the capitulation of Japan; hence the Dutch government was hardly prepared to meet the problems in its huge dependency on the other side of the world. A week before the surrender, nationalist leaders Sukarno and Mohammad Hatta were summoned to Saigon by the commander in chief of the Japanese armies in Southeast Asia to confer about an immediate proclamation of Indonesian independence. Within a few days the Indonesian leaders returned to Batavia (Djakarta), and on August 17, 1945, independence was declared. The Indonesian nationalists still had six weeks of unhampered freedom in which to consolidate their position. Not until September 29 did the British arrive with a small force to disarm and repatriate the Japanese troops.

The Dutch government was prepared to grant Indonesia a large amount of autonomy within an imperial union, but the representatives of the newly-proclaimed Indonesian republic demanded recognition as a sovereign state, after which, they declared, they would be willing to accept close political relations. After three years of intermittent negotiations, with two "police actions" by Dutch armed forces, followed each time by United Nations' intervention, an agreement was finally reached at a Round Table Conference at The Hague in November 1949. On December 27, 1949, sovereignty was transferred to the United States of Indonesia. The two sovereign states agreed to enter a Netherlands-Indonesian Union for "organized cooperation" in the fields of foreign relations, defense, and financial, economic, and cultural relations.

THE FEDERAL EXPERIMENT

The heart of the nationalist revolution was in Java and in certain areas of Sumatra. These territories constituted the core of the 1945 republic which the Dutch could not crack even though they penetrated them deeply in their "police actions." Outside Java and Sumatra the Dutch had little difficulty in reestablishing their authority, and there they proceeded to organize states which they planned to unite in a federal structure. The republicans felt that the "federalists" were pro-Dutch, not true patriots, and there was considerable hostility between them. But when the Rum-Van Royen agreement, signed on May 7, 1949, made it clear that the Netherlands was about ready to grant Indonesia independence, representatives of the republic and of the federal consultative assembly met in an inter-Indonesian conference to determine the main outlines of the provisional constitution for Indonesia. The draft of the constitution was completed at The Hague during the Round Table Conference. The Dutch were merely informed that the federalists and republicans had agreed on a constitution and were given a copy of the text.

The title assumed by the former Dutch dependency was the "Republic of the United States of Indonesia," and the first article declared it to be "a democratic state of federal structure." The position of the nationalist Republic of Indonesia in the federation was somewhat like that of Prussia in the German Empire. The republic had over 40 percent of the population of the country, and Sukarno and Moham-

Indonesia

mad Hatta, respectively its president and vice president, were chosen to fill the same offices in the federal republic.

It is impossible to know whether the republicans ever intended to give the federal government a real trial, for the movement to dismantle it began immediately after the transfer of sovereignty. The opposition to the federal system was powerfully aided by the attack on Bandung on January 22, 1950, by a rebel force under the leadership of a Dutch adventurer, Captain Raymond ("Turk") Westerling. According to the Indonesian government, this force contained or was assisted by a number of soldiers and officers of the Netherlands and Netherlands Indies army. Shortly thereafter, Sultan Hamid II of West Borneo, a leader among the federalists and a member of the cabinet, was arrested as the mastermind behind the plot. This affair fanned anti-Dutch sentiment and helped to discredit the federal system, which was largely regarded as originally an invention of the Dutch "to divide and rule" and, even after independence, was looked upon as tainted with colonialism. The federal system was not given a decent legal or constitutional burial; it was just abandoned.

A number of reasons were advanced to justify this action. It was asserted that the federal system was too costly, that it required a far larger number of experienced and trained personnel than Indonesia possessed, that the territories of the "states" or "units" were poorly drawn, and that the populations of the "units" were grossly unequal. It is certainly true that the federal structure as set up in the constitution had many weaknesses and defects, but it is difficult to escape the conclusion that the chief motivating force for its destruction was psychological.

The republican leaders felt that they had been deprived of a complete victory by being compelled by force of circumstances to go to The Hague and negotiate a settlement. The federal constitution was a symbol of that failure, and it had to go. For months, however, the government was paralyzed when much needed to be done quickly. Events, moreover, were soon to demonstrate that another important factor was the matter of positions. Most of the offices in the governments of the "federal states" were held by persons regarded by the republicans as cooperators with the Dutch. A quick means of getting the "cos," as the cooperators were called, out of all government positions and filling them with faithful republicans was to replace the federal with a unitary government. For a country with the geographic and ethnic structure of Indonesia, however, the creation of a highly centralized government may have been ill considered.

Indonesia as a federal state had only one cabinet. Hatta, who was vice president, was also the prime minister. He probably represented the best political leadership Indonesia possessed, and he had in his cabinet a number of very able men, but his government had to work under extremely unfavorable conditions.

UNSTABLE CABINET GOVERNMENT

The provisional constitution of the new unitary state went into effect on August 17, 1950, the fifth anniversary of the proclamation of the original republic. Mohammad Natsir, the leader of the Masjumi (Moslem) party, the largest in parliament, was its first prime minister. The Nationalist party, with the second largest number of seats in parliament, was not a member of the government coalition. Although it was on the whole a strong cabinet (which held a position of moderate liberalism), the life of the Natsir cabinet was short. It resigned March 20, 1951.

The Natsir cabinet had to struggle with a number of difficult problems, nearly all of which also plagued succeeding governments. There was, first of all, the question of Indonesia's relations with the Netherlands, including the dispute over West New Guinea. The Dutch and Indonesian representatives at The Hague had been unable to agree on the disposition of this vast jungle area of over 150,000 square miles with a population estimated at less than a million. Indonesians insisted that it be included in their domain, since it was a part of the former Netherlands Indies, but the Dutch maintained that this relationship had been only incidental and that the territory was not an integral part of Indonesia geographically, ethnically, or otherwise. In order to conclude the main business of the conference it was agreed that the "status quo" of the territory would be maintained with the stipulation that "within a year from the date of transfer of sovereignty . . . the question of the political status of New Guinea be determined through negotiations" between the parties. This was in effect an agreement to continue the disagreement, but with the immediate advantage with the Dutch, since the "status quo" left the Netherlands administering the territory. The unwillingness of the Netherlands to surrender the territory to Indonesia embittered Indonesian-Dutch relations.

Thirty-seven days after Natsir's resignation, the Masjumi and Nationalist parties succeeded in forming a coalition government. Headed by Sukiman of the Masjumi, this second government under the unitary system was regarded as conservative. It signed the treaty with Japan at San Francisco, instituted some monetary reforms, and devalued the rupiah.

The Sukiman cabinet came to grief, however, over a matter of foreign policy. The foreign affairs minister signed an agreement with the United States for Mutual Security Agency assistance involving only eight million dollars, largely in the form of badly needed equipment for Indonesia's internal security forces. When the agreement became public, a political furor instantaneously developed, for the Mutual Security Act required all governments receiving aid under it to agree to contribute "to the defensive strength of the free world." Practically every Indonesian political leader regarded the acceptance of even such a mild, vague commitment as a departure from his country's independent, or neutralist, foreign policy. The government submitted its resignation on February 23, 1952, after having held office for nearly ten months.

The third government following federalism's abandonment, which took office on April 1, 1952, represented a coalition of the Masjumi, Nationalist, and five smaller parties. The most important positions, however, were held by Nationalists; the prime minister, Wilopo, was a Nationalist. The Wilopo cabinet wobbled through one crisis after another until it finally fell on the issue of the handling of the land distribution problem on the east coast of Sumatra. But this was not the cause, only the occasion, of the downfall of the cabinet. The two major parties supporting the government became deeply divided on a number of issues, so that cooperation between them became impossible.

A harbinger of Indonesia's future political development occurred during the period of the Wilopo cabinet when in mid-October 1952 certain army elements in effect dictated a decision to the civilian leadership. From this time until its resignation on June 3, 1953, the Wilopo government existed in a "political oxygen tent." The minister of defense, Sultan Buwono of Djokjakarta, was carrying out plans for modernization of the army. The group of former guerrilla officers in the army disliked this policy, chiefly because of their inadequate training, and the large number of former guerrilla fighters within the army likewise feared the plan would mean their removal from the service when the strength of the army would be reduced from 200,000 to 100,000 men.

The issue was politically explosive. A foreign military mission—worse still, a Dutch mission—was advising and aiding the sultan in carrying out the plan. Opponents of the plan charged that the army was losing its revolutionary character and was again acquiring a "colonial" status. Apparently also involved was rivalry between President Sukarno and Sultan

Buwono. The former seemed to fear the role and ambitions of the latter.

When the issue came up in parliament voices were raised demanding changes in the defense ministry, whereupon a number of army officers petitioned President Sukarno to dissolve parliament, since it had no mandate from the people and therefore no moral authority to pass judgment on other departments of the government. (Members of parliament had not been popularly elected, but were appointed by the political parties according to a system of proportional representation established by a presidential committee.) On October 16, parliament passed a resolution, introduced by a member of the Nationalist party, calling for early withdrawal of the Netherlands military mission and the appointment of a committee "to bring forward concrete proposals for changes in the top echelons of the Defense Ministry and in the Armed Forces." On the next day the capital witnessed a wild popular demonstration against parliament and in support of the defense minister, with the army much in evidence. The crowds entered the parliament building, destroying furniture and finishings, and then marched to the presidential palace, demanding the dissolution of parliament and early elections for a new national assembly. With his customary skill in handling crowds President Sukarno succeeded in calming the demonstrators without promising anything more than that the first general elections would be held as soon as possible.

A few days after the October 17 affair three territorial commanders (in East Java, East Indonesia, and South Sumatra) were removed by subordinate officers, apparently in protest against what they believed to be the actions of the military clique in Djakarta. The usurping officers declared allegiance to President Sukarno while engaged in their acts of insubordination. The government in a public statement strongly rebuked the officers who had participated in the October 17 demonstration and promised "to restore integrity and unity" in the armed forces. However, instead of disciplining the rebellious officers, the new chief of staff formally appointed them to the positions they had usurped, over the protests of Defense Minister Buwono.

The resignation of the Wilopo government was followed by a 58-day political crisis. The succeeding coalition cabinet was composed of the Nationalist and a number of small nationalist and Marxist parties, with Ali Sastroamidjojo, at the time ambassador to the United States, as prime minister. Among the new ministers was Iwa Kusuma Sumantri, who had spent some time in Moscow and was imprisoned in 1948 for participation in the attempted Communist coup of that year; he was given the sensitive post of minister of defense.

An important factor which helps to explain the character and history of this first Ali cabinet was its peculiar relationship to President Sukarno. It seems clear that without his influence and active support it could not have been formed or remained so long in power. The cabinet was "presidential" in everything but name. Sukarno appeared to possess all the advantages; he enjoyed presidential government but did not have to accept the blame for any failures. The Ali cabinet remained in office two years, which was considerably longer than any of its predecessors. Ali weathered the loss of some support in parliament, a cabinet reshuffle, widespread corruption in administration, deteriorating economic conditions, continued internal insecurity, and a revolt in North Sumatra. It looked as if the life of his government was secure, at least until the general elections, which were scheduled for September 1955. But suddenly the Ali cabinet ran into political trouble and fell.

The manner of the fall of the Ali cabinet points up the political instability of the country. The prime minister, flush with the diplomatic festivities and honors enjoyed on an official visit to Communist China, suddenly found himself and his cabinet in serious trouble. When the minister of defense sought to fill the vacancy caused by the resignation of the army chief of staff, the deputy, serving as acting chief of staff, and seven colonels, all territorial commanders, refused to accept the newly appointed chief. The colonels successfully defied the prestige, power, authority, and combined efforts of President Sukarno and Prime Minister Ali. Not only did they refuse to accept the appointee, but they acted as if he did not exist, and the deputy continued to function as chief of staff. They rejected all offers of compromise. On July 26, 1955, the cabinet handed in its resignation.

Indonesia's government claimed to be democratic, yet more than five years after the transfer of sovereignty it was still operating under a provisional constitution and a parliament that was not elected. It no longer had moral authority. The army leaders apparently felt no strong obligation to respect the decisions of the Ali cabinet. Whatever the explanation, the affair revealed a critical situation. Natsir, the leader of the Masjumi party, succinctly summarized the gravity of it when he stated that Indonesia was confronted not only with a cabinet crisis but with "a crisis of authority." Following the fall of the Ali government, a new cabinet under the leadership of Burhanuddin Harahap, the chairman of the Masjumi party in the parliament, took office on August 13. The Harahap government, a coalition of 12 of the 20 parties represented in the provisional parliament, was conservative in character. The main parties in opposition were the Nationalists and Communists.

THE 1955 ELECTIONS AND THEIR AFTERMATH

The first general elections were held at long last in September 1955. Twenty-eight parties and individuals won seats—twelve winning only one seat. The results of the election were rather surprising. It was thought that the religion of the masses would work to handicap the Nationalist party and would favor the Masjumi, the leading Moslem party. However, in the country as a whole the Nationalists' vote surpassed slightly that cast for the Masjumi, and on Java the vote ran three to two in favor of the Nationalists. On the other hand, a splinter Moslem party, the Nahdatul Ulama (Moslem Schoolmen's League or Moslem Teachers' party), received nearly as many votes as the Masjumi. One of the most startling aspects of the election returns was the large vote of the Communist party—more than 16 percent of the total.

On December 15, 1955, Indonesia held a second national election, this time for members of the constituent assembly which was to draft a permanent constitution. In this election, in which fewer votes were cast than in the earlier one, the Nationalists received a larger and the Masjumi an even smaller percentage of the total vote. The two national elections seemed to indicate a strong trend toward extreme nationalism, radical economic policies, and militant, orthodox Islamism.

On March 16, 1956, Ali Sastroamidjojo succeeded in forming a government based upon the three largest parties in parliament—the Nationalist, the Masjumi, and the Moslem Teachers—and a number of smaller parties. Though the Ali cabinet started with a strong numerical backing in a parliament only recently elected by the people, it soon found itself in difficulty. In August the army, under authority of martial law, attempted to arrest Foreign Minister Ruslan Abdulgani on charges of corruption just as he was about to leave for a conference in London; he was subsequently cleared by a cabinet commission. The army also jailed a leading newspaper editor for criticizing the government. In November an army officers' group in Djakarta apparently sought to overthrow the Ali government, and in December there was a series of military revolts in Sumatra. Revolutionary councils set up in South Sumatra demanded the right to keep more of the revenues collected in the area for local use. In January the Masjumi and several small parties withdrew

Indonesia

from the ministry, leaving the Ali cabinet in a precarious position.

President Sukarno responded to these developments by publicly appealing for the "burial" of Indonesia's political parties and the replacement of the democratic political parliamentary system by "guided democracy." He regarded the formation of parties in 1945 as a grave mistake which had caused discord among the people. In opening the constituent assembly, he declared, "For the time being our democracy must be a guided democracy—thus not a democracy that is based on conceptions of liberalism." He suggested that, once the parties were dissolved, political leaders should decide "whether a one-party system should be formed, a mass movement, or some well-founded parties." He asserted that he did not want to become a dictator.

After many weeks of expectation the president on February 2, 1957, formally called on his countrymen to abandon the "imported" Western system of democracy. He proposed the creation of a cabinet which would comprise all the major parties, including the Communists, which had seats in parliament as a result of the 1955 elections. This cabinet would represent parliament, and a second body, a national council, composed of a cross-section of the people, would represent Indonesian society. The latter body, presided over by the president himself, would "advise" the cabinet. If his "plan" were adopted, Sukarno said, there would be an end to the opposition which had paralyzed Indonesian governments; instead, there would be only brotherly discussion. The Communists greeted the proposal with joy and immediately began a campaign to whip up enthusiasm for it. Political leaders opposing Sukarno's proposal received letters threatening them unless they changed their minds.

The opposition to Sukarno's plan for political centralism expressed itself sharply. On March 2, 1957, a dissident group proclaimed a military regime in East Indonesia. The leader of the revolt presented President Sukarno an ultimatum demanding the dismissal of Prime Minister Ali Sastroamidjojo and his cabinet and warning the president that the rebels would not tolerate Communists in the government. The spreading reaction against "Javanese centralism" was a very serious matter for the Djakarta government. Cut off from the rich tax-producing and large foreign exchange-earning outer islands, the government, situated in overpopulated Java, would soon experience financial strangulation. Yet another indication of the mounting political trouble was the rift between President Sukarno and Vice President Hatta, which had been developing for some time. Hatta became outspokenly critical of proposals advocated by the president. On December 1, 1956, he resigned.

Increasing dissidence in the outer islands, here and there breaking out into open defiance, forced out the Ali Sastroamidjojo cabinet in March 1957. President Sukarno promptly declared a state of war and siege, legally giving him virtual dictatorial authority. In April he appointed a cabinet headed by Djuanda as prime minister. This cabinet, which contained a number of extreme leftists, was more presidential than parliamentary. After the resignation of the Ali ministry parliament functioned ineffectively, with barely a quorum in attendance. The president was authorized by parliament to establish the national council which he had advocated as part of his plan for a "guided democracy," and in accordance with his previously expressed views, he included Communists in its membership.

Throughout 1957 efforts were made by the moderates to effect a compromise between Djakarta and the dissident areas in the outer islands and to bring about a reconciliation between Sukarno and Hatta. The high point of these efforts was a national conference in Djakarta in September 1957 attended by leaders of the central government and of the disgruntled and rebellious outer islands. Hopes centered on a possible reconciliation between the president and his former vice president. The estranged leaders signed a joint state-

Indonesia

ment in which they pledged to work with the Indonesian people in striving to realize the ideals of the proclamation of independence in 1945. While this vague statement of "agreement" really did nothing to solve the crisis, it did slow down the widening of the breach between Djakarta and the outlying regions. The conference also made an attempt to solve another of Indonesia's persistent problems, disunity in the army. The military participants in the conference, who included many "rebel" colonels, took an oath pledging to obey unconditionally the decisions made by a commission named by the conference.

Increasing dissatisfaction with the trend of affairs and deepening concern over the direction of President Sukarno's leadership finally led to the formation of an opposition government. In the closing months of 1957 more and more of the dissidents gathered at Padang in the western part of Sumatra. The group comprised a considerable number of military and some outstanding political leaders. It included the president of the Bank of Indonesia, Sjafruddin Prawiranegara, and two former prime ministers, Natsir and Harahap. The dissatisfied leaders deliberated for weeks and finally organized a council.

An indication of the tension which existed at the time was the attempt that was made on November 30 to take the life of President Sukarno. He escaped uninjured, but the hand grenade thrown at him killed eight people and wounded a number of others.

The revolutionary council based in Western Sumatra issued an ultimatum to President Sukarno and Prime Minister Djuanda on February 10, 1958. The council demanded that Mohammad Hatta and Sultan Hamengku Buwono of Djokjakarta be named to form a new cabinet to be composed of "men of integrity and free of atheistic influence," this cabinet to function until the next general elections in 1960. The rebels also insisted that Sukarno return to his constitutional position as president. The ultimatum, which was called a

"Charter in Defense of Freedom and Justice," was preceded by a long preamble in which the grievances and political views of the group were set forth. The Djuanda cabinet was charged with actions hostile to the legitimate desires of the outer regions and with disastrous economic and financial policies culminating in the abrupt liquidation of Dutch economic activities. Sukarno was charged with having gone abroad (following the assassination attempt), not to recuperate his health, but to try to purchase arms from the Soviet bloc, "apparently to crush the popular movements." The Sukarno-Djuanda regime was also accused of seeking "to strengthen the Communist position in the government while intensifying atheistic influence in the community, and to disrupt friendly relations with the Western world in order to bring Indonesia closer into the Soviet bloc."

The Djuanda cabinet rejected the ultimatum, President Sukarno returned from his "rest" trip on February 16, and the government ordered the arrest on treason charges of the prime minister of the counter-government, Sjafruddin, and five of its ministers. The Djakarta government went into military action against the rebels in the middle of March. Its navy blockaded the rebel ports, and the air force landed parachute troops at Pakanbaru, the oil center, with little difficulty. The rebels offered small resistance. Greater resistance was met by the central government forces when they launched an amphibious attack on rebel-controlled North Sulawesi, but by July the back of the rebellion had been broken.

There were many reasons for the failure of the rebellion. The leaders apparently expected to be joined by the military commander of the vital region of South Sumatra, and by the Achinese in the north of Sumatra and by other known pockets of discontent throughout the islands. Nor did they receive political aid from Mohammad Hatta or the Sultan of Djokjakarta. The counter-government movement fell between two stools: it tried to be both a regional and a national movement, but failed to be either sufficiently to rally real

Indonesia

support. Moreover, the armed forces proved to be surprisingly efficient.

TOWARD GUIDED DEMOCRACY

When the second cabinet of Ali Sastroamidjojo resigned in March 1957, the period of parliamentary or constitutional democracy came to an end and that of "guided democracy" can be said to have begun. It was hoped that the general elections, held in 1955, would bring improvement in the political process, but their outcome seemed rather to have hastened decline. Democratic political campaigns and elections in a society which lacks unity can be very divisive.

In July 1959, Sukarno began drastically to reorganize ("retool") the government along the lines of his *konsepsi* (concept) of "guided democracy." He decreed the dissolution of the constituent assembly, which for three years had worked unavailingly to draft a permanent constitution, and ordered the restoration of the revolutionary constitution of 1945, which concentrated power in the hands of the president and the armed forces. President Sukarno abolished the office of the prime minister, assuming its duties himself, making Djuanda his "first minister." In March 1960, he dissolved the elected legislature, replacing it some months later with an appointive "gotong rojong" (mutual help) parliament, in which debating and voting were barred, and decisions had to be unanimous. When unanimity could not be achieved, the president might decree a regulation. Political parties and newspapers were vigorously controlled, some permanently banned. The Masjumi and Socialist parties were banned as well as some other parties and organizations. A National Front, which was regarded as the personal party of the president and which Sukarno must have hoped would displace all the other parties, was launched with fanfare, but it did not become as great a force as was expected. Sukarno was elected president for life in 1963.

The position of prime minister, which was replaced by that of first minister in 1959, was revived in 1963, and President Sukarno named himself to the post. Three deputy prime ministers were appointed. The governmental structure was complicated and the relationship of the various leading organs was difficult to determine. These bodies, however, included a 45-member Supreme Advisory Council; a 77-member National Planning Council; a 281-member Gotong Rojong Parliament; and a People's Provisional Consultative Congress of 616 members. The cabinet was composed of 77 members. It is obvious that this strange structure was designed to diffuse functions and dilute powers so as to enable the president to make the important decisions and control the administration. The 1945 constitution called for a vice president, but none was appointed or elected. Elections were frequently promised, but none had been held six years after the "postponed" constitutionally scheduled 1960 balloting. The anti-Communists, who would normally have insisted upon early elections, were largely silent. An election might have produced new Communist gains and added to the latter's prestige and influence.

Communist influence in the government increased in the first half of the 1960s. In a cabinet reshuffle in August 1964, the first avowed Communist was included in the cabinet, though in a minor position. In March 1965, two leading anti-Communist cabinet members were demoted, while the position of Foreign Minister Subandrio, who had developed an informal alliance with the Communists, was strengthened.

While Sukarno remained the strongest single political force in Indonesia during the first half of the 1960s, his power was far from absolute. His position was dependent on maintaining a delicate balance between the army and the Communist party. In this three-cornered struggle for power each party commanded elements of strength. Sukarno still had his hypnotic power over the masses and was extremely skillful in exploiting the hostility between the army and the

Indonesia

Communist party, keeping in precarious equilibrium the desire of each for power. The rebellion of 1958 and confrontation with the Dutch over West Irian and with Malaysia over "neo-colonialism" strengthened the position of the army, which constantly grew in size and was well equipped. In a foreign crisis, Sukarno's dependence on the army was necessarily great. The strength of the Communist party largely consisted in its growing membership; it was said to be the largest Communist party in the world outside the Communist bloc, reportedly having a membership in excess of 2,500,000. Moreover, it appeared to be well organized and disciplined, and continued economic deterioration seemed to favor its growth.

The Sukarno government had three important achievements to its credit. It had put down rebellion, restored internal security, and won the struggle with the Netherlands over West Irian. But it did not solve two other very pressing problems: it failed to weld the various island peoples and conflicting ethnic and social groups into what was truly a nation, and it never seriously attacked the economic problems of the country. Instead of economic development there was steady deterioration. The economic situation became literally desperate, confronting Sukarno with a cruel dilemma. Only by a strident nationalism and the existence (or supposed existence) of threats from foreign countries could his shaky governing coalition and country be held together. Any serious attempt to tackle domestic problems, especially that of economic deterioration, might result in such strong clashes of interests that the governing coalition would fall apart and the country possibly break up. In this kind of crisis Sukarno might be forced to choose between the army and the Communist party. And this was a choice Sukarno wished to avoid. Sukarno held the country together, but his inability or unwillingness to cope with economic problems brought him to a dead end. Indonesia also appeared to face a second and equally unhappy dilemma. Without Sukarno it might be in serious danger of disintegrating; with him it faced almost certain economic disaster, with resultant massive social suffering.

ECONOMIC PROBLEMS

Political instability and economic stagnation have been the twin evils of Indonesia, each aggravating the other. No economic progress can be made until there is political stability, but the political instability is in part due to the difficulties of the economic problem, which is in turn the result of Indonesia's social, geographic, demographic and economic structure. Foreign adventures can only postpone and make more terrible the day of reckoning.

The rebellion of 1958-1961 in part reflected a difference in economic and political attitudes of the outer islands from that prevailing in Djakarta and Java. Most of the inhabitants of the outer islands had a more favorable attitude toward capitalism and foreign enterprise; they had experienced the economic and social benefits which came with foreign capitalism. With a more favorable relation of population to resources they could more easily see the value of individualism in economic activity. They feared the centralization of authority in a Java-controlled government.

The strong bias of most Indonesian political leaders against capitalism and in favor of socialism is not difficult to understand. In colonial days there was very little indigenous capitalism; it was practically all foreign, so quite naturally capitalism was associated with alien political domination. Indonesian nationalists accordingly concluded that it was impossible to get rid of one without the other. Some had more sophisticated reasons for their socialist views. They believed that rapid economic development could be achieved only through government leadership and action. There was a general if unexpressed fear that foreigners would exploit Indonesian disunity to advance their own purposes.

Indonesia

The Indonesianization of the foreign-owned enterprises is now almost complete. Belgian, Dutch, British and American plantations and industries have been taken over and the Chinese who are not Indonesian nationals have been forced out of many of their commercial enterprises. The Indonesianization of the economic life of the country has not resulted in greater production. The expulsion of the Dutch from the inter-island shipping business in December 1957 severely hurt the outer islands. Production in nearly all areas has declined; only in the oil industry, which remained under foreign control until 1965, has there been an increase of production over 1940. Food production has not kept pace with population increase. Serious inroads have been made on the forest reserves on Java, with erosion and flood problems as a result. Starvation conditions were reported to obtain on Java in the early months of 1964.

Indonesia has been depleting its capital assets. The foreign owners have lost heavily in the Indonesian takeover of their enterprises and the Indonesians have gained nothing. As production has declined, the properties have deteriorated and foreign exchange has dwindled. Large amounts of foreign economic aid and Japanese reparations amounting to several million dollars have likewise been consumed without lasting improvement of the economy as a whole. Inflation reached alarming proportions. From 1953 to April 1965, the cost of living index had gone up 6,500 percent. The value of the rupiah on the black market declined from 1,800-to-$1 in June 1964 to 10,000-to-$1 a year later. From 1959 to 1964 exports by value declined by half. Government expenditure in 1964 totaled 680 billion rupiahs, while public revenue came to only about 283 billion rupiahs.

The population pressure on Java, meanwhile, is becoming acute. The density per square mile is already about 1,200, with an annual increase of 2½ percent or about 1,500,000. The average peasant on Java cultivates less than an acre and a half of land. Many in the villages are landless, not because of large land ownership but because industry has not been developed to draw off the surplus population.

SUKARNO AND SUKARNOISM

Indonesia had known no other national leader than Sukarno as it passed the twentieth anniversary of its proclamation as an independent state on August 17, 1965. Sukarno had been at the head of the government since 1945, and for nearly two decades before that he was among the few top leaders of the nationalist movement. He early developed a hypnotic power over the masses with the spoken word. Coupled with this has been a compulsion to "philosophize." All of his many speeches have had a highly ideological content. This is especially true of his annual Independence Day addresses, which have not inaptly been called orations on the state of the universe. Sukarno has seen himself as the tongue of the Indonesian people. "The podium of the 17th of August," he declared in his 1964 address, "for me is the Peoples' Podium of the Revolution, the podium of the struggle, . . . the podium of the vigorous dance of the Nation's will." These addresses have had florid, mystical titles, such as "The Realization of the Message of the Peoples' Suffering" and "The Year of Living Dangerously."

The Pantja Sila (Five Principles) are regarded as the basic principles of the Indonesian state. They were laid down in a speech by Sukarno on June 1, 1945. The five principles he outlined constitute "the philosophy, the innermost idea, the soul, the deepest desire upon which to build the structure of an Indonesian Merdeka (freedom)." These principles (nationalism, internationalism, democracy, social justice, and belief in God) could be reduced to three, he said—namely, socio-nationalism, socio-democracy, and belief in God, and these three could again be compressed in one, "all for all." It is interesting to note with respect to democracy that he declared that no state is truly alive if its representative body

Indonesia

does not burn and boil like a cauldron, "if there is no struggle of convictions in it." He also stated that the head of state "should be chosen by the people." His views have changed. Since 1957 he has spoken a quite different language. He was opposed to American and European parliamentary democracy, he subsequently said, because it left the people at the mercy of the capitalists. He wanted a "politico-economic" democracy. With respect to the principle of belief in God he declared that the whole of the people should worship God in a "cultured," "civilized" way, that is, "without religious egoism."

The Pantja Sila must be seen as an effort to synthesize different streams in the political and religious life of the Indonesians. In spite of the fact that it was broad and vague, in some cases because of it, it failed to please everybody. Nationalist party leaders accepted it wholeheartedly, but many members of the Masjumi and others viewed it critically.

As early as 1949 Sukarno gave indication of a line of thought which was later to lead him to "guided democracy." He spoke favorably of Indonesian or Eastern democracy, "a democracy with leadership." In subsequent years he spoke contemptuously of "free-fight liberalism," "majocracy," and "50 percent plus one democracy." This trend reached its climax in his 1959 Independence Day speech, which bore the title, "The Rediscovery of our Revolution." Indonesia had sacrificed the spirit of the revolution in order to survive. "Through the Dutch, via the Round-Table Conference, we were made to dilute our revolutionary spirit; in Indonesia itself we had to compromise with groups which were nonrevolutionary: Dutchified groups, reformist groups, conservative groups, contra-revolutionary groups, chameleon and 'cockroach' (spy for the Dutch) groups. Until at last, in sacrificing this revolutionary spirit, we went away and left the 1945 constitution as an instrument of struggle. Indonesia had deviated from the Spirit, from the Principles and from the Objective of the Revolution." For this the 1950 constitution was largely to blame. It "pressed upon the spirit of the revolution, hampered and slackened the flow of the revolutionary current, killed the revolutionary way of thinking, provided the fertile soil for the growth of all kinds of conventional and conservative trends." The entire apparatus of the state had to be "retooled."

This speech can readily be seen as an after-the-event justification for dissolving the constituent assembly, abolishing the 1950 constitution and proclaiming the return to the constitution of 1945—all of which Sukarno had decreed only a month before. And yet it was more than that, for events were pushing him further in a radical direction. To maintain himself, he became steadily more dependent on the army and the Communist party and was forced to engage in foreign ventures as a means of holding this strange coalition together. As conditions grew worse his revolutionary fervor mounted. Unable to achieve anything constructive, his only emotional outlet was in revolution, perpetual revolution, revolution as an end in itself. Sukarno's 1960 Independence Day speech was a frenzied panegyric on revolution, reaching its height in the peroration:

"I tell you frankly, I belong to the group of people who are bound in spiritual longing by the romanticism of revolution. I am inspired by it. I am completely absorbed by it. I am crazed, I am obsessed by the romanticism of revolution. . . . That is why I, who have been given the topmost leadership in the struggle of the Indonesian nation, never tire of appealing and exhorting: solve our national problems in a revolutionary way, make the revolutionary spirit surge on, see to it that the fire of our revolution does not die, or grow dim, not even for a single moment. Come then, keep fanning the flames of the leaping fire of revolution! Brothers and sisters, let us become logs to feed the flames of revolution."

In his subsequent Independence Day speeches Sukarno elaborated this theme. He concluded his 1964 address, which he gave the title "A Year of Living Dangerously," by declaring that he had the capability to guide the multi-complex revolution "to magnify all of its strengths, to exalt all of its thoughts, to arouse all its romanticism and dynamism, to set all its powers to strike booming, to set noisily to work all its ability to sweat and toil, to step to the skies all its creative power, to forge and wield all its muscles of wire and bones of iron." This address was an even greater *tour de force* than any of his previous Independence Day speeches. Twenty-one thousand words in length, it took three hours to deliver. It was altogether appropriate that the title "Great Leader of the Revolution" should be conferred on him.

Indonesian national identity has been one of the things emphasized in Sukarnoism. Sometimes this took odd forms. In May 1964, National Education Day was celebrated by burning some 500 foreign books, which was said to symbolize Indonesia's opposition to "cultural subversion through ideas and theories contrary to Indonesian ideas and theories." In a country where colleges have practically no libraries and students no textbooks this act would seem excessive dedication to a principle. The Minister of Basic Education and Culture has criticized the use of foreign terms and practices. Objection was made to "beatle" and "bird-nest" hair styles, the latest Western clothing styles, and nicknames of Dutch origin.

The chief end of Sukarnoism was Indonesian socialism—"a just and prosperous society." Capitalism was condemned, the virtues of socialism extolled. Sukarno painted idyllic pictures of this future society. In a Mother's Day address in January 1961, he promised the women that in this Utopia there would be so many modern conveniences, including the latest kitchen appliances, that "you will have lots of time to be a sweetheart to your husband." "God willing, I promise each Indonesian woman one husband." "Under capitalist society," he declared, "marriage has become a difficult economic problem. Many men would like to marry, but they haven't the courage to do so because their income is so small."

Sukarno had never wasted kind words on capitalism, but at this time he became very hostile to it and held it responsible for nearly everything evil in the world. In April 1958 he declared, "The dangers of the A-bomb and the H-bomb—all born of the capitalistic system—should be wiped out." His thoroughgoing Marxism was evident in a statement in the same address, "The new era will be marked by socialism and the brotherhood of man and the fall of capitalism and imperialism which is an historical certainty. Those who cannot understand or oppose the trend of the times will be destroyed." He seemed determined to force Indonesians into a Marxist type of socioeconomic and political organization.

The principles set forth in the 1959 Independence Day address at once became the Political Manifesto, or Manipol. Subsidiary manifestos followed in a stream. Everything was abbreviated in slogan form: Manipol, Manipol-USDEK, NASAKOM, NASAKOMIL. The latter was a slogan calling for a coalition in the government of all the population elements: nationalism, religion, communism, and the military. If slogans could solve problems, Indonesians would be the happiest people in the world. Sukarno seemed to have convinced his fellow countrymen that slogans had a mystical quality, that they had an effectiveness in themselves. They had only to be uttered to produce results.

All public officials engaged in ideological propaganda. Next to President Sukarno the chief expounder of the revolutionary doctrine was Dr. Subandrio, formerly first deputy prime minister and foreign minister; according to an Antara news dispatch of March 24, 1964, he declared that there was something unique about Indonesia, namely that she did not imitate other countries. "While other nations, after obtaining independence, begin to bestow attention on economic and technical issues, Indonesia has spent much time in establishing a powerful national consciousness . . .

Indonesia

the Indonesian revolution is not only a great revolution compared to other revolutions undergone by many nations, it might even be the last revolution, [it] is adapted to the growth and demands of the present era, stage by stage, sometimes defying any rationalization."

Sukarnoism was taught in the schools and colleges. Students had to make a passing grade in it. But when a group was formed to propagate Sukarnoism it was proscribed. The movement was condemned because it used Sukarnoism as a "tool for dissension." Apparently the anti-Communists had tried to use the ideology of the Great Leader of the Revolution to combat Communism.

In banning the organization known as the Body for the Promotion of Sukarnoism, President Sukarno declared that he had secret information that the American C.I.A. was using the organization "to kill Sukarnoism and Sukarno." He ordered the dissolution of all organizations, newspapers and instruments that were "henchmen" of the banned body. In an address to the Indonesian Journalists Association he stated that "in a revolution there should be no press freedom. Only a press supporting the revolution should be allowed to exist."

When Dr. Subandrio was asked in the Netherlands (December 1964) what Indonesia was, he replied that he had no name for it, that he was not interested in names, "since they all emanate from your Western ideology." "We have no written textbooks nor piles of textbooks and dogmas. We are on the way searching for a form. We are accompanying ourselves, thinking, making efforts, experimenting . . . but what is going to be its shape politically and socially will be known only after thirty years."

Probably no better conclusion concerning Indonesia under Sukarno by the mid-1960s could be offered. Politically, socially, economically Indonesia was in flux. The internal situation was marked by an apparent tightening of the alliance between Sukarno and the Communist party by mid-

1965. At Sukarno's urging the Nationalist party in August 1965 purged its central organization of all moderate leaders, leaving the party in the control of the pro-Communist faction. The stage was said to be set for the continued gradual takeover of Indonesia by the Communists.

THE ABORTIVE COMMUNIST COUP OF 1965

The long-predicted Communist takeover has still to occur and may in fact never take place. Not that the Communists did not try. They did—and failed. An obscure commander of President Sukarno's guards, one Lieutenant Colonel Untung, nominally led the coup that was attempted the night of September 30-October 1, 1965, but the Communists were the instigators, and Untung's collaborators within and outside the armed forces were clearly pro-Communist. The takeover failed, however, for reasons that may never be wholly known. There were even those who stated that Sukarno himself was involved in the *putsch* against the army and had cold feet at the last moment—a hypothesis that might in fact be true.

The Communists were long known to have endeavored, with moderate success, to infiltrate the armed forces, but it was clear to themselves above all others, even before the failure of October 1, that their penetration of the military had not yet been extensive enough. For this reason the Communists, Sukarno's allies against the army, had been urging the president to add a new dimension to Indonesia's already large armed services—a "fifth force" of volunteers, whom they would seek to control. Sukarno, however, probably because he feared that such a force might eventually be used against himself, put only limited pressure on the soldiers to acquiesce in the Communists' proposal, and this clearly was not enough. But even this tactical failure does not explain the Communists' seemingly ill-prepared resort to

Indonesia

arms against the far more formidable military. Indonesia's number two strong man, General Abdul Haris Nasution, escaped assassination, but surely the Communists' hopes of success did not rest wholly on their ability to liquidate a single military figure. The conclusion seems inescapable, accordingly, that the Communists were caught by some sudden unexpected crisis and responded the way they did out of desperation. That crisis might have been a planned coup by the army as such or one or another of the top soldiers. The ailing health of the 65-year old Sukarno, the Communists' ranking political patron, might also have played a part since the Communists undoubtedly feared a move by the military against them in the event of Sukarno's demise—political or otherwise.

In any event the Communist action played into the soldiers' hands. Sukarno's ideological stand had previously rendered illegitimate all attempts—by the "Supporters of Sukarnoism," the army, and others—to put a halt to the growing influence of the Communists in the government. The Communists' resort to revolt, which included the brutal murder of six ranking military leaders, gave the army the excuse it needed to plow into its chief opposition. The results were brutal. Thousands of Communists were executed by the soldiers themselves. More important, the revolt, its failure, and the army's response were the cues needed by elements of the population previously oppressed by the Communists to engage in a wholesale bloodbath. Violent encounters had already taken place between Moslem and Communist student groups, but these were merely a prelude to what happened after October 1. Sukarno himself publicly admitted that more than 87,000 Communists were slain by angry elements of the population, mostly aroused Moslems, in the late months of 1965; other estimates ranged from 100,000 to 400,000. At least 45 members of the 50-person Communist party central committee were killed; the party's leader, D. N. Aidit, was believed dead. President Sukarno apparently earnestly sought to prevent the slaughter but to no avail.

There is reason to believe that the Communists sought to halt the would-be coup as soon as they realized how strongly the odds were against them. But the military leaders had long awaited this hour, and they would not be denied. The soldiers used their emergency powers to establish varied types of military rule throughout the archipelago.

The army did not immediately seek to topple Sukarno, long the Communists' chief protector. They needed him perhaps as a national symbol, they may have feared popular reaction, and he could come in handy as a scapegoat for Indonesia's persisting economic difficulties. But the soldiers did in effect take over the government, paying lip-service to Sukarno's paramount position but disregarding his orders and pleas. Army personnel replaced all civilian staff members in the important Supreme Operations Command, known as KOTI, which immediately became the real executive arm of the government in Indonesia, acting in Sukarno's name if not at his pleasure. General Nasution, already defense minister, became one of KOTI's three deputy commanders with top responsibility in the military field. Significantly, one of the other two deputy commanders was the well-known moderate, Sultan Hamengku Buwono, himself also a former defense minister. The army seemed to be in the process of taking over the government, but, like the Dutch in the early years of colonial times, the soldiers seemed reluctant to assume full governing responsibility unless it proved to be absolutely necessary.

The state of the economy was one reason for the army's hesitation. Things had been bad before the coup, but they worsened subsequently. A major decrease in exports followed the takeover try, with a resulting foreign exchange crisis. Prices in January 1966 were 15 times what they had been only a year before. The old rupiah was replaced by a new one in late 1965, the latter equalling 1,000 of the former notes. The move was taken to curb inflation, but it failed to do so. Prices doubled in the first month following the revaluation. By mid-January 1966 one American dollar could buy 60 new rupiahs—or the equivalent of 60,000 old ones. The long oppressed Indonesian masses, moreover, were beginning to stir. Widespread demonstrations took place against the prices of some items and the non-availability of important foodstuffs. The government searched frantically for rice in foreign markets, not aided by its reputation for failing to meet its credit obligations—possibly the world's worst. The Indonesian pot had never boiled like this before. Little wonder that the soldiers hesitated to assume direct responsibility for Indonesia's grossly mismanaged economy!

Sukarno showed surprising daring in the face of the obvious opposition to him. He attacked the Communists as "rats that have eaten a big part of the cake and tried to eat the pillar of our house." But he also threatened those who turned so violently on the Communists—to no avail; the slaughter continued. Those who attacked the Communists he termed "stooges" of the neocolonialist-imperialist powers. At the same time, however, he openly admitted that there were those who sought to remove him as Indonesia's leader, an admission that seemed to lack the old Sukarno defiance and to betray more than a little fear that his political end was near.

The main change, however, was less immediately in the role of Sukarno than in the position of the Communist party. It had been transformed almost overnight from a powerful government party into an organization whose members and sympathizers were hunted up and down the country by military and vigilante groups alike with a determination not unlike that which had shown itself in the 1945-1949 war against the Dutch. Important political figures, such as former Premier Ali Sastroamidjojo, who formerly fell over one another to display their friendship for the Communists, now engaged in almost passionate portrayal of their animosity toward their onetime allies. There was much pathos in the scene.

SUKARNO—AND THE FUTURE

Sukarno's position was clearly diminished, at least temporarily, by the events of October 1 and subsequently. His weapons were being reduced in number, being almost wholly his mass appeal and his related public image in early 1966, and yet he remained a political force of no little importance despite the reduction in his influence. The obvious disinclination of the soldiers to follow his leadership, however, seemed to be eroding even the long sacrosanct Sukarno prestige. The University Graduates Action Front questioned Sukarno's right to call himself "Great Leader of the Revolution" in April 1966, and a Moslem student leader protested Sukarno's title of "President for Life."

The first five months of 1966 saw three major showdowns in the struggle for political ascendancy in Indonesia—with the outcome still not definitively settled. In February Sukarno succeeded in ousting General Abdul Haris Nasution, generally regarded in the past as his number one rival, from his position as defense minister. Nasution had been tagged for assassination by the Communists in the October 1 affair but had escaped and subsequently played a major role in the trials before military tribunals of the chief figures in the abortive uprising. Sukarno's ouster of Nasution was said to show that the 65-year old Indonesian leader had by no means lost all his power, but it may also have reflected Nasution's unwillingness to take a strong public stand against Sukarno—which he appears to have avoided doing repeatedly through the years.

The balance of power within Indonesia was not appreciatively affected by this event, however, as Sukarno was not able to carry the day completely with the military's acceptance of his own nominee for defense minister. The

Indonesia

Nasution dismissal was counter-productive, in fact, as the popular soldier's ouster triggered massive student demonstrations which forced Sukarno to turn over even greater power to the country's military leaders in March. A new 30-man cabinet was named, but, more important, Sukarno also announced formation of a six-member presidium or inner cabinet. Three members of the latter body immediately came to dominate official decision-making in Indonesia, and this triumvirate was the *de facto* government in the country in early May 1966 on the eve of a long-awaited session of the People's Provisional Consultative Congress, supposedly the supreme body in the land. These three men were General Suharto, protege of Nasution, Army Chief of Staff and Defense Minister; Sultan Hamengku Buwono of Djokjakarta, Economics Minister, and Foreign Minister Adam Malik.

The leader of the government was now apparently General Suharto more than anyone else. Some said that Suharto was really a front for General Nasution, but there were indications that Suharto was increasingly a leader in his own right. A highly respected professional soldier, Suharto had been catapulted to the forefront of Indonesian politics by the assassination of six senior generals and the incapacitation of General Nasution in the unsuccessful coup attempt of September 30-October 1. It was Suharto who seized the leadership of the anti-Communist resistance to the takeover and capably and efficiently halted the would-be seizure in 12 largely bloodless hours. Sukarno subsequently focused his sights on Nasution, his longtime chief rival, and, in seeking to reduce his political importance, probably paid too little attention to Suharto. In any event, Suharto quickly became the chief spokesman of the post-October 1 Indonesian government and increasingly its single most important figure. Although technically only one of six deputy premiers (in charge of defense and security), he was probably the closest thing to Indonesia's real leader on the eve of the announced May 12, 1966, meeting of the People's Consultative Congress.

The 616-member Congress, never elected but selected personally by President Sukarno, was to have met in October 1965, but this was postponed because of the Communist coup attempt. The rescheduled May meeting was expected to be the scene of another clash between Sukarno and his political opponents, but this session itself was postponed at the last moment. Suharto had declared in April that Sukarno was subordinate to the Congress, and there were expectations that the May session might both further divest Sukarno of authority and at long last name a vice president to fill the vacancy created by Mohammad Hatta's resignation from that office a decade earlier. There was no official explanation for the abrupt postponement of the Congress, but it was clearly a tactical victory for Sukarno. Two explanations circulated widely in Djakarta: the triumvirate of Suharto, Sultan Hamengku Buwono and Adam Malik were said to have backed off from a final clash with Sukarno until they had solidified their position, and it was also claimed that General Suharto was concerned about the still strong position of the leftists in central and east Java—who might use the occasion of Sukarno's *de facto* deposition as an excuse to start new trouble.

Sukarno was still clearly struggling to retain as much power as he possibly could. He clearly opposed assumption of a purely ceremonial role. As he himself put it, "I have not sacrificed 50 years of my life to be a maharajah." But would the soldiers continue to allow him actively to oppose their policies? A Western embassy official put it this way: "There won't be peace in this country until the 'Bung' is gone or dead. He is a man who admits he is in love with the romance of revolution. But it's a new revolution here now." The time appeared to be approaching when Sukarno would have to accept a largely honorary status—or possibly destroy himself trying to hold on to real power. Sukarno was by no means down and out, nor was it sure that he could not hold on a

Indonesia

little longer. But time and history—after so many years—no longer appeared to be on his side.

The military might well have taken over in Indonesia long before this time, Sukarno's nationalist pre-eminence notwithstanding, if it had not been for its politically necessary preoccupation with West Irian—which gave the Communists time to build their strength. The soldiers took over in Thailand in the 1930s and again in the 1940s and have done so in Burma, South Vietnam, Pakistan, Iraq and many other emerging countries. The Communists and the use made of them by Sukarno were probably the chief obstacles to military rule in Indonesia during the decade 1955-1965. What seems to be happening in Indonesia today, in short, is what has happened earlier elsewhere for essentially the same reasons—civilian incompetence, political instability, economic mismanagement, internal disunity, and related causes.

FOREIGN POLICY

For over a decade relations with the Netherlands constituted the chief foreign policy problem of Indonesia. Indonesia made an insistent drive to obtain control over West New Guinea, whose final status had been left undetermined by the Round Table Conference. By 1962 Indonesia had virtually achieved this end, and in the process had terminated all The Hague arrangements for continued association between the two countries and had taken over the extensive Dutch economic interests in the country. The Indonesian triumph was complete.

The Dutch were psychologically ill-prepared to accept the fact of the "loss" of the Indies. They had been in the archipelago for about three and a half centuries, and many roots had become deeply embedded in Indonesian soil and many institutions in the Netherlands were dependent upon the economic, cultural, and political relationship with Indonesia.

Large numbers of Netherlanders had made Indonesia their home, either on a permanent or semipermanent basis, and Dutch investments in Indonesia were large, especially for a country of the size and population of the Netherlands. The Dutch therefore were insistent that some tie between the two countries be preserved.

The Indonesians indicated little enthusiasm for the Netherlands - Indonesian Union at the Round Table Conference, and that little was thoroughly dissipated within a year of the transfer of sovereignty. Though the language of the Union Statute clearly safeguarded the independence and sovereignty of the two members, the Indonesians feared that their country would be regarded as the junior partner. They looked upon the union as in some sense a vestige if not a continuation of the colonial relationship.

Negotiations to settle the political status of West New Guinea were conducted in 1950, but led to no result. The Indonesians were under the impression that the Dutch delegation at the Round Table Conference had insisted upon tabling the West New Guinea issue merely as a face-saving device which would enable the Dutch government to get the Round Table agreements approved by parliament, and that once this was obtained, Dutch public opinion on the issue would change and permit the government to yield to the Indonesian demand for West Irian. Instead, Dutch public opinion hardened rather than softened on the issue. On the Indonesian side, President Sukarno rarely made a speech, regardless of the occasion, without including a rousing demand for the "restoration" of West Irian to Indonesia.

The Indonesian government based its claim to the territory almost solely on the ground that it was a part of the Netherlands Indies, to which the Republic of Indonesia had become the successor. President Sukarno declared that the Indonesian national revolution would be incomplete until West Irian again became a part of Indonesia. The Netherlands government claimed that the territory had a geological,

Indonesia

biological, and geographical character of its own which could not be classified as Indonesian, and that from the point of view of culture, religion, language, and ethnology the Papauns, as the inhabitants of New Guinea are called, were quite different from the Indonesians.

For the Dutch it was an unequal contest. All of the advantages were on the Indonesian side. Indonesians did not value the Round Table agreements; they meant much to the Dutch. Large numbers of Netherlanders and very substantial Dutch investments in the erstwhile colony were exposed to hostile pressure.

The Indonesian government sought international support for its claim to the territory by asserting that the chief issue involved was "colonialism." Indonesia nearly succeeded in getting the 1954 session of the General Assembly to adopt a resolution requesting the Netherlands government to resume negotiations on the matter. It succeeded in getting the African-Asian Conference at Bandung in 1955 to adopt a resolution vaguely supporting its position. The matter was again before the General Assembly at its 1955 session, but when the Indonesian and Dutch governments issued a joint statement announcing early negotiations to settle differences between them, that body merely expressed the hope that the problem would soon be peacefully resolved. A similar resolution failed of adoption by the 1956 session. A resolution sponsored by 19 members inviting the Netherlands and Indonesia to seek a solution in conformity with the principles of the Charter and requesting the Secretary General to assist in negotiations between the two countries failed to receive the necessary two-thirds approval in the General Assembly when it came up for a vote on February 28, 1957.

When relentless pressure on the Dutch failed to induce the Netherlands government to yield on West Irian and positive support from the United Nations was not forthcoming, Sukarno and his government decided on drastic action. Relations between the Netherlands and Indonesia were already bad. The Dutch military mission had been withdrawn in 1953 at the request of the Indonesian government. In 1955 the latter unilaterally denounced the union and in 1956 it announced the repudiation of the debt to the Netherlands which it had assumed in the Round Table Conference agreements. The anti-Dutch campaign was sharply stepped up. The Dutch, with investments of over a billion dollars in Indonesia, were extremely vulnerable. Dutch enterprises were taken over, Dutch businesses were boycotted, all publications in Dutch were banned, consular offices were closed. Under extreme pressure thousands of Netherlanders hastily left the islands. In pursuance of the policy of "confrontation of all our national forces with those of the Dutch," President Sukarno in his 1960 Independence Day speech announced that he had broken diplomatic relations with the Netherlands.

The whole country was now mobilized in the "confrontation." Volunteers for the liberation of West Irian were trained by the army and a program of infiltration accelerated. Large supplies of military equipment were obtained from Russia. Actual hostile clashes between the Dutch defense forces and Indonesian armed parties were an increasing occurrence. Total mobilization was ordered by President Sukarno on December 19, 1961.

The Dutch response to Indonesian "confrontation" was an accelerated program of economic and political development and military reinforcement. But the Dutch people in the Netherlands were losing interest in West New Guinea and had little desire to become involved in a costly war on the other side of the world. Foreign Minister Luns in September 1961 proposed to the General Assembly that the United Nations take over the administration of West New Guinea. The Netherlands would continue to give financial assistance; in due course the people of the territory would be given the right to determine their future status. Indonesia

Indonesia

strongly objected to the proposal, which never came to a vote.

By the end of 1961 the situation had become acute; naval and military clashes seemed to indicate an early Indonesian attempt to invade West Irian. Secretary General U Thant of the United Nations sent a message urging the two countries to seek a peaceful solution. Negotiations finally began in March, just outside Washington, with a retired American diplomat, Ellsworth Bunker, as mediator. An agreement was reached in August 1962. An obstacle to agreement had been Dutch insistence on the right of self-determination for the Papuans. Indonesia accepted a provision for a referendum on whether the territory would remain with Indonesia or become independent; the plebiscite would, however, not be held until after Indonesia had acquired control over West Irian but before the end of 1969. In accordance with the agreement, the Netherlands on October 1, 1962, transferred the administration to the United Nations, which in turn on May 1, 1963, turned over to Indonesia the territory it had so long struggled to acquire.

After the settlement of this issue relations between the two countries began to improve. Netherlanders began to return to their erstwhile colony. Foreign Minister Subandrio visited the Netherlands in April 1964, and in July Foreign Minister Luns made a week's visit to Indonesia. Reparations for the nationalization of Dutch property and the possibility of joint business ventures were discussed. At his departure Luns announced that his government was willing to guarantee export credits for the year 1965 to the amount of one hundred million guilders.

Not long after the victory over the Dutch, Indonesia turned "confrontation" against Malaysia.* There were a number of motives behind this action, but certainly not least among them was the problem of national unity as well as the

---

* For further discussion of this subject, see Chapter 3 on Malaysia.

seeming need to escape from what appeared to be the nearly insuperable difficulties of economic deterioration. The situation presented Indonesia's leaders with a cruel dilemma. Some kind of bold action seemed necessary to hold the country together, but foreign adventures made impossible any serious attempt to attack mounting economic problems; rather they made for a more rapid deterioration. Indonesia's actions were self-defeating. As the economic situation became more acute, the greater was the unity, effort, and determination required to make an effective attack on the problem.

There were other contributing factors behind Indonesia's policy of "confrontation" towards the new state of Malaysia, launched on September 16, 1963. Malaysia was an avowedly anti-Communist country, and expansion of this progressive nation to include Singapore and the formerly British northern Borneo territories of Sarawak and Sabah was particularly strongly opposed by Indonesia's Communist party. For the army, confrontation was also a diverting task for the men who comprised its excessively enlarged ranks; for the Communists, it was a means of distracting the soldiers' attention from internal political developments. Malaya, parent state of Malaysia, was historically a Malay (or Indonesian) land, and Malays dominated its ruling elite; the contrast between the economic successes registered by this Malay country and Indonesia's economic failures disturbed President Sukarno and may even have been viewed by the Indonesian leader as a threat to his own position. The ties between the east coast of Sumatra and the western coast of the nearby Malay Peninsula were strong despite the fact that the two territories had been under different colonial rulers, and there can be no denying that some peninsular Malays viewed the riches of Sumatra with a near-imperial eye. Indonesian mass emotions, in addition, had been aroused by the West Irian campaign and had to be channelled off somewhere—better against Malaysia, Sukarno may have thought, than against the Indonesian political elite. Finally, there was Indonesia's

Indonesia

particular image of the world around it. Assertive and confident though the words of its leaders may have sounded, Indonesia nonetheless retained the fears and doubts born of recent colonial subjection. It is probably true that most of the Indonesian ruling elite generally regarded Malaysia as a "neo-colonialist plot" to "encircle" Indonesia. It was a means of retaining British influence in Southeast Asia. Malaysia was fronting for the imperial British. This Indonesia could not endure—particularly if it involved territories Indonesia itself desired, Sarawak and Sabah in northern Borneo. The policy of confrontation produced no gains for Indonesia, however—least of all the dismemberment of Malaysia—and in June 1966 the Army government took the first steps toward reconciliation with the Malaysians.

Indonesia's relations with the other Southeast Asian states were less troubled in the two decades which followed the Second World War.*

INDONESIA AND THE UNITED NATIONS

On September 28, 1950, Indonesia was admitted to the United Nations as its 60th member. To a young, underdeveloped country like Indonesia membership in the world organization enabled it to play a far greater role in world politics than if restricted to the traditional methods of diplomacy. The General Assembly provided it with a forum from which it could attack colonialism, present the views and needs of underdeveloped countries and offer solutions to the cold war. Indonesia sent strong delegations to the meetings of the General Assembly, generally headed by the Minister of Foreign Affairs.

The policy of Indonesia in the United Nations on the issues of the cold war was one of independence and neutralism. However, it did not view its role as passive or negative. It

---

* These—and Indonesia's relations with other powers interested in Southeast Asia—are discussed in Chapter 10.

sought to create a climate of peace, an atmosphere which would promote conciliation between East and West. Until 1953, when the moderates were in power, it was a neutralism which inclined to be pro-Western; from 1953 to 1956 a transition took place and after 1957, and especially after 1959, Indonesian policy became steadily more pro-Communist. In 1950 Indonesia voted for the Uniting for Peace Resolution and in 1953 for the extension of Trygve Lie's term as Secretary General; it also defended both Lie and Dag Hammarskjold against Russian attacks. As a small state, it supported all measures to strengthen the General Assembly.

Until Indonesia's withdrawal President Sukarno had kind words for the United Nations and expressed Indonesia's loyalty to it. In his 1952 Independence Day address he declared: "I myself am convinced that in the present conditions of the world the U.N. plays a very important role. In the circle of the U.N. all disputes can be discussed and a solution searched for. The history of mankind has reached the point where an international organization is extremely important to prevent weak nations from becoming victims of strong nations."

Even as late as 1960, when he addressed the General Assembly, President Sukarno had appreciative words for the United Nations. "If I may say so," he declared, "we of Indonesia have a very special desire to see this organization flourish and be successful. By the actions of this organization our own struggle for independence and national life was shortened. I say in full confidence that our struggle would in any case have been successful, but the actions of the United Nations shortened that struggle and saved both us and our opponents many sacrifices and much sorrow and destruction."

It would not have been surprising if Indonesia had after 1957, when it failed for the fourth time to get a resolution through the General Assembly calling upon the Netherlands

Indonesia

to resume negotiations on West Irian, turned against the United Nations, but Sukarno's expression of praise in 1960 revealed no bitterness. Yet Indonesia became the first member to withdraw from the United Nations. When in 1964, the General Assembly elected Malaysia to the Security Council, apparently with the object of indicating sympathy with that state in its conflict with Indonesia, Sukarno was deeply offended. The decision to withdraw was announced in the first days of January 1965. The withdrawal became formally complete on March 1. The letter of resignation explained that the step had been taken because of the seating of "neo-colonialist" Malaysia in the Security Council. "Our decision," the letter concluded, "may become the catalyst to reform and retool the U.N. in spirit and in deed, lest the present atmosphere of complacency shown by the neo-colonial powers . . . undermine the lofty principles of the U.N." Less than a year later, a new Indonesian foreign minister, Adam Malik, spoke of Indonesia's hope to return to the U.N., but President Sukarno took vigorous public issue with him. Many believed that this was the last foreign policy issue on which Sukarno would compromise. Indonesia's return to the U.N. may be delayed, but it will surely come in time.

PEKING-DJAKARTA AXIS

There were clear indications in 1965 that Indonesia would seek to organize a counter-world organization composed of the New Emerging Forces (NEFOS), as Sukarno called the anti-colonial, underdeveloped countries of the world. It was open to serious question, however, whether such an action seconded (and financially supported), as it was, by Communist China, could be made to fit into a policy of nonalignment. In his Independence Day speech on August 17, 1965, President Sukarno proclaimed that Indonesia was joining China, North Vietnam, Cambodia and North Korea in building an "anti-imperialist axis," with the object of putting pressure on Britain, the United States and other Western powers to "get out of the whole of Southeast Asia altogether."

Sukarno's actions were by no means consistent with the fears of many of his countrymen respecting China. Most Indonesians have regarded that country as the ultimate and real threat to their national independence. Was Sukarno ready to play the role of a junior partner in the axis or of a satellite state, or did he plan to break with China once their common aim of getting the Western powers out of Southeast Asia had been achieved? Whatever his plans, he was gambling for high stakes: the dominance of Southeast Asia and a leading role in world politics.

For the United States the movement of Indonesian foreign policy was ominous. Peking would use such an axis to outflank American containment positions in the Philippines, South Vietnam, Thailand and Taiwan. For months before the announcement of the axis, Sukarno seemed to be pushing for an open break with the United States. When Marshall Green, the new American ambassador, presented his credentials to President Sukarno in July 1965, he was treated to a lecture on worsening relations between the two countries which, the president said, had "declined to the lowest point." The reason for this was ascribed to United States support of Malaysia and the war in Vietnam. When the ambassador returned to the embassy, he was greeted by a "go-home" demonstration by 3,000 shouting youths. In July demonstrators stoned the United States consulate in Medan. In August a mob of 7,000 Indonesian youths stoned the consulate in Surabaya and smeared the walls with anti-American slogans.

Imagine the surprise accordingly of American newspaper-readers when they read in their papers in early October 1965 of anti-Communist—and pro-American!—street demonstrations in Djakarta. This was in the wake of the abortive September 30-October 1 Communist coup. Indonesian military leaders and others, moreover, charged Chinese Com-

Indonesia

munist complicity in the would-be takeover, and relations between Peking and Djakarta, so recently hailed as allies and leaders of the New Emerging Forces (NEFOS), immediately deteriorated. Communist China suspended all aid and trade with Indonesia—worth millions to the badly disrupted Indonesian economy. Official and other informed Americans reacted with justifiable caution, however, as well they should have done. General Nasution warned the "neocolims," as he called the allegedly neocolonialist-imperialist powers, not to assume that the Djakarta government would abandon its leftist political policies.

There were other reasons for caution. Street mobs that one day demonstrate against the United States and another day against Communist China are hardly to be trusted as an accurate barometer of a country's foreign-policy orientation. The road back to a friendly relationship with the United States is a long one. So, too, is the road back to the United Nations or the road back to economic respectability for a nation that defaults on its international obligations. The United States, which had given Indonesia $800 million in aid before cancelling its program in 1965 because of violent anti-Americanism, agreed in early 1966 to sell Indonesia 50,000 tons of rice at a cost of $8,198,000, but this was only the beginning of any new stable political relationship. Indonesian foreign policy will surely change with time, one way or the other, but it is too early to suggest major alterations in its basic world outlook. Indonesia's foreign policy, after all, was not only Sukarno's foreign policy—or that of the Communists—but also the foreign policy of General Nasution, as his remarks in the aftermath of the unsuccessful coup indicated, and of major interest and other groups in Indonesian society.

CHAPTER 3

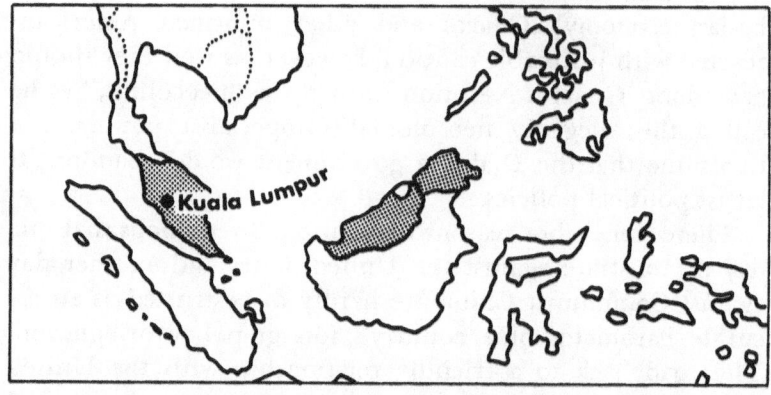

MALAYSIA
Crisis of Confrontation

MALAYSIA CAME INTO existence on September 16, 1963. It was really not a new state but came about by the incorporation into the Federation of Malaya (which had been granted independence in 1957) of three territories: the island of Singapore and Sarawak and Sabah (North Borneo), all former British dependencies. The extension of the federation to include these loose ends of the British empire in the region was generally greeted with approval but unfortunately with hostility on the part of its neighbors—the Philippines and Indonesia—mildly by the first and violently by the second. Instead of adding to the stability of Southeast Asia, as was widely hoped, the formation of the expanded federation led to extreme bitterness and an undeclared war.

HISTORICAL BACKGROUND

In contrast with its hostile neighbors Malaysia has not known long Western administration. Whereas Indonesia and the Philippines had been under Western rule for several centuries, Malaya escaped European penetration until the late wave of imperialism in the nineteenth century, and this in spite of the fact it lies on one of the world's most important water routes. Settlements and trading posts were established earlier at a few points, including the pendent islands of Penang and Singapore and the port of Malacca on the peninsula.

In 1786 the British East India Company obtained possession of the island of Penang from the Sultan of Kedah, who at the time, in trying to throw off the suzerainty of Siam, sought the aid of the British. When the East India Company failed to go to Kedah's assistance, the latter sought to recapture the island. The Company settled the matter by an agreement to pay the sultan and his successors 10,000 Malay dollars annually. As part of the deal Britain obtained Province Wellesley, a small area on the mainland opposite the island. Parenthetically it may be noted that a number of Malay sultanates, with a population of nearly a million, remain under Siamese rule to this day. No irredentist movement of any consequence has developed.

That Malacca occupied a strategic geographic position had been recognized long before the white man's arrival. Sultanates and empires had fought for its control. The Portuguese had taken it, and the Dutch in turn had wrested it from them in 1641. Singapore was maneuvered away from the Dutch in 1819 by the far-seeing Sir Stamford Raffles, who had been governor of Java during the British occupation in the Napoleonic wars. His views on the strategic position of the small island off the tip of the peninsula proved correct. It flourished from the day of its founding and is now one of the world's great commercial centers. In a trade with the Dutch for a small area on the west coast of Sumatra, the British in 1824 acquired Malacca.

Thus by 1824 Britain had control over the key points on —or just off—the peninsula, but hesitated to extend its control over the interior, which was ruled by over a dozen small sultanates. However, by 1873, matters had developed to the point where the British could no longer follow the policy of abstention. The opening of the Suez Canal in 1869, the introduction of the rubber tree from South America in 1877, the rapid development of tin mining and the influx of Western capital and Chinese and Indian labor greatly stimulated the commerce of Malaya. The internal situation in and among the petty states was not conducive to economic development. Britain obtained treaties with the sultans, in accordance with which the latter agreed to ask the advice of a British resident on all matters other than those touching upon the Islamic religion or Malay custom.

From this background there developed a bizarre pattern of governments: of Crown colony and protectorates, of directly and indirectly governed territories, of federated and unfederated territories, of eleven governments for an area the size of New York. The administration nevertheless attained a high level of efficiency. In comparison with that of neighboring territories its level of social services was high. The country prospered.

By the end of World War II this hodge-podge of feudalistic government had become thoroughly anachronistic. Unfortunately, a base on which a more modern government could be built was lacking. The whole system of treaty arrangements, on which most of the structure rested, could not be unilaterally swept aside. Though the war had brought some changes in attitude there was still very little political consciousness. There were sharp divisions among the various population groups, whose differences were not only ethnic but economic and religious. The native Malays, who constituted about half of the population, felt that the country belonged to them and resented the presence of the Chinese and Indians, whom they regarded as temporary residents with permanent interests in their homelands. Moreover, the Malays were peasants and fishermen; few among them had acquired middle-class status. By contrast, a considerable number of Chinese and Indians, especially the former, had amassed considerable wealth or had attained high professional status. The Chinese felt they had developed the country, while the Malays felt themselves aggrieved stepchildren in their native land. Economic power was in the hands of the British and the Chinese. Any shift from the existing feudalistic government to a more unified, democratic system could only result in giving the "outsiders" political power in addition to the great economic power they already enjoyed. This was the fear that haunted the Malays.

For the British this also presented a grave problem. The spirit of the times (and their own inclination) demanded rapid advances toward self-government, but there was no national group to whom they could turn over the reins. There did not yet exist a Malayan nation which could sustain and control a modern government. British policy in Malaya had not promoted the molding of the various ethnic groups into a single nation. Even if the policy had been different and the time to accomplish it greater, the results might have been almost the same, as the obstacles to nation-building under the existing conditions were great. The Japanese occupation had not tended to promote unity among the ethnic groups. The Malays continued to carry on the government under the Japanese much as they had under the British, while the Chinese were treated brutally. The Chinese regarded the Malays as collaborators.

THE "EMERGENCY"

The problem of instituting governmental reforms was made more difficult by the Communist insurrection, which strained the government's resources for over a decade. The British had trained and armed a nucleus of guerrillas before Singapore fell; Japanese brutality helped to increase their numbers. They became strong and were very effective in disrupting Japanese supply lines, but they fell more and more under Communist leadership. They punished collaborators, levied contributions on whomever they could, and collected them by fair means or foul. When the Malayan Communist Party in 1948 turned to organized violence to achieve its ends, it used this group as a base for a campaign of terror. Recruited mainly from young Chinese, it operated in the jungle behind a screen of agents in every village.

Though the number of guerrillas was not large—estimated at only 3,000 to 6,000—the campaign to suppress them was costly. Some 35,000 British soldiers and some airforce units, together with a large number of extra police and special constables, were mobilized. War against these Communists was difficult. Much of Malaya is jungle, which is ideal for guerrilla warfare. The large areas of rubber plantations offered much the same advantage. In addition, the guerrillas were aided by some half million Chinese who had squatted on the fringes of the jungle. During the depression in the 1930s Chinese laborers in tin mines and on the rubber plantations turned to the lands on the edge of the jungle for a livelihood; during the war their numbers were greatly increased by thousands of Chinese who fled from the towns. The squatters were in the clutches of the bandits; since they lived in areas where the police could not protect them, they were forced to furnish food, supplies, money and information. The guerrillas also obtained recruits from the squatters. Thus no real progress could be made against the bandits until something was done about the squatters. The solution was a resettlement program. The squatters were given small plots of land in accessible and protected communities where they could enjoy the advantages of education and social services.

The resettlement of so many people was necessarily an arduous and expensive task. It did not improve the relations between Malays and Chinese. Ninety percent of the guerrillas were Chinese, but the Chinese community did little to help suppress them. Few Chinese joined the police force of the federation. And in the resettlement program the government was spending huge sums on the section of the community which was economically least needy.

POSTWAR POLITICAL REORGANIZATION

According to the 1947 census, Malaya, including the Straits Settlements (of which Singapore was a part), had a population of 5,848,910. Of this number a little more than 38 percent of the total were Malays, about 5.5 percent were closely ethnically related Malaysians (chiefly Indonesians), nearly 45 percent were Chinese, and about 10.5 percent were Indians and Pakistanis; Europeans and Eurasians accounted for 0.3 percent each. The racial complexion of Malaya and Singapore separately was quite different. In Malaya, exclusive of Singapore, the Malays and Malaysians accounted for nearly 50 percent of the total population, the Chinese for a little more than 38 percent, and the Indians and Pakistanis for a little less than 11 percent. In Singapore the Chinese constituted nearly 78 percent, the Malays and Malaysians slightly more than 11 percent, and the Indians about 7.5 percent of the population. Singapore, with a population of 941,000 in 1947, and estimated at about 1,200,000 in 1957, is predominantly a Chinese city. Penang is also strongly Chinese, with over 55 percent of the population of that urbanized island belonging to that race.

The population of the country was growing rapidly, even though Chinese and Indian immigration during the depression and since the war had almost ceased. The rate of population growth was well over 2 percent—highest among the Chinese and lowest among the Malays. The fertility of all the communities was high, but the death rate among the Malays was much higher than among the Chinese and Indians.

About 60 percent of the Chinese in Malaya and about 50 percent of the Indians were locally born. The number returning to their native country was considerably greater among the Indians than among the Chinese. Since the Second World War, immigration has ceased to be an important factor in population growth. Religiously the population of Malaya was divided as follows: Islamic, 2,575,000 or 44 percent; Confucian-Buddhist, 2,560,000 or 43 percent; Hindu, 510,000 or nearly 9 percent; and Christian, 120,000 or about 2 percent. Religious divisions ran along racial lines; the Malays and Malaysians are Moslems almost to a man, the Chinese are Confucianist-Buddhist, and the Indians are predominantly Hindu, with a small number of Moslems and Sikhs. The literacy rate for the whole population of Malaya, including all ages, was 32 percent. It was highest among the Indians (40 percent) and lowest among the Malays (25 percent).

Malaya had, and still has, what is sometimes called a "plural society." The inhabitants of Malaya were not culturally and economically integrated; on the contrary, they were divided into sharply separated racial communities. The native Malays were the rice growers and small-holder producers of rubber. The lower and middle positions in the government were their patrimony. Few were found in wage-earning employment, in the professions, or in commerce. About 70 percent of the Indians and Pakistanis were laborers, chiefly on rubber plantations. A considerable number were in commerce and the professions. The Chinese were engaged in rubber cultivation both as laborers and as small holders, and they provided most of the laborers in the tin mines and a very large percentage of the factory workers. They also owned and operated tin mines, were strong in the professions, and very nearly dominated the commercial life of the country. The Europeans held the top positions in the government, were large producers of tin and rubber, and played a leading role in finance and shipping.

The economy of Malaya is heavily concentrated on the production of rubber and tin for export. These two commodities generally total over 80 percent of the value of all domestic exports and account for about a fifth of the national income. Singapore has a large entrepot trade. The Malayan per capita income is the highest in South and Southeast Asia.

The British government planned a thoroughgoing reorganization of the government of Malaya after the war in the direction of unification and democracy. The Malay aristocracy would be deprived of their privileged positions and the constitutional patchwork replaced by two governments—a Union of Malaya (which would include all the territories on the peninsula and the island of Penang) and Singapore. The latter was to be detached from the mainland and made a separate unit of government for two reasons. First, Singapore was a cosmopolitan free port, whose prosperity was in large part due to its entrepot trade. Its economic interests were not wholly tied to Malaya. Secondly, exclusion of Singapore from the union would give a majority to the Malays, the racial community least politically conscious and economically advanced.

The British plans were based upon the assumption that it would require a campaign of heavy fighting to drive the Japanese out of Malaya and that in the campaign British forces landing on the shores would be assisted greatly by Chinese guerrillas operating in the Japanese rear, with the Malay rulers, civil servants, and police giving passive if not active military aid to the enemy. The British prewar policy of "protecting" the Malays was regarded by the Chinese as unjustifiable favoritism. With the record of Malay collaboration with the enemy and active resistance by the Chinese, the old British policy could not be restored. However, the British did not return to Malaya in the manner expected.

The Japanese surrendered without the necessity of a campaign in Malaya; as a result the plan had either to be abandoned or carried out under unanticipated conditions. The British government decided on the latter course.

In pursuance of the decision to proceed with the plans, Sir Harold McMichael was sent to Malaya with essentially similar treaties for all the rulers to sign. The sultans apparently felt that they had no alternative, for all agreed to sign away most of the independence of their states and practically all of their own prerogatives. Strangely, the non-Malay communities, which stood to gain greatly by the proposed Malayan Union, did little or nothing in support of the proposal, but the response to it of the Malays, and especially of the Malay intellectuals, was immediate and strongly adverse. A United Malay National Organization (U.M.N.O., as it became popularly known) was formed under the leadership of Dato Onn Bin Jaafar to oppose the union proposals. Other organizations sprang up with the same purpose. Though the Malayan Union constitution was inaugurated in April 1946 and nominally remained in force for two years, some of its more important provisions were never given effect, and negotiations with the sultans and the U.M.N.O. for a revision of the constitution were begun almost immediately. Out of these negotiations emerged a new federation constitution which went into effect on February 1, 1948.

With the replacement of the union by the federation the Malay community had scored a victory over the non-Malay communities. The Malays were bitterly opposed to a democratic, unified government, for such a system would give the Chinese and Indians great influence, if not control, over the government. The intellectual Malays had no love for the old feudal system, but they were unwilling to see it swept away in order to open the door to political power for the non-native groups. They were caught in a dilemma. There was only a limited place for them in the old system, but a

Malaysia

more democratic system, they feared, would improve their position little. Citizenship and the right to vote were the crux of the problem. In the union proposals the provisions for citizenship were quite liberal—under the federation constitution more restricted. By excluding Singapore from the federation, the Malays were given an additional advantage on the peninsula.

DEMOCRATIC GOVERNMENT AND INDEPENDENCE

The Federation of Malaya, which was set up in 1948, comprised eleven units: the nine Malay States and the Settlements of Penang and Malacca. The federation agreement set up a legislative council composed of 75 members, of whom 50 were unofficial, 9 were the presidents of the state councils, 2 were from the settlement councils, and the remainder were ex officio and official members. The agreement also established federal citizenship "designed to draw together with a common loyalty all those who can be said to regard Malaya as their true home." The federation agreement provided that "as soon as circumstances and local conditions permit," legislation would be introduced for elections to the federal legislature and to the state and settlement legislative councils. Municipal elections, Malaya's first such voting, were held in 1951 in Penang, Malacca, and Kuala Lumpur.

A step forward on the road to democratization was a citizenship law which became effective in September 1952. By this law some 1,100,000 Chinese, between 50 and 60 percent of the federation's Chinese population, and 180,000 Indians, about 30 percent of the total, acquired citizenship. The Indians and the Chinese were not altogether pleased with the provisions of the law. It did not automatically grant citizenship to all persons born in Malaya, as the non-Malays demanded, but only to second generation non-Malays.

After these progressive steps the British government seemed

to hesitate. Oliver Lyttelton, the colonial secretary, warned in July, 1952, against moving too rapidly toward self-government in Malaya, stating that there was not yet enough fusion and unity to make self-government successful. Early in 1954 the colonial secretary rejected a request from the leaders of the U.M.N.O. and the M.C.A. (Malayan Chinese Association) for direct talks in London on federal elections and constitutional issues. The political leaders of Malaya reacted strongly. The strongest Malay party, the U.M.N.O., and the largest Chinese organization, the M.C.A., had already formed an alliance in order to present a common front. They were now joined by the Malayan Indian Association (M.I.A.). Sir Cheng-lock Tan, president of the powerful M.C.A., in December 1953 issued a strong statement in protest to the trend of the British pronouncements. He declared that if the transfer of power was delayed too long, the people might be provoked into impatience and hostility. The contention that national unity must precede self-government and that communal antipathies made such unity impossible, he said, would be interpreted as a policy of "divide and rule."

Regardless of the official British views on the feasible rate of progress toward self-government, events from 1952 moved rapidly and irresistibly toward that end. In the Kuala Lumpur municipal elections of that year the U.M.N.O. and the M.C.A. won nine of the twelve seats. The Alliance, as it came formally to be called, was so successful that it was expanded to municipal elections elsewhere in the country. In March 1953 the U.M.N.O., and the M.C.A. announced an agreement for the extension of the Alliance to the general elections for the federal legislative council. In August of that year the Alliance held a national congress which adopted a resolution making an independent state within the British Commonwealth and full responsible democratic government its goal and demanding that elections to the federal legislature be held the next year.

Malaysia

In 1954 yet another step was taken in the direction of self-government. The legislative council was enlarged to 98 members, of whom 52 were to be elected. The members of the executive council were to be subsequently appointed in consultation with the leaders of the group or groups commanding a majority of the elected members, thereby creating a sort of limited responsible government. In the elections held in July 1955 the Alliance, of which the Malayan Indian Association had also become a member, won 51 of the 52 elective seats. As a result of this triumph, the leader of the U.M.N.O. and of the Alliance, Tengku Abdul Rahman, was named chief minister.

Chief Minister Rahman and his Alliance now pressed hard for a timetable for independence within the Commonwealth. A Federation of Malaya Constitutional Conference met in London in January 1956 attended by representatives of the Malay rulers, the Alliance, and the United Kingdom. It was announced on February 6 that an agreement had been reached. The constitution for the new state was completed in the early months of 1957. The form of government remained federal, with an elected monarch as its titular head, the Yang di-Pertuan Agong, being elected by and from the group of Malay rulers for a term of five years. The legislature was bicameral, with a lower house (Dewan Ra'ayat) composed of 104 members and an upper house (Dewan Negara) of 38 members, two elected by the Legislative Assembly of each state and 16 appointed by the Yang di-Pertuan Agong. Each of the states and settlements had written constitutions and responsible government. The constitution during a transition period guaranteed the Malays special privileges, namely reservation of positions in the civil service, scholarships, business permits and licenses, and land. While the citizenship provisions were not as liberal as the Chinese and Indians desired, they did represent concessions by the Malays.

The Federation of Malaya became independent on August 31, 1957. It entered a defense treaty with the United Kingdom and became a member of the Commonwealth. Shortly after receiving its independence it was admitted to membership in the United Nations. Tengku Abdul Rahman, who previously had been chief minister, became the country's first prime minister. His cabinet of eleven members included three Chinese and an Indian. In the first federal elections under the new constitution, held in 1959, the Alliance won 73 of the 104 seats in the lower house. Although subject to considerable internal strains, the Alliance government seemed stable and strong. In 1960 it declared the "Emergency" ended.

SINGAPORE

Singapore became a separate crown colony in 1946, and it did not become a part of the new federation in 1948. The reasons for leaving it outside the new political organization of the peninsula were obvious. The Malays did not wish to include Singapore with its overwhelming Chinese population in the federation, while the British wished to safeguard their interest and that of the Commonwealth in the military, naval and air bases on the island.

Political reforms were begun in 1951, when the legislative council was reconstituted with a membership of 25. Of the 16 unofficial members, 4 were nominated by the governor, 3 were named by the Chamber of Commerce, and 9 were elected by constituencies. Only a fraction—48,000—of the persons qualified to vote registered, and of these only 52 percent actually voted. In 1953 automatic registration was introduced, whereby the number was increased to 300,000. A commission appointed in 1954 to advise on the amendment of the constitution recommended changing the name of the Legislative Council to Legislative Assembly and increasing the number of elective members to 25. These recommendations were adopted by the government, and elections under the new arrangements were held in April 1955. The leftwing parties, running on promises of repealing the emergency regulations, the immediate achievement of independence, and the creation of a socialist society, won 13 of the 25 seats.

David Marshall, who became premier by virtue of his role as unofficial leader of the Labor Front, hoped to achieve self-government for Singapore and the union of Singapore with Malaya. Tengku Abdul Rahman, the chief minister of the federation, rejected his advances for union. The Tengku had no desire to endanger the existing favorable political developments on the peninsula by bringing into the federation this urban center with its large Chinese population and its strongly leftist, if not Communist, tendencies. Marshall also failed in obtaining self-government for Singapore. He headed a delegation to London for a conference like that which had brought success to Rahman and his federation delegation only a few months earlier, but Singapore was a different story, due primarily to its position as an important military base. The British government offered extensive concessions, but not enough to satisfy Marshall, who said he wanted the whole loaf or none.

Marshall was succeeded as chief minister in June 1956 by Lim Yew Hock, a seasoned labor leader and an effective administrator. In his determination to put Singapore's house in order and then press for self-government, he was challenged by the Peoples Action Party (PAP), which encouraged strikes and political demonstrations. There was violence and bloodshed. In the campaign to eliminate criminal and subversive elements a large number of Chinese students, journalists, and trade union and PAP leaders were arrested. Negotiations for self-government were resumed. Agreement was reached in 1957 on a constitution to go into effect in 1959. The State of Singapore would be granted internal self-government while Britain would retain control over defense and external affairs. The problem of internal security in its relation to defense was solved by the creation of an

Internal Security Council composed of three British members, including the United Kingdom Commissioner, who would serve as chairman, the prime minister and two other members of the Singapore cabinet, and a nominee of the government of Malaya.

The constitution provided for a unicameral Legislative Assembly of 51 members elected from single member districts with compulsory voting. The first elections for the new assembly were held on May 30, 1959. The PAP received a clear majority of the popular vote and won 43 seats. Lee Kuan Yew, the leader of the party, did not believe that complete independence for Singapore was either practical or possible; its best hope, he thought, lay in a merger with the Federation of Malaya. Supported by moderates in the party, he sought to make the people of Singapore more Malayan-minded and to win the confidence of the people in the Federation by establishing conditions of law and order. As the leaders of the PAP became more moderate, left-wingers began to split off. By early 1962 the PAP's strength in the Legislative Assembly had dwindled to 26. It was obvious that Lee and his party would soon be swept aside by more radical forces unless they could achieve the merger of Singapore with the Federation.

NORTH BORNEO TERRITORIES

The Dutch had ample opportunity to make all of Borneo a part of their eastern empire, and had they done so there might today be no crisis of "confrontation." Between 1830 and 1840 there existed the opportunity for entering into political relations with Brunei and as late as 1859 Raja Brooke, Sarawak's European ruler, made proposals for the territory's transfer to the Netherlands. It was not until 1891 that a treaty with Great Britain was concluded establishing the boundary line between Dutch territory and the British protectorates of northern Borneo. By this agreement Britain obtained undisputed control over more than a fourth of the area of this large island.

SARAWAK

An adventurer, Sir James Brooke, laid the basis for British control of Sarawak. The Sultan of Brunei was having trouble with rebellions on the part of some of his subjects. In return for cessions of land, Brooke agreed to help him suppress the uprisings. In 1841 he was ceded several thousand square miles of land, which territory was greatly enlarged in subsequent years by additional cessions. In 1888 his successor placed the state under British protection. In 1946 the last of the "White Rajahs" ceded the state to the British Crown. This action was met by some protest in Sarawak.

Political reforms were begun in 1948 with the organization of local authorities. A new constitution was promulgated in 1956. It provided for a legislature of 45 members, of whom 24 were elective. Further electoral and constitutional advances in the direction of responsible government were made in 1963.

SABAH (NORTH BORNEO)

This territory also has a strange political background. In the 1860s an American company obtained a ten-year concession to a tract of land in North Borneo. Baron Overbeck, an Austrian, subsequently took over the concession of the American company from the Sultan of Brunei. Since the Sultan of Sulu also claimed rights of suzerainty over the area, Overbeck prudently obtained a concession from him, too. Control next passed to a British firm, which in 1881 consequently obtained a royal charter to organize the North Borneo Company. Britain assumed protection of the colony. The chartered company administered the colony until 1946, when it turned over its direction to the British Colonial Office.

Political life in the colony started slowly but moved rapidly when it began. From 1951 onward some progress was made in establishing local councils. In 1960 the advances were obtained of an unofficial majority in the Legislative Council and a decrease in official (and an increase in unofficial) membership in the Executive Council. By 1962 only seven of the 25 members of the Legislative Council were ex officio and official. As in Sarawak, further constitutional advances were made in 1963 in preparation for the state's membership in the Malaysian federation.

BRUNEI

The Sultan of Brunei once laid claim to jurisdiction over all of the territory of northern Borneo, but the area of his state was drastically reduced by the cession of Sarawak and North Borneo (Sabah) until it embraced only the present 2,226 square miles. The sultanate became a British Protectorate in 1888. By a treaty of 1906 the Sultan accepted a British Resident, who in effect ruled the state with the assistance of British members of the Malay Civil Service. Until 1959, when the Sultan promulgated a written constitution, there were no elections. Under the new constitution the post of British Resident was abolished and a Legislative Council set up, less than half of whose members were to be elected by District Councils. Elections were held in 1962.

Though small in area and population, Brunei is wealthy. The production of oil is the source of large revenues. Brunei not only has no public debt, but it has sizeable overseas investments. The state has a system of non-contributory old age pensions, something unknown elsewhere in Asia and by no means universal in the West.

Seeking an arrangement to bring the fragments of its empire in the region together so as to make them more viable after independence, Britain promoted "closer association" of the three northern Borneo states. Sir Anthony Abell, governor of Sarawak and high commissioner for Brunei, in February 1958, formally proposed a northern Borneo association, with a central authority, to deal initially with defense, external relations, internal security and communications. Little progress had been made by 1963, however.

FORMATION OF MALAYSIA

By 1962 the leaders of the Federation of Malaya, Prime Minister Lee of Singapore and his moderate supporters, and the British government were confronted with a critical situation, calling for difficult and far-reaching decisions. If Lee could not effect an early merger of Singapore with the Federation, he and his followers would be swept aside by a swift movement toward extreme radicalism, if not Communism. If this happened, what would be the fate of the city-island? And how would this affect the security of Malaya?

Prime Minister Rahman and his government were also faced with a hard dilemma. For the Malays, the idea of the inclusion in the Federation of Singapore with its overwhelming Chinese population had lost nothing of its old unpleasantness. In January 1957, Rahman gave utterance to the typical uncompromising Malay point of view. He declared that there would be no merger, pointing out that in independent Malaya, Malay would be the official language, Islam the religion and a Malay the paramount ruler—conditions unacceptable to the predominantly Chinese population of Singapore. In the following years he repeatedly declared his opposition to merger. But what were the possible situations with which Malaya might be confronted if it continued to refuse to admit Singapore into the Federation? In such a situation Singapore might look elsewhere for friends. An independent Singapore allied with or in control of a hostile power was not a remote possibility. The fear of a "Chinese

Cuba" off the southern tip of the Malay Peninsula clearly haunted Rahman. The problems created by Singapore's membership in the federation might be unusually thorny and sensitive, but the difficulties which would very likely arise with Singapore independent and hostile to Malaya would probably be even worse.

Quite understandably, the British government strongly favored merger. What would ultimately happen to the military base on Singapore if the island became independent? Merger would help solve this problem, and, if the Borneo territories could also be brought into an enlarged Malayan federation, so much the better. Britain was looking for solutions to at least two problems, and merger seemed the answer to both of them.

In an address on May 27, 1961, Prime Minister Rahman indicated a change of attitude. He suggested that Malaya, Singapore, Sarawak, Brunei and North Borneo "be brought closer together in political and economic cooperation." Rahman's suggestion was enthusiastically received in Singapore but with caution and hesitancy, and even opposition, in the Borneo territories. Negotiations began at once and proceeded intensively. Solutions had to be found to some difficult constitutional problems.

It is not difficult to see why Rahman was eager to include the Borneo territories in the merger. The Chinese constituted about 38 percent of the population of Malaya but more than 44 percent of the combined populations of Malaya and Singapore. Indeed, in the combined population of the two territories the Chinese outnumbered the Malays. According to government estimates the population of the two territories on December 31, 1963, was as follows: Chinese 4,195,329; Malays (including aborigines and Indonesians) 4,107,029; Indians and Pakistanis, 1,005,870; and others 194,692. For all of Malaysia, however—that is, inclusive of northern Borneo—the percentage of Chinese was somewhat lower. Nevertheless, even in Malaysia as a whole the

Chinese outnumber the Malays. In Sarawak the Malays constitute only about a sixth of the population and in Sabah even less. Could Rahman assume that the non-Malay indigenous peoples of these territories would always align themselves politically with the Malays? He was taking risks.

If the seats in the new federal parliament had been allocated in proportion to population, Singapore would have had 25 of the total membership of 159, a not inconsiderable bloc. Fortunately for Rahman and the Malays, it was not necessary to grant Singapore so large a number. Singapore wished to keep control of its educational and labor policies. In exchange for this concession of autonomy, Singapore's representation in the Malaysian parliament was set at only 15.

A difficult problem centered on the Singapore military base. Britain had undoubtedly contemplated with deep concern the possibility of the military base falling under the sovereignty of an independent Singapore. Merger removed this danger, but it did not solve the problem completely. While Malaya under Rahman was decidely pro-Western in its orientation, it shunned the Southeast Asia Treaty Organization (SEATO), of which Britain was a member. Britain and Malaya agreed to extend the existing defense agreement with the Federation to embrace the whole of Malaysia, and the Malaysian government undertook to continue to afford the British government the right to maintain the Singapore base "for the purpose of assisting in the defence of Malaysia and for the Commonwealth defence and for the preservation of peace in Southeast Asia." The defense installations were not to be used for SEATO purposes, but the defense of Malaysia, the preservation of peace in Southeast Asia, and SEATO purposes would seem not to be easily distinguishable.

Accession of the Borneo territories to the Malaysian union was by no means an easy task. There was considerable sentiment in these territories for their amalgamation into a new and independent state of North Borneo. The British and Malayan leaders made extensive efforts, however, to win the Borneans to Malaysia. A special British and Malayan commission under the chairmanship of Lord Cobbold, a former Governor of the Bank of England, was sent to Sarawak and North Borneo to ascertain sentiment about the proposed federation. It reported in July 1962, that majority opinion favored the federation.

In Brunei there was strong opposition to the proposed federation. The Party Ra'kyat, which favored a union of the three Borneo states under the Sultan of Brunei as a constitutional monarch, won all the elected seats in the Legislative Council in 1962. The chief spokesman for the party, a man named Azahari, who had spent some time in the Indonesian army, denounced the proposed federation as a device to reduce Brunei to a colony of Malaya. He became the leader of an armed rebellion which broke out in December 1962. British troops sent from Singapore put down the rebellion. It was probably because of this opposition, as well as the failure to reach agreement on the distribution of revenues and the question of precedence for the sultan with respect to his eligibility to become the Paramount Ruler, that Brunei decided not to join Malaysia.

Public opinion in Sabah and Sarawak moved in favor of the Malaysia plan. In Sabah the pro-Malaysia Sabah Alliance won an overwhelming victory in elections held shortly after the Brunei revolt broke out. Pro-Malaysian parties also won handily in elections held in Sarawak in July, 1962. As a result of constitutional changes made in 1963 both territories entered the federation with a system of responsible government and legislatures that were almost completely elective (either directly or indirectly).

The test of public opinion took a peculiar, though not necessarily dubious, form in Singapore. It was assumed that the general election of 1959 had been a referendum on the issue since merger had been one of the principal planks in the government's platform. The voters were accordingly given the choice of three alternatives: 1) merger under the terms of the government's 1961 agreement with Malaya, 2) unconditional merger on the same terms as the existing 11 states of Malaya, and 3) merger on terms no less favorable than those for the Borneo territories. In a referendum which was held on September 1, 1962, 560,000 votes were cast out of an electorate of 625,000. The first alternative received 397,626 votes. The parties opposed to merger urged the voters to express their opposition by casting blank ballots; 144,077 blank votes were cast.

Clear evidence of the very substantial popular support that existed for Malaysia at the time could be found in the elections for the Malaysian parliament held in May 1964. The Alliance won 125 and the PAP 13 of the 159 seats. Thus the two parties most responsible for the merger won an overwhelming victory.

CONFRONTATION

After two years of consultation, negotiation and compromise the stage was set for the Federation of Malaysia to come into existence. In accordance with the final agreement of July, 1963, between Britain and the Federation of Malaya, the new federation was scheduled to be launched on August 31, 1963. Because of the bitter opposition which had developed to the formation of the federation on the part of Indonesia and the Philippines, the date was postponed to September 16. Strangely, this hostility developed at the same time that the three countries were actively engaged in developing closer relations. In 1959 Malaya and Indonesia had concluded a Friendship Treaty. In July 1961, Malaya, Thailand and the Philippines formed the Association of Southeast Asia (ASA) for the purpose of establishing effective machinery for close economic and cultural cooperation and mutual assistance. And on August 5, 1963, when the formation of the Federation of Malaysia was nearly an accomplished fact, Presidents Sukarno and Macapagal and Prime Minister

Rahman announced in Manila that they had agreed to establish a new regional organization, Maphilindo, for the purpose of strengthening "cooperation among their peoples in the economic, social and cultural fields" and of combining "their efforts in the common struggle against colonialism and imperialism in all their forms and manifestations and for the eradication of the vestiges thereof in the region in particular. . . ." This agreement was interpreted at the time as indicating a relaxation of the opposition to merger, but this was not to be the case. As later used by Sukarno, it would appear that the Maphilindo agreement was regarded as a means of blocking the Malaysian merger. In any event, one of the grounds stressed by Indonesia in protesting the federation's formation was that it was done in violation of the Maphilindo principles.

Indonesia did not at first oppose the establishment of Malaysia. Dr. Subandrio, Indonesia's Foreign Minister, stated in the General Assembly of the United Nations in September 1961, that "when Malaya told us of her intentions to merge with the three British Crown colonies of Sarawak, Brunei and British North Borneo as one Federation, we told them that we have no objections and that we wish them success with this merger so that everyone may live in peace and freedom." However, the statement contained a passage which indicated a basic unhappiness with the movement. "Naturally," said Subandrio, "ethnologically and geographically speaking, this British part is closer to Indonesia than, let us say, to Malaya. But we still told Malaya that we have no objections to such a merger based upon the will for freedom of the peoples concerned." The sentiments born of ethnic and geographical ties seemingly triumphed in the end, however.

Indonesia's attitude toward Malaysia changed after the revolt in Brunei in December 1962. In a speech at Djokjakarta on January 20, 1963, Dr. Subandrio declared, "We cannot but adopt a policy of confrontation towards Malaysia because at present they represent themselves as accomplices of neo-colonialist and neo-imperialist forces pursuing a policy hostile towards Indonesia." Two days later a spokesman for the Ministry of Foreign Affairs declared that Indonesia's policy of confrontation amounted to a direct offensive against Malaysia in the economic and social spheres but involved no military activity. That the Federation of Malaysia was the product of British neocolonialism was given as the chief justification for the policy. L. N. Palar, Indonesia's chief representative at the U.N., declared in the General Assembly in September 1963, that Britain had helped to form Malaysia in order to perpetuate its sphere of influence in Southeast Asia, while Defense Minister General Abdul Haris Nasution declared in a nation-wide radio broadcast on October 4: "Malaysia is a state under foreign control politically, economically and particularly militarily. As a result, it is becoming the base for foreign domination in Southeast Asia and for subverting our economy and security." President Sukarno denounced Malaysia as a "neocolonialist conspiracy" and as a plot to encircle Indonesia militarily, to "corner" Indonesia. He vowed to "crush" Malaysia.

Privately Indonesians have said that their government was opposed to Malaysia because it would facilitate Chinese infiltration into northern Borneo and thus prepare the way for China taking over this strategic area. On the other hand, Prime Minister Rahman gave as one of the reasons for creating Malaysia that it would prevent China picking off these territories one by one. In June, 1963, it looked as if Indonesia and the Philippines had relaxed their opposition to Malaysia and that the former had made a significant shift away from its policy of neutralism. The Maphilindo agreement was widely interpreted as an anti-Peking pact. This interpretation was largely based on a paragraph of the joint communique issued at the conclusion of the conference of the foreign ministers of the three countries held at Manila from June 7 to 11, which stated: "The Ministers were of one mind that the three countries share a primary responsibility for the maintenance of the stability and security of the area from subversion in any form or manifestation in order to preserve their respective national identities. . . ." Whatever the reasons behind this statement, Indonesian policy did not move any further in this direction. Quite the reverse, the Indonesian Communist Party and Sukarno adopted a steadily more pro-Peking line.

The foreign ministers at their Manila meeting proposed that the Secretary General of the United Nations be asked to ascertain whether the peoples of Sabah and Sarawak wished to join the Federation of Malaysia. This recommendation was adopted by the two presidents and the prime minister at their meeting in Manila from July 30 to August 5. United Nations teams began their survey on August 26. To enable the Secretary General to make his report on the findings of the teams, Prime Minister Rahman postponed the date of inaugurating the federation to September 16. Malaya and the Philippines agreed to seek a solution to the problem of the latter's claim to sovereignty over parts of Sabah after the formation of Malaysia. Secretary General U Thant made his report on September 14. He concluded that the majority of the peoples of Sabah and Sarawak, after having given "serious and thoughtful consideration to their future, and to the implications for them of participation in a federation of Malaysia . . . wish to engage with the peoples of the Federation of Malaya and Singapore, in an enlarged federation of Malaysia through which they can strive together to realize the fulfillment of their destiny."

The Indonesian and Philippine governments refused to accept the United Nations findings as valid, and the former stepped up its confrontation against Malaysia. Raids were made on Malaysian territory in Borneo and paratroopers were dropped in Malaya. Several countries offered to mediate the dispute but all to no avail. A truce arranged by United States Attorney General Robert Kennedy in January, 1964, broke down when Malaysia demanded that Indonesia withdraw its guerrillas from Malaysian territory as a condition for a summit meeting on the dispute. Sukarno, on the other hand, declared that Indonesia would not withdraw its guerrillas from Malaysian territory until the political issues between the two countries had been settled.

In a letter of September 3, 1964, the Malaysian government informed the President of the Security Council of the United Nations that Indonesian paratroopers had been landed in south Malaya and requested an urgent meeting to consider this act of "blatant and inexcusable aggression against a peaceful neighbor." The Indonesian representative did not deny the Malaysian charges; he justified Indonesian actions as part of a campaign against imperialism and colonialism, as giving aid to the peoples of Malaysia who were seeking liberation. A mild Norwegian resolution which expressed no condemnation of Indonesia but merely deplored the incident of which Malaysia had complained and called upon the parties to refrain from all threats and use of force and to resume their talks, received nine votes. Only Czechoslovakia and the Soviet Union voted against it, but the negative Russian vote constituted a veto.

THE POSITION OF THE PHILIPPINES

Part of the explanation for the Philippine position is to be found in former President Diosdado Macapagal's personal interest in the claim of the heirs of the Sultan of Sulu to sovereign rights over a part of North Borneo. As a member of Congress he had introduced a resolution calling on the president of the Philippines to press the British government for the recognition of the sovereign jurisdiction of the Philippines over the territory. The resolution was adopted by the House of Representatives in 1950 but failed of passage in the Senate. When Macapagal became president, agitation for the "recovery" of North Borneo was revived and stepped up. The British government's brusque rejection of the claim may have stiffened Macapagal's position in the matter. The Philippine government was obviously embarrassed by the extreme belligerence of Indonesia and sought to dissociate itself from the latter position and to restore normal relations with Malaysia. Diplomatic relations were finally restored in June 1966.

The Philippine conduct in the affair may also be explained in part by the young republic's search for a distinctly national foreign policy. This quest led President Macapagal to seek to loosen Philippine attachments to the United States and to establish a position of greater influence in Southeast Asia. Such a policy involves dangers, especially in the present situation. Indonesia has three times the population of the Philippines and at the moment boasts large, well-equipped armed forces. Any weakening of the ties with the United States may expose the Philippines to the dangers of Indonesian expansionism. The "Sukarno-Macapagal doctrine"—that Asian problems should be solved by Asians in an Asian way—may mean that they will be solved in accordance with Indonesia's wishes. It was understandable that Sukarno should have placed so much stress on the doctrine, but was it wise for Macapagal to do so? The same may be asked about the paragraph in the joint statement of August 5, 1963, in which foreign bases were referred to as "temporary in nature" and the three signatories pledged to abstain from the use of arrangements of collective defence to serve the particular interests of any big powers. The wording may seem to be innocuous, but it could be used to weaken the American and British presence in the region, which can hardly operate to strengthen the independence of small states.

Malaysia

BASIC ISSUES OF CONFRONTATION

The basic differences which divide Indonesia and Malaysia are not superficial. They run deep. Malaysia suspects Indonesian leaders of expansionist aims, of a desire to revive a greater Majapahit Empire, while Indonesians are convinced that Malaysia is seeking to destroy their republic.[1] "From Singapore," said Dr. Sudjarwo, the Indonesian representative before the Security Council of the United Nations on September 9, 1964, "we suffered and continue to suffer economic subversion and manipulation, and both Singapore and Malaya . . . have provided not only a shelter but an active base for secessionist rebels against the Republic since 1958." Moreover, the two countries follow diametrically opposite economic and foreign policies. Indonesia neglected economic development in favor of armaments and confrontation, while Malaya chose economic development. Malaya is prosperous; Indonesia is in a desperate economic condition. Malaya encourages free enterprise and foreign investments and enjoys a high level of prosperity and social welfare; Indonesia has moved toward a "socialist" economy, discourages foreign investments and experiences dire poverty. To top it all, Malaysians have a democratic government, while Indonesia abandoned such a system for "guided democracy" with its restrictions of political liberty. Neighboring states following such different policies and having such different experiences, especially if one is much larger than the other, are quite likely to be mortal enemies.

The two states, however, had one thing in common, namely, a lack of national unity. This raised the question of which could better withstand protracted confrontation. Would confrontation promote integration or the reverse? Which state would stand up under continued pressure? Malaysia seemed to have many advantages: an efficient civil service, a sound and growing economy, the support of power-

---

[1] See *Indonesian Intentions Towards Malaysia*, with a foreword by Abdul Rahman, Malaysian Minister of Internal Security. Kuala Lumpur, 1964.

ful allies, and the sympathy of most of the free world. Malaysia enjoyed the second highest per capita income in Asia, being surpassed only by Japan. It was the world's largest producer of rubber and tin. These two commodities accounted for about 25 percent of the country's gross national product and more than 75 percent of its exports (rubber alone for over 50 percent), and they contributed nearly half the government's total revenues. While these two commodities added greatly to the country's prosperity, the importance of their production rendered the economy highly vulnerable. The price of rubber, moreover, was under heavy pressure from competition with synthetic rubber. Malaysia, in addition, produced only half of its food requirements. Thus, though the economy was flourishing, it had weak aspects. The severance of trade relations by Indonesia and the setting up of rival free ports in its territory hurt the economies of Penang and Singapore, though not seriously.

On the eve of the inauguration of the Federation, all elements of the population seemed united in favor of Malaysia. The resounding election victories of the PAP in Singapore and of the Alliance and its allies in the other territories strongly suggested such solidarity. Yet national unity in a state so consciously constructed would require years to achieve. The creation of the federation was an act of faith; its political structure was fragile. Bitter communal riots between Chinese and Malays broke out in Singapore in July 1964, and again in September. The riots were responsible for a score of deaths and several hundred wounded. The riots may have been provoked by Indonesian agents and local Communists, but they were made possible by basic antagonisms between the two communities—the Malay minority, which feels socially depressed, and the more energetic and better educated Chinese.

The situation was delicate. The political advantages enjoyed by the Malays and the special privileges guaranteed them in the Constitution created, and continues to cause, dissatisfaction among the Chinese. This can easily be exploited—as can also the Malay fear of Chinese economic power. Singapore's Prime Minister Lee Kuan Yen charged that "ultras" in Rahman's party were bent on preventing Malaysian-born Chinese from playing an equal role in governing Malaysia despite the fact that Malays constituted less than 40 percent of Malaysia's population. On June 3, 1964, Lee made a statement to the press in which he warned that unless attacks by the Malay-language press on him and indirectly on ethnic Chinese ceased "blood will flow again." Lee and his People's Action Party demanded a "Malaysian Malaysia" and not a Malaysia in which the Malays expected to control the central government indefinitely merely because they were the country's indigenous inhabitants. The Singapore prime minister was seeking to form a coalition opposition in the national parliament. He suggested the desirability of "other arrangements" for a new federation if the Chinese were not to be allowed to share equally in Malaysia's ownership and government.

OUSTER OF SINGAPORE

Prime Minister Rahman urged moderation on the Malays, but Lee's attack on the special rights of Malays caused a sharp reaction among the Malay ultra-nationalists. Suddenly, on August 7, 1965, the national parliament passed a resolution expelling Singapore from the federation. Lee was informed about the contemplated move only the day before. He and his cabinet signed a separation agreement only after they were convinced that the expulsion could not be prevented. Rahman justified the action on the ground that it was the only solution to the growing friction between Chinese and Malays.

The expulsion of Singapore came as the result of both internal conflict and external pressure. How much it was due to the latter is difficult to judge. The Indonesian embargo reduced Singapore's external trade by 15 percent. In any case, Sukarno and the Indonesians hailed it as a great triumph for their confrontation policy. Malaysia and Singapore, recognizing their economic need of each other, have agreed to carry on trade as usual. Trade between the two in 1964 totaled $1.7 billion. In 1962 Singapore's exports to Indonesia totaled $98 million and its imports $268 million. Indonesia proposed to renew trade relations with Singapore, but Prime Minister Rahman warned the latter against any attempt to establish diplomatic and trade relations with the former. He hinted that his government might cut off Singapore's water supply if it attempted to do so.

In their separation agreement Malaysia and Singapore agreed that Britain should retain the military bases on the island. British military expenditures in Singapore are important for the island's economy, but this is no guarantee that movement for the removal of the bases will not develop. Rahman has declared that Britain can build a military base on Malaysian territory. As long as the British military bases remain in Singapore, Indonesia will probably not wholly abandon its policy of antagonism toward the island-state—although it may seem to soften its hostility.

Prime Minister Rahman has warned Sarawak and Sabah that it would be foolish to try to secede from the federation, that they could not do it constitutionally, and that they could not survive as independent states.

THE END TO CONFRONTATION?

It is hazardous to predict the extent to which Indonesian hostility to Malaysia will be abandoned. Few would question the resourcefulness and doggedness of Indonesia's long-time President Sukarno—least of all the Dutch. But Sukarno is aging and ill, and his political power seemed to decline appreciatively in late 1965 and particularly in the first months of 1966. There are factors, however, which will

Malaysia

continue to tempt Indonesia's leaders, whoever they may be: Malaysian communal discord, internal Communist opposition to the Federation within Malaysia, the favorable terrain of north Borneo for infiltration, and the presence of over 30,000 Indonesians in Sabah. Indonesia, for its part, has seemingly sought to abandon the military dimension of confrontation because of its deteriorating economy and the fact that it is not itself lacking a danger of disintegration. The abortive pro-Communist coup of October 1, 1965—and the following killings of some thousands of Communists by aroused Moslems—clearly indicates that Indonesia, too, is internally troubled. Internal discord, on the other hand, could encourage renewed international adventurism as a means of relieving domestic pressures.

If either or both countries broke up, who would pick up the pieces? The odds would seem to be in favor of Communist China. For this reason, it seems likely that Indonesia's present leadership, which appears to have abandoned Sukarno's past policy of cooperation with Peking and genuinely wishes to employ Indonesia's resources in a more beneficial way, sincerely wants to improve relations with Malaysia, if it can do so in a face-saving fashion. President Sukarno continued to support confrontation even after the setback suffered by his internal Communist allies in late 1965; so, too, did General Suharto and new Foreign Minister Adam Malik, both acclaimed as moderates. But General Suharto also said that Indonesia "remained open to a peaceful settlement" but one based on the "needs of the revolution and the people." Confrontation has not accomplished what Sukarno said it would accomplish. The soldiers are tired of the policy, and the Indonesian masses are much more concerned with the persisting problem of earning enough to supply themselves with the necessities of life.

The proclaimed continued endorsement of confrontation by Suharto and Malik appeared by mid-1966 to have been part of an internally required policy of caution in backing down from the most vigorously proclaimed foreign policy of the late Sukarno years. Malik traveled to Bangkok to meet with Malaysia's Deputy Premier and Foreign Minister Abdul Razak, and on June 1 the two leaders announced verbal agreement on "practical steps" to end the undeclared war that had been raging between their countries for three years. Specifically, Malik and Razak agreed "to submit for approval to their respective governments the principles upon which practical steps to restore friendly relations between the two countries should be based."

Any settlement between the two nations, however, must be watched. The basic differences dividing them remain, and Indonesian abandonment of confrontation, if it fully takes place, will not mean an end to Djakarta's desire to dominate the whole of Borneo and to attain leadership of the broader Malay world embracing the Malay peninsula and even the Philippines. Containment of such irredentist aspirations will probably challenge both Malaysia and the Philippines—repeatedly—in the years and decades ahead.

CHAPTER 4

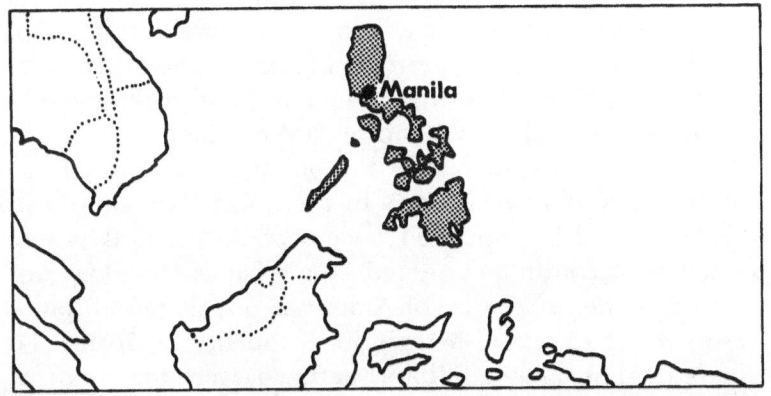

THE PHILIPPINES
Doubting Democracy

MORE THAN 450 years ago the Portuguese navigator Ferdinand Magellan, sailing in the service of Spain, discovered a chain of islands which the ancestors of the present-day Filipinos had found centuries earlier. What the Filipino of 450 years ago, if indeed he was a Filipino,[1] had not discovered, however, was himself and his fellow Filipinos. There was no common sense of identity among the ancestors of today's Filipinos, and it was the unifying effect of Spanish colonial rule which ultimately developed such a feeling. The Spaniards ruled the Philippines, or parts thereof, for nearly three and a half centuries—centuries of authoritarian government during the last years of which the impact of European liberalism presaged the attempted ouster of the foreign occupier.

The Spanish were followed by the Americans, who, depending on the interpretation, ousted Spain from the Philippines or seized the islands just as the Filipinos were about to oust the Spanish. In any event, the three and a half centuries of Spanish rule were followed by 50 years of American colonial government dedicated both to the early independence and maximum democratization of the Philippines. The result of these two quite different types of colonial rule is the modern Philippine nation—avowedly democratic politically, Catholic in faith, and more modern and united than any other Southeast Asian land.

The Philippines, in fact, is the oldest continuously functioning nonwestern democracy in the world. No country in Asia or Africa has operated a democratic political system for a longer continuous period. To what extent does this fact justify the imposition of American rule as the Filipinos were seeking to establish their independence of Spain? To what extent is today's Filipino nation largely the result of the experience of Spanish rule of the islands? And to what extent is the Philippines of today still Filipino in ways that evaded both Spanish and American proselytizers?

BEFORE COLONIALISM

The string of islands on which Magellan landed in 1521 numbered more than 7,000 and embraced a total area of nearly 116,000 square miles. The two largest of these are Luzon, the big northern island, and Mindanao, the big southern one, which, covering 40,814 and 36,906 square miles respectively, account for 67 percent of the total area of the archipelago. The eleven largest islands (including Cebu from which Magellan launched his attack against Lapulapu) make up 95 percent of the land area of the Philippines.

[1] A well-known Filipino historian raised the question in 1965 of whether the now revered chieftain Lapulapu, whose men killed Magellan, thought of himself as a "Filipino." The historian thought that he did not do so, but Gemma Cruz (Philippine beauty queen, "Miss International," and spirited nationalist) thought differently and abruptly left the professor's lecture. The professor, she said, was a "little brown Spaniard."

The Philippines

Situated 200 miles south of Formosa, governed today by the Chinese Nationalists, and 700 miles east of Vietnam, which was even then threatened by China, the Philippines represented a Pacific gateway then—as now—to the rest of Southeast Asia to the west and to the Asian mainland.

The Filipino whom Magellan encountered was by no means the first human type to inhabit the islands. Thousands of years earlier, more primitive peoples had come to the islands—including the ancestors of the pigmy negrito types still to be found in the country today. The brown-skinned Malays did not reach the Philippines until two or three centuries before the birth of Christ, coming from parts of present-day Indonesia. A more significant wave of Malay migration began about the start of the Christian era and lasted through the thirteenth century. These migrants were the ancestors of today's major Filipino peoples—the Tagalogs, the Ilocanos, the Visayans, and such. Still more Malays, these practitioners of the Moslem faith, came in the late fourteenth and fifteenth centuries, settling in Mindanao and the nearby Sulu archipelago.

Some of the ways of the pre-Spanish Filipino were no different from those of his descendant of today. The rural Filipino house, for example, was then, as now, built on piles high above the ground and made of wood, bamboo, and nipa palm—from which it gets its name, nipa-hut. But there were other important ways in which the ancestor of today's Filipino was most distinct from his twentieth century counterpart. And, even though he undoubtedly would have changed his ways even if the Spaniards had never come and imposed their rule over him, the fact is that there was a Spanish presence—and Filipino change took a particular form because of this presence.

There was nothing akin to the kind of centralized government, such as the Burmese and the Thai possessed, for example, before the coming of the Spanish. The basic unit of government was the *barangay,* more a kinship group than anything else and comprising as few as 30 and as many as 100 families. The head of this community was the *datu,* or chief, who made laws, carried them out, and adjudicated differences among his subjects. Alliances were frequently established among *barangays,* but they were also as frequently broken—and wars between chiefs and their armed followers were not uncommon. The Spanish in this sense brought unparalleled peace to the islands (for which they were rarely credited).

It would not be accurate to consider all Filipinos before the imposition of Spanish rule "free," as many nationalists are wont to do. There were three distinct classes in pre-Spanish times: nobles, freemen, and serfs. The former comprised the chiefs, their families and their friends—the ruling class—and they could behave more or less as they pleased (as, indeed, do many members of the same class in the Philippines today). The freemen were what their name implies—men free of any kind of bondage but by no means possessed of the range of privileges enjoyed by the ruling class. The serfs, who have also been called slaves and dependents, owed various kinds of service both to the nobles and the freemen. The serf could escape his status, however, and the freeman could fall into it.

Pre-Spanish Filipino life was not democratic, but then neither was life in contemporary Spain. Nor were many Filipinos free except in the sense that no foreigner ruled over them. The lot of the average Filipino, however, was no worse than that of the ordinary man in most other Southeast Asian lands. In fact, free from military attack from outsiders, such as the Chinese—a freedom not enjoyed by the Vietnamese, Burmese or Javanese, for example—the Filipino probably fatalistically regarded his as the best of any possible life.

THE SPANISH PRESENCE

Magellan came upon the islands known today as the Philippines in 1521 while on an expedition to circumnavigate the

The Philippines

globe. They were claimed by him for Spain and named in honor of Prince Philip, later Philip II—a circumstance which continues to irk some Filipino nationalists down to the present time (a handful of these desiring to change the name of their country in order to remove what they regard as a degrading reminder of their past colonial servitude). Not until about half a century after Magellan's discovery of the archipelago, however, did Spain establish any permanent settlements in the Philippines. These settlements were established on the island of Cebu in 1569 and at Manila, present-day main city of the Philippines, in 1571, following an expedition sent out from Mexico under the command of Miguel Lopez de Legaspi. Spanish administration was subsequently (if gradually) extended throughout the archipelago, though it never was really effectively established among the Moslems of the south. The diffusion of Spanish cultural influences also took place and resulted in many lasting changes. In 1611 the Royal and Pontifical University of Santo Tomas was founded in Manila; it is today the oldest university in Asia.

As a result of Spanish rule the Filipinos became Christianized and the most Westernized of the Asian peoples. Islam had come to Mindanao and the Sulu islands about two centuries before the Spanish arrived, however, and the natives of these islands have remained Moslems, numbering about one million today. About 90 percent of the population is Christian, 80 percent of these belonging to the Roman Catholic church. Filipino Protestantism developed as a result of the American colonial occupation, and Protestants today number 8 percent of the Filipino people. Pagans, constituting some 5 percent of the inhabitants of the islands, are found mainly in the mountain fastnesses of northern Luzon and Mindanao.

While the Spanish did practically nothing to advance or train the Filipinos in self-government, they indirectly created the conditions which were bound to produce a nationalist movement. Spain brought the peoples of the many islands under one administration and gave the upper classes a common language and the masses a common religion, thus gradually welding the different ethnic groups into a nation. The Spanish clergy also acquired great wealth, mainly in the form of landholdings, and this contributed to the growing social dissatisfaction which partly underlay the revolutionary outbreak of 1896. The increasing number of Filipinos who traveled to Europe for their education after the opening of the Suez Canal—among them the most revered of Filipino nationalist heroes, the subsequently martyred José Rizal—returned to the islands infused with liberal ideas, ideas which would soon fire the first nationalist uprising against European colonial rule in all Asia. It was a nationalist revolt which produced a very liberal, modern constitution and which might have succeeded if the United States and Spain had not fought a war in the Caribbean which spilled over into the far Western Pacific. The latter development may have been to the advantage of the Philippines, however, as it is by no means sure, as some Filipino nationalist historians assert, that the new Filipino nation would have been able to hold its own against all comers in a world in which European imperialism was still expanding.

The revolt against Spain broke out in 1896, was put down, and then re-emerged after the American military victory against the Spaniards in Manila Bay in 1898. The United States and Spain ended their war and came to terms in February, 1899, terms which included the cession of the Philippines to the former. The Filipino revolutionaries, however, had proclaimed their republic, naming their military leader General Emilio Aguinaldo as its president, only a month earlier and were in no mood to exchange one colonial master for another. The American government now found itself in the awkward position of having to put down a movement for national independence that had adopted both a constitution and a republican regime. Not until April 1901, did General Aguinaldo surrender.

AMERICAN RULE

The establishment of United States sovereignty over a territory many miles from the American mainland and inhabited by an alien people who were already engaged in a bitter struggle for independence presented a new departure in American policy, the meaning of which was not at once apparent to the American nation. Assuming responsibility for the destiny of the Philippines was not expansion into sparsely peopled areas awaiting American settlement but imperialism, and for this the American people were not prepared. As a result there was much inconsistency in America's Philippine policy. In many respects the distant tropical territory was treated as if it were to become a part of the American union. English was made the official language of the islands, even though another Western language, Spanish, already enjoyed wide use. Much of the American legal system was extended to the overseas territory, and as soon as the peace treaty with Spain permitted it, tariff barriers between the two countries were removed, and the economic life of the Philippines thus was made increasingly dependent upon the United States. On the other hand, there soon developed a general assumption that the Philippines was to be granted independence and that the only justification and function of the United States in the islands was to prepare the Filipinos for self-government as rapidly as possible.

For an understanding of American policy in the Philippines it is necessary to keep certain factors in mind. Americans never became conscious of their responsibility in the Philippines. There were reasons for this. The islands were a long way from the continental United States—some 8,000 miles—and few Americans visited them. Moreover, the area and the population of the United States was large in comparison with that of the Philippines, and there was little pressure on Americans to seek outlets for people or capital in the dependencies overseas. The cause of Philippine independence, moreover, had a major advantage, which Filipino nationalist representatives in the United States fully exploited, and that was the generally strong anticolonial sentiment of the American people.

The United States had been an immigrant-receiving country on an enormous scale, and in order to assimilate these vast numbers, the American people had unconsciously come to emphasize cultural assimilation and conformity. The situation was not one to develop sympathy for foreign cultures. In contrast with the Dutch, who did not try to Dutchify the Indonesian peoples, the Americans quite naturally followed a policy of cultural assimilation in the Philippines.

American rule in the Philippines, which began in 1899, became civilian government when William H. Taft, later to become president of the United States, assumed his position as governor of the islands in 1901. Governor Taft was assisted by a commission which included, besides himself, four other Americans and three Filipinos. This was the chief ruling body of the Philippines for the first six years of American civilian rule (1901-1907), its members serving collectively as a legislative body and individually as heads of departments. Thus were Filipinos given responsible positions in government from the first days of American civil administration. The Philippines was also authorized by congressional action in 1902 to send two resident commissioners to Washington with seats in the House of Representatives but without the right to vote. In 1907 a fully elective assembly was established, assuming the role of lower legislative house while the appointive commission served as the upper chamber. The same act that established this

The Philippines

elected legislative body also expanded the civil service system, which had been established in 1900 on the merit principle and was in many ways much in advance of its American model.

Independence was a major issue in the first general Philippine elections of 1907. The Nacionalista Party stood for "immediate independence of the Philippine Islands to constitute it into a free and sovereign nation under a democratic government." Led by Manuel Quezon and Sergio Osmena, the Nacionalistas won an overwhelming victory. So much did the Nacionalista party increase its strength in succeeding elections that by 1916 the Philippines had in effect a one-party political system. The tireless and resourceful Quezon was to serve as the leader of this party during the next quarter of a century and was to become the major architect of Philippine independence.

Far more than any of his predecessors or successors, Woodrow Wilson, who assumed office as president of the United States in 1913, was strongly committed to a policy of independence for the Philippines. His appointee as governor general, Francis Burton Harrison, eagerly carried out the president's directive to do everything possible to prepare the territory for ultimate independence and "to move forward toward that end as rapidly as the safety and the permanent interests of the islands will permit." As an immediate first step the commission was reconstituted to give the Filipinos a majority in that body. In 1916 Congress, prodded by Wilson, provided the Philippines with a new organic or governing act, which in the preamble declared that it had always been "the purpose of the people of the United States to withdraw their sovereignty over the Philippine Islands and to recognize their independence as soon as a stable government can be provided them." An elected senate replaced the appointive commission as the upper house of the legislature as a result of the act. Directly or indirectly, however, all bills, including appropriations, could still be vetoed by the president of the United States. But Governor General Harrison interpreted the new law very liberally in favor of Filipino self-government. He also vigorously pursued the policy of increasing the number of Filipinos in the administrative branch of the government with the result that by 1920 it was almost completely Filipinized.

The Republicans, who came to power in the United States in 1921, did not share the views of Wilson and Harrison, expressed a year earlier, that the dependency was ready for independence. The Filipino drive to independence was resultingly stalled for more than a decade. The depression brought a major change in the attitude of many politically important Americans, however, a change that was not wholly welcomed by the Filipinos (who feared the economic effects of too sharp a break with America). Panic stricken by the great economic calamity, several important sections of the American public wished to deprive Philippine products of the advantages they enjoyed on the American market because of the 100 percent tariff preferences between the two countries. With such economic interests groups joining the idealists in championing the independence cause, the national freedom of the Philippines was assured.

THE COMMONWEALTH AND INTERNAL SELF-GOVERNMENT

The Tydings-McDuffie Act, signed by President Franklin D. Roosevelt on May 24, 1934, and accepted by the Philippine legislature on May 1, provided for full independence for the Philippines on July 4, 1944. The Philippines thus became the first of the Western colonies to be promised its freedom by the ruling imperial power. As noted, this was in part a reflection of a traditional American ideology opposed to colonialism as well as a reflection of the economic pressures of the depression years. It should not be forgotten, however, that the Filipinos won the promise of their independence as early as they did partly because of the maturity

The Philippines 117

of their nationalist movement. Nationalism came first to the Philippines of all the Southeast Asia colonial holdings, and it almost succeeded in freeing the Filipinos from their politically subjected status under Spain. Too much credit accordingly can be given the Americans in this respect—which is not to detract at all from the farsightedness and liberalism of the American position.

The Philippine independence act was a particularly enlightened document, providing as it did for a transition period from benevolent colonial rule to full self-government. And Filipino nationalist leaders, including both Quezon and Osmena, showed great wisdom in acquiescing in a period of internal self-government prior to Filipino assumption of full responsibility for the governing of the islands.

The government that was to rule the Philippines in the years between 1935 and 1944 was called the Philippine Commonwealth. In accordance with the act that established the commonwealth and pledged independence, a constitution was drafted by a popularly elected convention and ratified in a popular referendum. Foreign relations during the interim period were to remain under the control of the United States government. Instead of the former American governor general there was established the office of the high commissioner of the United States. Free trade between the two countries was continued for the first five years, but beginning with the sixth year the Philippine government was to levy an export tax of five percent "of the rates of duty which are required by the laws of the United States to be levied, collected, and paid on like articles imported from foreign countries." The rate was to be increased by an additional five percent each year, and with the termination of American sovereignty the United States would levy the same import duties that it levied on goods coming from other foreign countries. For the purpose of the regulation of immigration, a major reason for American labor's support of independence for the Filipinos, the Philippines was immediately regarded as a foreign nation and was granted a paltry quota of 50 immigrants a year. During the commonwealth period the president of the United States had a limited authority to suspend laws, contracts, and acts of the commonwealth government.

The constitution which the Philippines adopted was basically the United States Constitution with such changes as some political scientists and progressive reformers have from time to time suggested be made in it. Its legislative body, called the national assembly, consisted of a single house. The president's term of office was six years, but he was not eligible for immediate reelection. The president was clearly a strong executive, made more so by the great popularity of the first holder of the office, the nationalist leader Manuel Quezon; the chief executive, as an example of his power, possessed the authority to veto items of appropriation bills. The supreme court, the third major organ of government after the American model of the tripartite separation of powers, was specifically accorded authority to declare laws (and ultimately treaties) unconstitutional—but only with the concurrence of two-thirds of all the members of the court. Changes were made in the constitution just before the war, presidential tenure being altered to eight years and the unicameral legislature being converted into a two-house lawmaking body. The institutions of present-day Philippine government are basically those of the commonwealth era. Moreover, many of the leaders of that period were to gain experience which would serve their nation well when long-sought independence finally came.

THE CHARACTER OF AMERICAN RULE

With the establishment of the commonwealth the primary responsibility for the government of the Philippine islands passed from the American to the Filipino people. How well

The Philippines

had the United States discharged the stewardship it had so freely assumed in 1899?

First of all, the United States was generous—financially—with the Philippines. For example, it bore the total cost of defense, a burden which in most other colonies was borne by the colony itself. This enabled the Philippines to spend a larger percentage of governmental income for welfare and education than was the case in other dependencies. On the other hand, even this laudable American attitude may have had its negative side: Filipinos in the post-colonial years were not to distinguish themselves by a high level of self-taxation for the benefit of their republic and its people. And most of them felt that the United States failed to reward them in the cold war years that followed the end of colonial rule as well as it treated many allegedly less worthy countries. Such attitudes may have been born of an American policy that did not sufficiently encourage Filipinos to draw upon their own resources as much as they could for their self-betterment.

The United States also gave a good account of itself as colonial steward of the Philippines by rapidly reducing the number of Americans in the Philippine service and replacing them with Filipinos, even in the highest government positions. This was in sharp contrast with the policy of the French in Indochina, of the Dutch in Indonesia, and even of the British in Malaysia. The number of Americans in the classified service of the Philippines reached its peak in 1905, when the total was 3,307. By 1914 the number had declined to 2,148. Under the administration of Governor General Harrison the number shrank rapidly. In 1921 there were only 614 Americans in the service of the Philippine government, and about half of these were teachers. In 1913 all but two or three bureaus were headed by Americans; in 1921 nearly all the bureau chiefs were Filipinos.

The story was the same in the policy-making branch of

the government. From a minority in an appointive commission in 1901, the Filipinos were granted ever greater self-government until on November 15, 1935, they assumed almost full responsibility for the internal self-government of their islands. They were promised independence by July 4, 1944, and they were to receive it only two years behind schedule in spite of the fact that the ten-year commonwealth period had been interrupted by the Second World War and a Japanese occupation that brought particular destruction and horror to the Philippine islands.

The way the Filipino took to political life American-style is suggestive of his native competence, particularly in such areas as bargaining and electioneering. At the same time, it needs to be pointed out that few former colonies anywhere in the world made the transition to self-government and subsequently conducted themselves as responsibly as did the Filipinos both in 1935, when the commonwealth began, and in 1946, when independence came. The freedom of Filipino political institutions today is perhaps the best tribute to the wisdom and skill of American rule—qualities which the Americans also displayed in occupied Japan after the war, suggesting more than an ordinary gift for helping subject peoples adjust themselves to the ways and demands of democratic politicking.

Good as the American record was in a political sense, however, the United States shared with the other colonial powers in Southeast Asia the failure to develop economic and social conditions which are necessary if democracy is to grow and have its fullest meaning. That American policy failed to lay the socioeconomic basis for a sound democratic society is evident from the data on social conditions revealed by the 1939 census reports and official reports since the war. Over half of the wage earners in 1939 received less than 35 cents a day. Aliens conducted 87 percent of the business of the country and controlled more than 85 percent of the invested capital. Farm tenancy increased during the period

The Philippines

of American rule. In spite of the great effort made in the field of education, only 41.4 percent of the children between the age of 7 and 10 were in school. Moreover, the holding power of the schools was low. Half of the children entering the first grade dropped out of school before they completed the third grade, and only about a tenth of them remained to complete the seventh grade.

The annual national income was low, and it was very unequally distributed. About half of the Filipino people received an annual income, largely in kind, of about $62.50 per family, and, although only one percent of the people received an annual family income of over $500, their combined incomes amounted to about one-third of the total national income.[2]

The United States did little in a positive, direct way to improve economic conditions. By measures to improve health and by releasing funds for education the American government indirectly did much to improve social conditions, but this was in considerable part nullified by the policy of preferential tariffs between the United States and the Philippines. Americans liked to call it a free-trade policy, but it was free only for Americans and Filipinos. For others it was a door very nearly completely closed: about 80 percent of the Philippine exports in value was artificially channeled to the United States, and about 60 percent of the islands' imports came from this country. By encouraging Filipino producers to concentrate on a few specialized export crops, this policy tended to keep the economy of the islands predominantly dependent and agricultural. Sugar alone accounted for over 40 percent of the exports in value, while the four chief export commodities—sugar, abaca (Manila hemp), copra, and coconut oil—accounted for three-fourths of the

[2] Shirley Jenkins, *American Economic Policy Toward the Philippines* (Stanford, Calif., 1954), 41. Her statement is based on the Report and Recommendations of the Joint Philippine American Finance Commission, H.R. Doc. 390 (Washington, July 8, 1947), 11. The estimated figures are for 1938.

total exports in value. The country had so specialized on a few export commodities that it failed to produce enough food to feed its own people, even though it was predominantly agricultural. The "free trade" relationship with the United States also tended to discourage industrialization of the Philippines.

Speaking of the results of American rule for the toiling man, President Quezon declared in 1937: "His hopes have been raised, his vision has been broadened, and his outlook has been painted in bright colors. But 35 years of American regime has brought him only disappointment and sometimes despair. . . . The poor man has still to drink the same polluted water that his ancestors had drunk for ages. Malaria, dysentery, and tuberculosis still threatened him and his family at every turn. His children cannot all go to school, or if they do, they cannot even finish the whole primary instruction for one reason or another. Roads from his barrio or his little farm to the town there are none. Only trails are within his reach—trails that have been formed by the daily pressure of his bare feet and not because they have been constructed. As he works from sunrise to sundown, his employer gets richer while he remains poor. He is the easy prey to the heartless usurer because usury is still rampant everywhere despite legislative enactments intended to suppress it."[3]

And yet Quezon himself as president of the commonwealth provided only limited leadership for socioeconomic reform, setting a pattern that was to be followed by postwar Filipino chief executives.

Agrarian unrest was to be expected under such conditions, and develop it did (as it was to do again after independence had been attained). In 1935, the year the Americans transferred most of the reins of government to the

[3] *The Second Annual Report of the United States High Commissioner to the Philippine Islands. Covering the calendar year 1937.* Manila, September 1, 1938. (Washington, 1939).

The Philippines

commonwealth leaders, the Sakdalistas, a minor leftist political party, staged an armed uprising in the provinces around Manila. Their leaders charged the government with indifference and insincerity toward the demands of the poor and advocated a drastic reduction in the taxes paid by the poor, a more equal distribution of property, and a division of the large landed estates.

Economic and social conditions were not such as to provide maximum support for a truly democratic political life. One-party government existed with Quezon very nearly the absolute boss of the party. The government became highly centralized; the larger cities had practically lost the right of self-government. The national assembly had not the prestige nor the power, and generally lacked the will, to check the president. By 1940, President Quezon had come to espouse what he called "partyless democracy." As he saw it, political parties were not necessary to democratic government. The view was suggestive of the stand another major Southeast Asian nationalist leader, Indonesian President Sukarno, was to take nearly two decades later. If the Filipino political experiment had not been interrupted by Japan's attack in December 1941, would there have been a drift toward authoritarian government in the islands? Was Filipino democracy after the war a second try at democracy rather than a continuation of the prewar experiment, as is generally asserted? Or would the Philippines have moved ever forward in a democratic direction if the commonwealth period had not been ended by invasion? No matter what the answer, it is difficult to escape the conclusion that the United States was in a major way responsible for the shape of Philippine political development.

THE WAR AND JAPANESE OCCUPATION

Some people in the United States had been in favor of granting the Philippines independence out of isolationist sentiment. Japanese aggression in Manchuria in 1931-1932 had caused Americans grave concern over the possibility of war in the Far East. Some believed that the danger of involvement in future hostilities in the Western Pacific would be greatly reduced by the United States' withdrawal from the Philippines. Whether or not Japan would have attacked Pearl Harbor if the United States had not retained sovereignty over the Philippines will probably never be known. But the American-Filipino quarrel over defense responsibility in the islands is a matter of history, President Quezon arguing that accountability for any war in which the Philippines might become involved rested with the United States in view of its continued sovereignty over the islands and its exclusive control over Philippine foreign relations. Pearl Harbor found Philippine defenses inadequate in any event, but the fighting spirit of the American and Filipino defenders denied victory to the enemy until May 6, 1942.

Because of the advanced political development of the Philippines, Japan quickly "granted" the islands their "independence" and allowed the establishment of a puppet government headed by José P. Laurel as president. (Quezon and Vice President Osmena had established a government-in-exile in Washington.) Many other Filipino leaders collaborated with the Japanese, whatever their motives may have been. As elsewhere, they sought to justify their acts or excuse themselves with the claim that their object was the protection of their fellow Filipinos from worse Japanese treatment. In contrast with the collaboration of such leaders was the heroic conduct and resistance of many of the ordinary Filipino people.

The occupation years had greater importance than merely testing the mettle of various of the country's leading political figures, however. The destruction wrought by conquest, occupation, and liberation left the country a shattered reflection of what it had been in 1940. Food production was reduced, output of export crops was interrupted, and roads

The Philippines

and other vital components of the country's not inconsiderable capital plant were destroyed or badly damaged. Law and order—and personal discipline—suffered, too, perhaps the single most important negative legacy of the wartime years. A people who had been largely law-abiding before the war now committed thievery and worse crimes in an effort to harass and destroy the occupying enemy, a far more cruel colonial master than the Filipinos, with much experience under foreign rulers, had ever before known. It became a virtue to commit acts that used to be considered crimes in the minds of men as well as before the law. The end became the justification, as men—and women, too—took the law into their own hands. Democracy, more than any other approach to the governing of man, requires discipline. This valued quality was lost to many Filipinos during the war years, and not all of them regained the lost treasure with the end of the occupation and the coming of independence. It was perhaps an unavoidable development, but it was a sad one. Many Filipinos today regard the alteration of moral values during these years as their country's greatest national tragedy in modern times. It is probably at the root of much of the lawlessness that today afflicts the struggling Philippine republic.

INDEPENDENCE ATTAINED

Independence came to the Philippines in 1946 under circumstances quite different from those anticipated at the time of the passage of the Tydings-McDuffie Act of 1934. The worst war the world had ever known had taken place, and the Philippines was one of the most ravaged of the world's nations. President Manuel Quezon did not live to see his country gain its freedom. Quezon died in August, 1944, in the United States and was succeeded by his vice president, his longtime colleague (and rival), Sergio Osmena. A distinguished and devoted nationalist leader, Osmena lacked the remarkable resourcefulness and force of Quezon. Would the more flamboyant Quezon have obtained better terms of independence? No one, of course, will ever know, but this Roosevelt-like patrician politician might have tried to do so—as he did in the 1930s when he rejected the first independence bill passed by the American Congress, the Hare-Hawes-Cutting Act (only to obtain the very slightly different Tydings-McDuffie Act).

Osmena returned to a country which had suffered severe war damages and was plagued with financial, economic, social, and political problems. Chief among the latter was the issue of collaboration with the Japanese. President Roosevelt had declared that the collaborators must be punished, and President Truman criticized Osmena for his failure to take action against the leaders of the Japanese puppet government. But the matter was never vigorously pushed for a number of reasons. Except among dissident groups, including the Communist-led Hukbalahaps, there seemed to be little popular demand for it, and firmer action might have played into Communist hands through destruction of an elite, many members of which were in fact collaborators. When General Douglas MacArthur personally exonerated Manuel Roxas, who was in charge of obtaining food for the occupying Japanese army, the collaborationist issue lost all logic and force. Roxas defeated Osmena for the presidency in the first postwar election in April 1946.

The United States has been sorely criticized for its alleged failure to set new economic directions for the Philippines after liberation and for the terms of its grant of independence to its island colony. Both charges possess much truth, but both are also often overstated by Filipino nationalists and American scholar-commentators who show more understanding of Philippine needs than of American difficulties in grappling with a multiplicity of new problems as unanticipated world leader in the wake of World War II. It is also true that United States policy toward Japan during these

The Philippines

years appeared more enlightened than American actions in the Philippines. But it must be remembered that the Philippines was a friendly country, that it had a legislature elected before the war and called back into session after liberation, and that the pattern of dependence that had developed between the United States and the Philippines meant that there were important American interests vitally involved in Filipino economic life. There were also American domestic interests that fully knew, or thought they knew, the economic challenge presented to their well-being by Philippine products.

The system of preferential tariffs between the Philippines and the United States during colonial and commonwealth times meant that the former was almost wholly dependent on the American market. As U. S. High Commissioner Paul V. McNutt observed at the time, Philippine economic dependence on the United States was greater than that of any single American state of the union as a whole. The Tydings-McDuffie Act had contained a formula for the progressive alteration of the Filipino-American economic relationship, but the war had interrupted this schedule. It had also made possible, however, some reorientation of Filipino economic life. Was it America's responsibility—in so short a time— to assume responsibility for so momentous an action? Could the United States have done as much in this respect as has been frequently claimed by critics of American policy?

It is true that, when political independence came to the Philippines on July 4, 1946, the country had still to gain its economic independence. But this was also true of Indonesia as it freed itself from the Dutch or of Burma at the time of liberation from British rule. Some of the same persons who criticize the subsequent sharp rupture in Indonesian-Dutch economic relations as well as the Indonesian leadership's failure to restore and develop agricultural production attack the United States for retaining as close ties as it did with the Philippines and for not taking the leadership in preventing re-establishment of the prewar "colonial economy." In Japan the United States sought to prevent the re-emergence of a militarist-led industrial nation and to break the back of a quasi-feudal land-owning class. In the Philippines many of the old economic elite were good friends of the United States. And the Philippines was a colony on the threshhold of independence—not an occupied recent enemy-state. Be all this as it may, the fact remains that the war had completely severed trade between the two countries, and much of the Philippine economy had been badly damaged. Might it still not have been wiser not to have reinstituted trade preferences? The United States could still have helped the Philippine economy by means of subsidies. However, trade preferences were reinstituted and the colonial character of the economy perpetuated.

Economic relations between the new Republic of the Philippines and the United States were regulated by the Philippine Trade Act, passed by the United States Congress shortly before independence came to the islands. The act provided for reciprocal free trade until July 3, 1954, followed by increasing duties (five percent each year) until July 3, 1973, when the full rates would become effective. Seven of the most important exports of the Philippines, however, were made subject to absolute quotas. The act also contained the so-called "parity clause" which guaranteed to nationals of the United States the right to exploit the natural resources of the islands and to operate public utilities on equal terms with Filipinos. Another restrictive provision tied the peso to the dollar. The Philippine government could not change the value of its currency in relation to the dollar—nor suspend the convertibility of pesos into dollars, nor impose restrictions on the transfer of funds from the Philippines to the United States—without the agreement of the American president.

Filipinos had protested the institution of trade preferences in 1909 but pleaded for their continuation in 1945 and 1946. They believed that this was the surest and quickest way of securing the rehabilitation of their country. "Parity," on the other hand, was widely regarded as too high a price to pay for the hope of American investments to expand the economy and was, moreover, in conflict with a provision of the Philippine constitution which restricted the exploitation of natural resources to citizens of the Philippines or to corporations in which at least 60 percent of the capital was owned by Filipinos. President Roxas, however, won popular approval of the necessary referendum on a constitutional amendment giving American capital equal rights with Filipino capital in developing the country's resources and acquiring franchises for public utilities. A major factor in the vote was the widespread impression that further American aid for rehabilitation and reconstruction depended on acceptance of parity. The Philippine Rehabilitation Act passed by the United States Congress in 1946 limited payment on any war-damage claim to $500 until the Bell Act went into effect, while the latter act was dependent on Filipino acceptance of "parity."

Congressional passage of the Military Assistance Act in 1946 indicated that the Philippines would continue to be dependent on the United States for its defense as well as its economic welfare. By another agreement, which took effect in March 1947, the United States was granted a number of naval and military bases for 99 years.

The military tie was desired by the political leaders of the Philippines, and only "parity" was immediately attacked among the economic provisions related to the granting of independence. Criticism of these and other aspects of American policy should not obscure the important fact that the United States was the first of the colonial powers to set an Asian territory free. Being the first of the imperial powers to take such action, it naturally had no precedents to follow. Moreover, American preoccupation with its new worldwide responsibilities meant that the nation was truly taxed by an unparalleled range of problems and perhaps lacked the opportunity to accord the Philippine problem the attention it warranted. All of this explains the American position, but it does not justify it. It does not make trade preferences or parity either beneficial or desirable.

FROM ROXAS TO MARCOS

The candidate of the long dominant Nacionalista Party in the April 1946 elections, the first following the Japanese occupation, was Sergio Osmena, who had succeeded Quezon in exile in 1944. His opponent was Manuel Roxas, a key figure in José P. Laurel's wartime government. Both had been Nacionalistas, but the senior Osmena was assured the party's presidential nomination—so Roxas founded his own party, the Liberals, as the only way to become president. And he became president, the independent Philippines' first, defeating Osmena mainly because he appeared to have convinced a majority of the voters that he could get more aid from the United States.

Nineteen years later, Roxas and Osmena were still in the thick of the never-ending Filipino politicking—that is, Sergio Osmena, Jr., son of the second and last commonwealth president, and Gerardo Roxas, son of the first president of the independent Philippines. Roxas was the vice presidential running-mate of re-electionist President Diosdado Macapagal, Osmena the ranking senatorial contender of the same party. This party was the Liberal party. Before and right after the war the older Osmena and Roxas had been Nacionalistas, the two men were on opposite sides of the political fence in 1946, and by 1965 their offspring were key figures in the Liberal party. The younger Roxas was a party regular, Osmena a recent Liberal convert trying to advance his own position through a party clearly seeking to exploit his influence among his fellow Cebuenos (one of the country's key ethnic groups). The Roxas-Osmena family political sagas suggest much about the nature of Filipino politics.

The intervening years from Roxas to Ferdinand E. Marcos,

The Philippines

who defeated incumbent President Macapagal (and his vice presidential running-mate Ferdinand Lopez, the younger Roxas) in 1965, had been fateful ones for the Philippine republic. Democracy largely maintained itself in the islands—indeed, expanded in some respects—a somewhat uncommon experience in a world of growing authoritarianism in the so-called "new states." Some basic social and economic problems were attacked, moreover, but probably more failed to find solution or even adequate attention. This was a reflection in part of the range of problems confronting the Filipino political leadership and of the limited means and experience with which this leadership faced such problems. It also reflected the absence of concern on the part of a quite conservative elite which was not pained by the country's main problems as was the common *tao*, the ordinary rice-growing Filipino peasant.

President Roxas died suddenly in April 1948 before he had really had time to leave his mark on the new republic. Recovery and rehabilitation were the main needs of the first years of independence, and Roxas emphasized solution of these problems above others. Only too many members of the prewar political and economic elite which had by this time re-established itself were more concerned with restoration of their own well-being, however, than that of the nation. Elpidio Quirino, the vice president who succeeded Roxas, was not a member of this elite, but, sincere and well-meaning man though he may have been, he was required to do the bidding of the regular party leadership. During the Quirino years the government of the Philippines nearly collapsed. Economic and financial conditions became so bad that Quirino appealed to President Truman for help. The economic survey mission dispatched to the Philippines by President Truman reported that the basic problem in the country was inefficient production and low incomes. Although population had increased by 25 percent in the previous decade, agricultural and industrial output in 1950 was still below the prewar level and the standard of living of most people was lower than before the war. Inequalities in income had become greater, the disillusioned Philippine farmer saw no escape from the various types of exaction to which he was subject, Communist-led Hukbalahap rebels sought to exploit this discontent, the financial status of the country was critical, corruption was increasing in government, and public confidence in the leadership was rapidly declining. The Bell mission recommended various reforms, including major changes in the tax system, as well as United States financial aid in the amount of $250,000,000, chiefly on a project basis and subject to supervision in order to guarantee effective use of the funds. President Quirino was able to get the Philippine congress to pass the reforms in question but not without strong opposition and in somewhat diluted form. Quirino, whose reputation at one time was the lowest of all the postwar Philippine presidents, showed considerable statesmanship in this hour of great national need and subsequently provided admirable leadership in the field of economic policy. He is only now coming to be more justly appreciated by his countrymen.

One reason for Quirino's unpopularity was the alleged corruption and incompetence that marked his regime. Another was the nature of his victory over wartime president José P. Laurel in the 1949 elections. Only four years after the end of the war Laurel, the chief collaborator with an enemy still much hated in the islands, was chosen as the presidential candidate of the historically most important Filipino political party, the Nacionalistas. By using all of the great powers of the presidential office and by exerting great pressure on officials and voters alike, President Quirino managed to win the election—at least officially. The Laurel forces charged that the election had been stolen.

The economic problem lessened after Quirino's re-election, but the threat from the Communist insurgent Hukbalahaps mounted. Smoldering discontent had regularly broken out

The Philippines

into violence in Philippine history from the earliest days of Spanish rule, and the postwar uprising fitted the pattern. There were peasant risings under American rule in northwestern Mindanao in 1923-1924, in northern Luzon (the Philippines' most important and most populated island) in 1931, and in 1935 in the provinces surrounding Manila by a movement called the Sakadalistas. All of these uprisings reflected deep, bitter discontent among the peasantry, the source of the wealth of the landowning rural elite but the recipient of a negligible share of the output of their own labor. Everybody and everything seemed to be on the landlord's side as the tenant saw it: the moneylenders, the politicians, and the government and its agents, the national constabulary and the army. There was little recourse but revolt.

The Huks were ready to tap this discontent. The name "Huk" was an abbreviated form of Hukbalahap (*Hukbong Bayan Laban Sa Hapon,* which is Tagalog, a main Filipino language, for People's Anti-Japanese Army). The Huks had been formed shortly after the invasion and fought valiantly against the Japanese. Peasants constituted the base of the group, whose leader was the Communist Luis Taruc. When denied their postwar demand that they be taken into the armed forces as a unit, the Huks went underground and waged a steadily worsening war against the national government. Efforts of both Roxas and Quirino to contain the rebels—whether by conciliation or force—failed.

The situation had become desperate by 1950. The Huks seemed to be everywhere; their strength was estimated at 40,000 fully armed members, with about 2,500,000 reserves. They made attacks on towns on the outskirts of Manila, and this seat of government and commerce itself seemed in danger. At this critical juncture President Quirino appointed a vigorous young congressman as secretary of defense—Ramon Magsaysay. Magsaysay reorganized the army and got it to pursue the Huks deep into the jungle. He rooted out inefficiency and corruption. Convinced that misery, bad government and landlord exploitation were at the heart of the discontent upon which the Huks fed, he followed a policy of friendship for all who were prepared to surrender (as well as force against the Communist corps of diehards). Surrendered Huks were resettled on farms. Within a year the back of the rebellion had been broken.

Ramon Magsaysay, the man who defeated the Huks and set new standards of vigor and honesty in his administration of the defense department, became a national hero. The Nacionalistas, seeing certain victory in his nomination, named him their presidential candidate only weeks after he had left the government of Liberal President Quirino and quit the Liberal party. It was the Roxas story all over again—only this time it was the party which saw a presidential victory in a new man rather than the man seeing victory in a new party. Party-jumping was to become chronic in subsequent years; Roxas and Magsaysay helped set the pattern. Quirino, as expected, won renomination by the Liberals.

Magsaysay carried the campaign into the *barrios* (villages), which was something new in Philippine politics. Previously Filipino national politicians had dealt only with the rural bosses, who fairly successfully delivered the vote in a manner not dissimilar to old-style American city bosses. Magsaysay revolutionized Filipino electioneering behavior—which will never again be the same. And he and his newly embraced Nacionalista party won an overwhelming victory, receiving more than two-thirds of the vote cast. Magsaysay had a clear mandate from the voters to carry out the reforms he had advocated, such as agrarian reform and expanded educational and welfare services, but he almost immediately ran into trouble with the Nacionalista old guard, which had endorsed his candidacy because of his vote-getting capacity rather than because of any sympathy with his progressive outlook. These regular Nacionalistas were reluctant to accept Magsaysay's leadership, and Congress delayed and sometimes diluted his bills.

The Philippines

One of Magsaysay's bills which Congress did enact, although more than a little hesitatingly in view of the involved interests of many of the legislators, was the Agricultural Tenancy Act, which sought to regulate the relationship of the landowner and the sharecropper or leaseholder, giving greater security to the tenant and farm worker. The law limited the rate of interest on loans to tenants to eight percent. An agrarian court, modeled after the court of industrial relations, was subsequently created. And a land-tenure law was enacted to permit expropriation of large estates and their distribution where "justified agrarian unrest exists."

Magsaysay was a populist who sought to remove social evils and injustice for the betterment of the common man. He also endeavored to convince the people that the government was their government by inviting everybody in the land, whatever his economic or social status, to bring his complaints to Malacanang Palace, the official resident of the president. And he frequently went out personally into the villages to adjust the complaints himself. This made Magsaysay very popular with the masses and lifted their confidence in government, but trying to solve everybody's little problems left "The Guy," as Magsaysay was affectionately known, little time or energy to work on large national problems. Magsaysay, however, brought a new and higher moral tone to the presidency than it had ever before known or was to know under his immediate successors. The Magsaysay years, which began with the successful prosecution of the war against the Huks, ended in an airplane crash on a Cebu mountainside in March 1957. Few national leaders have ever been more genuinely mourned.

Carlos P. Garcia, Magsaysay's vice president, succeeded to his nation's highest political office and, although not previously a major power in the party, won nomination in 1957 as the Nacionalista presidential candidate through skillful political manipulation. The young reformers who had backed

Magsaysay in 1953 broke with the party as a result of the nomination of this old-style boss-type politician and founded the Progressive party. Ex-newspaper publisher Manuel Manahan was the Progressive presidential nominee, but his main function—along with another protest party candidate—was to draw votes away from one of the two main candidates (the Liberal nominee being sugar baron José Yulo). Garcia won a plurality victory, largely the result of record spending, but the Liberal vice presidential candidate, young congressman Diosdado Macapagal, edged out Garcia's running mate, House of Representatives Speaker José P. Laurel, Jr., son of the wartime president. The Garcia administration was marked mainly by greater corruption than ever before in Filipino politics. The reformism that had distinguished President Magsaysay's years in office had no appeal for the great populist's successor, and implementation of major Magsaysay programs, such as land reform, was halting and ineffective.

The election of a vice president of party persuasion different from that of the president had no precedent in Philippine political history. President Garcia can be forgiven accordingly for not knowing what to do with his unwanted executive colleague. He decided to do nothing—that is, to ignore him—which was probably the worst thing that he could have done. Thus freed from any administrative or other responsibilities, Vice President Macapagal used the four years of his occupancy of the nation's second highest office to campaign for the only position that outranked his own—the presidency. He received the Liberal party nomination in 1961 and went on to defeat Garcia in one of the most hotly contested Philippine elections of the postwar period.

Garcia tried to buy victory but failed. The 1961 presidential election was the costliest ever, however, in a country famed for lavish spending by candidates for public office. Money is very often the decisive factor in Philippine politics, but it is more decisive in local elections, including provincial

The Philippines

gubernatorial races, than in national voting—and certainly more decisive in races for the house of representatives than for either the senate or the presidency. Few, if any, senatorial races have ever probably been bought and no presidential elections. The 1949 Quirino victory notwithstanding, irregularities in national polling in the Philippines are probably much less decisive than many observers have suggested. The main reasons for Garcia's defeat in 1961 were probably the rampant corruption in his government and Macapagal's vigorous exploitation of this issue.

Macapagal was hailed by many as a second Magsaysay, but such claims betrayed ignorance of the path of his rise to prominence within the Liberal party. He was a party regular, and his government, not surprisingly, contained very few new faces in Filipino politics. His policies, on the other hand, were innovational, in many ways more so than Magsaysay's. Like the last Liberal president (Quirino), Macapagal sought to break new ground in the area of economic policy. He immediately ended most foreign exchange controls, removing what he called "a vital source of graft," and placed the peso on the free market—both highly beneficial actions. Macapagal also asked Congress for various remedial measures to alleviate resulting inflation, measures which Congress failed to enact in the subsequent four years and for which Macapagal blamed the Nacionalistas in the senate in his bid for re-election in 1965.

Macapagal faced a problem American presidents have encountered one out of three years in American history—a Congress of opposite political persuasion. The Nacionalistas won control of the house of representatives in 1961, but Macapagal subsequently gained control of that chamber by persuading enough members of the opposition to switch sides; the president called them "patriots," but many others referred to these new "Liberals" as turncoats. The Liberal party had won six out of the eight senatorial births at stake in 1961, but a strong Nacionalista majority among the solons not seeking re-election meant a tie between the two parties in the upper house. Although Liberal Senator Ferdinand E. Marcos, who was to become Macapagal's presidential opponent in 1965, was elected senate president in 1963, the Liberals held fewer seats than the Nacionalistas by the time of the 1965 elections—defections, which helped the party in the house in 1962, later hurt it in the senate.

Perhaps the most notable accomplishment under Macapagal's leadership in 1962-1965 was the Land Reform Act of 1963—which went beyond the earlier legislation passed under Magsaysay. This law replaced the old landlord-tenant relationship with a new lease arrangement governed by contract according to specific regulations designed to protect both parties. A land authority was given the power to expropriate land in order fully to utilize all agricultural lands and to reduce large landholdings. Landowners were to be compensated in cash, tax-free bonds, and shares in a land bank to be set up for the purpose. This newest Philippine agrarian reform legislation was changed far less than expected by Congress but has failed to be actively implemented—partly because Congress has not adequately followed it up and partly because of Philippine financial resources.

Macapagal's opponent in the 1965 presidential election was Senator Ferdinand E. Marcos, who had contested the 1961 Liberal party nomination against Macapagal and quit the Liberals to join the Nacionalistas in 1964 because he had been denied that party's presidential nomination anew by the re-electionist Macapagal. Corruption, as in almost all previous elections, was again a major issue. It was not the only problem as Filipinos conducted their sixth presidential election since the war, however. The cost of living was at an all-time high and steadily rising. Smuggling accounted for perhaps one-third of all Philippine imports. A record amount of rice had to be imported in 1965, presumably to make sure that a shortage of the grain did not hinder Macapagal's re-election bid. Law and order appeared to be deteriorating. Politically, the Philippines remained very much a democracy. Economically and socially, there was less of which Filipinos could be proud.

Macapagal's effort to retain office in 1965 proved to be a futile one as he lost decisively to his Nacionalista challenger, the never-defeated Marcos, who became the sixth president of the republic on January 1, 1966. The triumph was clearly one for Marcos over Macapagal rather than a party verdict, Macapagal's Liberals emerging with a majority in the house of representatives despite their leader's defeat. Most Filipinos sighed with relief that the election campaign had finally come to an end—and the business of government could begin again. So preoccupied was Macapagal with politicking, for example, that vast credits made available by the United States, Japan and Germany had gone untouched.

But why did Marcos defeat Macapagal if the latter, as incumbent chief executive, was possessed of such greater resources and had devoted such an extraordinary amount of time to campaigning? The most important single factor was probably a sort of national frustration that the main problems which have long plagued the Philippines were not being alleviated. The Philippines has never re-elected a president since independence, apparently for this reason—and Macapagal, like Garcia and Quirino before him, fell victim to the jinx. It is almost as though the Filipino electorate must have a change every four years, irrespective of the candidates—so deep is this frustration with presidents who can not, or will not, solve their nation's problems. There were also other factors, however: the strong geographical base on which Marcos could build in his well populated and highly parochial native Ilocos region of northern Luzon and his connection with the long important Romauldez political clan in the Visayan, or central, Philippines through his wife, daughter of the late House Speaker Daniel Romauldez.

Macapagal's defeat was more Marcos' opportunity than his victory, however. His victory, if it comes, will have to be over the multiplicity of problems that plague the Philippines economically, educationally and otherwise. Marcos is unquestionably a competent politician. But the problems which the ever-victorious new president now faces may turn out to be more formidable than his past political opponents.

"IN'S" VERSUS "OUT'S"

Philippine politics is an almost classic example of seemingly eternal jockeying for power between the "in's" and the "out's." New President Marcos, once head of the Liberal party, quit that body in 1964 only because of the alleged refusal of Macapagal to honor a promise made to him in 1961 not to seek re-election and to support the latter's bid for the presidency. Marcos presided over the senate as one of Macapagal's leading legislative lieutenants, but he joined the opposition Nacionalistas in a practically undisguised attempt to win that party's presidential nomination. The man he defeated for the nomination, incumbent Vice President Emmanuel Pelaez, had been Macapagal's running mate in 1961 but split with the president ostensibly over a slur on his political honor. Pelaez, besides also being a very recent Liberal, was a man, however sincere and honest (as claimed by his followers), who had changed parties more than any other living Filipino politician.

When President Macapagal forced a large enough number of Nacionalista members of the house of representatives to join the Liberal party and give that party a majority in the lower chamber in 1961, these so-called "patriots" included two of Cebu's less illustrious congressmen. Three years later, these legislators returned to the Nacionalista fold because Cebu city Mayor Sergio Osmena, Jr., the ranking Liberal senatorial aspirant and himself a recent party convert, demanded that Macapagal refuse to proclaim them as official Liberal candidates. One newspaper columnist noted that the "turncoats" had become "return-coats," another that the "patriots" were now "repatriates."

For four years Vice President Diosdado Macapagal campaigned for the presidency as the officially spurned second ranking Philippine national executive officer, defeating re-electionist President Carlos P. Garcia in 1961 partly because of this strenuous campaigning. The next four years saw President Macapagal taking his cue from Vice President Macapagal as he campaigned for re-election as no incumbent Philippine president had ever done before him. Macapagal was on the campaign trail in 1964 and 1965 for a much greater time than he remained in Manila to lead the government. He even asked the voters to re-elect him because, ineligible to succeed himself a second time, he would spend the next four years in Malacanang doing the things a Philippine president was officially supposed to do. Macapagal's quest for office—and perhaps office more than power—was part of the same pattern as the party-jumping of new Nacionalistas Marcos and Pelaez and, before them, the Liberal party's founder, first president Manuel Roxas.

So eager were the candidates in the 1965 campaign to gain their party's endorsement of their bids to be (or remain) president that the national nominating conventions were held a full year before the actual balloting. This gave the Philippines probably the longest officially proclaimed election campaign in democracy's history. The Nacionalistas, who fell out among themselves contesting the nomination, used most of this time to try to mend the differences among themselves—so bitter and brutal was their nomination contest. They never did restore unity to the party—if unity there was before the 1964 Nacionalista nominating convention.

Why this frantic quest for public office—a quest that characterizes local politics, even school and club elections, as much as it does the national political process?

The answers to this question are probably to be found in various areas. One such area is the rewards of public office. So-called "congressional allowances," whether accurately labeled or not, rose rapidly in recent years, reaching a peak of 250,000,000 pesos a year by 1965—or $250,000,000 for a four-year congressional term. President Macapagal vetoed the portion of the budget providing such funds in August 1965 at the height of the presidential campaign, but cynics asserted that the allowances would return in 1966—no matter who was elected president. The "in's" fight harder than the "out's" to stay in, some assert, because they have so much to lose—while the "out's" have much to gain but little to lose.

Another answer may be found in the Filipino's psychological make-up. The Filipino politician takes defeat as a personal rejection—which is why he frantically seeks renomination for another bid at the office he lost (or failed to gain). A policy setback (on a congressional vote, for example) is a minor thing compared to a defeat at the polls. Before the Japanese war, civic organizations had to recruit vigorously to obtain office-holders; today the competition for such posts can be as keen as in provincial gubernatorial races. Once elected, moreover, the successful candidate—having obtained, after all, what he really sought—is inclined to rest on his laurels and ignore the duties for which he was presumably elected. Practically everybody knows, of course, that this was not at all why he sought private—or public—office.

Then there is the matter of power—sought to reward one's friends and supporters rather than to advance more general public policy goals. This is not really the defense of the interests of a particular ruling class, as some have claimed. For there is no difference between the two major political parties in the Philippines, the Liberals and the Nacionalistas, and it is these parties that have alternated in power since independence. The interests represented by the two parties are the same, and there is no difference in the social background of their leaders or their followers. Indeed, most of the big names in recent Philippine politics have been members of both parties at one time or another—Roxas, Magsaysay, Marcos, and Pelaez, among others.

Senator Raul S. Manglapus, defeated 1965 presidential candidate of the third-force People's Progressive party (made up of many of the followers of the late President Magsaysay), described his country's political structure as a "two-faction one-party system," a very accurate description of what it is today (and has been since 1946). But Manglapus himself is a former Nacionalista, an ex-Liberal, and a member of the reformist "Grand Alliance" that contested the 1959 senatorial elections. Even those who protest the system bear its marks.

This is not to say that there are not interests in the Philippines which seek governmental action—or inaction—on their behalf. These there surely are, and they dominate the two main parties. But they probably dominate them to about the same extent. They also dominate the process of formal political communications, controlling the nationally circulated Manila newspapers, TV stations, and the country-wide radio networks. These communications moguls frequently clash with one another but rarely, if ever, on general or ideological grounds. A few years ago one of the nation's leading commercial and industrial figures purchased a newspaper wholly for the purpose of defending himself as a person against the attacks of another newspaper owned by a second important commercial and industrial family. The two families belong to the same elite, however, an elite that endeavors to perpetuate its power—and resulting pleasures.

Can the Philippines be considered a democracy under such circumstances?

That there is much that is undemocratic in Filipino political life cannot be denied. It should be remembered, on the other hand, that democracy is not a "way of life," as is so frequently and glibly asserted; it is a particular mode of selecting public office-holders which takes place in a setting sufficiently free to allow genuine competition for the offices in question. And nobody could ever call Filipino politics noncompetitive! The Filipino masses, moreover, play an unprecedentedly large role in Filipino politics at the present time. Magsaysay revolutionized Philippine political campaigning, and Macapagal outshone even "The Guy" in this regard between 1958 and 1965. Vote-buying may take place in the Philippines in both subtle and not so subtle ways, but the *tao* showed in 1953 and 1961 in particular that, when he wants to turn a government out, he can do so.

This, however, is one of the great problems of contemporary Philippine politics. The widespread popular support for the late Ramon Magsaysay excepted, the Filipino almost always votes against the government in power and not for a more attractive alternative government or program. This happens in many political systems, of course, but the result in the Philippines has been the rotation in office of two practically indistinguishable groups of politicians. There has accordingly never been a real change of governments in the Philippines since independence—if by change one means even a modest change in policy. Presidents have differed more than their parties in this respect, and, more often than not, it has been the parties not the presidents which have prevailed.

If there has never been a real change of governments, there has been a perceptible change in the political system of which government is only a part. And this means that it is only a matter of time until government begins to mirror this change. Indeed, there are signs that this is already happening, but the signs are almost equally evident in both of the two coalitions of office-seekers known as the Liberal and Nacionalista parties. Probably the most important of these changes is the increasing activity and importance of modern-style interest groups. The Philippine Chamber of Industries, the Chamber of Commerce of the Philippines, and the

The Philippines

Chamber of Agricultural and Natural Resources are among the most important interest groups in the country today. Although labor's power does not rank with these giants of influence, partly because the trade union movement is divided, it is nonetheless greater than it has ever before been. More specialized economic interests are also active—the Philippine Sugar Association, the United Philippine Coconut Producers Federation, the Virginia Tobacco Association of the Philippines, and others. And there are teachers' groups and others, including the powerful Roman Catholic Church and the unitarian Iglesia in Kristo, an indigenous sect, that allegedly votes as a bloc.

The power of these groups is growing at the same time that certain family-groups and other highly personalized factions are claimed to be establishing themselves as a semi-perpetual ruling class. Some of the members of the more important economic groups also belong to this ruling class, but not all of them. One of the chief tensions within this ruling group, moreover, is the division between the emergent industrialists and those who represent traditional agricultural interests. Fortunately for Philippine democracy, one of the important groups in the society that is not a contestant for control of the government is the still civilian-controlled army.

PROBLEMS UNSOLVED

Filipino preoccupation with politics, meaning the struggle for public office, has probably had the result of insufficient attention to many of the country's most pressing problems. Some of these problems are long-range ones and could not be wholly alleviated during the term of a single president. Others have their roots in the deficiencies of past American colonial rule, and Americans for this reason should only modestly criticize Filipinos for their failure adequately to alter conditions left behind in the islands by the United States. Still others, however, are partly the making of the postcolonial Philippine leadership, while some have worsened during the 20 years since the Second World War.

Chief among the country's unsolved problems is the food situation. The Philippines is a fairly rich agricultural land, and yet it does not grow enough food—particularly rice, the overwhelming favorite of its population—to feed itself. Rice imports have risen sharply in recent years. In fact, the 1965 importation of the grain was greater than in any previous year since independence—a fact which was not unrelated to Macapagal's presidential re-election bid. This suggests the political context in which such problems are viewed by the national leadership. Very little, for example, has been done to increase domestic rice production.

Economic growth in general, however, has been moderately impressive. Discounting the inflated claims of Macapagal's former official propagandists, the economy probably grew about five percent in 1964 and appeared on the way to repeating this performance in 1965. Export prospects for such key crops as sugar and copra were good, and industrialization has proceeded modestly but surely. But much of the impressive economic gains on paper have been offset by the country's high population growth rate. The Philippine population has been increasing at a rate of 3.8 percent annually, which is about equal to one million new Filipino mouths to feed each year—and ultimately a necessary increase in new jobs. Unemployment and underemployment are chronic in the country—not the least in the teeming, dirty governmental and commercial city of Manila.

Although some of the problems cited in the Bell report of nearly 20 years ago have been alleviated, others have not. Income distribution, for example, is at least as unequal as formerly, and the gap between the rich and the poor may actually be increasing. There were signs of revived Huk activity in central Luzon in 1964-1965, but this was still of a most modest character. However, unless peasant grievances are relieved, new outbursts of revolutionary activity are not only possible but ultimately almost certain. Implementation of Macapagal's land reform legislation was slow—far too slow in proportion to the problems it was designed to solve.

Prices, meanwhile, have risen to an all-time high, probably the single most important issue against the Macapagal administration in the 1965 election. Real wages in 1965 were about 15 percent below what they had been a decade earlier. A pathetic attempt to raise the minimum wage in 1965 hardly solved the problem. It not only hurt a large number of marginal firms, forcing some actually to close, but it also resulted in the discharge of many workers, who became too costly for their employers to retain.

Smuggling was probably a major factor in the Philippines' economic problems as well as a reflection of the state of law and order in the country. Ironically, the increase in smuggling occurred during the Macapagal administration partly in response to measures adopted by the president to improve the economy. In 1962 President Macapagal lifted foreign exchange controls and placed the peso on the free market, thus eliminating a wide range of long existing financial irregularities. Macapagal simultaneously boosted tariffs to provide a substitute for the protection previously accorded by the exchange controls. Money was more easily available than before, but importing was more expensive because of the increased tariffs. The result was a sharp rise in smuggling, depriving the government of probably a greater amount of revenue than it actually received from customs collections (a major source of income for the Philippine government).

A large percentage of this smuggling was "technical smuggling"—misdeclarations, wrong classifications, and such (all done in connivance with the officials involved). Whether corruption is quantitatively as great in the Philippine government today as it was in the worst days of the Quirino and Garcia administrations is open to question, but it is definitely more widespread. Even the Macapagal government had to admit this! And the consequences have been extremely harmful economically. Besides the loss in government revenues, the industrial boom of the 1950s has been slowed, and many young industries have been hurt. Philippine assemblers of electronics equipment, for example, can hardly be expected to compete effectively with duty-free Japanese transistor radios.

But smuggling was only one sign of deteriorating respect for law. The ever-present security guard patrolling the residences of all who could afford such protection was another. So, too, were the frequent gun-battles in Manila's streets and throughout the country. Many more guns were said to be illegally in the hands of nonofficial Filipinos—not to mention appropriately registered firearms—than were possessed by all of the various armed forces and national and local police elements!

Possibly the most important long-range social problem was the still incomplete integration of the southern Moslems of Mindanao and the Sulu archipelago into the national life of the republic. Most southern Moslems still distinguish between themselves and the majority Christian Filipinos. Reports in 1965 of increased illegal Indonesian immigration into the southern Philippines clearly alarmed the national leadership, but suggestions of Filipino Moslem disaffection were summarily denied. However, it is just this imperfect integration that makes such infiltration the danger that it is. Many Moslems probably feel as close to their brother Islamic Indonesians as they do with the Catholic majority of the country of which they are legally nationals. This might produce a most serious situation.

REASSERTION OF THE FILIPINO

There were always at least two levels of Filipino behavior under colonial rule—the imported and the indigenous. The former appeared to be almost always dominant in the days of the Spanish and the Americans because, even in seeking to throw off foreign dominance, the Filipino had to deal in the foreigner's terms. He had to use Western military means in his revolt against the Spanish, and he had to learn to use American institutions and invoke American values to free himself from the presence of the United States in his islands. The phenomenon is familiar to colonies.

But the Filipino outdid most subjects of colonial rule. No other Western colony was so nearly wholly converted to a foreign religion as was the Philippines. In no other Western imperial holding did the alien's language take as strong a hold as did English in the Philippines under the Americans. Most important of all, perhaps no other conquered peoples in the era of European imperialism so loudly and appreciatively proclaimed, "We've been conquered! Look! We're Westernized!"

The response was a measure of both the Spanish and the American impact, and it reflected the modest level of Filipino cultural development before the Westerner's arrival. All the same, it was still unnatural. And now with the colonial embrace gone, the Filipino's non-Western face is beginning to appear. He still idolizes Quezon, as yesterday's heroes are always idolized, but he likes his present-day politicians with much less Spanish blood in their veins. He also likes them with less Spanish and American manner and values. The Western component of the present-day Filipino may be higher than that of the Indonesian, but his Filipino side is reasserting itself, and Filipino behavior will be increasingly difficult to comprehend for those who do not realize this.

FOREIGN POLICY

Manuel Roxas, first president of an independent Philippine Republic, declared in 1946: "We are not of the Orient except by geography. We are part of the Western world by reason of culture, religion, ideology, economics. . . . We expect to remain part of the West, possibly as the ideological bridge between the Occident and the Orient." This orientation toward the world beyond the Philippines has marked Filipino foreign policy during the 20 years since independence came on July 4, 1946. But there has also been a change in the Filipino outlook toward the world, and, although fairly slow in revealing itself and even more halting of expression in formal policies of the Manila government, this change has proceeded through the years and is likely to increase its momentum.

Although the Philippines only became a sovereign state in 1946, its government had actively participated in international politics before that date. Commonwealth President Quezon signed the United Nations Declaration in 1942, and the Philippines was a participant in the San Francisco Conference which drafted the Charter of the United Nations and became one of the original members of that organization. The chief of the Philippine delegation, General Carlos P. Romulo, took an active part in the movement of the small states to restrict the great power veto and to make the provisions of the articles on non-self-governing territories as broad as possible. Romulo's attitude at San Francisco established key dimensions of the pattern of Philippine foreign policy. While in many matters the island republic would follow American policy closely, it was to show marked and consistent independence in others.

The Filipino self-image of a people more Western than Asian, which was probably accurate in several respects for the elite (but certainly not of the vast masses of the Filipino people), was a major obstacle to the government's proclaimed desire to serve as a "bridge" between East and West. Filipinos, mainly because of this self-image and the way it expressed itself, were not generally popular with other Asians—as a nation, that is. Many such Asians felt that Filipinos considered themselves superior to their geographical neighbors. These Asians regarded Filipinos as too Westernized, as alienated from their native culture. Filipinos were caustically characterized as the strange product of three centuries of life in a Spanish convent followed by forty years in Hollywood. President Sukarno of Indonesia, in an address to Congress on the occasion of an official visit to the Philippines, chided the Filipinos for their desertion of their indigenous Malay culture. The countries of Southeast Asia which followed neutralist or anti-Western foreign policies, moreover, viewed the Philippines' pro-Western orientation with distrust for other reasons. They considered the Philippines a client state of the United States.

Although the Filipino-American relationship has had its moments of disagreement and resentment, the two allies, on the whole, have cooperated fairly harmoniously through the years—probably more so than any other former metropolitan ruler and an ex-colony. The bonds that link the two countries have been misunderstood by many other governments, however. And they appear to be misunderstood by some Filipinos today, such as left-wing students who apparently believe that the United States would—indeed, could—help to defend the Philippines against foreign attack as much without bases on Filipino soil as with such facilities.

The change that has slowly marked the evolution of Philippine foreign policy during the last 20 years has had its roots in a steady retreat from the idea that the Filipino is more Western than Asian and in the related emergence of a powerful tide of egalitarian nationalism released in large measure by that highly influential intellectual politician, the late Senator Claro M. Recto. President Macapagal, who tried so hard (if unsuccessfully) to develop a pattern of close and satisfactory relations with Indonesia, reflected these twin trends more than any previous Filipino president, which suggests, among other things, that the trends are probably developing ones. Recto was inaccurately regarded by many as anti-American, but the worst of his ideological sins was probably that he was passionately pro-Filipino. He wished to make the Filipinos truly and fully independent, which meant reduced dependence on the United States.

A certain tension has been introduced into Philippine foreign policy as a result of these conflicting tendencies. On the one hand, the Filipino is increasingly alert to his Asian identity—culturally, economically and ideologically—and he wishes as much *de facto* independence as possible. On the other hand, however, he realizes that independence is not possible in the present-day interdependent world, nor can he escape the fact that his country is the third largest English-speaking nation in the world, one of the leading Catholic lands, and a far more Westernized country in some respects than even Japan.

This tension reflects itself in Filipino security policies. The Philippines entered into base and military assistance pacts with the United States in the wake of independence. It signed a mutual defense agreement with the Americans in 1951, and it became a founding member of the Southeast Asia Treaty Organization (SEATO) in 1954. The rise to power of the Communists in China in 1949 reoriented Filipino fears that the threat from the north was mainly Japanese. The subsequent expansion of the war in Vietnam in which China is involved, though less directly and more modestly than the United States, heightened Filipino concern in this respect. The impact of President Johnson's efforts to probe the possibilities of a peaceful end to the Vietnamese war in 1965-1966 was minimized in the official pronouncements of the ranking architects of Philippine foreign policy who feared that the United States might withdraw in favor of the Communists and leave their nation isolated. On the other hand, there were some Filipinos, including not a few journalists, who vigorously deplored growing American military involvement in Vietnam.

A major controversy developed in 1965 concerning Presi-

The Philippines

dent Macapagal's request for congressional authorization of the dispatch of 1,000 Filipino soldier-engineers to Vietnam accompanied by another 1,000 army personnel to provide protection for them. There was a cry that this would invite Communist retaliation, and the measure lapsed in view of the fact that it was an election year (but it was subsequently revived in 1966). This is not to say that the Philippines is not prepared to carry its modest share of restoring as well as maintaining the peace of the world. The Philippines sent troops to Korea, Filipino civic-action teams performed yeoman duty in South Vietnam, and the Manila government endeavored to mediate Indian-Pakistani differences not long before the outbreak of fighting between these two South Asian powers in 1965.

The Philippines has also sought security in regional selective defense. The objective of SEATO, founded at the Manila Conference of 1954, was the prevention of Communist—meaning mainly Chinese—expansion in Southeast Asia. But only three of the eight SEATO countries were Asians: Thailand, Pakistan, and the Philippines. Hence, Filipino membership in SEATO brought Manila's foreign policy into conflict with other important Asian states—not least of which was assertive next-door Indonesia. The independent Asian stream of Filipino foreign-policy thinking clearly ran counter to the Western-oriented dependence current.

Filipino participation in the 1955 Bandung Afro-Asian Conference, where Indonesia was host, was followed by goodwill visits to Djakarta of Senators Pelaez and Recto and to Manila of Indonesian Foreign Minister Subandrio. Presidents Macapagal and Sukarno later exchanged visits. The Philippines sought to draw Indonesia into either pan-Malay or regional cooperation, but agreement concerning "Maphilindo" (linking Malaya, the Philippines and Indonesia) in August 1963 was followed by new and expanded differences among the states concerned. The Philippines, as well as Thailand, Japan, Cambodia and the United States, tried unsuccessfully to mediate Indonesian-Malaysian differences. Filipino patience with Sukarno expired when Indonesia began attacks against the Malay Peninsula in its limited war, called "confrontation," against the new state of Malaysia in 1964. President Macapagal in particular had tried to be friends with Sukarno, but he and most other members of the Filipino elite subsequently found themselves even more frightened than previously of their big neighbor—so frightened, indeed, that the Manila government sought American aid to establish a new major naval base in the southern islands. It was hard to be "Asia-oriented" and "independent" in such circumstances.

The Philippines also sought closer relations with other regional neighbors, particularly Malaya and Thailand. These three states formed the Association of Southeast Asia (ASA) in 1961, but the grouping subsequently foundered on Filipino-Malayan differences regarding the expanded Malayan state of Malaysia's incorporation of the north Borneo territory of Sabah, a former British dependency also claimed by the Philippines. There was no sentiment in Sabah for absorption into the Philippine state, but the Filipinos still pressed the issue to the disadvantage of closer relations with another mainly pro-Western state also opposed to Indonesian expansionism. Narrowly oriented nationalism seemed to be the motivation.

There were also other areas of ambivalence in Filipino foreign policy. The two Chinas represented one of these areas. As already noted, the Philippines has been unalterably opposed to Communist China; a succession of Filipino governments have opposed a seat for Peking in the United Nations or its recognition by the United States and other countries as well as itself. Manila has been even more vehement than the United States in defending the myth that Formosa is China. But relations between Taipeh and Manila have been also frequently strained, reflecting Filipino fears of the large aggressive Chinese minority in the

The Philippines

islands and doubts about its loyalty. Filipinos also fear Japan, a legacy of occupation and gross mistreatment during the Second World War. Japan finally agreed in 1956 to reparations in the form of $550,000,000 worth of capital goods, services and cash over a 20-year period and $250,000,000 in long-term development loans. Some Filipinos feared, however, that such reparations might result in Philippine economic subordination to Japan. A pattern of economic specialization between the two countries is in fact developing.

"SPECIAL RELATIONS" WITH AMERICA

Filipinos and Americans alike speak of the ties between their two countries as "special relations." By this they mean that each theoretically treats the other more advantageously than it does any other country. The United States probably does enjoy greater privileges in the Philippines than in any other nation on earth. But the relationship is by no means reciprocal as the Filipinos, or increasing numbers of them, see it. The Philippines has not received as much foreign aid proportionately from the United States through the years as have various former enemy and present-day "neutralist" states. American military forces have been stationed in the Philippines under terms more restrictive of Filipino sovereignty than those to be found in comparable agreements with the several NATO countries or Japan. And the United States has a more favored investment position in the Philippines than any nation has in any other country anywhere in the world. "Special relations," accordingly, is a term not infrequently used sarcastically in the Philippines.

Yet despite these "irritants," as the Americans have called them in an apparent attempt to minimize their importance, relations between the two nations have remained both cordial and cooperative. The problem for the future is whether the United States will be able to answer new demands from the Filipinos for more equal—let alone "special"—relations.

The two chief areas of persisting disagreement between the Philippines and the United States have been military and economic relations. The military assistance and bases agreements came into being in 1947, while the bilateral mutual defense pact was signed in 1951. According to Article IV of the latter treaty, "Each party recognizes that an armed attack in the Pacific area on either of the parties would be dangerous to its own peace and safety and declares that it would act to meet the common danger in accordance with its constitutional processes." Neither this pact nor the Manila Treaty establishing SEATO provide for automatic response by an ally or allies of the attacked state in the event of aggression. But American presidents and secretaries of state have repeatedly affirmed that the United States would treat an invasion of the Philippines as an attack against its own territory—most recently President Johnson on the occasion of President Macapagal's 1964 American state visit.

The American bases have irritated Filipinos in two respects. The first of these concerned the question of jurisdiction. The United States possessed jurisdiction over all crimes committed on the bases except when both parties were Filipinos; the Philippines had jurisdiction over American personnel outside the bases unless they were on official duties. These terms were more restrictive of Filipino sovereignty than those of agreements with other countries, and Filipinos were also periodically aroused by the shooting of scavengers on base property by American military personnel —a situation over which the Philippines had no legal control. Talks between the two countries in 1956 and 1958-1959 failed to resolve the problem, but agreement was finally reached in 1965 on terms essentially the same as those of the so-called "NATO formula."

The other major irritant respecting the bases concerned the degree of consultation necessary for their use in any military action. The 1959 talks apparently resulted in satis-

The Philippines

factory agreement on this issue, but the matter was raised anew in 1964-1965 when it was claimed that aircraft from Clark Air Base had participated in strikes against Communist North Vietnam. Other problems have also been solved through the years, such as a reduction in the term of the leases from 99 to 25 years as well as in the number of base-sites. But foreign bases almost always produce friction, they can be used by various types of agitators, and their very presence seems to some persons to be an affront to a nation's sovereignty.

Agitation has also persisted through the years for renegotiation of Philippine-American economic ties. Demands for revision of this relationship as determined in 1946 increased as the time approached for the graduated imposition of duties on trade with the United States in 1954. Some Filipinos believed that this aspect of "special relations" was mainly responsible for the retarded condition of their economy and that it prevented the industrial development of the Philippines by keeping the country dependent on a few export crops. Young industries in the islands could not hope to compete in the home market against duty-free goods from the United States, the most advanced industrialized country in the world.

The result of trade talks between the two countries was the Laurel-Langley Agreement, which was signed September 6, 1955, and went into effect January 1, 1956. The new pact was generally regarded at the time as more favorable to the Philippines than the old relationship. United States control over the exchange rate of the peso was eliminated, while "parity"—which allowed Americans to exploit natural resources and to operate public utilities—was made reciprocal. "Parity" was also extended, however, to permit Americans to compete in business on the same terms as Filipino nationals, a concession which more outspoken Filipino nationalist elements attacked in the mid-1960s as a reason for unilaterally abrogating the Laurel-Langley Agreement. The new pact also gave the Philippines the right to accelerate the imposition of import duties on American manufactured goods, while the United States agreed to impose duties on Philippine goods at a slower pace than under the 1946 agreement. But full tariff rates were still to be applied by both countries in 1974 (as in the agreement of 1946).

Another irritant in Philippine-American economic relations was the Retail Trade Nationalization Law of 1954. This act was passed by the Philippine congress as a means of ending Chinese domination of retail trade in the country, but it provided for a 10-year adjustment period before it became wholly operative. A Filipino firm had to be fully Filipino-owned, according to the act, to qualify for exemption under the law. But what about American firms in view of "parity"? Did the act cover them? The question arose in 1964, and the American firms and the United States government replied in the negative. They were excluded because of "parity," and, besides, an earlier Philippine president had stated that the law did not apply to Americans. But, since few American firms were wholly American-owned in view of the open sale of stocks to persons of all nationalities on American exchanges, this meant that Americans were "more equal" economically than Filipinos in their own country. The issue was a troublesome one. The United States declared in 1965 that it would not seek extension of "parity" beyond 1974, but a lot of agitation and ill will could develop before then.

The adjustment of differences between the two countries over the base jurisdiction issue in 1965 left the several-sided economic question as the main problem confronting them. Further renegotiation of the trade relationship before the 1970s was deemed likely by many observers; it was likewise felt that the retail trade law could be applied to American firms if the Philippines wished to push the issue. These differences notwithstanding, however, few countries have been as faithful to an ally during the 20 years since the Second World War as the Philippines to the United States—or the

The Philippines

United States to the Philippines. If the United States was not always sufficiently sympathetic to the demands of Filipinos, this was by no means mainly the result of the continuation of a colonial mentality, although there was just a little bit of this in the American attitude. The main problem was that the United States was the close ally of many states—the Philippines of only one. Filipinos expected to loom as large in America's eyes as Americans did in their eyes. But this never could be.

CHAPTER 5

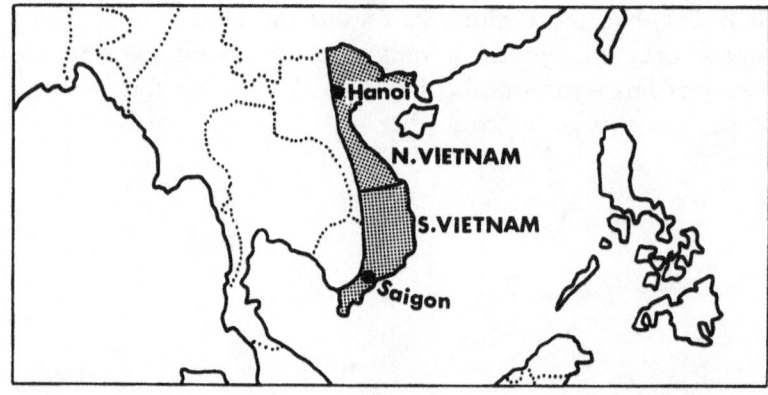

VIETNAM
Cork in the Bottle?

ON VIETNAM, little known to most of the world's peoples only a few years ago, today have converged almost all of the main forces of international politics as part of the persisting efforts of competing powers to expand their influence and limit that of their adversaries. Ever since the occupation of Indochina by the Japanese in 1941 the world's political leaders have been very conscious of the strategic position of this territory in the southeastern corner of Asia. The defeat of Japan did not bring peace to Indochina; it brought in new contestants and intensified hostilities. The Japanese pushed Indochina toward the vortex of world politics; since then it has been fitfully pulled and pushed nearer the center. Today the bloody struggle for ascendancy in Vietnam ranks as the most threatening crisis since the Second World War,

Vietnam

stimulating fears of a Third World War and a direct American confrontation with Communist China. The Vietnamese civil-international war could continue for years, according to some observers.

The struggle for supremacy in Vietnam has steadily drawn the United States into its most thankless commitment in the years since World War II and the assumption of leadership against the forces of tyranny and aggression manifested in international communism. By mid-1966 approximately 255,000 American fighting men were serving in Vietnam, and official and private sources alike were suggesting that this figure might be doubled within the year. Nine cents out of every dollar in the budget presented to the Congress by President Johnson in January of 1966 was earmarked for Vietnam. The war in Vietnam was costing the United States heavily in financial outlay, casualties and, not least of all, prestige in the eyes of the other nations of the world.

World reaction to United States policies and actions in connection with Vietnam was mixed. Many of America's friends were openly critical of our efforts to use military means to force a political settlement. Even some of our supporters backed us quietly, almost in half-clandestine fashion—like Thailand. At the same time, however, many of these very nations would lose faith in America's ability to provide leadership to the non-Communist nations if the United States were suddenly to withdraw or to suffer defeat on the battlefield.

The situation was an unprecedented one for the American democracy. The First and Second World Wars had been in the American mind holy causes conducted by allies against tyranny. In Korea the United States had been the officially designated leader of a legally authorized United Nations international fighting force. But Vietnam was different. Ho Chi Minh was not Adolph Hitler. And the war was a civil war, for all its international significance and foreign support of the two sides. Nor could Communist North Vietnam or the guerrilla Vietcong in South Vietnam be said to threaten the United States in any immediate sense.

FRENCH COLONIAL RULE

Geographically Vietnam is in the shape of an "S," very narrow at the center and with a bulge at each end. It is about 1,500 miles north and south, about 300 miles wide in the north, 300 in the south, and only 40 in the center, where the mountain range which separates Vietnam from Laos pushes toward the sea and narrows the coastal plain to a mere strip. The delta of the Red River constitutes the heart of the northern bulge, while the Mekong River delta at the lower end gives the south a very rich agricultural area.

Vietnam borders on China and intermittently has been under heavy Chinese pressure. For over a thousand years (186 B.C.-939 A.D.) Annam, as the country was then known, was under Chinese rule. The Vietnamese accepted much of Chinese culture as is evident from their religion and literature and—until recently—the imperial political structure and mandarin bureaucracy. The long period of Chinese rule was followed by an uneasy independence under a succession of Vietnamese emperors. The division of Annam in 1673 into the two states of Tonkin and Cochin China led to a long series of dynastic quarrels which encouraged foreign intervention. In 1789 a Catholic bishop landed a party of French soldiers to support one of the warring factions. This action did not, however, lead to French control. A new emperor succeeded in uniting all of Annam, and French influence declined. Seventy years later the persecution of missionaries furnished the excuse for determined French intervention. Saigon was taken in 1859, and by treaty of 1862 the Emperor of Annam ceded a large part of Cochin China, the rice-rich delta region, to France. In 1864 Cambodia became a French protectorate. Desiring to open a road to south China, France extended its control to the north. In 1884 the rest of the country became the protectorates of Annam (central Vietnam) and Tonkin (northern Vietnam). By the establishment of a protectorate over the kingdom of Laos in 1893, the French conquest of Indochina was complete.

The French administration of Indochina, which had an area approximately the size of France itself, was both complex and simple. Tonkin, Annam, Cambodia and Laos were protectorates, while Cochin China (south Vietnam) was a colony and as such sent a deputy to the French Parliament. The difference between colony and protectorate was largely a theoretical one, for a powerful governor general, appointed by Paris and rigidly subject to its control, ruled over a highly centralized administration which included all five territories. French policy in Indochina was characterized by extreme assimilation, economically, culturally, and politically. The French tariff, which was highly protectionist, was extended to Indochina and since its rates were designed to benefit home industries the industrialization of the colony was retarded. France educated an elite who became thoroughly Frenchified in culture but who became dissatisfied because few administrative positions were open to them and opportunities for advancement in business and commerce were made difficult by the sharp competition of the numerous Chinese. France reluctantly and slowly developed representative institutions. The aim of France was to draw its dependencies closer to the metropolitan country as parts of a highly integrated empire dominated by Paris. This policy left little scope for the employment of Vietnamese intelligentsia, who in their frustration became bitterly anti-French and revolutionary.

Opposition to French rule was present from the start but it was slow in gaining momentum. During the First World War this resistance began to assume the form of Western-type nationalism, transmitted to distant Indochina through French literature and civilization. Nationalism as a movement gained further strength as a consequence of France's use of more than 100,000 Indochinese troops in Europe, where they came into direct contact with Western democratic concepts and ideas. The next two decades witnessed ever-increasing agitation for the ending of French imperial rule in Indochina. The movement gained momentum in the years leading up to World War II.

WAR AND POLITICS: 1945-1954

The explosion came shortly after the conclusion of the Second World War. The French administration in Indochina had acquiesced in the Japanese occupation of the land, although more for reasons of expediency than affinity with Japan's aims. It continued nominally to govern Indochina until almost the war's end, but Japan was the real ruler of the country. Probably realizing that their doom was sealed, the Japanese in March 1945 suddenly arrested the French officials and in a broadcast declared that "the colonial status of Indochina has ended." The Emperor of Annam, Bao Dai, issued a declaration of independence, but the Viet Minh, the anti-Japanese resistance movement under the leadership of the Communist Ho Chi Minh, refused to recognize Bao Dai's government. It issued a declaration of independence of *Viet Nam* (land of the south) and established its government at Hanoi. After the war, Indochina was occupied by British and Chinese (Nationalist) troops, with the sixteenth parallel as the dividing line. As in the case of Korea, this line of demarcation became politically significant in large part because of the different policies followed by the occupying powers. The British helped to restore French control, the Chinese impeded it. Early in 1946 the British and Chinese forces withdrew but the latter not until France had given China generous concessions and promised to accord Chinese residing in Vietnam special treatment. The Chinese hoped to gain control of the Vietnamese republic, but Ho retained it.

Vietnam

When the French returned to Vietnam in September 1945 they found most of the country in Viet Minh hands. The French were able to drive the revolutionaries from the cities and to establish their rule once again in the urban areas, but the countryside, for all practical purposes, remained Viet Minh-governed territory. By an agreement of March 6, 1946, the French recognized the Democratic Republic of Vietnam as "a free state with its own government, parliament and army, and finances, forming part of the Indochinese Federation and the French Union." The two sides disagreed over whether Cochin China should be included as part of Vietnam, which otherwise consisted of Tonkin and Annam, both protectorates under the prewar arrangements. The French, however, pledged themselves to hold a referendum on the question.

In April 1946, a month after the agreement had been signed with the Viet Minh, representatives of the two sides met at Dalat, Cochin China, to discuss, among other matters, diplomatic relations between Vietnam and other states, French economic and cultural interests in Vietnam, and the future status of Indochina as a whole. No real agreement was reached on any of these topics, although the Vietnamese did agree that there should be some kind of a federal assembly for all the Indochinese states and that there might also be a customs and monetary union among them. The French reiterated their promise to conduct a referendum in Cochin China.

On June 1, in apparent direct violation of the French pledge, Admiral Thierry d'Argenlieu, high commissioner for Indochina, announced French recognition of the "free republic" of Cochin China—without the holding of a referendum. Termed "provisional" by the French, the move was not necessary for France's administration of the area pending agreement upon its fate. Representatives of the Vietnamese republic and France met in July at Fontainebleau in France to discuss two of the thorniest problems facing them, the status of Cochin China and the position of Vietnam within the Indochinese Federation, a federal political grouping which the French envisioned as including Vietnam, Cambodia, Laos, and possibly Cochin China. While the Fontainebleau talks were in session, Admiral d'Argenlieu convened a second conference at Dalat in Indochina of representatives from Laos, Cambodia, south Annam, and Cochin China—but not the Viet Minh, which had not been asked to attend. So incensed were the Vietnamese delegates at Fontainebleau by this highhanded conduct of d'Argenlieu's that they walked out of the conference in protest.

All but one of the members of the Vietnamese delegation returned home. Ho Chi Minh remained behind in Paris and on September 14 finally signed with Marius Moutet, minister of France overseas, a modus vivendi providing for the cessation of hostilities and the settling of certain cultural and economic questions. To Moutet, Ho is reported to have said, "Don't leave me this way. Give me some weapons against the extremists. You will not regret it." Whether or not Ho was sincere in his protestations of opposition to the "extremists," French concessions were always too little and too late, and the extremists won the day.

The September 14, 1946, modus vivendi was the last agreement to be signed by France and the Viet Minh until July 21, 1954, when signatures were affixed to the now-famous Geneva Accords. Skirmishes between the French and the Vietnamese had been continuing since France's return to Indochina, but they were a far cry from the type of warfare which was to engulf the unfortunate peninsula in the years which lay ahead. War broke out in full force after November 23, when the French bombed Haiphong, killing or wounding thousands of persons. In December the Viet Minh retaliated with a surprise attack on French forces in north Vietnam. From then through the summer of 1954, war raged in Indochina.

The aims of the two parties could not be reconciled. The

French could not give up the idea of a greater France, for France by itself would cease to be a world power. As Premier Ramadier put it, "a nation of traditional size is condemned to be a satellite unless it becomes the center of its own constellation." The French Union in some fashion had to be preserved. Ho and his Vietnamese were willing to make some concessions to the French over cultural and even economic matters but they would not compromise with respect to their demand for the integration of Cochin China into Vietnam and the recognition by France of complete Vietnamese sovereignty.

Indicative of its intentions was France's action in bringing back Bao Dai to Vietnam in 1949. Rather than attempting to seek a settlement with Ho Chi Minh, the French decided to establish the abdicated emperor of Annam as "head of state" of Vietnam, hoping that the Vietnamese would rally around the emperor, a personage of traditional veneration, and so cut down popular support for the Viet Minh. But Ho Chi Minh's prestige was of such stature that it would have taken a real patriot and politician to rival him in the affections of the Vietnamese people. This Bao Dai was never able to do, having had little association with his people, lacking in political ability or inclinations, leading a life of luxury, and spending considerable periods of time away from Vietnam in the sunny resorts of southern France.

At the same time that France enticed Bao Dai from his Hong Kong nightclub life to be the "head of state" of a pro-French Vietnam, it attempted another political sleight of hand, so-called "associated statehood." Abandoning earlier proposals for an Indochinese federation, the French billed associated statehood as something akin to independence—only better because of its continued bond with Paris. Vietnam, Cambodia and Laos were to comprise the Associated States of Indochina, in which they would possess "internal sovereignty," as the French called it. Each was to be theoretically sovereign in internal matters, except for affairs best handled on an Indochina-wide basis. Externally, control over foreign affairs and the armies of the three associated states was to be in the hands of Paris. The Elysée agreements, ratified by the French national assembly in late January 1950 made Vietnam an associated state, and other agreements gave a similar status to Cambodia and Laos.

Much had happened since March 6, 1946. There is little in the record, however, to indicate that anywhere in the long years of tragedy and chaos the French had given up their primary objective of retaining at least a degree of colonial hold over Indochina.

THE COMMUNIST ROAD TO POWER

But even though the French were not fighting Communism as their primary objective, they were battling against it in pursuance of their main aim, for the Ho Chi Minh-directed Viet Minh was a Communist as well as an anti-French nationalist movement. There was no doubt that Ho Chi Minh, redoubtable leader of the Viet Minh in its war with France, had been a Communist throughout the long years of his struggle against French imperialism in Vietnam. As early as 1917 Ho organized the first Vietnamese Marxist group in Paris. In 1920 he joined the Communist International (Comintern) and the next year he organized the Intercolonial Union, which was sponsored by the French Communist party. Two years later the Vietnamese revolutionary attended the Congress of International Peasantry (Krestintern) in Moscow. In 1925 Ho—then known as Nguyen Ai Quoc—appeared in Canton, in south China, where he not only worked as translator-assistant to Michael Borodin, Russian adviser to the Chinese Nationalists, but also formed the Revolutionary Youth Fraternity of Vietnam. The uneasy alliance between the Chinese Nationalists and Communists came to an abrupt end, however, when Chiang Kai-shek turned on the Communists, who were out to infiltrate his movement as a means of taking over the Chinese revolution. Ho fled to the Soviet Union with many of the Russian and Chinese Communists.

In 1928 Ho Chi Minh returned to his native Vietnam, where he commenced active agitation in behalf of Vietnamese independence. Two years later he organized the Vietnamese Communist party at a conference of previously rival revolutionary groups in Hong Kong. The Ho Chi Minh-directed Vietnamese Communist party was to occupy a position of prime importance in the country's nationalist movement until its dissolution in 1945, a move designed to win the support of non-Communists for the Vietnamese revolution.

The *Viet Nam Doc Lap Dong Minh Hoi* (Vietnam Independence League), or Viet Minh, was founded in May 1941. It represented a coalition of sixteen revolutionary groups which had as their common objective the abolition of French and Japanese rule in Vietnam. Communists were included in it, as were a variety of other organized groups, but they constituted only a minority of the movement's members and had no more than a corresponding voice in its policies and activities. As the war years progressed, Ho Chi Minh emerged as the coalition's leader, but he led the movement as a nationalist—not as a Communist. Similarly, the very able General Vo Nguyen Giap, victor at the tragic battle of Dien Bien Phu in 1954, commanded the liberation army formed under Viet Minh auspices, but he also owed his position to his nationalist rather than his Communist orientation.

When avowed Communists like Ho Chi Minh and Vo Nguyen Giap emerge as the leaders of a political grouping, it is not unnatural to assume that the movement they head is Communist as well. Perhaps in an area of the world like Southeast Asia where individual leadership has showed itself to be so decisive in recent years, it is misleading to distinguish between the leaders of a movement and the movement itself, including those who support it. Yet in Vietnam this differentiation does appear to have had considerable pertinence. The crux of the problem for the West in Vietnam was—and continues to be—the difficulty in determining where nationalism ends and Communism begins. Communists came to dominate completely the Viet Minh movement, but they received the support of a large proportion of the Vietnamese people because they were conceived of as unselfish and devoted supporters of Vietnamese nationalism. Ideologically, Ho Chi Minh was clearly a Communist; politically, the movement he headed was undeniably nationalist in terms of its mass support. This is what made Vietnam the problem it was during the years from 1945 through 1954—and is still today.

A major result of French efforts against the Viet Minh movement was to drive the non-Communist moderates from positions of influence within the movement and replace them with Communist extremists. What had once been a predominately nationalist coalition with important Communists in some key positions became in the years between 1945 and 1954 an overwhelmingly Communist organization which played upon the nationalist sympathies of the Vietnamese people.

Could the French by a more flexible policy have driven a wedge between the genuine nationalists and the committed Communists? This is a question that cannot be answered. Plausible arguments can be made each way; in any case it would seem that the triumph of Communism in China may have guaranteed the ultimate ascendancy of the Communists in North Vietnam.

THE GENEVA CONFERENCE OF 1954

The French and Vietnamese military campaign against the Viet Minh was an uphill struggle. By 1953 it was costing France more than a billion dollars a year and a steady and mounting loss of human lives. Beginning in August 1950, the United States sent an increasing stream of military aid to the French and the Vietnamese, bearing by 1953 about a third of the cost of the war. In spite of this great expenditure and effort the military situation had deteriorated. The climax and crisis came with the battle of Dien Bien Phu in April and May 1954 with victory for the Viet Minh. Utterly discouraged and weary of the war, France was determined to withdraw.

The military reversals and their effect on French morale in the spring of 1954 were particularly painful for the Eisenhower administration. The Republicans had severely criticised the Roosevelt and Truman administrations for the loss of China in the 1952 elections and for the "no-win" war in Korea. The Eisenhower administration, moreover, had cut military expenditures, reducing the armed forces, including American troops abroad. At the same time the United States had become deeply involved in the war in Indochina. In the last months America was bearing about 75 percent of the cost of the military operations in that unhappy country; altogether it had given about $2,500,000,000 worth of assistance. Secretary of State John Foster Dulles stated in a radio and television address on May 7, 1954, "We are now paying at the rate of about $800,000,000 a year, plus a very large provision of military equipment."

Secretary Dulles' dilemma was a painful one; he had promised that the United States would not again become bogged down in local wars, but he had also pledged to hold the line against the Communists. It was in this setting that Dulles proclaimed his "instant, massive retaliation" threat—which frightened and alienated America's friends and provided its enemies with propaganda. When the military situation worsened and the French at long last decided to get out of the war in Indochina at once, the administration apparently seriously considered the idea of sending American troops into the war conditional upon allied support and the approval of Congress. The attitude of the Senate was not very constructive, however; most senators were opposed to direct military intervention but also to making any concessions which would help reach a compromise settlement.

A conference of American, British, French and Russian foreign ministers which met at Berlin in January and February 1954 suggested calling a conference on Korea and Indochina to be held at Geneva in April. The United States government was unhappy about the conference, and its policy with respect to it was uncertain. Secretary Dulles, obviously frustrated by the trend of events, flew to Europe and publicly appealed for a "united action" policy to stop Communist aggression in Indochina. The result was a public rebuff. Britain, influenced by domestic public opinion, as well as by the views of Commonwealth members, and a sincere desire on its own part to attempt a peaceful settlement with the Communist countries, refused to participate in any such action "in advance of the results of Geneva." The European fear was that Dulles wanted to scuttle the Geneva Conference. But it is quite clear that he wished only to strengthen the anti-Communist position in order to get a more favorable settlement. The response of America's European allies was a major reason why the United States took such an inactive part in the Geneva Conference. The allies seemed to be working at cross purposes. As a United States senator put it, the French wanted to get out of Indochina, the British wanted to stay out, and the United States, it seemed, wanted to get in.

American military strength and American sentiment had much to do with the final settlement reached at Geneva in 1954 despite the modest level of United States participation in the conference. The Communists did not dare to press their demands too far for fear that they might drive France into the arms of the United States and arouse America to large-scale intervention. The Geneva agreements meant in effect the practical withdrawal of France from Indochina, the evacuation of the Communist Viet Minh forces from Cambodia and Laos as well as South Vietnam, the temporary division of Vietnam at about the seventeenth parallel, and a planned plebiscite in two years to determine the future status of the whole of Vietnam. An International Control Commission, composed of Canada, Poland and India, with the latter as chairman, was established to supervise the execution of the accords.

The United States clearly suffered a setback in Indochina, though it is not clear what other results might have been obtained given the Communist military victories and American reluctance, when the chips were down, to intervene unilaterally. China gained an important ideological ally (and a foothold in Southeast Asia) with significant mineral resources, strategic location, and 15,000,000 people. The plebiscite scheduled for July 1956 was never held. The tragedy is that the United States a decade later was struggling to force the Communists to agree to the holding of such a vote. By the mid-1960s, however, the Communists were even stronger in South Vietnam (not to mention North Vietnam) than they had been at the time of the 1954 Geneva Conference.

President Eisenhower, in a statement on the results of the 1954 Geneva Conference, declared that he was glad that agreement had been reached to stop the bloodshed in Indochina. The "role of the United States at Geneva had been at all times to try to be helpful where desired and to aid France and Cambodia, Laos and Vietnam to obtain a just and honorable settlement." The Americans would not accede to the conference declaration, however. The United States was not itself a "party to or bound by the decisions taken at the conference. The agreement contains provisions which we do not like." In a press statement on July 23, Secretary Dulles declared that the "important thing from now on is not to mourn the past but to seize the opportunity to prevent the loss in northern Vietnam from leading to the extension of communism throughout Southeast Asia and the Pacific Southwest."

The United States attitude toward the Geneva Conference, and its policy there, reflected the basic dilemma in which the Americans found themselves in Vietnam and which has dogged them ever since. The Korean armistice did not remove the conflict with China (or the Communist world); it only shifted the center of conflict from the north to the south. In Korea the conflict had been direct; in Vietnam it was war by proxy. Secretary Dulles feared that the unfavorable French military situation greatly favored the Communists in negotiations. Much as it wished to stop the advance of Communism, however, the United States was reluctant to become involved in another Korean situation, least of all in a terrain as unfavorable as that of Indochina. The United States therefore would not commit ground troops. It was probably prepared to go to the aid of the French and the Vietnamese with its air and naval power, but it is extremely doubtful whether this could have been decisive. Secretary Dulles had earlier warned China that if it continued to aid the Viet Minh the United States might respond with massive retaliation. This threat apparently was not taken seriously for it had no effect. During the conference the United States intermittently talked of direct military intervention of some kind and of a united display of force. Unless massive direct outside aid were immediately forthcoming, the French military position would continue to deteriorate, but direct outside intervention might also precipitate a global war. This was the dilemma.

SOUTH VIETNAM UNDER DIEM

The virtual partition of Vietnam at roughly the seventeen parallel gave South Vietnam an area of about 66,000 square miles and a population of about 13,000,000. It is separated from North Vietnam by a boundary of less than 50 miles but has a long border with Laos and Cambodia. South Vietnam is predominately agricultural with a sprinkling of light industry. The southern half of truncated Vietnam faced almost insuperable difficulties following partition. Some 900,-000 refugees, nearly all Catholics, came down from the north, requiring an expensive resettlement program. The strangest kind of feudalism, moreover, prevailed in the country. Political and military authority was exercised by three groups— two unique and powerful religious sects, the syncretist Cao Dai and the allegedly reformed Buddhist Hoa Hao, and the Binh Xuyen, river pirates who dominated the police and gambling establishments of Saigon, the capital city. All three groups had their own armies. In addition, there were pockets of the disciplined Communist Viet Minh's own army, a violation of the 1954 Geneva Accords. The emperor, Bao Dai, conducted his office most of the time from his residence on the Riviera, while the commander of the army acted as if he were responsible to no one but himself. Economic conditions were bad. The outlook for South Vietnam was gloomy.

In June 1954, Bao Dai appointed Ngo Dinh Diem as premier, but actually gave him little authority. In Diem's favor was his reputation as a nationalist leader. He had had some administrative experience. His biggest asset probably was the backing of the United States. He deposed his disloyal army commander. By various methods and devices, including intrigue, persuasion and military action, he reduced the power of the Binh Xuyen and the sects. He succeeded in consolidating the power of the government. Substantial economic progress was made. Diem also made political progress of a sort. In October 1955, a plebiscite was held in which the voters were asked to choose between the absent Emperor Bao Dai and Diem. The latter won an overwhelming victory. On October 26 the Republic of Vietnam was proclaimed with Diem as its first president, and on March 4, 1956, elections were held to choose a 123-member National Assembly. A constitution was promulgated on October 26, 1956. It invested the president with broad powers and specifically outlawed Communism.

The solid achievements of Diem may be easily forgotten because of his last years. In 1959 his work was quite generally praised. Ernest K. Lindley in *Newsweek* declared that South

Vietnam had made "more progress in more ways than any other Asian nation I have so far visited." He further observed: "In five years, these are some of the achievements: The armed sects have been destroyed or disbanded. Most of the Communist nests have been wiped out. The nearly 1 million refugees have been resettled and are earning their living. More than 52,000 people have been moved into the previously almost empty plateau area where they make Viet Minh infiltration more difficult and produce fiber crops. The second largest land reform of free Asia, involving the conversion of 300,000 former tenants into small landowners, is two-thirds completed. A nation-wide agricultural credit system is operating. Rail lines and bridges have been repaired, and new highways are being built. Rice exports have been resumed. Rubber exports have risen, and new higher-yielding trees are being planted. Schools and other social services have been expanded. A start has been made on assimilating 700,000 Chinese."

Tillman Durdin, in a series of articles in the New York *Times* in April 1959 surveyed the situation in South Vietnam. If not laudatory of Diem, he was certainly not critical of him. He pointed to many advances in the country. When the U. S. Freedom Foundation gave its special leadership award in 1961 to Diem for his effective resistance to Communism, the New York *Times* declared editorially that this resistance has "up to this point, been more successful than many persons would have imagined possible. Free Vietnam is still free, and is forging ahead. The tactics that President Diem has used, therefore, are worthy of analysis. They may work elsewhere." He achieved "some degree of actual physical unification within his country," he turned "into reality some of the social and economic reforms that had always been high on the list of unfilled Communist promises," and probably "the most important in the long run, he has set into motion a vigorous program to give his people a fresh spiritual outlook. He is meeting the Communists on the ground of the contest for the minds and the spirit of his countrymen. Thus far he is winning." The editorial ended with the statement: "What President Diem and his associates are trying to do is to establish a revitalized Vietnamese moral culture. This, they believe, is the best way to meet and defeat the amoral materialism of communism."

President John F. Kennedy likewise praised Diem and the Vietnamese for their achievements. On the sixth anniversary of the Republic of Vietnam Kennedy sent a message to Diem, in which he stated: "Mr. President, in 1955 we observed the dangers and difficulties that surrounded the birth of your republic. In the years that followed, we saw the dedication and vigor of your people rapidly overcoming those dangers and difficulties. We rejoiced with you in the new rice springing again from fields long abandoned, in the new hospitals and roads and schools that were built, and in the new hopes of a people who had found peace after a long and bitter war. The record you established in providing new hope, shelter and security to nearly a million fleeing from Communism in the north stands out as one of the most laudable and best-administered efforts in modern times."

But at the peak of Diem's prestige and power there were ominous signs. In November 1960, an attempt was made by a military group to overthrow his government. Communist guerrilla activities, which had greatly diminished, were being rapidly revived. This was probably a tribute to Diem's success. The Communists could not afford to allow his government to become stronger. While Communist pressure was rising, however, Diem's government was becoming increasingly unpopular. Although Diem was recognized as an incorruptible patriot, there was steadily mounting dissatisfaction with his authoritarian character and strongly dictatorial tendencies. Vigorously disliked was the family nature of his regime. Members of his family held virtually all the levers of power in the government. One brother, Ngo Dinh Canh, was the overlord of central Vietnam; a second, Msgr. Ngo Dinh Thuc, as bishop and later archbishop of Hue, was head of the Roman Catholic hierarchy in South Vietnam; a third, Ngo Dinh Luyen, was South Vietnam's ambassador at London; while a fourth brother, Ngo Dinh Nhu, was the president's chief political adviser and head of the secret police. And not the least influential member of the family was Nhu's wife, a member of the National Assembly and an authoritarian feminist who was said to wield extraordinary power behind the scenes.

The almost militantly Catholic character of the regime (when the population was 70 percent Buddhist and only 10 percent Catholic) was bound to create resentment. Buddhists, and others felt that Catholics and Catholic projects were given privileges, that Catholics advanced faster in government, and that the regime was trying to establish Catholicism as a kind of state religion. As his government became more insecure, Diem became more intolerant of political opposition and resorted to increasingly oppressive measures. The situation became critical when on May 9, 1963, government forces fired on a Buddhist demonstration in Hue and killed nine persons. This incident marks a political watershed for the Diem regime. The Buddhist protest became a facade for a general movement of opposition to the government. Instead of seeking conciliation, as the United States had urged, the government in August raided Buddhist temples, herded monks and nuns into trucks and took them away. With this the situation became explosive. How much Diem had to do with this assault is not certain. Nhu may at this time have executed a palace coup and taken over from his brother.

The government justified its crackdown on the Buddhists by declaring that it was strongly determined not to tolerate the exploitation of religion for political purposes. Madame Nhu charged the Buddhists with being dupes of the Communists. For the United States government the situation was extremely difficult. It was not in South Vietnam to govern but to help the Vietnamese government to suppress Communist infiltration, subversion and guerrilla warfare. But an unpopular Vietnamese government greatly impaired the effectiveness of these efforts. The Diem regime had become a distinct liability. The mounting hostility against it was beginning to extend to the United States. Communist propaganda was tarring the two governments with the same brush. The United States had urged moderation on Diem but without result. If it exerted great pressure, the United States would lay itself open to the charge of "colonialism," of having reduced South Vietnam to a satellite. Dissociating itself from the oppressive Diem regime also had its dangers. It might lead to Diem's overthrow. There was no assurance that anything better would replace it.

The United States did resort to mild pressure on the Diem regime. In August 1963, it sent Henry Cabot Lodge, Jr., former senator and United States representative at the United Nations, to Saigon as its ambassador. He replaced an ambassador whose policy had been inflexible support of Diem. Lodge, apparently, was to reverse this policy. Some basic military aid was suspended. President Kennedy in a televised interview on September 2 said, "I don't think that the war can be won unless the people support the effort. And in my opinion, in the last two months the government has gotten out of touch with the people. . . . With changes in policy and perhaps in personnel I think [popular support] can [be regained]." On October 2 the White House issued a statement on the report of Secretary of Defense Robert S. McNamara and General Maxwell D. Taylor, who had just returned from a visit to South Vietnam to survey the situation, which contained the following assessment: "The political situation in South Vietnam remains deeply serious. The United States has made clear its continuing opposition to any repressive actions in South Vietnam. While such actions have not yet significantly affected the military effort, they could do so in the future."

These acts and statements could only be interpreted as a rebuke to the Diem government. Were they also interpreted by the opposition in Saigon as an encouragement to overthrow it? In any case, a group of generals seized control of the government on November 1. Diem and his brother Nhu were killed. The military junta in a broadcast to the nation accused the Diem government of abusing power, of thinking only of personal ambition, of slighting the fatherland's interests, of trampling on the people's lawful rights, and of incompetence.

NORTH VIETNAM

The 1954 division gave the North 61,293 square miles of territory as compared with 65,948 for the South. However, the population of the North is probably two and a half million greater—about 15,500,000 to 13,000,000 (1966 estimate). The North has a better base for industrialization than the South, possessing large deposits of coal, iron and phosphates, and some deposits of copper, lead, manganese, zinc and other metals. On the other hand, the North is deficient in the production of rice, the staple food of its people, whereas the South under peaceful conditions would have large amounts for export.

After 1954 the Ho Chi Minh regime, which had clandestinely ruled much of the territory since 1945, became the official government. It began with a government in form modeled after that of the Western democracies but in fact controlled by an oligarchy of Communists. In 1960 the Democratic Republic of Vietnam adopted a new, Communist type constitution. A popularly elected National Assembly meets for very brief sessions. It elects the president and delegates the exercise of its authority between sessions to a Permanent Standing Committee. The controlling power is held by the Political Bureau and Central Committee of the ruling Workers party (Lao Dong). The leaders of the party are also the top men in the government. The veteran Communist leaders Ho Chi Minh and Pham Van Dong are president and premier respectively. In contrast with the parade of governments in the South since the fall of Diem, the political leaders in the North have been stable fixtures.

The adoption of the new constitution marked a determined drive to socialize the economy. Russia and China and other Communist countries had given aid to rehabilitate the country after the ravages of the war and also helped it to industrialize. Communist bloc grants and loans to North Vietnam totalled over a billion dollars from 1955 to 1961. As is evident from the large number of factories which have been built since 1960, considerable progress is being made in industrialization. Land reform may have been pressed too hard, for there were peasant uprisings in 1956. The emphasis upon industrialization in the first Five-Year Plan, at the cost of rural development, apparently again caused peasant disturbances in 1961.

North Vietnam's foreign policy, especially within the Communist bloc, has been beset with difficulties. Population pressure and the need for the surplus rice of the South make reunification of Vietnam the primary object of government policy. Since China has a similar problem the two can readily agree on revolutionary action to "liberate" the South Vietnamese. On the other hand, North Vietnam fears Chinese domination and hence would like to balance Russia against China, but China is next door and Russia is far away. Furthermore, North Vietnam needs both Russian help to industrialize and its military aid. It was quite natural therefore for Ho to try to follow a neutral policy in the controversy between China and Russia; he has even tried to mediate the dispute. Yet North Vietnam moved more and more in the direction of China. In not signing the test-ban treaty it openly sided with China, which was bitterly critical of this agreement. There were many reasons for siding with China. There was an acute food shortage in 1963 in North Vietnam, which looked to China for relief. In their consuming desire for reunification, the North Vietnamese Communist leaders naturally supported China's aggressive doctrine of armed revolution for "liberation" of peoples from imperialist control and rejected the Russian policy of coexistence with the capitalist world. China vigorously supported the revolution in South Vietnam; Russia wanted peace and was loathe to disturb relations with the United States. Hanoi and Peking both desired to eliminate American power and influence in Southeast Asia. The explosion of an atomic bomb by China undoubtedly also had its influence. North Vietnam is probably no longer free to negotiate or make peace against the wishes of Peking, even if it wished to.

Russia was in a difficult position. Engaged in a bitter struggle with China for prestige and power in the Communist world and among the uncommitted nations, it could hardly be deaf to the pleas of a fellow Communist state, and it could not afford to let China use the situation to advance its own position and to discredit the Soviet Union. Peking attacked Soviet leadership for not having taken a more active role in support of North Vietnam and the Vietcong guerrillas. It charged Moscow with wanting to "strike more bargains with the United States and betray the Vietnamese people's revolutionary cause." Unless relations between China and Russia improved greatly, Russia could get no advantages from Communist gains in Southeast Asia, for this region is China's sphere, and whatever the Communist harvest there might be, it would be reaped by China. Yet Hanoi does not wish domination by Peking and still apparently hopes to play off the two Communist giants one against the other—as evidenced by North Vietnam's high level representation in

*Vietnam* 183

1966 at the 23rd Soviet Communist Party Congress, which the Chinese denounced and boycotted.

DEVELOPMENTS SINCE THE MILITARY COUP OF 1963

The overthrow of the Diem regime in South Vietnam brought neither political stability nor military progress. Since the first military coup the political history of South Vietnam has been one of grave instability. Governments, torn by factions, succeeded each other in rapid succession. Some were purely military regimes, others weak civilian governments backed by the military—all caretaker administrations at best.

Meanwhile, the military situation deteriorated. What may be called the second Indochina war began in 1957 with the assassination of a few South Vietnamese officials by terrorists. At first there were only a few scattered armed bands backed by a fairly extensive secret political organization. From this small beginning the Communist Vietcong expanded into a formidable fighting force equipped with modern infantry weapons. In the Mekong Delta, where South Vietnam's population is concentrated, more than half of the people live under a Communist shadow government which engages in activities much like a regular government, including the collection of taxes.

How the military situation worsened can be seen from the increase of American troops in South Vietnam. Before 1961 there were fewer than 700 men but in that year their number was more than doubled to a total of 1,650. President Kennedy took this action upon the recommendation of his chief military adviser, General Maxwell D. Taylor, who had made a survey of the situation in Vietnam. By the end of 1962 there were 11,000. There were 15,500 American fighting men in Vietnam at the end of 1963—and 23,000 by 1964's end. There was a rapid buildup in 1965. In May there were nearly 46,000, a few months later 75,000, and by the end of the year 200,000

—a ten-fold increase over December 1964; the latter figure was exclusive of American servicemen on ships off the Vietnamese coast or flying missions from Thailand, Guam or other locations. By mid-1966 the figure had risen to more than 255,000. South Vietnam had 345,000 men in the regular army and 350,000 in police and para-military forces. The Vietcong force was estimated at 90,000 "regulars" (full time) and as many as 120,000 "irregulars" (guerrillas).

The role of the American forces in South Vietnam has undergone a steady change. The basic United States position until 1965 was that its members served only as "advisers." American military men were not to shoot unless shot at. When North Vietnam attacked United States naval vessels in the Gulf of Tonkin on August 5, 1964, President Johnson ordered a "positive reply." American forces made air attacks on North Vietnamese naval installations. On February 6, 1965, Communist guerrillas staged infantry and mortar attacks on American installations at Pleiku air base. Seven Americans were killed and 109 wounded. Charging that North Vietnam had directed and made the raid possible, the United States and South Vietnamese air forces launched joint "retaliatory attacks against barracks and staging areas in the southern area of North Vietnam which intelligence has shown to be actively used by Hanoi for training and infiltration of Vietcong personnel into South Vietnam." A few days later the Communists raided American barracks at Quinhon with further loss of American lives. In announcing the retaliatory attacks in the latter instance, President Johnson stated that the United States sought "no wider war" but added that "whether or not this course can be maintained lies with the North Vietnamese aggressors. The key to the situation remains the cessation of infiltration from North Vietnam and the clear indication by the Hanoi regime that it is prepared to cease aggression against its neighbors."

The retaliatory air bombing attacks on North Vietnam became steadily intensified in fire power and scope and lost any real relation to specific attacks by the Communists. It is obvious that the hostilities in South Vietnam had a civil war—and an international war—character, but in 1965 the latter clearly became dominant. The United States government justified the shift in its policy in a white paper issued by the State Department on February 27. In this statement it is said that "the hard core of the Communist forces attacking South Vietnam are men trained in North Vietnam. They are ordered into the South and remain under the military command in Hanoi. Special training camps operated by the North Vietnamese Army give political and military training to the infiltrators. Increasingly, the forces sent into the South are native North Vietnamese who have never seen South Vietnam. . . . It is . . . apparent that infiltrators from the North—allowing for casualties—make up the majority, and probably the overwhelming majority, of the so-called hard core Vietcong. Personnel from the North, in short, are now and have always been the backbone of the entire Vietcong operation."

The white paper stated that since 1959, 20,000 Vietcong officers, soldiers and technicians were known to have entered South Vietnam "under orders from Hanoi," and that probably 17,000 more infiltrators entered the South. The State Department document countered the argument that this number is small in comparison with the total size of the South Vietnamese armed forces by pointing out that "in guerrilla combat the burdens of defense are vastly heavier than those of attack. In Malaya, the Philippines and elsewhere a ratio of at least 10 to 1 in favor of the forces of order was required to meet successfully the threat of the guerrillas' hit and run tactics."

The hostilities in Indochina took on an increased international character when American planes late in 1964 began bombing the Communist supply line running from North Vietnam through central Laos to South Vietnam. Was this a violation of the 1962 Geneva agreements which guaranteed the neutrality and independence of Laos and specifically forbade the entrance of foreign troops into the country? The State Department justified reconnaissance and bombing missions in Laos on the ground of continuing Communist violations of the agreements. The United States as well as Communist China and North Vietnam are signatories of the agreements.

PEACE PROPOSALS

There was profound concern throughout the world that the limited war in Indochina might escalate into a general war. Many efforts were made to bring about negotiations for a peaceful settlement. On February 12, 1965, U Thant, the Secretary General of the United Nations, made an appeal for "shifting the quest for a solution away from the field of battle to the conference table," and on February 25 he said at a news conference that he had presented "concrete ideas and proposals" to "some of the principal parties directly involved in the question of Vietnam." Apparently, some months before he had attempted to arrange secret informal discussions between Hanoi and Washington. Pope Paul VI on February 20 disclosed that he had tried to make contact with political leaders to plead for a peaceful solution in Vietnam. In April, 18 non-aligned states made an appeal for negotiations without conditions to end the fighting in Vietnam, and in June the conference of (British) Commonwealth prime ministers proposed the sending of a peace mission, headed by Prime Minister Harold Wilson of the United Kingdom, to the countries involved. There were other attempts to bring about peace talks: France's proposal for a new Geneva Conference, Soviet endorsement of a Cambodian Conference which could serve as a backdoor approach to the Vietnam problem, and India's plan for a cease-fire policed by an Afro-Asian force.

Probably as a result of great pressure both at home and abroad to clarify United States aims in South Vietnam and its conditions for a peaceful settlement, President Johnson in an address at Johns Hopkins University on April 7 made important concessions and proposals. He stated that the United States was prepared for "unconditional discussions" on peace in Vietnam. Heretofore, he had demanded that the Communists cease their attacks in South Vietnam before any discussions could take place. The American objective in Vietnam, he declared, was an independent South Vietnam free from outside interference and attack, "tied to no alliance, a military base for no country." As an inducement to restore peace he proceeded to offer one billion dollars for launching a huge regional development plan, a Mekong River project that would dwarf even the Tennessee Valley Authority. He hoped that "all other industrialized countries, including the Soviet Union," would join in the plan. In an address on May 13 President Johnson called on every industrialized country to join the United States in forming an Asian Development Bank to help finance the economic development of Southeast Asia.

Several times President Johnson has reiterated the offer of the United States to hold discussions "with any government anywhere and without any conditions." As proof of its willingness to negotiate the United States informed Hanoi through Canada that it was ordering a cessation of any bombing for an indefinite period. When there was no response from Hanoi after a six-day pause, air attacks were resumed on May 18. In his address to the 20th United Nations anniversary commemoration at San Francisco on June 26, President Johnson made an ardent plea for negotiations on Vietnam. He said: "I call upon this gathering of the nations of the world to use their influence, individually and collectively, to bring to the tables those who seem determined to make war. We will support their efforts, as we will support effective action by any agent or agency of these United Nations."

This plea seemed directed at rallying world opinion to exert pressure on Peking and Hanoi to negotiate. They rejected all appeals, demanding that the United States withdraw from Vietnam before there could be discussions.

Even after the decision was made in July—after high level White House conferences—to commit more American armed forces to the struggle in Vietnam, President Johnson at his news conference on the 28th stated: "I have stated publicly and many times, . . . American willingness to begin unconditional discussions. . . . But there has been no answer."

The President further stated that he had directed U. S. Ambassador Arthur Goldberg to present immediately to Secretary General U Thant "a letter from me requesting that all the resources and the energy and the immense prestige of the United Nations be employed to find ways to halt aggression and to bring peace in Vietnam."

THE JOHNSON PEACE OFFENSIVE AND THE FUTURE

The United States itself brought the Vietnam problem before the Security Council of the United Nations on February 1, 1966, but not until the American President had made another and more determined effort to ascertain if there was any willingness on the part of the North Vietnamese government to negotiate a settlement. For 37 days the Americans held off bombing North Vietnam despite the continued flow of men and materials from the North to the South. During this period emissaries of President Johnson visited most of the world's main capitals and talked to many of the world's leading statesmen. The United States sought negotiations with North Vietnam "without conditions." The Americans were willing to withdraw their forces from South Vietnam as soon as that territory was "in a position to determine its own future without external interference." South Vietnam's future government and reunification of the two Vietnams, if it should take place, should be determined by free elections. Ho Chi Minh's government termed the American peace offensive "a trick, merely the repetition of old themes." The bombing of North Vietnam was resumed on January 31, 1966.

According to Secretary of State Dean Rusk, the bombing moratorium would have been extended by the United States if Hanoi had responded to the American overtures with any kind of peace gesture. There was none. In ordering resumption of the bombing, President Johnson stated that the move "does not mean the end of our pursuit of peace."

The peace offensive had not been successful in bringing about immediate negotiations among the protagonists. But its failure provided a springboard for the appeal to the U. N., and it may have convinced some doubting nations—but by no means all—that the United States sincerely sought negotiations. South Vietnam's Premier Air Vice Marshal Nguyen Cao Ky clearly feared that Washington might go too far in such negotiations, stating publicly, "No other nation is qualified . . . to decide on our destiny." As for the Communists, they not only turned a deaf ear to the American peace proposals, but they also used the bombing lull to repair previously damaged roads and bridges and to move new men and material into the South—probably as many as 2,500 reinforcements in January, 1966.

The Johnson peace offensive reflected in large measure the American concern at the rising cost of the war in Vietnam. The 1,432 American fighting men who lost their lives in combat in Vietnam in 1965 represented more than a ten-fold increase over the previous year. The United States probably spent in excess of six billion dollars for Vietnam in the same year, an outlay of $16.5 million daily, and President Johnson's 1966-1967 budget called for an increased expenditure of $10.5 billion annually. And the United States was building new major military installations in or near South Vietnam, three major jet airfields, a navy base at Camranh Bay, and another sizeable naval installation at Sattahip on the Gulf of Siam in Thailand. The war ahead looked like a long one.

The first half of 1966 saw a major increase in the intensity of air strikes against North Vietnamese targets but no signs that the enemy was yielding in its determination to fight. Even conservative military estimates stated that no decisive action could be expected until the end of the anticipated American buildup to 400,000—or more—fighting men in late 1966 or early 1967. Meanwhile, as many American servicemen lost their lives in the first four months of 1966 as in all of 1965. Leading American legislators and commentators were asking whether the war in Vietnam was worth its cost, and President Johnson had to respond to such criticism, although it is undoubtedly also true that the President desired a peaceful solution of the Vietnamese problem—if this was possible.

Probably most politically influential of the many such appraisals was the report of the study mission headed by Senate Majority Leader Mike Mansfield, who has long followed developments in Vietnam closely. According to the Mansfield report, "A rapid solution to the conflict in Vietnam is not in immediate prospect." The report continued: "Indeed, if present trends continue, there is no assurance as to what ultimate increase in American military commitment will be required before the conflict is terminated. For the fact is that under present terms of reference . . . the question is not one of applying increased U. S. pressure to a defined military situation which is, in effect, open-ended." The "alternative prospect" to peace talks, Senator Mansfield and his colleagues asserted, was a "continuance of the conflict in the direction of a general war on the Asian mainland." These conclusions shocked many Americans who believed Secretary of Defense McNamara when he stated his hope in 1964 that "the major part of the U.S. military task would be completed by the end of 1965"—or Secretaries Rusk and McNamara when they declared a year earlier that American troops would begin leaving South Vietnam by late 1964. The expectations of ultimate triumph implicit in the McNamara-favored buildup of American fighting men in Vietnam to 400,000 or more in 1966 could be no less falsely rooted than the defense secretary's earlier expressed anticipations. Both Secretaries McNamara and Rusk had been wrong before—dead wrong.

The fact was that the war was still going against the United States in Vietnam in 1966. The pro-American Saigon government controlled a lesser area in January 1966 than it had a year earlier, although the deterioration in the situation which was so evident in the first months of 1965 had been at least temporarily halted. In February 1966 the Saigon government itself admitted that it controlled only 10 percent of the land area south of the seventeenth parallel; nearly half the people in the South lived outside this area. The war was still defensive by any type of measurement, moreover. And Americans were playing a growing—and South Vietnamese a decreasing—role in it, relatively speaking. Moreover, there were new actors on the scene by mid-1966: about 20,000 North Vietnamese army "regulars," who had moved south to join the Vietcong guerrilla fighters, and at least two dozen Chinese Communist MIG-21 jet fighters stationed near Hanoi. There were no Chinese fighting units in North Vietnam, but C. L. Sulzberger of the New York *Times* claimed in April that "some 20,000 uniformed Chinese"—"logistical type units"— were in the country helping to maintain rail links with China. Soviet surface-to-air guided missiles had earlier been installed in North Vietnam. And in mid-May 1966 Peking claimed that one of its aircraft had been downed by missiles from an American plane over Chinese soil. Chinese Premier Chou En-lai had only days earlier pledged Hanoi "all-out support" whatever the extent the United States "may widen the war and whatever cost we may pay." Some feared that a direct American-Chinese clash was imminent.

The South Vietnamese military situation brought in its wake other problems. More than 700,000 refugees fled to urban areas from the countryside in 1965—about 600,000 more than Vietnamese officials were prepared to receive and almost as many as came from the North in the wake of the 1954 Geneva Accords. Desertions from the South Vietnamese armed forces increased sharply, reaching 8,000 monthly by the end of the year. More than 6,000 village officials were assassinated by the Vietcong in 1965. And South Vietnam, a rice-exporting country under peaceful circumstances, was forced to import considerable quantities of the grain to feed its urban population.

Some—like American Senator Ted Kennedy, brother of the late president, who visited Vietnam to study the refugee problem—declared that South Vietnamese officials were indifferent to the mass suffering occasioned by the war. Others charged that the generals were still jockeying for power, a claim that seemed to be substantiated by Marshal Cao Ky's dismissal of Brigadier General Nguyen Chanh Thi, ambitious commander of I Corps in the Danang-Hue area in central Vietnam, in March 1966. The Cao Ky government, however, proclaimed its intention to implement a vigorous "rural pacification" campaign designed to alleviate peasant hardship and win the support of the rural masses in 1966, and the United States agreed to finance such an effort in an expanded aid program. The Honolulu meeting between President Johnson and Premier Cao Ky in early 1966 symbolized American determination to support the Vietnamese leader's efforts to cope with economic and social problems as well as the war with the Communists. But the Honolulu talks appeared subsequently to backfire. It looked to only too many that it was the United States which was taking the initiative concerning reforms, unintentionally implying that the Saigon government was incapable or unwilling to do so. It appeared that Cao Ky had been summoned to Honolulu, President Johnson's embrace of the 35-year old Vietnamese premier indicating that he was "America's boy,"—"a puppet of the imperialists," as the Communists were to put it.

Premier Cao Ky sacked General Thi soon after his return

from Honolulu, reflecting the continuing political rivalries among the country's military leaders. The Buddhists, who had played an important role in the earlier fall of President Diem and who were strong in the area formerly commanded by General Thi, rushed to the streets to demonstrate in defense of the ousted soldier, their support being merely an excuse to express their opposition to the Saigon government and to advance their own political fortunes. The Buddhists also probably reflected a mounting war weariness in the country in general. Led by the monk Thich Tri Quang, they scored a tactical victory against the Cao Ky regime. Cao Ky had previously promised a constitution by late 1966 and elections the subsequent year. But, pressed by the demonstrating Buddhists, the Vietnamese premier indicated that voting would take place earlier than had been indicated—probably well before 1966 ended. This seemed to settle the situation, and work commenced on framing an election law.

Cao Ky himself reopened the controversy by stating in a press conference in early May that he would probably retain the premiership for another year. His promise to the Buddhists, he said, had been to hold elections for a constituent assembly to draft a constitution—there was nothing in that pledge that could be construed to allow such an assembly to transform itself into a legislature. It would still probably be mid-1967 before an elected civilian government would take office, according to Cao Ky. The Buddhists were visibly upset by Cao Ky's interpretation of the concession which they had obtained from him, and demonstrations began anew. The more optimistic of observers believed that the constituent assembly vote would be so anti-government that there would be no stopping the constitution-makers from staying on as legislators. They at least would have more of a mandate than the Cao Ky regime if a vote were not blocked by boycott or fraud. Vietnam's problem was fragmentation—and alienation—and a popularly selected civilian government might go a long way towards solving the second malady. The question was whether agreement was possible among feuding Buddhists, Catholics and soldiers.

To many there was a touch of "Alice in Wonderland" in the notion that South Vietnam could hold meaningful democratic elections for a constituent assembly or a legislature—in 1966, 1967, or even subsequently—given Communist control of most of the countryside. But without such an attempt to establish a popularly endorsed government it was difficult to see how the Saigon government could rally support to its side. This is not to say that the government was altogether lacking in supporters, however. Too much can be made of the Vietcong's so-called "rice-roots" support. Elections were held in selected areas of the country in May 1965, and more than 73 percent of the eligible voters participated—despite Vietcong threats of reprisal. Moreover, the Vietcong have yet to make significant inroads in the urban areas, such as Saigon, where hostile mob action would be fatal to the government. The South Vietnamese leaders themselves, in addition, give no evidence whatsoever of any early willingness to join hands with their adversaries in a coalition government. Their fear, indeed, is that the Americans will make concessions on their behalf—which they may not be able to countermand.

This fear is not unreasonable, but it is unfair. There is every reason to believe President Johnson when he says, as he did in his January 1966 State of the Union message, that "we will stay in Vietnam because a just nation cannot leave to the cruelty of its enemies a people who have staked their lives and independence on America's solemn pledge." What was holding up peace, as Johnson saw it (and so stated later the same month in a speech honoring former President Harry S. Truman in Independence, Missouri), was "the mistaken view on the part of the aggressors that the United States is going to give up our principles, that we will yield to pressure, or abandon our allies, or finally get tired and get out." As the President put it, "It takes more than one to sign an agreement. . . . If the aggressors are ready . . . let them come to the meeting place, and we will meet them there."

The North Vietnamese clearly were not willing to come to any meeting place on the terms—which were so unconditional as not really to be terms at all—suggested by Johnson. Replying to a message from Pope Paul VI, received during the period of the American peace offensive, the Communist Vietnamese leader Ho Chi Minh said, "The U. S. government must completely and unconditionally end its bombings and all acts of war against the D.R.V. [North Vietnam], stop its aggression in South Vietnam, withdraw its troops and armaments from South Vietnam, and let the Vietnamese people settle their internal affairs themselves." Concerning the latter point, Premier Pham Van Dong had earlier told the North Vietnamese National Assembly that "the internal affairs of South Vietnam must be settled by the South Vietnamese people themselves, in accordance with the South Vietnam National Front for Liberation, without any foreign interference." The United States was probably in tactical error in insisting that the Vietcong or National Liberation Front (NFL) not be allowed to participate in peace talks; the Vietnamese Communists, after all, were entitled to as much of a voice in determining their country's future as the alien Americans. But, it was not a "voice" for the NFL, the political arm of the guerrilla Vietcong, that Pham Van Dong demanded but rather settlement of the internal South Vietnamese situation on NFL, or Communist, terms. This was hardly a basis for negotiations between the two sides in the war.

It was in such a setting, and after such a response to his December 1965-January 1966 peace offensive, that President Johnson called on the United Nations for help in ending the war in Vietnam and bringing a peaceful settlement to that badly scarred Southeast Asian land. Pope Paul VI had proposed arbitration through the U. N. by representatives of the

Afro-Asian countries. Most of these, however, were held suspect by one or the other side in the conflict—or themselves suspected one of the two sides or its supporters (China and the United States). The Communists, moreover, could hardly be expected to give up at the conference table what they had won on the battlefield. The Soviets had forced them to accept the 1954 Geneva Accords but not without legitimatization of their *de facto* power position in North Vietnam and the promise of elections (which they probably would have won) in all of Vietnam in 1956. The Communists surely will not disgorge any of their hard won military gains in the South.

Likewise, the United States is not likely to abandon its South Vietnamese ally, however much Washington may wish it had never gotten itself into such a commitment. The Communist Vietnamese cannot dislodge the United States from Vietnam and so cannot achieve their goal of a united Communist Vietnam as long as American determination holds out. Retired General James M. Gavin thinks that American aims are beyond our capability and in a letter to a leading magazine advocated reduction of our military activity to holding operations along the coast of South Vietnam. Others—the "war hawks," as they have been popularly designated—call for enlarged and sterner military action, such as bombing or mining Hanoi's port, Haiphong. But whether this would bring Hanoi to its knees is problematical. Articles in two leading North Vietnamese publications in early 1966 indicated a "pacifist minority" opposed a "long and likely" war. But James Cameron, an experienced British newsman, reported in late 1965 that the main effect of American bombing raids north of the seventeenth parallel was to unite the people behind their government and against the intruding and destructive alien.

There was growing doubt in the United States, meanwhile, concerning the wisdom of the American response in Vietnam. A Louis Harris poll in May 1966 indicated that less than a

Vietnam

majority, 47 percent, of the American people rated President Johnson favorably on his handling of the situation. Four times as many bombs fell on South Vietnam than on the North in 1965. The United States pursued a veritable "scorched earth" policy in the South, destroying 80,000 buildings of one kind or another and planning to destroy 200,000 acres of crops in 1966. The problem in Vietnam was one of political fragmentation and alienation. The question was raised as to the appropriateness of the American response to this problem. Even more fundamentally, it was asked whether a foreign power could in fact effectively control the direction of political development of a territory, or country, like South Vietnam.

There was growing agreement in the West and most of Afro-Asia in mid-1966 that negotiations would be the best way to end the fighting in Vietnam, and the United States was by this time clearly willing to participate in another conference on Vietnam. Such a conference might be the only face-saving way out of Vietnam for the Americans. But, as the 1961-1962 Geneva Conference on Laos and subsequent activities in Laos clearly indicate, it is extraordinarily difficult—if not impossible—to guarantee a nation's neutrality. If, on the other hand, the United States abandons South Vietnam on the battlefield or at the conference table, this will surely make a mockery of the long vigorously expressed American commitment to the Saigon government and raise serious doubts in the minds of the leaders of other allied nations respecting Washington's willingness to stand by them when the chips are down.

The fact is that 1966 was not 1954, 1960, or even 1964. The situation had changed drastically in South Vietnam in the years since the first Geneva Accords. A situation possibly capable of being salvaged a decade earlier had sorely worsened. The anti-Communists were by no means a bankrupt force in the country, however, and might ultimately triumph. After all, the anti-Communists have not done so badly in

Laos since 1962. At the same time, the reality must be faced that it is the Communists who have been winning in the South and who each year of the 1960s have expanded the percentage of the territory under their control. It may well be that the United States and such states as are willing to take a stand against Communist aggression in Southeast Asia—like South Korea, Australia and New Zealand, the Americans' principal outside partners in the war against the Vietcong— should devote their attention more to containing tomorrow's Vietnam, whether Communist or not, rather than attempting unsuccessfully to guarantee either the internal political complexion or foreign policy orientation of South Vietnam.

Vietnam stands out among all the Southeast Asian countries as the land whose political development appears to have been most decisively influenced by foreigners. This impression is an erroneous one. The men who govern North Vietnam today—the 76-year old Ho Chi Minh, General Vo Nguyen Giap, Premier Pham Van Dong, party secretary Truong Chinh, and the influential Le Duan—are Vietnamese who have been actively pursuing particular political ends since the years of the Japanese occupation. Some of them, most notably Ho, have labored even longer for a certain kind of Vietnam politically. These are not foreigners, and their war with Ngo Dinh Diem, Nguyen Cao Ky and the other southern anti-Communist leaders has not been any kind of "invasion." The role of the chief Communist nations, China and the Soviet Union, and of the United States has been minimal in its impact compared with the importance of these men. Moreover, the regime which they have established in North Vietnam—and hope to extend to all of Vietnam— is less different from the governments of some of the other Southeast Asian states (Burma in particular) than many Americans are willing to admit.

The United States wisely decided not to intervene in the Franco-Vietnamese colonial-Communist war in 1954. It tried to shore up the administration of the late President Ngo

Vietnam

Dinh Diem in the South after 1954, and Diem, with American help, succeeded to a much greater extent than is today generally recalled—for a while. The failure to date of the United States in Vietnam—if "failure" it can really be called—reflects the fact that there were limits to what Americans could accomplish in that country, given the state of affairs within Vietnam, the length to which the United States was willing to go in seeking to attain its ends, and the ideological and moral climate of the world in which it found itself (as well as its own moral values). Vietnam is not yet lost to the Communists. The Communists may win in South Vietnam, or they may lose—or they may win and subsequently turn out to be no more frightening than Communist Poland or Yugoslavia. It is important, of course, if Vietnam becomes a Communist country, but it is primarily important to the United States and Vietnam's neighbors in Southeast Asia in terms of whether or not the Vietnamese Communists choose to pursue a peaceful or aggressive foreign policy. It may still be possible to prevent Vietnam from going Communist. But, if it is not, it is probable that the forces opposed to Communism, if they can coalesce, can prevent Vietnamese Communism from spilling over into most of the rest of Southeast Asia. If, however, the countries of the region—Laos, Cambodia, Indonesia, Burma, the Philippines, Thailand, Singapore and Malaysia—are not willing to take a united and determined stand, then it is open to serious question whether the United States could or should take on the task alone.

CHAPTER 6

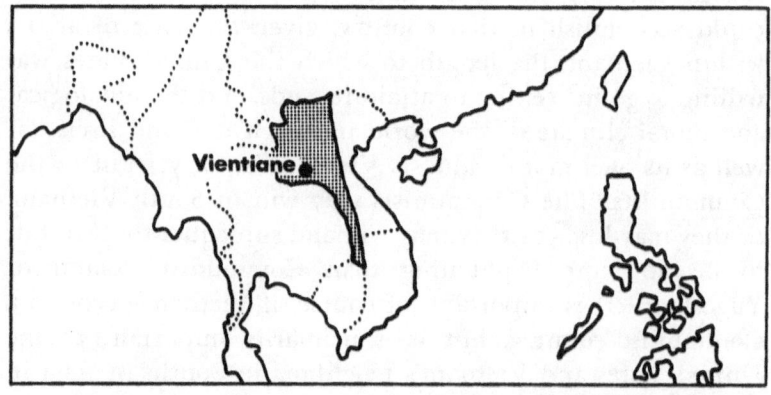

LAOS
Captive of Conflict

LAOS IS A SMALL, landlocked, underdeveloped country, sparsely populated by a collection of tribes without a national history. As a state it is an artificial entity. Such a country would seem destined for a role of insignificance in international relations, yet within a decade it has been the subject of two international conferences—in 1954 and in 1961-1962. At the earlier conference it shared the spotlight with the three other states which constituted the old French Indochina, but in the later one it monopolized the stage. As in the case of the whole of what was Indochina, its geographic position has made it important in world politics. The ancient rivalries of the region, suppressed in the days of Western colonial rule, have broken out afresh, and in addition Laos has been subject to the pressures of the world-wide conflict between the Communists and the anti-Communists. In short,

Laos

Laos is in the cockpit of intense competition for local supremacy and international ascendancy.

The two million people of Laos inhabit an area of about 91,000 square miles of mountainous country, only about 8 percent of which is suitable for agriculture. There is virtually no industry and very little commerce. Annual per capita income is only about $50; food consumption is among the lowest in Asia. About half of the population are Lao Thai, an ethnic group which also inhabits northeast Thailand. In fact, more Lao Thai live outside of Laos than in it. There are also small numbers of Chinese, Indians, and Vietnamese. Buddhism is the predominant religion, but many of the primitive people are animists.

After three centuries as a unified kingdom, Laos split in the seventeenth century into the kingdoms of Luang Prabang, Vientiane, and Champassak. Siam (now Thailand) early in the nineteenth century established control over these kingdoms. On the grounds that the territory east of the Mekong River had belonged to Annam (Vietnam), France in 1893 put forward a claim to it. When France made a display of force, Siam yielded and surrendered the territory. Laos became a French protectorate, though in fact all of the territory except the small kingdom of Luang Prabang was under direct rule by France. In 1904 Siam ceded some territory west of the Mekong River to Laos. Under Japanese "mediation" this area was receded to Thailand in 1941. With great reluctance Thailand returned the territory to Laos in 1947, yielding only after the French threatened to veto Thailand's application for membership in the United Nations unless the Thai government recognized the nullity of the transfer agreements of 1941.

There were no discernible signs of Laotian nationalism before World War II. The Japanese occupation undoubtedly inspired some anti-French sentiment and a mild nationalism. When the Japanese in March 1945 broadcast a declaration that "the colonial status of Indochina was ended," the nationalists demanded that King Sisavong Vong of Luang Prabang issue a declaration of independence. He did so reluctantly. After the surrender of Japan, when the Chinese Nationalists occupied the country, the king was forced by the Free Laos movement to abdicate, but later he was allowed to return to the throne as a constitutional monarch. France concluded an agreement with the king on August 27, 1946. While this agreement strengthened the king's position, it meant the reestablishment of French control over the country.

Laotian nationalism at the end of World War II was feeble, and it is still weak two decades later. Whatever nationalist sentiment existed was used by rival aristocratic Lao families for control of the country. In view of the social conditions which prevail, this is not surprising. A genuine, broad-based Laotian nationalism will take time to develop. During their occupation the Japanese gave both Laos and Cambodia virtual self-government, and the Laotian elite were determined not to lose these gains. Some of the nationalist elements took to the bush under Communist leadership in hopes of duplicating the Viet Minh feats in neighboring Vietnam. Other nationalists agitated for freedom from colonial rule under non-Communist leaders. As a consequence of the efforts of the latter group primarily, Laos moved slowly forward on the road to self-government. On October 22, 1953, it signed with France a treaty giving it "full independence" within the French Union. Laos was still not a completely sovereign state, but it appeared headed in that direction.

The obstacle to the realization of Laotian national aspirations was not France but the Viet Minh. They made unprovoked thrusts into Laotian territory in 1951 and in 1953-1954 and allied themselves with the initially weak Pathet Lao rebels. Prince Souphanouvong, a pro-Communist, had tried to persuade the non-Communist Lao Issara dissidents to cooperate with the Viet Minh but failed, was expelled, and turned to building up the Pathet Lao. The Lao Issara dissolved, but the Pathet Lao firmly established themselves as a resistance movement against both the French and the royal Lao government. Reinforced by North Vietnamese troops, they made themselves secure in the north of the country along the border with what is now North Vietnam, and by the end of 1953 they had fought their way to within a short distance of Luang Prabang, the capital. They then withdrew to the northern provinces of Sam Neua and Phong Saly.

THE 1954 GENEVA CONFERENCE

The situation and events which led to the Geneva conference have been discussed in dealing with Vietnam. In contrast with its attitude toward Vietnam, the expressed desire of the conference was that Laos not be divided—even temporarily. The Pathet Lao were to be integrated into the national community, and royal authority was to be restored in the provinces of Phong Saly and Sam Neua. According to Article 13 of the Cessation of Hostilities Agreement, "pending a political settlement, the fighting units of Pathet Lao shall move into the provinces of Phong Saly and Sam Neua." And according to Article 15, "Each party undertakes to refrain from any reprisals or discrimination against persons or organizations for their activities during the hostilities and also undertakes to guarantee their democratic freedoms." In addition, the government of Laos made a declaration that it "resolved to take the necessary measures to integrate all citizens, without discrimination" and affirmed that all Laotian citizens might freely participate as electors or candidates in general elections by "secret ballot." Unfortunately, this declaration also contained a vague provision to the effect that until the general elections were held, the Pathet Lao would have special representation in the administration of the provinces of Phong Saly and Sam Neua. All in all, the conference went fairly far in seeking to regulate the internal affairs of Laos.

In a second declaration Laos declared that it would "never join in any agreement with other states if the agreement includes the obligation . . . to participate in a military alliance not in conformity with the principles of the Charter of the United Nations . . . or, unless its security is threatened, the obligation to establish bases on Laotian territory for military forces of foreign powers." On their part, the members of the conference individually undertook to respect the sovereignty, the independence, the unity, and the territorial integrity of Cambodia, Laos, and Vietnam "and to refrain from any interference in their internal affairs." In stating that it was not prepared to join in the final agreement, the United States declared unilaterally that it would "refrain from the threat or the use of force to disturb" the various agreements and the final declaration and "would view any renewal of aggression in violation of the aforesaid agreements with grave concern and as seriously threatening international peace and security."

The provisions of these agreements were rather vague and somewhat contradictory, and it is no wonder that there were difficulties in carrying them out. While the object was national unity, the Pathet Lao were given quasi-recognition as a political unit with their own territory, at least during the transition period. Laos was not to enter a military alliance unless its security were threatened, and it was not to request foreign military aid "except for the purpose of its effective territorial defence." But France was allowed to maintain limited military establishments in the country. This permitted a wide range of Western interference. The Pathet Lao, for their part, entrenched themselves in Phong Saly and Sam Neua, built up their military forces, frequently violated the cease-fire agreement, and developed their subversive apparatus. They continued to receive aid across the unpatrolled border from China and North Vietnam. Negotiations between the government and the Pathet Lao moved slowly. Each suspected the other of being a front organization in the East-West conflict. Because of the delay in reaching an agreement, the government postponed the August 1955 elections. The elections were held in December, even though there was still no agreement, but without the participation of the two provinces controlled by the Pathet Lao.

After a long crisis Prince Souvanna Phouma assumed the premiership. An agreement with the Pathet Lao was reached in December 1956. In its foreign policy Laos would follow a policy of "neutrality," described by Souvanna Phouma as "more neutral than neutralism." The Pathet Lao were integrated into the government, including the cabinet and the army; the provinces of Phong Saly and Sam Neua were officially transferred to the Lao government by Prince Souphanouvong in December 1957. The National Assembly was enlarged from 39 to 59 members, and supplementary elections for the additional National Assembly seats were held in May 1958. The Pathet Lao front, the Neo Lao Hak Xat (Patriotic Laotian Front), was permitted to "undertake their political activities in the legal forms as the other political parties." The Pathet Lao made an excellent showing in the 1958 election, winning nine of the twenty-one seats. A coalition government was set up, with Souvanna Phouma as prime minister. His half-brother, Prince Souphanouvong, the leader of the Pathet Lao, became minister of economic planning and another Pathet Lao leader became minister of religious affairs.

FAILURE OF COALITION

American economic aid began to flow to Laos as early as 1951. The program was greatly expanded in 1955. From January 1, 1955, through June 30, 1959, the amount of aid totaled $190,281,000. Most of it went for the support of the

Lao army, police, and certain governmental services. Some of it was in the form of technical assistance. Unfortunately, instead of promoting political stability and national unity, United States aid seems to have had the opposite effect. The Pathet Lao held that a policy of neutralism meant the establishment of diplomatic relations with China, North Vietnam, and the Soviet Union, and the receipt of aid from these countries, too. This was opposed by the United States, which threatened to withdraw its economic assistance. Serious mistakes were made in administering the aid, moreover, and there was much corruption. This led one of the Lao political leaders to comment that the greatest danger of Communist subversion arose from "the bad use of foreign aid we receive." "It enriches a minority outrageously while the mass of the population remains as poor as ever." The Pathet Lao made political capital of this situation. Because of mounting criticism in the United States Congress, aid was suspended on June 30, 1958. After reforms were instituted and profiteering drastically curbed, economic assistance was resumed in October.

Stating that he had lost faith in the former rebels who had joined his government, Prime Minister Souvanna Phouma on July 22, 1958, submitted his resignation to the Laotian king. If asked to form a new cabinet, he said, he would try to keep out Pathet Lao representatives "because I have doubts of their political views." He was succeeded by Phoui Sananikone, who was pro-Western and pursued a bold anti-Communist policy. On January 14, 1959, the National Assembly authorized him for the next year to carry out "a sweeping program of social, economic, and political reform . . . without reference to the legislature." The main object of these reforms was to counteract Communist subversion and influence. In February the Phoui Sananikone government renounced the Geneva agreements on the ground that all of their provisions had been fulfilled. The reason for the renunciation, it would seem, was to permit greater American military aid. About this time the Laotian government received its first delivery of military supplies from the United States; American military personnel were also desired. Another reason for the renunciation of the agreements was to prevent the reconvening of the International Control Commission.

The Pathet Lao reacted to this policy by a return to its former methods, including open fighting. When the government troops in May 1959 surrounded the two Pathet Lao battalions which had not yet been fully integrated into the royal army and gave them the choice of surrender or annihilation, one unit gave up but the other fought its way out of the trap and moved toward the North Vietnamese border. The Laotian anti-Communist policy was met by increased pressure on Laos by the Communist countries. They demanded the return of the International Control Commission, and North Vietnam massed troops on the Laotian border.

In August the Laotian government, asserting that outside Communist aid was being given to the Pathet Lao in a variety of ways, asked the United Nations to send a team of observers. A month later it brought charges of North Vietnamese aggression. The Communist governments contended that what was involved was solely civil war and that the proper answer was the return of the International Control Commission. The Security Council, over the objections of the Soviet Union, voted to set up a subcommittee to probe the Laotian charges. The subcommittee reported that while it found evidence of Communist aid in the form of arms and supplies, the "ensemble of information . . . did not clearly establish whether there were crossings of the frontiers by regular troops." In November, Secretary General Dag Hammerskjold visited Laos and appointed S. S. Tuomioja, a national of Finland, as his personal representative in Laos. Hammarskjold apparently advised the Laotian government to pursue a policy of neutralism, for, shortly after talks with the U.N. secretary general, Phoui Sananikone bluntly stated that Laos would "remain neutral and not become a base for any foreign power bloc."

During 1959 there developed increasing dissension in the cabinet between the older moderate leaders and a group of young rightist reformists. On December 30 Phoui Sananikone resigned, and the king placed the country under the temporary control of the army. Whether or not this was a military coup is not clear. A cabinet to govern the country until the quadrennial national elections could be held was appointed. The elections, four months overdue, were held in April. The progovernment party won a sweeping victory, capturing 56 of the 59 seats in the National Assembly. Defeated leftwing candidates charged that the elections had been rigged.

On the night of August 9, 1960, a quite surprising event took place. A royal army paratroop battalion commanded by Captain Kong Le staged a coup in Vientiane, the administrative capital of the country. After a brief but sharp struggle the troops took over the government and military installations. In a radio broadcast August 11, 1960, Kong Le said that infiltration by a "foreign power" was increasing daily and "every organization in the country has a group attached to it." "Even my own battalion has ten Americans whom the government has allowed to infiltrate us." He accused the country's leaders of having "led us completely astray" and of having induced the people to "accept the money of a great power." The rebels proclaimed a neutralist policy and pledged to maintain the monarch and the constitution.

Captain Kong Le and his followers called for the resignation of Premier Tia Somsanith and the appointment of Prince Souvanna Phouma as his successor to "lead our country on the path of neutrality." Souvanna Phouma formed a coalition government with General Phoumi Nosavan, formerly defense minister in the previous cabinet, as deputy premier, but when Kong Le denounced the coalition, Phoumi withdrew to Savannaket, formed with Prince Boun Oum a revolutionary committee, and threatened an offensive against Vientiane. Phoumi was supported by his uncle, Premier Sarit Thanarat of Thailand, who instituted an economic blockade against Vientiane. General Phoumi and his rightwing group feared a Communist takeover. Late in September the United States accorded diplomatic recognition to the Souvanna Phouma government, but while it gave this government economic assistance, it continued giving military aid to General Phoumi. When Souvanna Phouma announced that his government would establish diplomatic relations with the Soviet Union and enter into negotiations with the Pathet Lao for the purpose of forming a coalition government, the United States on October 7 suspended its aid program and warned Souvanna Phouma that unless he broke off talks with the Pathet Lao and reopened negotiations with General Phoumi and Boun Oum, American help would be permanently withheld. When Souvanna Phouma declared that if the United States refused to give his government aid, he would get it elsewhere, American economic and military assistance was resumed, but apparently military help continued to go to General Phoumi, too. On November 16, 1960, Premier Souvanna Phouma charged the United States with supporting the rightist regime. Asked if a compromise with General Phoumi Nosavan were possible, he declared, "It does not depend on me anymore. Everything depends on the United States. There is no longer a national problem. It is an international problem."

Premier Souvanna Phouma's position became steadily more difficult. Several units of the army defected to Phoumi, among them the one stationed in the royal capital, Luang Prabang. Souvanna Phouma could not make peace with both the rightists and the Pathet Lao, and he was fast losing the army to the former. He announced plans to send goodwill missions to North Vietnam and Communist China and to ask aid from the Soviet Union. Fuel, food, and, later, military equipment were sent. When Kong Le in December again seized the city of Vientiane, Russia airlifted artillery and ammunition to the insurgent forces, but the rightwing troops under General Phoumi Nosavan drove them out after a few days of severe fighting. Kong Le retreated to the north, but en route he captured an important airfield complex. He made contact with the Pathet Lao forces and became associated with them, but he and his men kept their identity as supporters of Souvanna Phouma and neutralism. When Premier Souvanna Phouma, accompanied by most of his cabinet, fled to Cambodia, King Savang Vatthana withdrew authority from Souvanna Phouma and conferred temporary governmental authority on the revolutionary committee of Prince Boun Oum and General Phoumi Nosavan. The United States quickly recognized the new regime.

With the flight of Souvanna Phouma and the association of Kong Le with the Pathet Lao, the moderates disappeared as a force, at least for a while. The three-cornered fight gave way to confrontation between the rightists and the pro-Communists and Communists. The role of the United States had been somewhat ambiguous, if not ambivalent. While it had recognized Souvanna Phouma's neutralist regime as the legal government of Laos, it had favored the rightist insurgents and gave them aid, interrupting military shipments to them only when they began fighting the government and not the Communists. The situation had become explosive internationally. The Russian government in a note of December 13, 1960, accused the United States of "open actions against the lawful Laotian government of Prince Souvanna Phouma" and thus of undermining the Geneva agreements. It concluded that it could not "ignore the threat to the peace and security in Southeast Asia arising as a result of gross United States intervention in the domestic affairs of Laos." In its reply four days later, the United States categorically rejected the charges and condemned "as a violation of every standard of legal conduct the recent Soviet action in airlifting weapons and ammunition in Soviet planes

Laos

to rebel forces fighting the loyal armed forces of the royal government in Vientiane. Thus the responsibility for the present fratricidal war in Laos, about which the Soviet Government claims to be concerned, rests squarely and solely upon the Soviet Government and its partners." Joining in the diplomatic correspondence Peking warned the British and Russian governments that the situation in Laos had "developed to extremely dangerous proportions" and that China would "have to consider taking measures to safeguard its own security."

THE GENEVA CONFERENCE OF 1961

Differences began to develop among the Western powers. The British and the French believed that no Laotian government which did not include representatives of the neutralists and the Pathet Lao offered much hope of stability, but the United States feared that this course would open the door to intrigue and an early takeover by disciplined Communists. Because of the jungle and mountainous terrain and the long border with Communist China and North Vietnam, the British and French saw no possibility of any Laotian government preventing hostile infiltration without a massive and extremely costly military effort. A broad-based government, they believed, offered the best hope for order and peace, and a neutralist Laotian government would be the best guarantee against the enlargement of the conflict involving the great powers after the pattern of Korea.

The British urged the United States to back the reestablishment of the International Control Commission. The United States, after the National Assembly gave the Boun Oum government a vote of confidence in the first days of January 1961, declared itself prepared to have the commission revived. The British government then presented such a proposal to the Soviet government. The latter in a note of January 16, 1961, proposed "a conference of states of the type of the

Geneva Conference of 1954, joining with the efforts of those countries sincerely striving for a peaceful settlement in Laos."

The next important move came from King Savang Vatthana. On February 19 he proclaimed "once more the policy of true neutrality that Laos has always sought to follow. Laos would not join in any military alliance. Within the framework of this neutrality, Laos will not have on its territory either foreign forces or military bases." His country, the king said plaintively, "for more than twenty years has known neither peace nor security." He asked all nations "to renounce all intervention in the internal affairs of the kingdom, even in the form of aid, if the latter has not been sanctioned by international agreements entered into by Laos. We further ask them to make such intervention impossible." To assure this neutrality the king hoped that Cambodia, Burma, and Malaya would form a commission "which would come to Laos in order to establish that this country threatens no one and aspires solely to peace. This commission would have as its mission the denouncing of all foreign intervention, direct or individual, open or camouflaged, which would result in the imperiling of the kingdom's independence, integrity and neutrality."

The United States and British governments welcomed the statement and the plan, and the former urged Moscow to support it. The Soviet Union had refused to recognize the Boun Oum regime and was giving the Pathet Lao large amounts of military aid by airlift. With this support the Pathet Lao by May had gained control of nearly half of Laos. This undoubtedly was an important factor in the change of the American position. In spite of extensive United States aid, the rightist regime was steadily losing ground. A neutral Laos was better than losing it altogether to the Communists or becoming involved in a big power war over it. President Kennedy pressed hard for a settlement. At his news conference on March 23 he stated that the United States "unreservedly supports the goal of a neutral and an independent

Laos tied to no outside power or group of powers, threatening no one, and free from any domination." He demanded a cessation of the present "armed attacks by externally supported Communists." If the attacks did not stop, the United States would look to the Southeast Asia Treaty Organization powers to take the lead in dealing militarily with the situation. The SEATO Council meeting in Bangkok passed a resolution on March 24 stating that if the efforts for a cessation of hostilities and for peaceful negotiations to achieve an unaligned and independent Laos failed, and there continued "to be an active military attempt to obtain control of Laos, members of SEATO are prepared, within the terms of the treaty, to take whatever action may be appropriate in the circumstances." Finally, on April 24 the British and Soviet governments, as cochairmen of the 1954 Geneva Conference on Indochina, issued a message to all the military authorities, parties, and organizations in Laos calling for a cease-fire; another to India, as chairman of the body, to convene the International Commission for Supervision and Control in Laos; and a third to the members of the earlier conference requesting them to send delegations to a conference to deal with the Laotian question to meet in Geneva in May.

The military setting of the Laotian problem remained, however. When the Pathet Lao forces defeated some rightist forces and were moving toward the Thai border, Premier Sarit of Thailand in May 1962 called on the United States to send troops to his country. President Kennedy responded by ordering 4,000 ground and air forces to Thailand "to help insure the territorial integrity of this peaceful country."

The Geneva Conference on Laos opened on May 16, 1961, but final agreements were not reached until a year later, on July 23, 1962. Three sets of negotiations went on simultaneously. The conference itself was concerned with the nature of neutrality for Laos, and the means of guaranteeing and supervising it. Secondly, there were the discussions between the three princes, leaders of the main Laotian groups, on the domestic aspects of settling the civil war. The princes were able rather quickly to agree on the desirability of setting up a Government of National Unity whose policy would be neutrality, economic development, and reconciliation internally, but agreement on the actual composition of the government was more difficult and was reached only in June 1962. The coalition cabinet was composed of eleven neutrals, four rightists, and four Pathet Lao, with neutralist Souvanna Phouma as premier and minister of defense, the leftist Souphanouvong as deputy premier and minister of national economy and planning, and Phoumi Nosavan as minister of finance and also a deputy premier. Prince Boun Oum was reappointed for life as inspector general of the kingdom. A third set of negotiations was carried on by political and military representatives for an agreement on a permanent cease-fire.

The royal government of Laos made a formal Declaration of Neutrality, which was approved by the conference. Laos undertook not to "enter into any military alliance or into any agreement, whether military or otherwise, which is inconsistent with the neutrality of the Kingdom of Laos; it will not allow the establishment of any foreign military base on Laotian territory, nor allow any country to use Laotian territory for military purposes or for the purposes of interference in the internal affairs of other countries, nor recognize the protection of any alliance or military coalition, including SEATO." Laos was not to allow any foreign interference in its own internal affairs "in any form whatsoever," and it would require the withdrawal from its territory of all foreign troops and military personnel. There was a minor exception to the last provision, namely that if the Laotian government considered it necessary, France could leave in Laos "for a limited period of time, a precisely limited number of French military instructors for the purpose of training the armed forces of Laos."

Laos

The states which were members of the conference declared that they would recognize, respect, and observe "in every way the sovereignty, independence, neutrality, unity and territorial integrity" of Laos. This undertaking was spelled out in ten separate clauses of Article 2 of the 1962 Geneva agreement. In case of a violation or threat of violation of the agreement, the signatories agreed to consult jointly with the government of Laos "and among themselves in order to consider measures which might prove to be necessary to ensure the observance of these principles and other provisions of the present declaration."

AFTER GENEVA II

The 1962 agreements did not bring unity and peace to Laos. For a few months after the coalition government came to power there was relative calm, but by the end of 1962 feuding had developed among and within the various factions. The Pathet Lao began to squeeze out the neutralist forces of Kong Le by cutting off supplies to them. Premier Souvanna Phouma called for aid from the United States, which promptly responded, first with provisions and later with military equipment. In Vientiane a conflict developed between Souvanna Phouma and Quinim Pholsena, the foreign minister, who was an ardent pro-Pathet Lao neutralist and used his position to further the interests of the pro-Communists. On April 1, 1963, Quinim Pholsena was assassinated in retaliation for the murder of one of Kong Le's officers. Unable to subvert the coalition, the Pathet Lao withdrew from the government and went over to full-scale belligerence. They attacked and drove Kong Le's troops out of the Plaine des Jarres region and successfully attacked rightwing positions in south-central Laos.

All of Premier Souvanna Phouma's efforts to settle differences with the Pathet Lao came to nought. In despair he announced in April 1964 that he would resign. At this the commander of the national security police and the commander of the rightwing army units in the Vientiane area invested the capital and put the premier under arrest. The foreign reaction was probably not what they expected. The United States refused to support them, and they had to back down. With such confusion on the government's side, the Pathet Lao made easy progress against the royal Lao armed forces. By the beginning of 1965 the Pathet Lao controlled about two-thirds of the territory, but the government held the Mekong Valley, which supports about two-thirds of the country's population. The United States responded by supplying additional fighter bombers for the Royal Laotian Air Force. Unarmed American planes, moreover, made reconnaissance flights over Pathet Lao-held areas, and, when such a jet was shot down in June, American fighters accompanied subsequent missions. North Vietnam clearly was aiding the rebels. Lao government troops, in fact, captured some North Vietnamese regular troops. Premier Souvanna Phouma in September 1964 declared that 12,000 North Vietnamese regulars were operating inside Laos. The United States in late 1964 began air-bombing of key points in Laos, in particular along the Ho Chi Minh Trail (from North to South Vietnam), which runs through Pathet Lao-controlled territory.

In the summer of 1965 there was a lull in hostilities—following the first spring in several years in which the Pathet Lao had not mounted a major offensive during the last month of the dry season. As a result, the Communists did not significantly enlarge in 1965 the amount of territory they controlled, as they had done in previous years. The reason for the failure, or inability, of the Communists to take major offensive action was unquestionably the impact of the escalated war in Vietnam. The Royal Laotian Air Force distinguished itself by effective attacks on Communist-held areas, but much more important was the bombing by American jet aircraft of road links to Pathet Lao supply bases in North Vietnam. These attacks supplemented American bombing of supply and infiltration routes from North to South Vietnam through Laos. In addition, North Vietnam was increasingly limited in its ability to support Pathet Lao operations against the Laotian government as a result of United States air attacks against its own territory.

The Laotian government itself was also strengthened as a result of a showdown in early 1965 between ambitious rightwing General Phoumi Nosavan and military forces loyal to Premier Souvanna Phouma. Phoumi and General Siho Lanpouthacoul, young police commander, failed in their coup attempt against the government and subsequently successfully sought political refuge in Thailand. The personal para-military organization maintained by Siho, co-leader of the also unsuccessful 1964 coup try, was brought once again under the control of the ministry of interior. The use by Phoumi of his portfolio as minister of finance for patronage purposes and to amass a personal fortune had hurt the weak Laotian economy. Young and efficient Sisouk na Champassak, leader of a reformist "Young Turk" faction, succeeded Phoumi as finance minister and worked effectively to improve the economy. The currency was stabilized, and corruption was curtailed.

The situation appeared to have stabilized sufficiently to permit the government of Souvanna Phouma to declare the tripartite regime involving neutralist, rightwing and Communist participation—but from which the Communists had long since withdrawn—ended with the expiration of the mandate of the sitting National Assembly on April 24, 1965. The union government was a result of the agreement among the leaders of the rival Laotian factions in 1962, when the Geneva Accords attempting to neutralize Laos were signed. Conditions were calm enough to hold elections to the succeeding National Assembly on July 18 without serious incidents. Voting took place in all of the provinces except Phong Saly. The Pathet Lao denounced the elections and boycotted them. Only about 14,000 persons, mostly officials of one type or another, were declared eligible to vote. The candidates were carefully screened, and the king had the power to reject elected individuals and appoint other persons as he saw fit. Under such circumstances only a pro-government victory was possible. The 59-member legislature subsequently endorsed continuation of the leadership of Premier Souvanna Phouma. Souvanna Phouma stated that the assembly would sit until general elections were possible.

As might be expected, economic conditions in Laos leave much to be desired. With so much of the territory under Pathet Lao control, exports have about disappeared. For 1963 exports came to only $1,000,000, while imports totaled $29,000,000. In this year the kip, the Laotian monetary unit, declined in the black market from a rate of 150 to one United States dollar to about 700. With help from Australia, Britain, France, and the United States, the kip was stabilized in 1964. Laos had been receiving from $30,000,000 to $40,000,000 in aid yearly from the United States, but in 1965 this was increased to $50,000,000 exclusive of military aid.

There can be no peace or real economic stability in Laos until there is a change in the regional and global international situation. The difficulties in Laos are inextricably related to the hostilities in Vietnam and the expansionist pressure of China. The Laotian frontier has no reality, certainly none from a military point of view. With the control of eastern Laos by the Pathet Lao, the Vietcong in South Vietnam were assured of a free supply line until American planes began bombing the Ho Chi Minh Trail. But the terrain through which this route runs is such that air-bombing is not always effective. Clearly there can be no settlement in Laos without a settlement in Vietnam. And, if the Vietnamese settlement is the wrong kind of settlement, the problems afflicting Laos may increase rather than diminish.

Realizing this, Premier Souvanna Phouma took the initiative in 1965 in seeking international support for another attempt at settling the disturbed situation in what was once fairly tranquil French Indochina. The Laotian leader visited Britain, France and India—and in particular sought British support for the reconvocation of the 1954 Geneva Conference (for Vietnam and Cambodia as well as Laos). The Communist nations, however, were not yet willing to sit down again at the peace-table for "Geneva III." Not to be outdone by his international adversaries, Souvanna Phouma also made a strong effort at home to obtain a cease-fire and peace talks with his half-brother, Communist leader Prince Souphanouvong, but this attempt, too, failed.

The Communist response being what it was, Souvanna Phouma might have given up the fight or thrown his weight fully on the side of an open alliance with the United States. The first alternative was not a real one, however—Souvanna Phouma was too much of a Laotian nationalist to turn over his country, practically speaking, to the Vietnamese Communists. And the second alternative had already failed in 1958-1960 and had led directly to the Pathet Lao victories of the early 1960s that had given the Laotian Communists such a large portion of the national territory. Doggedly—and it required determination—Souvanna Phouma declared anew his government's intention to preserve as much of Laos' precariously maintained neutrality as it could. In December 1965, the Laotian premier took a strong public stand against the proposed introduction of American ground forces in Laos to halt the supply of men and materials from North to South Vietnam by means of the Ho Chi Minh Trail. The objective circumstances were far from conducive to neutrality, but Souvanna Phouma was trying just the same. The legitimate leadership of Laos seemed to be seeking to remain genuinely neutral, but the country appeared to be the almost inevitable captive of conflict.

CHAPTER 7

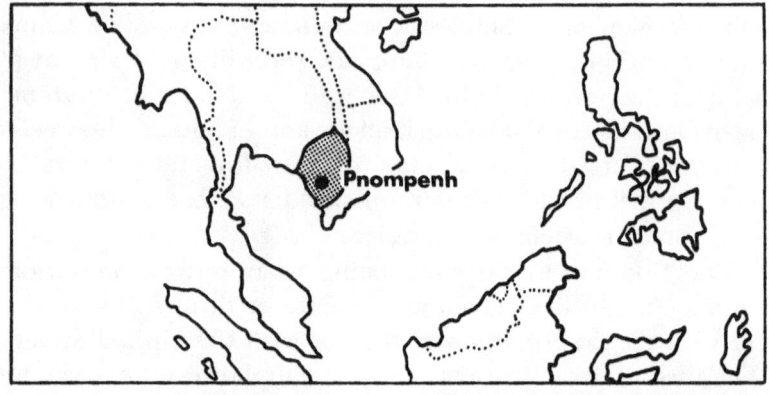

CAMBODIA
Land of Strange Politics

CAMBODIA IS A kingdom of about 70,000 square miles wedged in between Thailand, Laos, South Vietnam, and the Gulf of Siam. Its population of more than 6,000,000 is rapidly growing. Between 85 and 90 percent of the population are Khmers, whose ancestors moved down from the northwest into the Mekong Delta two thousand years before the Christian era. Their culture and religion were strongly influenced by Hinduism over a long period, beginning in the first century A.D. The Khmers were under pressure from various peoples, but about the year 800 there emerged the Khmer kingdom of Kambuja (now Cambodia), with its capital at Angkor, which developed a great civilization as evidenced by its surviving monumental structures, chief of which is the temple at Angkor Wat, the world's largest religious building.

From the twelfth century on, the Khmer kingdom was

subjected to steadily intensified pressure from the Thai people in the north. Angkor fell in 1431. Khmer culture declined; Hinayana Buddhism was adopted from the Thai. In the seventeenth century the Khmers began to experience pressure on the east from the kingdom of Annam in present-day Vietnam which by 1700 had won control over the Mekong Delta. A remnant of the Khmer people constitutes an important minority in South Vietnam today and serves as a reminder of the earlier greatness of the Khmer kingdom, while the presence of some 400,000 Vietnamese in Cambodia keeps alive the fear of Vietnamese aggression. Caught between the rival forces of the Thai and Annamese (or Vietnamese) kingdoms, Cambodia in 1846 became a vassal of both. The establishment of the French protectorate over the kingdom in 1863 probably saved it from extinction, although France in 1887 ceded several northern provinces to Thailand, only to exert pressure on Thailand two decades later (1904 and 1907) to return them. During the Japanese occupation the ancient pressure from the north reasserted itself. In 1941, Thailand, with Japanese connivance and support, recovered most of this territory, only to surrender it again after the war.

There were few people with a formal education in Cambodia before the Second World War; virtually no native middle class existed, and there was no nationalist movement of any consequence. The king was Norodom Sihanouk, who came to the throne in 1941, at the age of 19. A few days after the Japanese coup of March 9, 1945, the king repudiated the existing treaties with France and proclaimed the independence of his country, but shortly after the French troops in October occupied Phnom Penh, he declared his loyalty to France. However, he also assured his people that he had not forgotten their aspirations for independence. On January 7, 1946, Cambodia and France signed an agreement reestablishing French control over the country. France sent technicians and furnished capital to help develop the country, and used its influence to induce Thailand to restore the "lost provinces." Relations between the two countries for a few years were cordial. By a treaty of November 8, 1949, France recognized the *de jure* independence of Cambodia, but retained considerable control over foreign relations and the army.

The king after the war had resolved to change the government from an absolute to a constitutional monarchy as rapidly as possible. In September 1946, a Consultative Assembly was elected, and in December 1947, elections for the first National Assembly were held. A dispute arose over the relationship of the executive to the legislative branch, involving chiefly the 1949 treaty with France. The majority of the National Assembly, under the control of the Democrat party, opposed the treaty. Unable to resolve the difficulty with his parliament, the king ordered new elections. These were held in September 1951, but with results no more favorable to the king. The Democrats won two-thirds of the seats. The king was in an unpleasant position. The French insisted that he remove all anti-French elements from the government, but the majority of the National Assembly demanded complete independence at once, while dissident groups outside the government incited the people to defy French rule and take up arms, if necessary, for independence.

Caught between these conflicting forces, King Sihanouk abandoned the attempted role of a constitutional monarch and took matters into his own hands. He dismissed the Democrat ministry and asked the National Assembly to approve emergency powers for three years. When the Assembly refused, he dissolved it and in January 1953 declared martial law. He then set out for France in a crusade for independence. Slighted in Paris, he returned home to engage in a dramatic propaganda move. In June he went into voluntary exile in Bangkok, declaring that he would not return to his palace in Phnom Penh until France had granted his country complete independence. He stated that

Cambodia

he would ask Thailand to bring the case of Cambodia's independence before the United Nations. Deeply embarrassed, the French were at last ready to negotiate seriously. After a week in Bangkok, Sihanouk took up his residence in Battambang, in northern Cambodia, and from there directed negotiations. He won a complete victory. On November 8, 1953, he returned in triumph to his capital.

EMERGENCE OF SIHANOUK AS LEADER

The internal political situation continued to cause the king concern. His antagonists, the Democrats, still exercised a wide popular influence. He hesitated to call a national election, but he could not cling to his emergency powers indefinitely. He used his influence to bring a number of small political groups into a Union party, but apparently he felt more decisive action was needed. He urged constitutional reforms aimed at greater governmental stability. He was willing to allow the National Assembly to have the right to call for the resignation of individual ministers but not to turn out a whole cabinet by adverse vote. He said that he wished to save the people "from the kind of democracy that weighs them down."

King Sihanouk apparently believed that heroic measures were necessary. On March 3, 1955, he abdicated and organized his own party. In a broadcast he declared that he would never return to the throne or accept any public office such as that of premier or president of the National Assembly. It is not surprising that Prince Sihanouk did not adhere to this declaration; he has established a solid reputation for frequent changes of mind. An important factor which led him to make this drastic move was the opposition of the International Control Commission, which had been set up to supervise the Geneva Agreements, to his proposed reforms, which would have disenfranchised many of his political opponents. Prince Sihanouk appointed his father, Prince Norodom Suramarit, as his successor to the throne. The party he formed and headed he called Sangkum Reastr Niyum (Peoples Socialist Community). In the election held on September 11, 1955, Prince Sihanouk's party won 83 percent of the votes and all of the seats in the National Assembly. Though he left nothing undone to win a resounding victory at the polls, he apologized for "too complete a victory" for his party.

Since the 1955 election Prince Sihanouk has been the undisputed political leader of his country, but this has not meant stability of personnel at the head of the government. There were nine cabinets within two years, with the prince himself popping in and out of the premiership in a bewildering fashion. There were rival factions within the ruling Sangkum party, and there were continued disputes between parliament and executive over the division of power. To cope with the recalcitrant Assembly, the prince ingeniously instituted the National Congress, a biannual forum to which the people were invited to meet with him and his advisers to discuss current issues and air their grievances against legislators and government officials. In 1957 the Congress was given a constitutional basis; the government and the National Assembly must execute the decisions of Congress, and deadlocks between the National Assembly and the executive must go to the Congress for resolution.

Elections for the National Assembly were again held in March 1958. The candidates for the Sangkum party were carefully selected by the prince and his advisers, and he campaigned vigorously throughout the country. The Sangkum received all but 400 of 1,646,897 votes cast. But political tranquillity still eluded the country. A financial scandal, an alleged plot to overthrow the government, the death of the king, and heightened tension between Cambodia and its neighbors, Thailand and South Vietnam, led to ministerial crises. These critical situations did not lessen the prestige of Sihanouk; he emerged from each with enhanced power.

Cambodia

The problem of the succession to the throne was solved by the creation of a new office, the chief of state. By a popular referendum on June 7, 1960, Sihanouk was "chosen" for this office.

The domination by Sihanouk of Cambodian politics is almost complete. In three successive elections—those of 1955 and 1958 and the most recent voting of June 10, 1962—his political movement, the Sangkum, has captured all of the seats in the National Assembly. As "chief of state," the prince heads a kingless monarchy, supported by popular veneration of royalty but having attained his political position by means other than the accident of birth. The small elite he heads is a fairly closely knit one, and Sihanouk relies in part on the support of others of royal blood. The prime minister (and concurrently foreign minister) is a cousin, Prince Norodom Kantol. As for opposition, there is comparatively little, and much of this has been absorbed by the Sihanouk-controlled Sangkum. When the Sangkum was originally formed, many Democrats defected to its ranks. And in 1962 Sihanouk encouraged some of the most outspoken younger critics of his leadership to stand for office under the sponsorship of the Sangkum. There was value, as he saw it, in having his opponents within the party he almost single-handedly led.

The result of all this is a land of remarkable stability located literally next to the world's number one trouble spot, war-ravaged Vietnam. The strength of the indigenous Communist movement is probably less than anywhere in Southeast Asia. Although Sihanouk has chosen to cooperate closely with Communist China and has recognized Ho Chi Minh's "Democratic Republic of Vietnam," he has vigorously opposed such few native Communists as his country possesses. Although the latter represent no immediate threat to his leadership, Sihanouk went out of his way in 1965 to rebuke Cambodia's handful of Communists for their obstructionist behavior and their anti-government propaganda.

While not an imminent challenge to the existing regime, Sihanouk faces somewhat more formidable opposition from the Khmer Serai dissident movement based both in South Vietnam and Thailand, Cambodia's neighbors to the east and the west. Anti-Sihanouk broadcasts have been beamed from both locations, and there have been reports of Khmer Serai guerrilla activity along the Thai border. Sihanouk has publicly termed these activities part of an American plot against his government, and there can be no denying that there is more than a little justification for his suspicions. The dissidents have been given sanctuary on Thai and Vietnamese soil by the Bangkok and Saigon governments, and both of these are close allies of the United States.

Such opposition clearly helps Sihanouk. His resistance to such foreign interference sharpens the image of him as a dedicated patriot striving to develop his realm as a land increasingly capable of dealing with the problems of the second half of the twentieth century. That Sihanouk is able to do this is in a sense surprising. His initial participation in politics suggested a decidedly pro-French bias, and few have been the reformers who have come from the ranks of the royally born in the world's history. To be sure, candidacies for public office under the banner of the all-victorious Sangkum are controlled by Sihanouk, and the political opposition outside the party has been checked in various ways through the years. For these reasons it is not possible to describe Cambodia as a democracy, Sihanouk's claims to the contrary notwithstanding. That the prince and his party are almost universally popular among the Cambodian masses, however, is incontestable. Sihanouk's is popular as contrasted with democratic government in the sense that the masses participate in the politics of the realm and have clearly endorsed the prince's leadership, however unique the means by which they do this. Sihanouk, like the Philippines' late Ramon Magsaysay, has a knack for communicating with the ordinary people. He goes out to meet them, to discuss with them their grievances, and to explain to them what his government is trying to do. He also takes to the airwaves and talks to his people as a father talks to his children. This, however, may be Sihanouk's greatest failing. He is father to his people—an almost irreplaceable father. But what happens when he must be replaced? He has not prepared for this day —constitutionally, institutionally, or otherwise. He is what he is partly in reflection of the underdeveloped status of Cambodian politics. But he has done little to help develop his country politically. His country enjoys almost unparalleled prosperity and tranquillity in its part of the world—in large measure as a result of his leadership. But can it stand the challenge of tomorrow led only by Sihanouk or, worse still, without Sihanouk?

FOREIGN POLICY

If the antics Sihanouk sometimes employed in domestic politics were odd, those he frequently pursued in the conduct of foreign relations were no less strange. Yet here, too, Cambodia has been fortunate, however it may be explained. It has been spared the infiltration and consequent bitter strife which has been so ruinous in Laos and South Vietnam. It is not that there is no material in Cambodia for the Communists to work with. The 400,000 Chinese and a larger number of Vietnamese who inhabit the country offer excellent material for subversion by Peking and Hanoi. There are also indigenous dissident groups.

In its own eyes, at least, Cambodia follows a policy of thoroughgoing neutralism. It claims to be "neutral even against neutrals." Prince Sihanouk, the architect of the policy, has at various times explained why Cambodia follows this policy. In an article in *Foreign Affairs,* in July 1958, he declared: "Our neutrality has been imposed on us by necessity. A glance at a map of our part of the world will show that we are wedged in between two medium-sized nations of the Western bloc and only thinly screened by Laos from the scrutiny of two countries of the Eastern bloc, North Vietnam and the vast People's Republic of China. What choice have we but to try to maintain an equal balance between the blocs?"

Sihanouk was not always of this view. Revival of the ancient pressure from Thailand and Vietnam, which came with the disappearance of European colonialism in Southeast Asia, caused King Sihanouk to look to the West for protection. The threat from Vietnam came in the form of Viet Minh forces which invaded Cambodia in the early months of 1954 and sought to make common cause with the dissident Free Cambodians. Sihanouk turned to the United States for both military and economic help. With its experience in Korea fresh in mind and that of the French in Indochina vividly before it, the United States was reluctant even verbally to commit troops in a situation from which it might not be able easily to extricate itself. The Southeast Asian Treaty Organization (SEATO) provided further evidence of the unwillingness of the United States to make concrete guarantees to any country in the region except the Philippines, with which the United States had historical ties and for whose security it felt some moral obligation and which furthermore was situated at the southern end of its defensive arc in East Asia. Disappointed in the direct American response and in SEATO, Sihanouk began to turn to neutralism as a policy. An important factor in his shift may have been the influence of India's prime minister, Jawaharlal Nehru, who visited Phnom Penh in November 1954. From about this time the move toward neutralism became noticeable.

Cambodia's representatives at the Geneva Conference of 1954 won a diplomatic victory. The Viet Minh, supported by Russia and China, wanted Conference recognition of the Khmer Resistance government and, failing that, wished to obtain a regroupment area for their allies in the kingdom

Cambodia

and neutralization of the state—arrangements which they obtained in the case of Laos. The Cambodian diplomats held off the discussions on their country until the last night, when the assembled nations were under great pressure to bring the Conference to an end in view of the promise by French Premier Pierre Mendes-France to his people to have a solution to the Indochinese problem by July 20 or resign. The Conference yielded to the Cambodian wishes. Cambodia undertook not to join in any agreement with other states "as long as its security is not threatened" and not "to establish bases on Cambodian territory for the military forces of foreign powers." Assuming that Cambodia reserved the right to determine when its security was threatened, this provision really imposed no restriction on its freedom of action.

AMBIVALENT NEUTRALISM?

Prince Sihanouk has traveled extensively in the diplomatic interests of his country. He visited Communist China in February 1956 and signed a friendship pact which embodied nonaggression, mutual respect for national integrity and sovereignty, noninterference in the internal affairs of other countries, peaceful coexistence, and equality and mutual benefit. Cambodia and China also agreed to strengthen economic and cultural relations and to work for the "removal of doubts" in international relations. In March, Cambodia sent a delegation to negotiate commercial agreements with the government of Mao Tse-tung. Under the terms of an agreement signed in Peking on June 21, China was to invest $22,400,000 in the construction of textile, cement, paper, and plywood factories in Cambodia, with work on the several projects to begin before the end of 1957.

Sihanouk next made an "unofficial" visit to the Soviet Union, where likewise an agreement for economic and industrial aid to Cambodia was concluded. The Soviets agreed to supply industrial equipment and technician-instructors to Cambodia, and to build, equip and staff a hospital in the Cambodian capital of Phnom Penh. Sihanouk manifested his appreciation of the Soviet promises by declaring that the hope of his people "rests in the Soviet Union for the realization of our desires for peace and prosperity."

Meanwhile, prominent Cambodian spokesmen were criticizing United States assistance as designed to "buy the country." On a trip to the Philippines in early 1956, as an example of the Cambodian attitude, the easily aroused Sihanouk openly declared that the hospitality the Filipinos had heaped upon him was part of a United States plot to woo his country into the Southeast Asian Treaty Organization. Upon his return to Cambodia, the prince declared that in the Philippines he had seen many tractors and wonderful hospitals built with United States aid. To Cambodia, however, the prince told his people, the United States had given only refrigerators and automobiles. He ignored the fact that the United States had equipped and was then paying three-quarters of the salary of the Cambodian army; that the United States had started irrigation, school, health, and road projects in his country; that when the Cambodian rice crop had failed, the United States had rushed 20,000 tons of rice to the onetime French protectorate; and that in the fiscal year of 1956, American assistance totaled $50 million, slightly more than half of which was in the form of military aid to build up the newly organized army. The prince later retracted his statement that the United States assistance consisted mainly of luxury items, but he already had put himself on record for the Communist propagandists to quote.

If at times Sihanouk patronized the Communist countries, he also occasionally turned on them. In January 1959 he declared to the annual congress of his party, "I want to proclaim in advance that many countries have not believed in the mortal danger of communism, and when the evidence became clear to them it was too late and impossible for them to come to their senses. Look at Hungary," he continued, "if the moment comes when we must die or be taken over by the Communists, we will accept inevitable death with the conviction of not having betrayed our country." The Cambodian ambassador to Moscow was called home, and steps were taken to stop propaganda activities of the Soviet embassy and the Chinese trade mission in Phnom Penh.

On a state visit to Cairo in November 1959, Sihanouk explained Cambodia's policy. He preferred the term "neutrality" to "neutralism"—a neutrality "patterned on the model of the Swiss"—to describe the foreign policy of his country. Sihanouk would not want his country to join a bloc even if it were neutral. He said that Cambodia was receiving aid from the United States to develop its armed forces and emphasized that it had been offered "free of any conditions." Cambodia could not very well accept aid from the United States and the West without also taking some from the Soviet Union and the East. "We cannot forget," he said, "that we have two Communist neighbors, North Vietnam and Communist China."

Cambodia has found its "neutrality" profitable in terms of economic and military assistance. Between 1954 and 1959 it received foreign aid to the amount of $335 million, with $288 million coming from the United States, over half of which went to help develop Cambodia's armed forces. The United States financed at a cost of about $35 million a highway from the capital to a new harbor on the Gulf of Siam, the country's first seaport. Vessels of up to 3,000 tons sail up the Mekong River to Phnom Penh, but since South Vietnam controls the mouth of the river, this route is vulnerable. With relations between the two countries anything but cordial, this alternate route was highly welcome to Cambodia.

In spite of generous United States aid to Cambodia, relations between the two countries have deteriorated, primarily because poor relations exist between Cambodia and its neighbors, Thailand and South Vietnam, to whose defense the United States is committed. The aggressive Vietnamese and Thai gnawed away at the territory of the old Khmer kingdom in the past until it was much reduced in size. There is too much history too well remembered. In November, 1958, Cambodia suspended diplomatic relations with Thailand; the latter responded by recalling its ambassador and closing the frontier. Cambodia charged Thailand with infiltrating troops into its territory, and the latter held the former responsible for the border area activity of bandit and Communist elements. As a result of the mediation of a representative of the United Nations, diplomatic relations were resumed in February 1959. Clashes between border guards continued, however, and diplomatic relations were again broken in 1961. In December 1961, Sihanouk charged its pro-Western neighbors of "almost daily" violations of Cambodian territory and airspace. He declared that his country had been saved from attack largely by "the response of the Chinese Peoples Government which promised the firm and clear support of its forces in case of an invasion of Cambodia by its neighbors." He hailed Communist China as "the only effective support and real brother" of Cambodia. For years Cambodia and Thailand also disputed the possession of an abandoned temple on a mountain top on their common frontier. Fortunately they agreed to submit this issue to the International Court of Justice, which awarded it to Cambodia by a decision of June 15, 1962.

Cambodian relations with South Vietnam are even worse than those with Thailand. Thailand and South Vietnam regard Cambodian neutralism as a sort of Trojan horse in the region. The South Vietnamese government has asserted that the Vietcong, the Communist guerrilla forces, use Cambodian territory as a haven from which to make raids on Vietnamese outposts. American military advisers to South Vietnam formerly did not assert that the Vietcong had bases or camps in Cambodian territory but claimed that they slipped over the border when pursued and later returned to the attack in South Vietnam. In view of the fact that the frontier between the two countries is poorly defined and much of it runs through jungle, it is not surprising that there are repeated border incidents. It was quite clear by 1966, however, that there were major Vietcong supply, regroupment and hospital facilities within Cambodia's frontiers despite Sihanouk's past denials. This was but one of several indicators that real Cambodian neutralism may have become a thing of the past.

Cambodian bitterness toward its two neighbors is extended to the United States because of the latter's close military association with them. The United States could, it holds, restrain its allies, and failure to do so makes it indirectly responsible for the border incidents and other charges. If the United States cannot guarantee the integrity of Cambodia's borders, the Cambodians say that they will call on Communist China, which is willing and able to do so. As Prince Sihanouk becomes more outspokenly critical of the United States, his attitude toward Communist China becomes steadily more friendly. Sihanouk has backed Cuba in its continuing controversy with the United States and supported China in its border dispute with India. Cambodia was also the only non-Communist government to congratulate China on the explosion of an atomic bomb. After his return from a visit to Communist China in October 1964, Prince Sihanouk declared that China was Cambodia's "number one friend."

On November 12, 1963, Prince Sihanouk announced that Cambodia wished no further American economic and military aid after January 1, 1964, and that American and French military missions would also have to leave. He also announced the immediate nationalization of the import and export businesses and of Cambodian banks the following June. These moves he called part of his program of "advanced socialism" for his country. He would engage five

Chinese Communist experts to help organize "state control." Since 1955, Cambodia had received some $365 million in United States aid. The amount in 1963 was $31 million. Sihanouk charged the United States with having supplied secret radio stations in South Vietnam with transmitters to wage a campaign against him. He also accused the United States Central Intelligence Agency with having aided the Free Cambodia rebel movement with arms and funds. The foreign minister of Communist China immediately pledged "resolute support" for Cambodia in its "just and patriotic struggle against imperialism."

Prince Sihanouk the year before had proposed a reconvening of the Geneva Conference of 1954 to consider guaranteeing Cambodia's neutrality and territorial integrity. Subsequently urging a nine-nation conference for the same purpose, Sihanouk declared in February 1964 that, if the United States did not agree by May to attend such a conference, he would sever diplomatic relations with America; Cambodia would also have to consider assistance pacts with "certain great friendly countries." France, which advocated the neutralization of all of Indochina, became the most popular Western country in Cambodia. The United States was cool to the proposal, probably fearing that demands would be made at the conference for the neutralization of South Vietnam as well. Sihanouk then urged a four-power conference—Cambodia, South Vietnam, Thailand, and the United States—to reach an agreement on guaranteeing Cambodia's territorial integrity and neutrality. The United States and South Vietnam were favorably inclined to hold such a conference, but Thailand disliked the proposal.

CAMBODIAN APPEAL TO THE UNITED NATIONS

In May 1964, Cambodia brought charges before the Security Council of the United Nations that United States and South Vietnamese forces had committed acts of aggression against its territory. The United States and South Vietnam contended that the frontier incidents had resulted from the Vietcong guerrillas' use of Cambodia as a sanctuary and base for attacks on South Vietnam and that border violations had been committed unintentionally because maps had been misread by troops pursuing Communist guerrillas who took refuge in Cambodian territory. They urged that the United Nations station a force on the frontier to prevent further incidents. By a vote of nine in favor and two abstentions, the Security Council on June 4 passed a resolution which, after taking note of the apologies and regrets tendered Cambodia, requested that just and fair compensation should be made to the government of Cambodia, and provided for dispatch of a three-member commission "to the two countries and to the places where the most recent incidents have occurred in order to consider such measures as may prevent any recurrence of such incidents."

The Security Council mission, after visiting the areas where the incidents were alleged to have occurred, made its report on July 28. It attributed the tension between the two countries to "ancient rivalries and suspicions" and to differences of policy—Cambodia's neutralism and South Vietnam's "unequivocally" pro-Western position. "The two main problems to be solved," said the report, "are the resumption of political relations and the dispatch of international observers." Cambodia had broken off diplomatic relations with Saigon on August 26, 1963, because of purported ill-treatment of Buddhists in South Vietnam. Respecting international observers, the mission recommended the appointment of an unarmed United Nations civilian group to operate in Cambodian territory to watch for possible incursions. South Vietnam had proposed the establishment of an international force or an observer group "with sufficient personnel and resources to keep the frontier area under surveillance," but Cambodia was unwilling to accept such a drastic measure.

Border incidents continued with increasing intensity, reflecting the heightened level of conflict in South Vietnam. The United States and South Vietnam acknowledged on October 28, 1963, that their aircraft had fired on Cambodian targets at least five times in the week preceding, justifying their actions on the ground of increased Vietcong activity from Cambodian bases. A United States spokesman confirmed reports that an American military transport plane was shot down over Cambodian territory, with the loss of eight crewmen. Prince Sihanouk threatened to break off diplomatic relations with the United States and to extend recognition to North Vietnam and to the South Vietnamese Liberation Front, the political agency of the Vietcong. In reply to a message from Sihanouk, Communist China declared that "it cannot ignore any acts of aggression endangering the security" of Cambodia, but it made no specific promise of support.

Another sign of the mounting tension in the region was the announcement on November 10 by Secretary General U Thant that at Thailand's request and with Cambodia's acquiescence the United Nations peace mission to the two governments would be discontinued. When Cambodia and Thailand severed relations for the second time, in 1961, Thant had sent a special representative to try to induce them to reestablish relations. The mission was a failure—tensions had risen rather than subsided.

World-wide interest was aroused in 1965 by revival of the idea of a conference on Cambodia. It was hoped that such a conference might also take up the problem of South Vietnam or offer the occasion for its discussion collaterally. On April 3 the Soviet Union proposed to the British government that their foreign ministers, as cochairmen of the 1954 Geneva Conference on Indochina, issue a joint statement proposing an international conference on the neutrality and territorial integrity of Cambodia. Such a conference was earlier urged by the "Indochinese Peoples Conference" con-

Cambodia

vened by Sihanouk in Phnom Penh in March. Communists from both Vietnam and Laos played a dominant role in its deliberations, and the Soviet position was consistent with their actions. The British government on April 26 formally accepted the Soviet draft text of the proposed joint message, but Moscow did not respond. The reason very probably was that the governments of China and North Vietnam had subsequent doubts concerning the agenda and composition of the conference. They also insisted upon representation being accorded to the National Liberation Front of South Vietnam, and this the United States adamantly opposed.

CAMBODIAN-AMERICAN DIPLOMATIC BREAK

Relations with the United States continued to deteriorate. In September 1964, Prince Sihanouk declined to accept an American ambassador-designate; thereafter the head of the American diplomatic mission at Phnom Penh was a chargé d'affaires. On November 15 it was reported from Phnom Penh that Prince Sihanouk had called a special session of the Cambodian National Assembly to debate whether to expel the staff of the United States embassy. It was also reported that no more American journalists would be permitted to enter Cambodia until their attitudes toward the country had undergone "a drastic change" and that some journalists already there might be invited to leave. Sihanouk held the embassy staff responsible for circulating material for the dispatches which offended him. To reestablish good relations between the two countries, Sihanouk declared, the United States would have to obtain a firm agreement from Saigon that it would stop the attacks on the Cambodian border. On November 16 the National Assembly postponed indefinitely a decision on whether to close the United States embassy, and on the following day Sihanouk announced that representatives of the two governments would meet in New Delhi to discuss means of improving relations between themselves. The talks in New Delhi, begun on December 8, ended in a deadlock on December 17.

The final break between the two governments came on May 4, 1965. The prince attributed the action to an attack on two Cambodian border villages on April 28 by four Skyraider fighter planes of the South Vietnamese Air Force and an article in an American magazine derogatory of the queen mother. The Cambodian government was willing to continue consular relations, but this was rejected by the United States government.

"Neutral" Cambodia has become a showcase for coexistence with Communist China—from the Chinese point of view. The United States, however, is unhappy with the situation. China's influence in Cambodia has grown steadily as Prince Sihanouk has moved from reliance on the United States and the West toward the courtship of the Communist East; the psychological pressure on Thailand and South Vietnam has increased; and the Western position in Southeast Asia has deteriorated badly, for once the Western presence has disappeared from a country, only extraordinary developments can restore it. Perhaps the movement of Prince Sihanouk toward closer relations with Peking can be explained by the conviction on his part that China is going to dominate the region and that Cambodia must accommodate itself to the coming situation.

CHAPTER 8

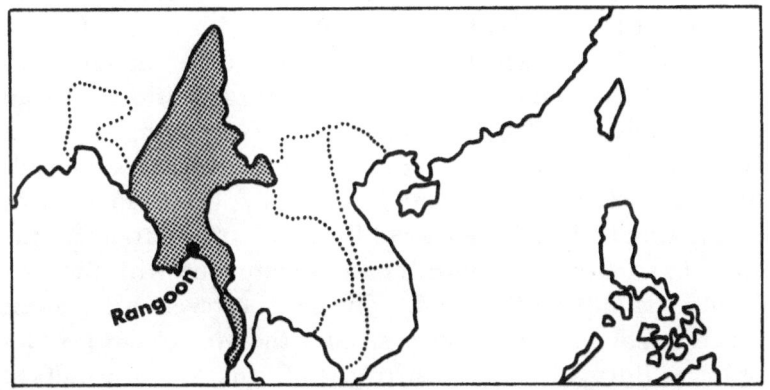

BURMA
From Buddha to Mars

BURMA HAD A democratic government—certainly in intention if not always in fact—from 1948 to 1958, the country's first ten years of renewed independence after liberation from British colonial rule. Its leader during these years was one of the most colorful and charismatic political figures in all the newly emergent lands of Asia and Africa, the intensely devout Buddhist U Nu. Nu sought the effective democratization of his country, the liberation of its people from poverty and injustice through socialism, and the revival of Buddhist values as the basic governing force in Burmese life. To do these things, however, a several-sided insurgency first had to be put down, and this meant an army had to be created. But this army, led by General Ne Win, a very minor nationalist figure before the Japanese occupation during the Second World War, subsequently became discontented with the way in which Nu and the other politicians were running the country. And so the soldiers took over from the politicians in 1958, restored them to power in 1960, and then toppled them again in 1962. Thus were U Nu and his men of Buddha replaced by Ne Win and his men of Mars.

The land over which these two quite different men successively governed is a comparatively large nation with an area of nearly 262,000 square miles. Geographically it is isolated. Overland communication with India is difficult because of formidable mountains; jungle-covered ridges, high mountains, and vast stretches of hilly country separate Burma and China; mountains form a natural boundary with Burma's eastern neighbor, Thailand. The sea, however, has proven much less of a barrier, and as a result the Mongoloid peoples of lower Burma have been strongly influenced by the culture of nearby India. The heart of the country is the central Irrawaddy-Chindwin river valley and its delta, in which is located Rangoon, the capital and largest city.

Burma's population today is about 24,000,000. Of this number about two-thirds are Burman—the name by which the majority people are known (as contrasted with Burmese, the name for nationals of the country). Other important ethnic groups are the Karens, the Shans, the Chins, and the Kachins. The first two peoples may constitute as much as a tenth and an eighth of the country's total population respectively. Before the Second World War there were more than a million Indians in Burma, but their numbers have drastically dropped in recent years as a consequence of the progressively mounting hostility of successive governments. The Chinese population in Burma does not exceed half a million.

Economically, Burma is a rich country. Before the war it exported three and a half million tons of rice annually. It took 20 years to restore this level after 1945, however, partly because of the difficulty of recovery from the war

Burma

and various continuing insurrections and partly because of the fact that there are 50 percent again as many Burmese to feed as there were before the war. Rice dominates the Burmese economy, three out of four working Burmese being engaged in its production. Burma also has significant petroleum deposits and a wide variety of mineral products including silver, lead, tungsten, tin, copper, and precious stones. The country is probably underpopulated at the present time in terms of its resources.

HISTORICAL INFLUENCES

Burma is what it is today politically and otherwise largely because of what it was yesterday. This Burmese past comprises three distinct eras in terms of their contemporary impact: the precolonial rule of the Burmese kings, British colonialism (beginning in 1826), and the wartime Japanese occupation. Each of these periods, which are of widely differing lengths but of no less importance because of this, left their imprint on the independent Burma of U Nu and Ne Win.

The history of Burma as a distinct political entity began with the great ruler Anawrahta, who founded the early Burmese kingdom of Pagan in 1044—before William the Conqueror conquered Burma's later British conquerors. Anawrahta also established Buddhism as the official religion of the realm. Pagan perished in 1287 before the Tartar armies of China's infamous Kubla Khan, and the next four and a half centuries were marked by the absence of even the semblance of unity in Burma except for the reign of Byinnaung (1550-1581). This era of disruption came to an end in 1754, when Alaungpaya rose to defeat the last of the kingdoms of the Mons, who now survive as one of Burma's lesser minorities, and established the last Burmese dynasty. Alaungpaya's Burma, like that of Anawrahta, was not a state in a modern sense, but it was sufficiently united to serve as the nucleus for the development of the present Burmese national state.

Later Burmese nationalists were to attack the arbitrary character of British colonial rule, but the Englishman was never as authoritarian as the successive governments of the Burmese kings, good or bad. There was little concern for their subjects on the part of the Burmese kings of old—and certainly no thought whatsoever for such needs as are today called social welfare. But there was a genuine interest in the religious welfare of the people, and this was a major distinction between precolonial and British rule in Burma. The Burmese monarch was the promoter of the Buddhist faith of his people, and this gave his rule a religious character and sanction. He ruled with an iron hand, but he also defended the faith. His latter role clearly provided a model for U Nu in his efforts to reestablish Buddhism as a vital force in the national and political life of his country.

British rule provided a different kind of model for U Nu and the other Burmese political leaders. And it also lasted for a relatively brief period compared with some of the other colonial administrations in Southeast Asia and elsewhere (such as the Spanish in the Philippines or the Dutch in Indonesia). Britain's conquest of Burma spanned sixty-two years, beginning in 1826, when the British East India Company, acting for the throne, took possession of the Arakan and Tenasserim coastal strips as a consequence of the attempted Burmese invasion of British India in 1824. In 1852 the governor general of India was provoked into sending another expedition against Burma, the immediate cause of his action being the treatment of British subjects and shipping in Rangoon. Britain thus acquired the remainder of coastal or lower Burma. On January 1, 1886, following Burma's defeat in the third Anglo-Burmese war, Britain announced the annexation of the rest of Burma. Incorporated into the British Indian Empire, Burma was administered as a province of India until 1937, when it became a separate colony.

British rule of Burma had several effects. The economic development of the country took place as a function of the British presence and policies. A national administrative structure and a transportation network were developed, directly encouraging such political, social, and economic integration as took place in Burma under the British. But the most important British contributions were probably the stimulation of Burmese nationalism and the encouragement of democratic political tendencies, however inadvertently.

The precise origins of nationalism in any land are difficult to date, and Burma is no exception. Nationalism did not emerge as a political force in Burma until after the First World War, but the seeds for its development were sown well before that time. British abolition of the local office of chieftain after the rebellion that followed the third Anglo-Burmese war created a vacuum into which some new allegiance inevitably had to move. The introduction of commercial rice cultivation, upsetting traditional village economic self-sufficiency, necessitated a more broadly focused political orientation. Increasing foreign domination of the country's economic life, including the growing stranglehold over the land possessed by Indian immigrants, was also a major factor stirring the Burmese to protest. And British withdrawal of governmental support of the Buddhist religion made the government more remote and foreign than it had ever before seemed. Something had to take its place as a focus of loyalty.

These events within Burma were matched by others outside the country, such as Japan's victory over Russia in 1905, which provided vivid evidence that the white man was not invincible. The protest activity of the Congress party of Gandhi and Nehru in India, of which Burma was a part until 1937, was another important factor encouraging the emergence of a vital Burmese nationalism.

Cultural nationalism preceded political nationalism in Burma as elsewhere in Southeast Asia. The Young Men's Buddhist Association, modeled after the Y.M.C.A., was an early institutional reflection of this. The step that bridged the gap between cultural and political nationalism was taken in 1921, when the General Council of Burmese Associations sought to direct mounting nationalist sentiment into political channels and openly declared home rule as its goal. But Burmese nationalism did not achieve the assertive and demanding character that was to carry the country to independence until the middle thirties, when young firebrand agitators like Aung San, the Communist Than Tun, and Nu came together in the *Dobama Asiayone,* or "We Burmans Association," to advocate immediate and complete political freedom and radical economic measures.

Simultaneous with the emergence of Burmese nationalism was the establishment of British-style parliamentary institutions on the national level of government in Rangoon. A national legislature, 79 of the 103 seats of which were filled by elections, came into being in 1923. A fully elected 132-member lower legislative house followed separation from India in 1937, and a Burmese prime minister and cabinet members were responsible to the parliament in almost all internal matters. Burmese utilization of these imported instruments of government was quite competent and meaningful. No other colony in the world possessed instruments of self-government as advanced as those of Burma in 1937 except America's Southeast Asian holding, the Philippines. Such experience in directing their internal affairs should have prepared the Burmese for the many problems of self-government when independence came (earlier than even wildly anticipated before the Second World War) in 1948. But the experiment in self-government was a brief one, and the leaders who were to govern independent Burma were not the same ones who participated in the parliamentary experiment of 1937 and subsequently.

Burma

The men who were to guide independent Burma were the younger Thakins (meaning "master") of the *Dobama Asiayone* radical nationalist protest movement. The most vigorous and probably most competent of these was Aung San, who went to Japan as leader of the "Thirty Comrades" who later returned to Burma with the invading Japanese as the nucleus of the "Burma Independence Army." One of the other Thirty Comrades was a comparatively obscure young nationalist who adopted the name Ne Win, meaning "Bright Sun." Ne Win was to distinguish himself as a competent military figure and steadily to rise in the Burma Independence Army, later renamed the "Burma Defense Army." Although Dr. Ba Maw, first premier after separation from India in 1937, headed the nominally collaborationist Burmese regime, he was firmly backed by such Thakins as Nu and Than Tun as well as Aung San. The Burmese nationalists hoped to use the Japanese to oust the British and gain their independence. To their sorrow, they discovered that they had exchanged a liberal colonial master for a far more cruel and exacting one. So the Ba Maw government became mainly a vehicle for protecting the Burmese from the harshness of Japanese rule.

Disheartened by their belief that Japanese rule would never willingly give way to true Burmese independence, the younger nationalists in the Ba Maw government organized a new movement to rid their country of this latest species of colonialism. This became the Anti-Fascist People's Freedom League, the main political party after independence. The A.F.P.F.L., a major legacy of the Japanese period, was to govern the country from 1948 until 1958. But it was not the only legacy of the war years that would influence the first decade of freedom, for the arms dropped by the British to aid the anti-Japanese resistance movement would be used after the war by various types of insurrectionists. The complete wartime breakdown of law and order, moreover, was to make the problem of a stable postcolonial Burma even more difficult than would otherwise have been the case.

RETURN TO INDEPENDENCE

Independence returned to Burma on January 4, 1948, at the astrologically propitious hour of 4:20 a.m. But it was independence that came with sorrow. Aung San was not there to witness the event for which he had striven so wholeheartedly. He and six other leading politicians, all destined to play major roles in the new independent government, had been assassinated six months earlier by agents of the crazed prewar political leader U Saw. Aung San's role as political leader of the new nation was taken over by U Nu—a mild, largely untested minor political figure of strong Buddhist religious conviction. Aung San's place as military leader of the nation would be filled later by Ne Win.

There was additional cause for sorrow on that momentous January morning. The omnibus nationalist movement, the A.F.P.F.L., was in the process of splitting; national independence was to bring with it national disunity. The Communists, members of the A.F.P.F.L., had denounced the independence and related agreements as shams, perpetuating British imperialism in fact if not in form. The truth of the matter, however, was that the break between Burma and Britain was greater than it needed to be. Burma decided not to join the Commonwealth, although India, Pakistan, and Ceylon determined differently, and so became the third colony in history to sever completely its links with its former British imperial master. The other two were the United States and Eire.

"ELDER BROTHER" NU AND THE A.F.P.F.L.

U Nu, independent Burma's first premier, was "elder brother," by no means the same as George Orwell's famous "Big Brother," to Burma's other leading political figures. These men—Nu, Kyaw Nyein, Ba Swe, and others—had worked together in the 1930s as agitators against British rule and

Burma

again in the forties as opponents of Japanese colonialism. Nu was older than most of them, and so he was given deference because of his age, even though he was only 40 when he became prime minister. As premier, Nu was much more than "first among equals." He was *Kogyi* Nu, "Elder Brother" Nu, to his associates, and "Mr. Burma" to the outside world. He personally dominated Burmese politics for ten years until a split in the ruling party in 1958 brought an end to the Anti-Fascist People's Freedom League and to Burma's most sustained attempt to establish democratic government.

Burma began its independent existence in difficult circumstances. The country's economy had been badly disrupted as a result of the Japanese invasion and subsequent occupation. Lawlessness was rampant in the land. The Communists and elements of most of the minority peoples had risen in revolt against the central government of Nu and the A.F.P.F.L. In 1949, Burma's second year of independence, many feared the imminent collapse of what was facetiously called the "Rangoon government" because it effectively controlled only the capital city of Rangoon.

But three factors mitigated against the dissidents. One was their own disunion. If they had coalesced, the insurgents might have toppled the government. But they sought different objectives, their moves were not coordinated, and so they failed to bring about the collapse of U Nu and his government. Equally important, however, was the courage of Nu and others of the ruling group. Nu never yielded in the crisis, believing that right would triumph—and so it did. Nu's skill as a political leader was matched by the competence of Ne Win in taking a Burmese army plagued by desertions and making it into a formidable fighting force. Finally, the rebels were unable to obtain foreign support. The Chinese, new to power in Peking, did not intervene on behalf of the Communist insurrectionists. Nor did the British give the Karen rebels the backing they sought in their struggle for a separate state free from what they considered as Burman domination. The Rangoon government controlled access to the outside world, and that world not only continued to recognize solely the Nu regime but also aided it in its struggle against the insurgents. The back of the several rebellions was broken by the mid-1950s, but the various revolts continued as major nuisances even down to the present time.

One consequence of the rebellions Burma faced beginning in 1948 was the delayed application of many of the grand socialist schemes which the Thakins, later to become the nucleus of the A.F.P.F.L., had long planned as they dreamed of the day of a more equal Burma as well as a Burma freed from foreign control. On the other hand, a number of actions were taken, such as the nationalization of the previously British-owned Irrawaddy Flotilla Company, which controlled inland water transportation, as well as of one-third of Burma's privately owned timber concessions. But the land reform program could not be implemented so long as the government controlled only a fraction of the national domain. The much-hated Indian moneylender-absentee landlord was slow to return, however; frequently when he did return, he was unable to claim land which had previously been his legally. The main prewar agrarian complaint—peasant indebtedness to Indian moneylenders and resulting land alienation—was never revived in its former dimensions, accordingly, because of the turmoil of the war and the subsequent grant of independence.

The recession of the insurgent threat in the early 1950s set the stage for Burma's most ambitious effort to transform the economy and generally to uplift the country—the eight-year development plan of 1952. The *Pyidawtha* ("happy land") plan had a proposed expenditure of more than $1,575,000,000 and was designed to advance industrialization, increase rice output, improve education, and promote social welfare, among other objectives. Curiously enough, it was drawn up by a team of consultants from nonsocialist America of whom Prime Minister Nu had learned from a newspaper. The plan was premised on a continuation of a generous level of American foreign aid and a seller's market in rice, Burma's leading—and near-exclusive—export commodity.

The bottom fell out of the rice market, however, and the Nu government terminated the American aid program, the first such country ever to do so, in protest against alleged United States support of military action by Chinese Nationalist irregulars (who had retreated before the Communists) on Burmese soil. As a result, the ambitious development program had to be pared. Pet projects of various leading politicians could not help but be affected, which increased differences among them. This was one of several reasons underlying the split which destroyed the long-ruling Anti-Fascist People's Freedom League in 1958.

There were other reasons for the 1958 split in the A.F.P.F.L. One of these was its particular organizational structure. The league had begun as an omnibus nationalist coalition designed to oppose continued Japanese rule of Burma. After the war it became the main vehicle for liberation of Burma from the colonial grip of the returned British, but defections from the league began almost immediately to take their toll. When independence came, the A.F.P.F.L. assumed responsibility for ruling the country as the government party. But there were further defections —the Communists, the leftwing of the People's Volunteer Organization (the veterans of Aung San's Burma Defense Army), and others.

The A.F.P.F.L. soon became a coalition mainly of members of the Socialist party, a party within a party led by Kyaw Nyein and Ba Swe, and independents (of whom the most illustrious and important was Premier Nu). The Socialists, however, were themselves divided into rival factions of "educated" and "uneducated" Socialists, the distinction between the two having more to do with their attitudes toward the conflicting claims of industry-first and proagriculture interests and on the importance of Buddhist religious values than with the extent of their formal education. Increasingly, Nu and the other independents sided with the "uneducated" Socialists.

The main leaders of the A.F.P.F.L. during these years were Nu as prime minister and his deputy premiers, Kyaw Nyein, Ba Swe, and Thakin Tin. Each of these leaders had his own organized following, Tin being the perpetual head of the All-Burma Peasants Organization and Ba Swe of the Trade Union Congress (Burma). The latter organizations were not autonomous spokesmen for important interests in Burmese society; rather they were means of communication between particular political leaders and the specialized publics to which they endeavored to make their appeal. For Ba Swe it was labor; for Thakin Tin, the peasantry. U Nu never built up such specialized public support, in contrast with his general popular appeal, nor did Kyaw Nyein succeed as well in this respect as Ba Swe and Tin despite his efforts to organize the youth of the nation on his behalf.

The A.F.P.F.L. breakup was more a split between Kyaw Nyein and Thakin Tin than anything else. Ba Swe tried to mediate the differences between the two men but to no avail. Tin called on Premier Nu to rally to his side, and Nu, paying off a political debt which he imagined that he owed Tin, did so. The debt in question illustrates the important role of personality in Burmese politics. In 1956 Nu had resigned the premiership to devote his full efforts to ridding the A.F.P.F.L. of corrupt elements. Ba Swe served as prime minister for this brief period, and he, Kyaw Nyein, Ne Win, and others talked of suggesting to Nu that he become president (hitherto a very nominal position in Burma's government) upon his return to public life. No political offense was intended; rather the other leaders hoped to enlist Nu's unquestioned unifying influence on his people without burdening him with day-to-day administrative problems. Tin, seeking to discredit Kyaw Nyein and Ba Swe, told Nu

Burma

that the others were plotting against him, and Nu believed Tin and returned to the premiership, foreswearing the presidency. Nu had always been a very suspicious person, of which Thakin Tin clearly took advantage on this occasion.

The A.F.P.F.L. openly split in April 1958, and a parliamentary showdown in June found U Nu's "Clean" A.F.P.F.L., supported by the Communists, winning a no-confidence vote posed by the Swe-Nyein "Stable" (or "Real") A.F.P.F.L. A partnership that had been born before independence was shattered by the weight of conflicting interests, organizational rivalries, and suspicious personalities after ten years of self-rule. And when the A.F.P.F.L., split, so did the whole nation.

Political partisans of the old united A.F.P.F.L. had been organized into vigilantelike armed groups at the height of the "multicolored insurrection," as the Burmese picturesquely called their several simultaneous rebellions. Some of these were controlled by one of the two major factions of the party, others by the other faction, and still others were torn by the rivalry between these two groups. When the party split, these armed auxiliaries split, too. Up and down the land, rival armed bands of the two factions faced each other. The nation was on the verge of civil war involving the various forces that had saved it from disintegration in 1949-1952.

The Communists and other insurgents did not fail to take advantage of this growing division in the ranks of their most formidable opponents. They became bolder and struck more frequently, and incidents were again reported not far from Rangoon. This alarmed the Army, which had fought so hard and sacrificed so much to contain the insurrectionists. Now the Army felt itself threatened by the resurgence of rebel activity and was genuinely disgusted with the seemingly senseless jockeying for power among the politicians. So it was that the Army seized power in September-October 1958 and established a caretaker government to restore law and order in the country preparatory to holding "free and fair elections" to determine its successor. It was a unique coup, however, for the Army in September told Nu that he had to step down, but he told the Army he would do so in October and made it pledge to return power subsequently to the civilians.

The failure of the civilians to continue to maintain a satisfactory level of law and order was only the single more important immediate cause of the Army takeover in Burma. There was also a growing gap between Nu personally and General Ne Win and other Army leaders. Nu was placing too much emphasis on obscurantist traditional values, Ne Win complained to his associates, urging plaintively that Nu "stop building pagodas and spend more time on our real problems." But Nu, who organized the Sixth Great Buddhist Synod in 1954-1956, spent more and more time in religious meditation as the years passed. And he consulted astrologers with greater frequency respecting the timing, if not the substance, of major policy pronouncements and inauguration of particular programs. Nu, once the revolutionary was becoming more and more conservative in terms of the values by which he lived and tried to lead his countrymen.

The Army realized this—or at least the more sophisticated elements in the armed forces did so—particularly the colonels who urged Ne Win to seize the government in September 1958. The takeover undoubtedly would have come in time even without the particular set of circumstances that prompted its occurrence. The fact of the matter is that the forces of traditionalism and modernization, previously fused in the person of U Nu, had become opposed to one another by the late 1950s.

The central figure in this conflict was, of course, Nu himself. Previously Nu had led both the drive to socialism and Burma's Buddhist revival. The split with Kyaw Nyein and Ba Swe within the A.F.P.F.L., however, separated Nu from the most dedicated civilian modernists and allied him

Burma

with Thakin Tin and others of more traditionalist orientation. The sycophants in the Tin camp played—both before and after the split—on this phase of Nu's personality. Clearly the burden of reconciling the old and the new in Burma was a heavy one, too heavy probably to rest on the shoulders of a single man. When that man faltered, much that had seemed secure collapsed. And the soldiers took over.

THE EIGHTEEN-MONTH ARMY INTERLUDE

General Ne Win took over Burma's government in 1958 to restore law and order to the country. But the evidence suggests that the colonels who assisted him—indeed, who prompted him to make the move in the first place—wanted Ne Win to remain in power and tried to prevail upon him not to allow the civilians to return to office.

The first Ne Win government, which took office on October 28, 1958, and restored the reigns of government to the civilians on April 1, 1960, was not a revolutionary regime. It sought no major changes. Rather it devoted its attention to ordering the existing apparatus and programs of government. It sought to put the pieces back together again in order that the civilians might have a second chance to prove their ability to govern the nation. Ne Win himself was not a professional soldier but a minor nationalist political figure turned soldier as a result of the unplanned circumstance of the wartime Japanese invasion. Nu, Ba Swe, Kyaw Nyein, and the rest were his former cronies—indeed, they had been much more important than himself in the nationalist movement. Ne Win, moreover, was a constitutionalist who had accepted the British notion of the subordination of the military to the policymaking civilian branch of government. The 1958 coup was, more than anything else, an interruption in the ordinary method of running the government rather than any kind of basic or dramatic alteration of the governing system.

The caretaker Army regime gave Burma the best government it has ever known. It was efficient and effective government. Corruption was greatly reduced; prices were controlled; Rangoon became again a city of beauty. Law and order was once more restored to the land, or to as much of it as had ever known law and order since independence came. The professional people—the doctors, the lawyers, the professors, and the like—largely applauded the soldier regime as did most Burmese who genuinely wanted to see their country modernized rather than returned to an age of astrologers and pagoda builders. The masses, on the other hand, were strongly opposed to the soldiers. In the first place, they had ousted the most genuinely beloved Burmese of all time, U Nu—Buddha-in-the-process-of-becoming, translator of the new aspirations into the old idiom, and apparent personification of all that was good and noble in the Burmese Buddhist value structure. And secondly, the soldiers demanded discipline—lines in front of poultry shops and such—and this the far from disciplined ordinary Burmese could not endure.

Lack of popular support was probably the main reason why the colonels could not convince General Ne Win to remain in office after he had ousted U Nu. There was another equally important reason, however. Nu wanted to return to power and was prepared to spare no means in attaining this end. In May 1959 he plotted a nationwide Gandhian-style civil disobedience movement. Nu's lieutenants were scattered throughout the country. There is no doubt that the masses would have rallied to his support. The country would have been divided again, which would have undone all that the Army had accomplished in containing the insurgents and in reestablishing law and order after the takeover. Nu was on the loose politically, he was a superb mobilizer of mass opinion, and Ne Win had to reckon with him.

So Ne Win announced that elections would be held in February 1960. It was widely believed even as late as Sep-

Burma

tember 1959, when the decision on elections was publicly proclaimed, that the "Stable" A.F.P.F.L. faction of Ba Swe and Kyaw Nyein would emerge victorious in the voting. The Stable party was alleged to be better organized, and it was known to be favored by the Army. But U Nu was U Nu, and no Burmese ever campaigned more vigorously—and Thakin Tin was Thakin Tin, and every bit as competent an organizer was he as Ba Swe or Kyaw Nyein. The result was a landslide victory for Nu and the "Clean" A.F.P.F.L. The Stable A.F.P.F.L. did not even win enough seats to enable it to move a parliamentary vote of no-confidence. Ba Swe and Kyaw Nyein were both defeated. So it was that Burma began its second attempt at democratic government.

THE RETURN OF U NU

A frequently offered criticism of the first Nu government was that too few attempted too much in too short a time. And the competent political figures in the A.F.P.F.L. in the first ten years were indeed few in number. The prewar politicians, who had gained some experience with parliamentary institutions between 1937 and 1941, were either discredited or ignored by the younger men. Seven of the abler younger men, moreover, including Aung San, were assassinated on the eve of independence. Unfortunately, the first decade of independence did not produce any new political figures who might have added fresh blood to the inner circle of the ruling elite. New men there were, of course, but none of the stature of the chief leaders—even in their younger years. And these younger years were not far behind them: Ba Swe and Kyaw Nyein were still in their 30's when independence came; Nu was only 40 when he became prime minister. An extremely youthful leadership group seemed to block the way for even younger men.

The second Nu government was in the hands of even fewer and less competent men. Ba Swe and Kyaw Nyein,

Nu's two most important lieutenants in the early and middle fifties, were absent even from the parliamentary opposition. Most of the best men in the old A.F.P.F.L., moreover—the likes of Nu, U Raschid, and a few others excepted—had sided with the Stable A.F.P.F.L. In terms of education, modernist orientation, administrative know-how, and such, Nu's Clean A.F.P.F.L., since renamed the Union party, clearly included the least impressive of the second-line political figures. These were the men, led by the unquestionably dedicated and democratic Nu, who would try for a second time to make democracy work in Burma.

Taking his cue from the retiring military caretaker government, Nu initially indicated that he would inaugurate no new major economic programs, but it was not long before he proclaimed a new sixteen-year plan that would quadruple Burma's national income. The words and the deeds, as previously, were at variance. Real income actually declined, as prices rose more than 10 percent in the first year and a half of the second Nu government. Nu, moreover, sought to reduce the growing economic ascendancy of the Army in the country. The military had its hand in almost every conceivable type of economic activity from importing and servicing foreign cars, to catching and marketing shrimp, to running a department store. Nu endeavored to undercut this economic power in order to lessen the Army's involvement in nonmilitary matters. There can be little doubt that General Ne Win was fully aware of what Nu was trying to do.

Because the Army leadership did not basically want to retain power (least of all Ne Win) and probably could have done so only with the spilling of much blood in view of Nu's planned passive resistance movement, the soldiers sought to influence the future political development of the country by indirect means. National Solidarity Associations were established throughout the land, and these were to serve as political vigilantes checking excessive behavior on the part of the politicians. There was some talk of N.S.A. candidates in the February 1960 elections, but this fizzled—probably because the Army realized that such men, identified with itself, would be defeated. The N.S.A. movement itself lapsed into virtual oblivion only months after U Nu's return to office in April 1960. The means available to the Army to control politics were becoming fewer and fewer.

Three problems in particular confronted U Nu during his second premiership. The first of these concerned relations among the politicians in his own camp. The Union party's victory had been too decisive. There was no reason to stick together. The A.F.P.F.L. split had come at a moment of minimum challenge to the party and unparalleled tranquillity in the country. Having gotten the Army out of office and defeated the Ba Swe-Kyaw Nyein Stable A.F.P.F.L., the Union party politicians likewise began to quarrel and scheme among themselves. The truth of the matter is that the Union party was never united in anything but name. And much energy, including Nu's, was wasted in senseless jockeying for power among the leaders of the party.

Nu's second major problem was largely self-made. This was the state religion question. Nu promised early in the election campaign that he would reestablish Buddhism as the official religion of the realm if his party gained control of the government. He probably would have won handily anyway; but he had made the promise, he apparently believed in the desirability of such a move, and he would keep it. Many non-Buddhists were alarmed at the prospect of an official religion, however, and new elements joined the ranks of those in revolt against the government—such as the Kachins. Nu subsequently obtained passage of a constitutional amendment guaranteeing religious freedom in the country —against which some Buddhists, including clergy, now demonstrated. If national unity were Nu's aim, as he so often proclaimed, his actions in the state religion controversy hardly advanced this end. They also increased Army suspicions of Nu.

National unity as such was Nu's third—and chief—problem. The religious question was only one dimension of this. Practically every minority had some of its members in revolt against the government at some time since independence came in 1948. The Karens, the most formidable of the ethnic insurgents, remained very much in the field. The religious dispute had added the Kachins to the ranks of the rebels. But the most dangerous challenge at this time came from the Shans, related racially to the Thai and inhabitants of that part of Burma adjacent to Thailand. The Burmese constitution gave the Shans the right of secession after ten years of independence, and some Shans were clearly threatening to invoke this right. Nu's response was to offer concessions of greater autonomy to the minority peoples, and he was in the process of doing just this when the Army again seized power on March 2, 1962.

The Army said that it could not allow the dismemberment of the union. Burma was falling apart; it might soon be divided like China, Vietnam, or Laos. Preservation of the nation as a single unit was the paramount necessity, the Army leaders declared.

THE PRESENT REGIME

Two factors in particular distinguish the present Ne Win government from the one headed by the same general which ruled Burma for eighteen months in 1959-1960. The most conspicuous difference is that the present regime is by no means a caretaker one. It has the avowed intention of revolutionizing the basic economic and social order. It has given no indication whatsoever as to when it will give up office; it probably has not even thought in such terms. The soldiers tried to mend things for the politicians once, but the politicians proved themselves incapable of adequately governing—in the eyes of the soldiers. So the soldiers took over again.

Burma

The second important difference is that these are not the same soldiers. General Ne Win headed both military governments, and he is every bit as much the boss of this regime as of the previous caretaker administration. But his lieutenants are different men this time. The men who urged him to take over from Nu in 1958, Brigadier Aung Gyi and Colonel Maung Maung, have long since left the ranks of the Ne Win's top advisers. These more or less liberal socialists have been replaced by the likes of Brigadier Tin Pe, a far less educated and much more doctrinaire and even vindictive socialist. There was a human quality to the Army regime previously, particularly as personified by Aung Gyi, that seems sadly lacking today.

Finally, the 1962 coup was well conceived and executed. It was not hastily organized, and it was related to a quite specific postcoup strategy. Even if the Army had not been willing to relinquish power in 1960, it would have been hard for it not to have done so with U Nu on the loose politically. Now Nu is detained—and has been since March 2, 1962. Most of his chief lieutenants have also been detained, with the result that there is practically no overt opposition to the Army regime in the country except, of course, the many and diverse insurgent groups.

Previously Burma had one of the most democratic governments in Southeast Asia. Today it has one of the most authoritarian. The liberal constitution that came with independence has been abandoned, the parliamentary institutions have been overthrown, and in their place stands an autocratic military Revolutionary Council headed by General Ne Win. The decisions which this Council makes frequently are ruthlessly carried out. The arbitrary behavior of the present ruling military elite would appear to be consistent with pre-British Burmese government, and so far today's Burmese subjects have been unable to do anything about it.

At first, General Ne Win and his subordinates allowed political parties to exist, though their precise function was open to some question in view of the absence of parliamentary institutions. Subsequently only one party was permitted, the government's Burma Socialist Program party. The government apparently thought that all the civilian politicians would rally to this single party's ranks, but the independent-minded Burmese politician did not do so. The Burma Socialist Program party, accordingly, has not really played any significant role at all since its establishment.

Opposition to the Ne Win government has come from at least five sources. The Communists, first of all, have been just as much the enemy of this Burmese government as any of its predecessors. There is a strong—indeed, extreme—leftist tinge to the Ne Win regime, and some of its participants clearly have thought in communistic terms. But they are not Communists, and those who are clearly the mainstream of Burmese communism remain as much in revolt today as a decade ago under U Nu. Ne Win tried to arrange peace terms with the Communists, but as they have done so many times previously, they balked.

The Ne Win government's relations with the ethnic minorities have both improved and worsened—depending on the minority. At long last the 16-year-old Karen rebellion seemed to have been ended in 1964 with the successful negotiations between the leadership of the Karen National Defense Organization, representative of the largest number of Karen insurgents, and the government. The terms on the government's side were generous, and Karen rebels immediately began to lay down their arms. The most militant —if minority—arm of the Karen insurrection continues, however. These Karens have for the last several years been closely allied with the Communists, probably more than a marriage of convenience.

The Shans, who are related to the neighboring Thai, have been the military regime's biggest headache. The Shans have always resisted full absorption into the Burmese union, fearing both Burmanization culturally and loss of freedom politically and economically (not least of all with respect to cultivation of opium-yielding poppies). Through his years as premier, U Nu enjoyed the confidence of Shan leaders. The Ne Win caretaker government of 1959-1960, a model of propriety before foreign eyes in Rangoon, frequently conducted itself in a high-handed fashion in the more distant parts of the country, probably nowhere more so than in the Shan states. In fact, the Shan problem in its present form began largely as a response to the behavior of the first Ne Win regime. The Shans wanted greater autonomy, resultingly, to protect themselves against such abuses. Their demands partly prompted the return of the soldiers to power, which circumstance in turn increased Shan intransigence. Today the Shan National Army is a fairly formidable force with about 5,000 men in the field. Geographical and other considerations make Shan secession a virtual impossibility, but it is also unlikely that the Army will quell Shan resistance to its vigorous reformism *cum* conformism in the immediate future.

The earliest opponent of the Ne Win regime—the press, an opponent that was both outspoken and subtle—has been quelled. U Law Yone, long a distinguished and courageous figure in Burmese journalism, was jailed early in the Ne Win regime because of his outspoken opposition to the way the soldiers governed. Later, U Sein Win, for many years editor of the influential *Guardian,* was placed under arrest. The press, meanwhile, has been nationalized—meaning that it is now run by the government, as in Communist and other totalitarian countries. It no longer serves as a critic of government as it did in the days of U Nu and the high-riding A.F.P.F.L. and Nu's subsequent Union party government. This is particularly tragic, since Burma once had one of the freest and most courageous presses in the world, which performed magnificently in two periods (1948-1958 and 1960-1962) when there was no significant legitimate, or parliamentary, opposition to the government of the day.

As might be expected, the Buddhist clergy has also been unenthusiastic about the Ne Win government. In the first place, the soldiers ousted and still detain U Nu, probably the greatest patron Burmese Buddhism has ever known. In addition, Ne Win overthrew the constitution that had been amended to make Buddhism the state religion, and his opposition to such a status for Buddhism is widely known. Finally, unlike Nu, Ne Win is pursuing a policy of maximum rapid modernization rather than seeking to effect a unique Burmese accommodation between the historical ethos of his people (including their religious outlook) and political, economic, and social change. Ne Win trumpets a "Burmese Way to Socialism," but there is nothing Burmese about it. Ne Win, moreover, attempted in 1965 to reorganize Burma's Buddhist clergy, not especially organized to begin with, and to give the government responsibility for maintaining discipline among the monks. Many *pongyis,* as such monks are called, resisted such efforts and demonstrated against the regime, destroying the headquarters in Rangoon of the Burma Socialist Program party. Ne Win then cracked down on the monks, arresting nearly a hundred of them.

Shortly after the roundup of the monks known or alleged to be opposed to the Army government, an almost equal number of leading and second-line politicians of the pre-coup days were arrested. The result of the latter action was to place under detention practically anybody of influence politically before the second Army takeover, including Brigadier Aung Gyi, former socialist politician and righthand man of Ne Win during the 1959-1960 caretaker regime, who resigned in 1963 to pursue religious meditation in the Kachin country (after clearly losing influence to Brigadier Tin Pe within the government). How much real plotting against the Ne Win government there has actually been is hard to say. Burma is a virtual police state today, the domestic press is closely controlled, and foreign newsmen have less access to Burma than to most of the Communist countries. But the detention of the monks and the arrest of the politicians and Aung Gyi clearly suggest that the foundations of the Ne Win government are still shaky, however stable an appearance the regime seeks to give. Its control is almost wholly by force, and the big question is how long such a government can exist without either mass backing or support from other key sections of the nation's elite. So far there are no signs of an early fall of the regime.

There are signs, on the other hand—lots of them—of the lack of success to date of various of the policies associated with the Ne Win loudly proclaimed Burmese Way to Socialism. Ne Win is a much more xenophobic type of nationalist than his predecessor U Nu, and the socialism of his confidants is seemingly of a heartless character. The first tendency of the regime, however, was not to nationalize everything in sight; indeed, it called for the support of private businessmen and promised them participation in certain types of economic activity in the short run. But the moderates in the Revolutionary Council, led by Aung Gyi, lost out to Tin Pe's more numerous leftist extremists, and wholesale nationalization became the order of the day. Practically every type of economic enterprise was nationalized, except for a handful of highly individualized activities (such as tailorshops).

The results were immediately catastrophic, and improvement has subsequently come about only slowly. Unemployment shot up approximately 25 percent almost immediately. The government did not have the skilled hands to do the job for which it had assumed responsibility, a circumstance that also existed in the beginning A.F.P.F.L. days when an early attempt was made to effect nationalization. The civilian politicians burned their hands and learned, but Ne Win apparently was not profiting by this, for he tried the same thing a decade and a half later. By the 1963-1964 fiscal year the gross national product, the value of all goods and services produced in the country, was the same as the 1961-1962 precoup level—a period of which the Army regime had been extremely critical from an economic point of view as well as otherwise. Industrial output was down 11 percent; the value of foreign trade, 13 percent. Agricultural production also declined by 5 percent. Production in the supposedly expanding public sector of the economy was off one percent; in the sorely restricted private sector, 13 percent. These figures add up to only one thing (at least in the short run)—gross economic failure. A better tomorrow is still possible economically, but it is a distant tomorrow at the rate at which Ne Win and the soldiers are moving. Unemployment and consumer goods shortages, occasioned by the wholesale nationalization moves of the soldier regime, were somewhat alleviated in 1965 by the decision to allow the private sector to share the distribution of consumer goods with state shops.

The government's rapid expansion of the public sector of the economy had its roots in two considerations: an intense desire to eliminate foreign control of the economy and the aspiration to foster a socialist order based theoretically on justice (though some of the brigadiers and colonels show little interest in seeing that justice is done when they get down to cases). Thousands of Indians have been forced out of business and so out of the country (which was the government's objective). These Indians have even been denied the right to take some of their most personal possessions with them—even their children's toys. One departing Indian went so far in protesting such treatment as to disrobe himself completely at Rangoon airport and proceed to the waiting plane "with nothing on that I could possibly be considered as taking from your dear Burma." Granted that the Indian exploited the Burmese, he also contributed some very necessary skills that played a major role in the country's economic development. Now these skills are gone or going.

That the Ne Win regime is basically totalitarian is quite evident from its action in mid-1965 in commencing the nationalization of the country's private schools, taking over

129 of these in July in both Burma proper and the outlying states. Previously, there had been roughly equal numbers of state and private schools on the high and middle levels (about 850 of each). The schools themselves, however, may have played a precipitating role in their nationalization. The government-issued uniform syllabus was not closely followed by many of the private schools, and this may have forced the regime to move faster than it may once have intended. "Education plays a vital role in the socialist education," Education Minister Colonel Hla Han stated at the time of the takeover, declaring that the objective of the action was to "enable all to receive education which made for socialist life and morality." According to the government's *Working People's Daily*, "The existence of so many private educational institutions run by so many different types of individuals or organizations has resulted in a proliferation of a diversity of objectives, some of which might not support the national objective." Half the schools taken over in the capital city of Rangoon were missionary schools, the best in the country; six others were Chinese, and five, Indian. Many foreigners taught in the missionary schools as well as in the Chinese and Indian schools. With nationalization, however, no foreign instructional personnel will be retained. The racist as well as ideological conformism of the soldier regime is nowhere more evident than in this dimension of its educational policies.

THE OLD AND THE NEW

The Ne Win and U Nu governments offer contrasts in the ways differing Burmese political leadership groups have combined the old and the new in the complicated process of catching up with the much more advanced world beyond Burma. When Nu was prime minister, it was widely (and rightly) noted that he sought to give meaning to ancient Buddhist religious and social values through the medium of the democratic socialist state. Socialism, in freeing the Burmese peasant from the exploitative grasp of capitalism, would give him time for religious meditation, allow him to acquire merit to achieve a better being in the next incarnation, and so aid him to escape the endless wheel of rebirths that is the Buddhist notion of existence. Socialism was the modern means to achieve ancient Buddhist goals, according to Nu.

Nu also was a democrat, perhaps the most dedicated that postwar Southeast Asia has known. During the 1959-60 Ne Win caretaker government Nu put his political neck and personal freedom very much on the line as he fought courageously to see that Ne Win would keep his promise to return the civilians to power. The socialism Nu admired was not the Communist kind to be found in the U.S.S.R., where men were not free to choose their leaders, but rather the British, Norwegian, or Israeli sort. The purpose of socialism was to free man economically; of democracy, to free him politically. Traditional Burmese man had been free in neither respect, and Nu had no desire to return to the old ways despite his efforts to revive the Buddhist religious values of a past era.

Ne Win tried less consciously to preserve the old, and yet in some ways he did so far more than did Nu. Ne Win also endeavored to establish socialism in Burma, a more thoroughgoing and rapidly effected socialism than that of Nu, as a matter of fact. Like Nu, he, too, sought the industrial development of the country, but in less grandiose terms than the eight-year *Pyidawtha* development plan of 1952-60. But Ne Win was neither democrat nor Buddhist. Like Sukarno of Indonesia, Ne Win frankly attacked the applicability of Western-style parliamentary institutions to Burma. These had been tried twice and found wanting, Ne Win said. So he did away with them, as completely as any nation has ever abandoned a particular set of political institutions.

Buddhism was a different matter, however. It was not imported, it had roots among the people, it could not be thrown out. The monks were there as a force to reckon with, the people's faith could not be diminished in the short run, and the pagodas could not be closed. But there were still actions that the government could take. U Nu could be kept in detention, for one thing, and not permitted to rally the Buddhists against the government—a possibility that surely must have struck fear into the soldiers' collective hearts in the wake of the Buddhists' self-burnings and other demonstrative actions in Vietnam in 1963 and subsequently. The government could also seek to control the priesthood. In December 1964, accordingly, the Revolutionary Council repealed a parliamentary act of many years earlier that allowed the clergy to bring religious conflicts before their own ecclesiastical court. Henceforth, a government agency would decide such disputes. Moreover, an order was issued forbidding monks to transport rice and oil given to them as alms from one district to another. A draft constitution was endorsed by most of the monks attending a government-sponsored ecclesiastical conference to establish a *Buddha Sasana Sangha* organization for the enrollment of all clergy. And the government-run People's Shops stopped selling monks articles inappropriate to the priesthood, a probably justifiable slap at the way many younger (and temporary) clergy have adhered to their vows in recent years.

The Ne Win government has so far by no means diminished the hold of the Buddhist faith on the Burmese masses as a whole. Nor is it clear that this is really its objective. It certainly has not proclaimed any such aim—which, of course, it would not do even if this were the case. But it has begun to restrict the autonomy of the faith and its clerical adherents. And Ne Win has certainly not tried to use Buddhism as a link between his reforms and the more known past as Nu used to do or as Cambodia's Prince Norodom Sihanouk still does.

Ne Win's link with history is his autocratic method of government—quite frankly, the traditional way of governing in Burma. Democracy, as Nu, Kyaw Nyein, Ba Swe, and the others sought to make it function, was wholly alien to the Burmese past prior to the advent of the British. Even after the British came, it was not until 1923 that the first semblance of self-governing institutions was introduced—and then only because of Burmese demands that reforms granted India, of which Burma was then a part, be extended to Burma, too. Even after internal self-rule was for all practical purposes inaugurated in 1937, the governor still held considerable reserve powers. The fact is that government in Burma in precolonial and colonial times was always arbitrary. Ne Win may not have consciously reestablished autocracy as a link between the past and today, but he is clearly using traditional-style authoritarian government as a means of effecting his economic and social reforms. It may be that this mode of government is in fact more appropriate to Burma's needs than U Nu's type of democracy.

The economic doctrine of the Ne Win regime is the self-styled Burmese Way to Socialism. It sets forth the goal of a "socialist society of affluence where justice shall prevail" and asserts the desirability of the nationalization of agriculture, industry, domestic and foreign trade, and communications. The state is proclaimed the main owner of the means of production and distribution. This is socialism clearly enough, but hardly Burmese. The suggestion implicit in the very title of the doctrine that this is a unique Burmese way of achieving socialist goals is grossly deceiving. The last thing the Burmese Way of Socialism can rightly be considered is a way of reconciling the old and the new in present-day changing Burma.

And yet there is such a process of reconciliation constantly in operation. Social change would not be possible without it. The old and the new are being blended—sometimes consciously, other times spontaneously. In the early days of the A.F.P.F.L. it appeared as though the new held the upper hand; then the forces of traditionalism increased in strength, and it looked as though they were becoming dominant. Ne Win today is introducing new ways but by traditional means. The face of Burma will never again be the same.

CHANGE AND CONTINUITY

It is popular to characterize Burma as having had since 1948 a civilian government, then a soldier one, then a civilian regime again, and finally military rule once more. The importance of these changes cannot be ignored, of course. At the same time, however, it is possible to make too much of them. That is to say, there are important similarities between the two civilian administrations of U Nu and the two military regimes of General Ne Win.

Both the civilian and military governments, effectively speaking, were oligarchies. The few ruled in both instances. This is the ordinary state of affairs in all countries, but the term "oligarchy" is more precisely employed when the few are comparatively narrowly based and the elite is a fairly closed one. By this yardstick, the Ne Win military regimes were more oligarchical than the two U Nu civilian governments, but the difference is one of degree rather than of substance. Proportionately speaking, far fewer ruled in Burma—or tried to influence those who ruled—than was the case in two other Asian states which have also tried, more successfully than Burma, to operate democratic political institutions, the Philippines and Ceylon.

One consequence of this situation in Burma is the fact that the gap has remained great between the rulers and the ruled. The ordinary Burmese voted in four elections after independence, particularly decisively in 1960 when he chose U Nu's Clean A.F.P.F.L. over the Swe-Nyein Stable faction by a most decisive margin. And the Burmese in the rice-paddy probably felt a unique communion with his leader,

U Nu. This having been said, however, the fact still remains that the gap was a wide one in A.F.P.F.L. times, and it has widened under Ne Win.

Both civilian and military governments in Burma have shown a tendency to be arbitrary—the latter much more so than the former, however. It is true that Nu, Kyaw Nyein, Ba Swe, and the others tried to establish a functioning democracy, but this did not mean that they did not frequently act in an undemocratic fashion. Nu often did so, telling the parliament on one occasion to stop picking fault with his programs. Both civilian and military governments were intolerant of opposition and criticism, both sought to silence criticism, and both were not above taking actions that had no basis in any existing laws.

The ends of both the Nu and Ne Win governments were not only similar but indeed identical. Both sought, above all else, to modernize the economy and to increase the control of the Burmese over national economic life. Both also tried to advance national unity by force and persuasion (though in differing combinations in the two circumstances). The policies pursued toward these ends, moreover, were surprisingly similar. Socialism was the means to a modern economy and as well to a more just society as perceived by both Nu and Ne Win and their associates. Both also sought to lift the level of education. The differences between the civilians and soldiers were less in terms of ends and means than in the style by which they went about the job and, frankly, their appraisal of the other's style.

Burma is today legally a one-party state, which in form if not in fact is actually more than some of the Communist countries are. This is a significant difference between the military regime of today and the three preceding administrations. Yet for all practical purposes even the latter were one-party governments. In the old A.F.P.F.L. days, the years from 1948 through 1958, there was only one party for all practical purposes—the Anti-Fascist People's Freedom League, which won all its elections by such a margin that there was no effective parliamentary opposition. During the first Ne Win regime there was no participation in the government by the existing parties. And in 1960 U Nu's Clean A.F.P.F.L. triumphed so decisively that the legislative opposition did not have enough strength even to move a vote of no-confidence against the government.

Finally, the problems faced by the civilian and military governments are very much the same, and so is the environment in which the attempted solution of these problems must proceed. Building a nation politically and economically—where there is still not one socially—remains the paramount task of the country's leadership. The other problems are also the same old ones: expansion of rice production, sale of rice abroad on the best possible terms, containment of the insurrections, industrial development, education, and the like. And these exist in the same setting of a backward country with limited domestic communications threatened by internal disunion and, despite Burmese reluctance to discuss the subject, lying within the shadow of large and resurgent China.

ESSENCE OF BURMESE POLITICS

Burma is the least developed of the Southeast Asian countries politically with the probable exception of Laos. There are only two interests that today influence policymaking in the country to any significant extent. Buddhism is a negative force in the sense that it sets limits to what can be done rather than positively promotes goals it would like to see embodied in public policy. The military, on the other hand, is itself the government.

This situation is not so different from what it was under U Nu's A.F.P.F.L. and Union party governments. That is to say, neither the soldiers nor the civilians were ordinarily influenced by what others wanted. They decided themselves what was best for the society. These ends may have been in the best interests of the society and not for the purpose of the self-aggrandizement of the leadership group (as happened so frequently in Latin America), but they almost always originated with the men who ran the government. Of politically active specialized publics or interests there were none. The public's function was not to originate but to be mobilized on behalf of goals already decided by the leadership group.

Similar conditions exist, of course, in all the Southeast Asian countries as well as in other developing lands elsewhere in the world. But they are clearly more pronounced in Burma than, say, in the Philippines or Thailand or Indonesia.

The explanation is probably to be found in a complex of factors. One of these is the backward nature of the economy and its lack of diversification. The near-primitive level of communications, which have not improved perceptibly since the war except for air travel, is another factor. It is also most important that the major economic interests have been largely foreign until the recent nationalization moves, and Burmese xenophobia has prevented such interests from giving natural expression to their wants. Whatever the cause, however, it is quite clear that Burma is a long way from being the type of political system in which autonomous interests largely determine public policy. It may be decades before this is the case.

FOREIGN POLICY

Burma's foreign policy has been neutralist almost from independence, but it has nevertheless undergone important changes in subsequent years. When Burma gained its freedom from Britain in 1948, China had yet to have a Communist government, and Burmese fears of their large resurgent neighbor had yet to take shape. U Nu and his polit-

Burma

ical associates expected to find their friends among both the Western countries (which they knew) and the Communist countries (which were also opposed to capitalism and so might be expected to sympathize with a new socialist nation).

But the ascent of the Communists to power in Peking changed things. The U.S.S.R., moreover, initially showed little sympathy for Burma's political leadership and was clearly partisan to the Communist insurgents who raised the standard of revolt in 1948. This frightened the Nu government, and it sought protection and assistance from the West. Military aid was obtained from both Britain and India to help Burma in the struggle against the various insurrectionist groups. The British and the Burmese also entered into an agreement prior to independence for the former to provide a training mission for the Burmese army.

The United States in particular was not yet ready in 1949 to assume a major commitment in Southeast Asia on behalf of Burma or any other country except the Philippines, its own former colony. Dr. E Maung, Burma's foreign minister, sought a pattern of regular consultations with America and Britain and military as well as economic aid, but neither Washington nor London was interested. It is interesting to speculate as to the possible subsequent course of Burmese foreign policy development if the West had responded to Burma's overtures in the late 1940s. It can truthfully be said that Burma turned to neutralism only after it found that it could not obtain the level of support it desired from the Western nations, with which U Nu and the other leaders felt a bond of sympathy in view of their common democratic aspirations.

Burmese neutralism had its origins, then, in the early 1950s as a second choice among possible foreign policy alternatives, although it probably would have developed anyway. There were several reasons for the adoption of this particular foreign policy orientation. Initially, of course, there was the fact that the West would not give Burma the kind of guarantees which its leaders apparently sought. Increasingly important, however, as the years advanced, was the fact of China's adjacency (with a long inadequately demarcated common border) and the growing aggressiveness of Chinese foreign policy. Burma feared offending China, which it could avoid doing by not favoring China's leading foes in international politics. The Burmese also hoped for maximum economic and other support from both sides in the cold war —meaning mainly the United States and the U.S.S.R. in the 1950s—and to favor one over the other would prejudice such a possibility. There was, moreover, the growing trend toward neutralism among the emergent states, and Burma could not help but be influenced by this development. Finally, there was U Nu's basically pacificist orientation born of his Buddhist outlook, his desire to see conflict of any kind controlled, and his image of himself as a potential mediator of differences between the larger powers (such as the United States and China, whom he tried unsuccessfully to reconcile in the early and middle fifties).

American economic aid to Burma began in 1950, two years after independence, but was small in amount—eight to ten million dollars for the fiscal year 1950-1951, about one-fifth of what the Burmese had requested. And the aid was terminated by the Burmese in 1953. Chinese Nationalist irregulars, refugees from the war with the Communists, had settled in northeastern Burma and were proving a domestic problem and a potential foreign one. Burma prevailed upon the United States to use its influence with Nationalist China to remove these elements. The American response was modest in comparison with what it might have been; the reasons for this have never been clear. As a result, American aid was discontinued. When it was resumed in 1956, the momentum had been lost. For a second time in less than a decade, Burma's leaders had reason to question the validity of American protestations of friendship. American leaders would regret these mistakes in the years to come.

If relations between Burma and the United States worsened through the years, those involving the Burmese and the U.S.S.R. improved in the middle fifties and have not subsequently approached the depths of the first years of independence. The change began with the death of Stalin in 1953. Nikita S. Khrushchev, who became Stalin's successor after a brief struggle for power within the Russian leadership group, aggressively sought to woo the emerging countries, not least of all Burma. The willingness of the Soviets and their satellites (as well as China) to take surplus Burmese rice in the mid-1950s as a result of a series of barter arrangements filled a gap created by the drop in the international rice price. U Nu traveled to Russia in 1955, and Soviet leaders Khrushchev and Nikolai Bulganin returned the visit only a month later. Many thought that Burma was caught in a pro-Communist drift. Nothing could have been further from the truth. The trade agreements, with which the Burmese were far from satisfied, resulted from economic necessity. Burma preferred cash sales and would gladly have sold its surplus rice to the United States, but the Americans —with a rice surplus of their own (and, more importantly, a rice lobby!)—could not oblige. It was yet another instance of Burma's turning in another direction after having been rebuffed by the United States. Burmese-Soviet relations subsequently became quite cordial, as did those between Rangoon and the Eastern European countries, but Burma never became a supporter of Soviet foreign policy aims or any other kind of Russian accomplice.

Burmese-Chinese relations, on the other hand, deteriorated during the same period. This is not evident from the public speeches and agreements between the two states, but these hide a very real and justified Burmese fear of Communist China. Burma was the first non-Communist country to recognize China, saying at the time, however, that recognition did not mean approval. U Nu was much impressed with the peaceful protestations of Chinese Premier and Foreign Minister Chou En-lai in particular, and the two leaders pledged their support of the five principles of peaceful coexistence. Chinese border crossings in 1956, however, alarmed Nu and the other Burmese leaders. Nu tried to reach agreement with the Chinese, but it remained for the Ne Win caretaker government to do this in 1960. The latter agreement, for the most part, recognized Burma's version of the border—which raises the question of Chinese intentions in the whole matter. In all probability, the Chinese wanted to strike a little fear into Burmese hearts in the first place and then found it expedient to reach an agreement with Rangoon to bolster its argument that Indian intransigence was at the core of Chinese-Indian border difficulties.

Burma was a strong supporter of the United Nations throughout the two Nu governments and the Army caretaker regime. The Burmese also approved the U.N. intervention in Korea in 1950, supported practically all disarmament moves, attended and took an active part in the 1955 Bandung Afro-Asian Conference, cooperated with the Colombo Plan group of nations in furthering regional economic development, and, as the years passed, became increasingly identified with the neutralist bloc of nations (not all of which were anywhere nearly as neutralist as Burma) such as met at Belgrade, Yugoslavia, in 1961.

The foreign policy of Burma during the years 1948-1962 was U Nu's foreign policy, the 1959-1960 caretaker government notwithstanding. Since General Ne Win's second takeover of March 1962, some claim that Burma has become advantageously neutralist from the Communist point of view.

Burma's neutralism is as neutralist as it ever was, from a technical point of view. General Ne Win is not pro-Peking, nor has he sought in any known way to undercut American policies in Southeast Asia. Burma has certainly not taken sides with either the Communist or Western camps in international affairs generally. The Ne Win regime agreed in 1965 to buy $5,000,000 worth of textile mills from China under a 1961 loan pact, negotiated by U Nu, but one-fourth of all foreign loans contained in the 1965-1966 budget were from Japan. Ne Win visited the Soviet Union in 1965, but he also visited India and Pakistan—and in 1966 he travelled to the United States. The Burmese soldier-leader also continued to pursue policies supporting general and nuclear disarmament, a "Geneva-type" settlement of the Vietnamese problem, and reconciliation of feuding Indonesia and Malaysia. Burma and the United States signed an agreement for American financing of construction of a modern teak mill, but relations between Washington and Rangoon remained cool.

All of this notwithstanding, however, there have still been changes—important ones—in Burma's approach to the outside world. In the middle 1950s Rangoon was a major cosmopolitan center in Southeast Asia—with international meetings, foreign experts in large numbers, and such—despite its comparatively primitive living and other accommodations. Today it is probably more difficult to enter Burma—and, more important, to stay even briefly—than all but the smallest handful of countries. Foreigners are not wanted anymore, as the ultranationalist Ne Win regime sees it. External influences, accordingly, affect Burma less directly than at any time since independence. Xenophobic considerations, resultingly, today dominate Burmese foreign policy to an unparalleled extent.

The consequences of Burmese neutralism, as currently expressed, are also of significance. As noted, Ne Win's neutralism is no more pro-Communist than was U Nu's. But Ne Win has diminished Western influence in his country to a post-1948 low, and this is exactly what Peking wants. China has types of influence which cannot be so easily reduced: its geographical nearness, its size, the Chinese minority in Burma, and the view in Rangoon that China is more capable and likely of ending Burmese independence than the United States. The result is that Burmese neutralism favors the

Communists—or, more specifically, China—more than it does the West or the United States. This is not Ne Win's seeming intent. It is, on the other hand, the apparent result of his policies. And in this case results are probably more important than intent.

CHAPTER 9

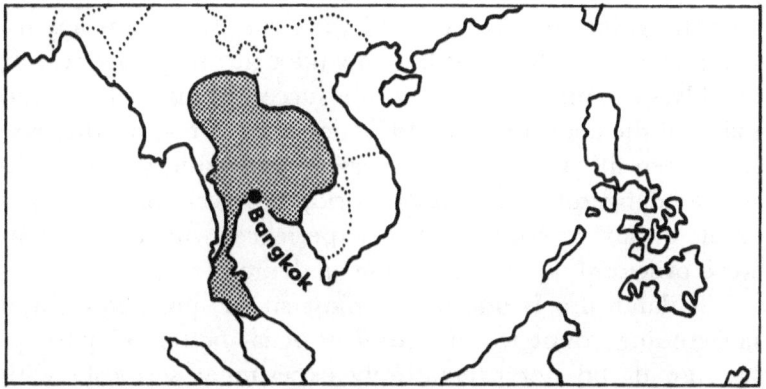

THAILAND
Soldiers in the Saddle

THAILAND IS THE ONLY Southeast Asian country that never has lost its independence to a Western colonial power. Partly as a consequence of this status unique in its part of the world, it experienced some of the same problems in the 1930s that other Southeast Asian nations were to encounter after the Second World War and the liquidation of the old imperial holdings. For example, soldiers played a part in making Thailand a nominally constitutional monarchy in 1932, and by 1938 the country had a fascistlike military dictator, perhaps farcically fascist, in the person of Field Marshal Phibun Songkhram. For more than thirty years now, soldiers have influenced—usually dominated—Thai politics. The military came to power in Thailand twenty years before the soldiers took over from the civilians in Burma—and probably for some of the same reasons.

Today Thailand is a firm ally of the United States in the complicated power relationships of Southeast Asia in particular and the Far East in general. But Thailand was once a neutral country—perhaps the first "neutralist," so to speak, playing off one great power against the other (first the British against the French and then the Europeans against the Japanese). The Thai have abandoned this policy, which, frankly speaking, was remarkably successful and achieved as many of the country's foreign policy aims as might otherwise have been filled. Thailand's present leadership sees neutralism as dangerous in today's world, however—perhaps as a result of having gone through experiences which states that were previously colonies did not undergo.

Thailand also is one of the most stable, prosperous, and law-abiding countries in Southeast Asia—better off perhaps because it did not prematurely experiment seriously with democratic and other political and social ideas that were not immediately relevant, at least in the past, to its particular level of development. Other states of Southeast Asia may learn from the Thai, who have made their share of mistakes through the years, although Thailand's experiences may be so unique that they are not applicable to the rest of present-day Southeast Asia.

BEFORE MODERNIZATION

The Thai, descended from an ethnic group closely related to the Chinese, lived first in south China and then migrated, forced by the pressure of the expanding Chinese, into mainland Southeast Asia. The first important Thai kingdom in Southeast Asia, which thrived in the thirteenth and fourteenth centuries, was located at Sukhothai. Celebrated in Thai literature and folklore as a kind of golden age, a second kingdom at Ayutthaya, north of the present capital city of Bangkok, lasted from the mid-fourteenth through the mid-eighteenth centuries. Bangkok became the capital of the

Thai kingdom only in 1782, on the eve of the expansion of contacts between the Europeans and Thailand. Although the Thai accepted Chinese suzerainty, they also repeatedly asserted their independence, an attitude they continue to display down to the present time. The Thai have equally repeatedly tried to conquer neighboring peoples, especially the Shans (of present-day Burma) and the Laotians, who are racially closely related to them. Cambodia accepted French protection, which became *de facto* French colonialism, in the nineteenth century primarily as a consequence of a fear of absorption by the expanding Thai.

Burma was probably Thailand's most important traditional rival, and it was the sacking and burning of Ayutthaya by the Burmese that led to the establishment of the present Thai dynasty, of which King Phumiphon Adunyadet is the ninth of the line, in Bangkok. The Thai king was an absolute monarch. He was a figure apart from, and above, his people—who rarely saw him, even those of his subjects who lived in the capital city of Bangkok. The king spent most of his time in his magnificent palace, and the gap between himself and his advisers, on the one hand, and the people they ruled, on the other, was tremendous. This gap, however, had a function. It seemed to justify the king's position; he was something above and beyond ordinary mortals. He was in fact a god-king after the Hindu-Buddhist model (found also in historic Burma and Cambodia). The king was at the heart of Thai life as the holy mountain was at the center of Indian cosmology, from which the Thai replica was drawn. The king's temporal and spiritual authority was to be seen in his ownership of all land and his direction of the affairs of the kingdom's Buddhist clergy.

The Thai king was absolute in theory and more absolute in practice than most of the other kings, sultans, and chieftains of Southeast Asia. But even Thai royal absolutism knew limits—limits imposed by geography and limits inherent in the human circumstance of a bureaucracy through which royal ideas and demands had to filter. The fact remains, however, that autocracy was the traditional Thai type of government and that Thailand, unlike the other countries of Southeast Asia, was not exposed to even the limited parliamentarianism that existed elsewhere under European colonial rule. Colonial governors were also autocratic, of course (certainly in theory if not always in practice in the case of particular individuals). But nationalists fighting against colonial rule sought legislative institutions— partly because of the inspiration of the domestic democratic model of the ruling power but also because of the opportunity this would allow indigenous elements to challenge the imposed external authority. In Thailand there was no imposed external authority to challenge, and so the tradition of authoritarian rule was less diluted by this type of experience.

Like other Southeast Asian societies, such as the Philippines, premodern Thailand was characterized by a distinction between freemen and slaves. Perhaps as many as one out of three Thai might be regarded as a slave. Even the freemen had his restricted place in the traditional Thai hierachy, however, and freemen could become slaves and slaves could become free—with the result that the distinction between the two groups was less sharp in practice than was conventionally the case.

Thailand on the eve of the Western intrusion, which affected the country even if not in the form of colonial rule, was a much more integrated society than most of the other Southeast Asian lands. The Chinese had already begun to migrate to the country, but the numbers involved were to increase in the years ahead. Thai absorption of Malays in the peninsular south was incomplete, but there was not then a united Malaya and no effective disintegrating counterpull. Thai unity at the time of the coming of the European was probably most fortunate in terms of the survival of the country as a free land.

Thailand

INDEPENDENCE RETAINED

During the second half of the nineteenth century, when a recrudescence of Western imperialism threatened the independence of Thailand (then known as Siam), the country was fortunate in having very able kings in Mongkut (1851-1868) and Chulalongkorn (1868-1910). King Mongkut opened his country to Western influence by signing a treaty of friendship and commerce with Britain in 1855. Similar treaties were negotiated with the United States and France in 1856 and with a number of other European countries in the next few years. Mongkut saw the need of modernizing his administration if his country were not to fall victim to Western imperialism. He brought in Westerners as teachers and advisers, who in many cases actually served as department heads. Most of his advisers were retired British officials from India and Burma, but he was careful to avoid getting too many from any one country. Belgians, Danes, Dutch, Italians, and Americans served in this capacity.

King Chulalongkorn was a progressive and reformer like his father. He abolished slavery, ended the practice of prostration in the royal presence, set up schools for the education of the children of the nobility, modernized the postal system, and reformed provincial administration and the administration of justice. The king traveled extensively and sent young aristocrats abroad for study.

The fact that Thailand alone escaped becoming a Western colony in Southeast Asia can be explained in part by the desire of both Britain and France for a buffer state between their respective territories, Burma and Indochina, in the region. Nevertheless, the story might have been different if the Thai had not displayed a remarkable cleverness in diplomacy. France put heavy pressure on Thailand to renounce control over Laos and the provinces of Battambang and Siemriep, which had once belonged to Cambodia. In 1883 the French blockaded Bangkok, after which the Thai yielded to most of their demands. Other concessions were made in 1904 and 1907. Thailand succeeded in retaining its independence from Western colonialism, but only at the cost of 90,000 square miles of its territory, including relinquishment of its hold over the northernmost states of what was quickly becoming British Malaya.

Thailand emerged from its diplomatic defense with a territory of nearly 200,000 square miles, its size today. A small strip of Burmese and Laotian territory separates Thailand from China in the north; in the south its territory extends almost two-thirds down the Malay Peninsula. Northern Thailand is mountainous, and the eastern part of the country is an infertile plateau. The large alluvial plain and rich delta of the Chao Phraya River constitutes the heart of the country. The population of Thailand, which is more homogeneous than that of Burma but less so than that of Cambodia, numbers about 25,000,000 and includes about 800,000 Malays in the south, 3,000,000 persons of Chinese ancestry, and, perhaps most troublesome of all despite their modest number, some 40,000 Vietnamese located in the northeastern portion of the country across the Mekong River from heavily Communist-infiltrated Laos. Repatriation of such Vietnamese to North Vietnam—the desired destination of a majority of these refugees from the Franco-Vietnamese colonial-civil war of 1946-1954—ceased in 1964 following the Gulf of Tonkin naval incident between the North Vietnamese and the Americans. Hanoi claimed that the shipping lanes were no longer safe.

THE 1932 COUP, PHIBUN, AND THE WAR

Until 1932 the government of Thailand was an absolute monarchy with official positions a practical monopoly of members of the numerous Thai noble families. Discontented young intellectuals joined leaders of the armed forces in that year in a bloodless revolution which ushered in a nominally constitutional monarchy. The political history of the country since then has been one of coup and counter-coup—some successful, more abortive. Constitution has followed constitution accordingly, but most of the time the government has been a thinly veiled, if fairly benevolent, dictatorship. Forces favoring the development of democratic political forms have tried again and again to assert themselves, but these have been thwarted by a combination of an initially rising and now entrenched military elite, an external threat (not always the same one!), and the apparent general unreadiness of the country for democracy—at least until the present time.

The political life of Thailand in the eighteen or so years which followed the first coup largely centered around the rivalry between two personalities: the soldier Phibun Songkhram and the lawyer-teacher Pridi Banomyong, both French-educated and exposed to liberal ideas incompatible with the values underlying the monarchy as it had existed. Pridi, the chief intellectual force behind the 1932 coup, shortly thereafter drafted a national economic plan that was clearly influenced by Soviet communism, though Pridi himself was unquestionably not a Communist. There was a strong reaction against the plan, and Pridi went into voluntary exile abroad. He subsequently returned to Thailand, was cleared of the charge of being a Communist, and quickly recovered much of his former political influence. Pridi still lost, however, in the struggle for political supremacy to Phibun, who had the backing of the army—which had been instrumental in the 1932 coup and had subsequently increased in influence and sought a more directly political role for itself. Phibun, who had acquired a favorable reputation by reestablishing order after an abortive proroyalist attempt to regain control of the government in 1933, became prime minister in 1938.

The constitution that had followed the coup of 1932 was a peculiarly democratic one. Taking real power from the previously absolute monarch, it vested public authority in a cabinet responsible to a single-house legislature. Initially, however, half of this parliament was to be appointed by the government, that is, the premier and the other ministers. The whole parliament was to be elected in ten years—or earlier, if half the eligible voters completed four years of school before that time. It was Thailand's first step toward democracy, and it was a grudging step. Intentionally or not, effective control of the government remained in the hands of the executive, royal or otherwise.

Although nominally a constitutional, semiparliamentary monarchy, the government of Phibun after 1938 was actually a dictatorship. A large number of the appointed members of the legislature and of the ministers were army or police officers, and officers of the armed services held the chief positions in the civil service. The press was rigidly controlled. Just enough debate was permitted in the legislature to create the impression that democracy was in the process of becoming in Thailand. In actuality, however, Thailand in the late 1930s was more akin to what was to happen a couple of decades later when the military assumed unprecedented importance in such other Southeast Asian states as Burma, Indonesia, Laos, and South Vietnam. The circumstances of the later emergence of the military as an important political force in these other countries may have differed, but the fact remains that the army gained unparalleled general significance in several Southeast Asian nations at roughly the same point in their political development.

As the Phibun government became increasingly fascist in character, its policy became more and more pro-Japanese. Under Japanese aegis it succeeded in obtaining the cession of a considerable area from Indochina, and with Japanese consent it annexed four Malay states and two Shan states from Burma. Thailand offered only token resistance to the Japanese when they demanded a military right of way through the country for their land attack on Malaya and Burma. A few days later Phibun entered into an alliance

Thailand 287

with Japan and shortly thereafter declared war on the United States and Britain. The British answered in kind, but the American government chose to ignore the Thai declaration of war and to treat Thailand as a victim of Japan. Phibun and his Thai political associates have been criticized abroad for their alleged collaboration with the Japanese, but the question should be raised as to the available alternatives. Neither America nor Britain was in position to defend Thailand. The responsibility of the Thai leadership was to the Thai people, and Thailand suffered less from the Second World War than any other Southeast Asian country.

During the war, however, some Thai did cooperate with the Allies. A Free Thai movement was organized among the few Thai abroad, which with the help of the United States and Britain gave aid to an underground resistance movement which was led by Phibun's longtime chief rival, Pridi. In August 1944, when Japanese troops were still in the country, Phibun's regime was overthrown, and a new government, secretly sympathetic with the Free Thai, came to power. Immediately after the collapse of the Japanese war effort, the Thai government issued a "peace declaration" in which the declaration of war against the United States and Britain was proclaimed null and void because it was made against the will of the Thai people. Seni Pramoj, minister to the United States and organizer of the Free Thai abroad, became prime minister, and a new, more democratic constitution was adopted. Phibun was arrested as a war criminal but was released after spending a few months in jail.

A satisfactory interpretation of these events is difficult. However the personal conduct of Phibun during the war might be evaluated, it would still appear that in the Second World War the Thai once again outwitted the great powers. With the Phibun government allied with Japan and the Free Thai cooperating with the United States and the other anti-Axis nations, Thailand could not lose—no matter how the war ended. After the war the United States obligingly intervened on behalf of the Thai with Britain, which did not feel kindly disposed toward Thailand, which, because of its collaboration with Japan, had contributed to British woes in Malaya. Malaya was badly in need of rice, and the British thought it not unreasonable to demand that Thailand contribute its surplus of that commodity. The British were outmaneuvered; Thailand got off very lightly in spite of its declaration of war on the Allies. There were rumors in Thailand, indeed, that the struggle between Phibun and Pridi was mere show and that they were actually in collusion. Such a policy of diplomatic reinsurance did not seem at all unreasonable to the Thai mentality—though such was probably not the case in actuality.

RETURN OF PHIBUN

Democracy's prospects seemed on the surface to receive a boost in 1946 with fully free voting to a wholly elected lower house of a bicameral legislature established under a new constitution promulgated the same year. The second chamber was elected by the members of the lower house, so that even it had popular roots. Pridi Banomyong, who was the logical person to head the government after the overthrow of Phibun but had not done so, became premier, supported by a substantial legislative majority. On June 9, less than three months after Pridi assumed the premiership, King Mahidol was found shot in his bed. Pridi's name became associated with the death of the king as a result of widespread rumors, the origin of which was not clear. The pressure became too great for Pridi, and he resigned in August 1946 (although he remained the power behind the scenes).

On November 8, 1947, the leaders of the armed forces overthrew the civilian government in the third successful coup since 1932. Pridi fled into exile, and Phibun, one of the members of the "Coup Group" (as it was called) which

Thailand

executed the November takeover, became prime minister five months later. The man who had declared war on the United States and Britain as an ally of Japan once again headed the Thai government. Pridi's and other forces tried unsuccessfully to overthrow the Phibun regime in a series of abortive coups in the unstable three-year period that followed Phibun's return to office.

In 1951 democracy's prospects in Thailand were further dimmed by the abrogation of the new constitution promulgated in 1949. Formulation of this document had begun before the military takeover, and the Coup Group allowed its proclamation but soon became disenchanted with the way the legislature behaved. The lower house was directly elected as under the 1946 basic law, but the upper chamber was nominated by the king—which marked the beginning of the return to political importance of the Thai monarch. This two-house legislature was replaced in 1951 by a unicameral one comprising 132 appointed members and 132 elected ones, the same situation as had existed under the 1932 constitution. In the elections of February 1952 approximately thirty opposition candidates won seats—hardly the stuff out of which vigorous opposition to the Coup Group could be formed. Twenty years after the first coup Thailand was no further along the path to democratic government institutionally.

A subsequent so-called democratization drive of Phibun seemed to be moving toward fulfillment with the announcement in November 1956 that the cabinet had accepted the prime minister's proposal for the elimination of "second category," or appointed, members of the legislature. Phibun's constitutional changes would also have made the parliament bicameral again (but these alterations were not to become effective until after the February 1957 election of half the membership of the otherwise appointed existing legislature). Elections to replace the appointed legislators under the new constitution were scheduled for May 1957, but these were never held. It has never been made clear why all the members could not have been elected in February.

Phibun was by no means the master of his government between 1948 and 1957 as he had been during his early premiership. The country was in effect ruled by the inner circle of the Coup Group, the body of senior officers who staged the 1947 coup, and Phibun's was only one of several important voices—probably the most important but not dominant. Political power at the center of the Thai government was shared by four men during these years, and their jockeying for supremacy constituted whatever competitiveness the Thai political process possessed. These men, in the order of their importance, were Phibun, no longer the dictatorial military figure that he once was but now a canny and effective politician; ambitious Police Director General Phao Sriyanon, the youngest of the four and head of a pseudomilitary organization that veritably rivaled the army; General (later Field Marshal) Sarit Thanarat, the army's commander in chief; and Field Marshal Phin Chunhawan, Phao's father-in-law, Sarit's predecessor as head of the army, and a decreasingly important figure because of his advanced age. Phao and Sarit so increased their strength between 1950 and 1957 that Phibun appeared to survive as premier only because he was able to maintain a balance between the two chief factions seeking to succeed to his authority.

It was during the later portion of these years that Phibun sought to introduce various democratic procedures into the Thai political process. His efforts were apparently sincere, the result perhaps of his impressions on visits to Britain and America and the reflection of his desire to go down in Thai history as the man who started democracy on its way in his country. On the other hand, Phibun might have been trying to mobilize mass opinion against Phao in particular—whom he apparently regarded as the chief threat to himself. Be all this as it may, Phibun established a Thai "Hyde Park" for

Thailand 291

soapbox public political oratory and adopted a most permissive attitude toward press criticism.

The February 1957 election, partly because of this greatly liberalized political environment, turned out to be more hectic than Phibun probably expected. The government party won a narrow victory amid charges of widespread corruption. Charges of irregularities in the Bangkok voting resulted in demonstrations by students and the now aroused political opposition, and a state of national emergency was declared March 2. Army head Sarit was named commander of all Thailand's military forces, including the national police, headed by his chief rival, Phao.

THE EMERGENCE OF SARIT

Sarit, addressing demonstrating students the day the state of emergency was declared, told them that the election was "completely dirty from all sides." This was an unusual position for a spokesman of the government to take and was the first major open sign of Sarit's bid for power. Although he was a ranking member of the ruling Coup Group, Sarit (unlike Phao and, of course, Phibun) had taken no part in the government party's bid for victory in the February voting. In fact, it was a Sarit supporter who first suggested impending irregularities on the eve of the balloting.

Jockeying for power of the sort that had characterized the preceding years followed the February election and disturbances, but Phibun and Phao were clearly losing. On September 16 Sarit struck, staging a lightninglike coup and dissolving the legislature and throwing out the constitution. The conventional Thai way of changing governments had once more expressed itself, and again it was neither constitutional nor democratic.

Elections were held in December—ostensibly to right the wrongs inherent in the irregularities in the February voting. The results were a foregone conclusion, however, and pro-

Sarit elements triumphed. Sarit, an extremely sick man, then departed the country, leaving his chief army deputy, General Thanom Kittikachon, in charge as prime minister. The problems, political as well as financial, were too much for Thanom, however, and a miraculously improved Sarit returned in October 1958 to seize control of the government again—in effect staging a coup against himself. Sarit proclaimed his second takeover a "revolution" and pledged himself to a program of reform and rejuvenation. Many Thai shook their heads at the words of the hard-drinking, high-living, self-indulgent military leader. They were words, they said, only words.

The Sarit era lasted five years and surprised practically everyone who had ever known the rough military leader. Sarit, who died in 1963 at the age of 55 as a result of years of prolonged dissipation, profited more than any contemporary Thai leader in terms of the size of the private fortune he amassed. But he also gave Thailand the most purposeful political leadership it had known since the great Kings Mongkut and Chulalongkorn. The civil service was mobilized as never before to execute a wide range of impressive development programs. The Thai government displayed unprecedented efficiency as Sarit instilled a new spirit of identification with the policymaking arm of government on the part of the administrative services. Power was increasingly centralized under Sarit, but the impact of the Bangkok government began to be felt in a meaningful fashion in the more distant countryside as well as in Bangkok, Chiengmai, and the other cities and areas adjacent to them. Sarit consulted regularly with the king, young Phumiphon, and the political stock of the royalists rose perceptibly. Phumiphon and his beautiful wife, Sirikit, traveled widely both within and outside Thailand and became an increasingly important domestic symbol of loyalty to the Thai state. Sarit's "revolution" was new in various major ways, but it also stressed

Thailand

important traditional institutions, such as the monarchy, and traditional values, such as Buddhism.

The Sarit years were also the most prosperous ones Thailand has ever known. The development plan adopted in 1960 resulted in major advances in the important fields of communications, transportation, power, and irrigation. Foreign investment, both public and private, flowed into the country despite the troubles in adjacent Laos and not so distant Vietnam. The stability of the Sarit era provided the kind of climate in which private foreign firms felt that they could invest in confidence. The government obligingly assisted with various sorts of incentives. Domestic capital also was effectively mobilized to contribute to the economic modernization of Thailand and to the uplift of its standard of living. Profitmaking was substantial, as might be expected in such boom circumstances, but corruption—Sarit's own record personal aggrandizement notwithstanding—was apparently less harmful to national development than previously, even if it continued to exist at a quite high level. The capital city of Bangkok seemed to change in appearance almost with each passing day as it moved toward becoming a modern industrial metropolis. A new university was begun in the key northern city of Chiengmai, the first such institution of higher learning outside Bangkok. Schools were built throughout the country, and a seven-year compulsory education program started. Thailand was changing under Sarit's leadership, and the change was increasingly being felt beyond the limits of the nation's capital.

The political change was in the new emphasis on good and competent government, which brought the regime the support of both the bureaucracy and the royalists. Together with the army, personally loyal to Sarit and very much the beneficiary of his financial favor, this gave the regime backing unparalleled for a government since the original 1932 coup. If there was stability and efficiency, however, there was also arbitrariness unprecedented in recent Thai history. Suspected Communists and arsonists, for example, were summarily shot. Unlicensed street stalls were rudely dismantled by police on orders from Sarit—after warnings to their owners to remove them were ignored—because Sarit had decided that the stalls were an eyesore and had to be replaced. The Thai leader behaved equally arbitrarily toward the elimination of pedicabs, bicycle-driven sidecars, from Bangkok's streets—probably a necessary move in view of the large increase in the number of automobiles in the capital city but an action taken without real concern for the welfare of the poor men who made their meager living pedaling such vehicles.

Sarit's concept of the modernization of Thailand was one of economic and technical modernization—not political modernization. Thailand's was an increasingly educated and potentially articulate population under Sarit, but no effort was made to allow the populace to have even an indirect voice in selection of the country's officials or the formation of public policy. An interim constitution was proclaimed in 1959 to replace the one overthrown in Sarit's second coup of October 1958. An appointed assembly was established in conformity with this constitution and was possessed of the dual duties of legislating and drafting a permanent constitution. The legislative function was not independently discharged, however, the assembly being more of a rubber stamp possibly than any such institution anywhere in the world. The task of constitution-making was no less freely pursued, Sarit having told the drafters of the document what they were to include in it. The draft as it progressed during Sarit's time bore the obvious imprint of the constitutions of Charles de Gaulle's France and, to a lesser extent, of Ayub Khan's Pakistan. The form of government would be presidential, and at one point it was indicated that the legislature would lack even the power to initiate bills. The constitution could easily have been completed long before Sarit's death, but this was not done—possibly partly as a reflection of the troubled international situation involving neighboring Laos and the internal manifestation of this in the proclaimed subversive threat in the underprivileged northeastern part of the country in which lives one-quarter of Thailand's population.

The late Sarit Thanarat was no democrat—quite clearly. Nor did he apparently advance the day when Thailand might become democratic except in the sense that various of his policies, such as in the fields of education and communications, may well have laid the groundwork for a more politically liberal Thailand tomorrow. Sarit was a military despot, however good a leader otherwise. Yet at the same time he was popular with his people. Like the attractive young king and queen, he traveled widely throughout the country, including the troubled and previously neglected northeast, from which he himself came. Neither Phibun nor Pridi, let alone any other past leader (least of all the murderous onetime national police chief, Phao), ever enjoyed such national backing. If Sarit was not a democrat, the masses of his countrymen, who had never known democracy anyway, could not have appeared to have cared less.

The apparent lack of opposition to Sarit—dissatisfaction with his policies or the way in which he ran his government—is the chief problem in gauging his regime in Thailand from 1958 through 1963. Since his death the personal fortune he acquired has been reviled by some of the same men who worked so closely with him (after the fashion of the criticism of Stalin by Khrushchev, who denounced the man under whom he rose to influence). But no one spoke out against Sarit when he lived. Nor did anyone denounce military dominance of almost all phases of Thai national life, including the economy, though it was obvious that many resented this state of affairs. The Sarit regime accomplished much good; it may have been the best possible government for Thailand at the time. But the natural interests of key sectors of the society were not able to express themselves, and this is never a healthy state of affairs.

AFTER SARIT

Sarit Thanarat was succeeded upon his death by his longtime and faithful deputy, habitually smiling Field Marshal Thanom Kittikachon—the same Thanom who proved unable to keep the political shop under control when Sarit was abroad for medical treatment in 1957-1958. There was widespread expectation accordingly that Thanom would be only an interim successor to strongman Sarit. General Praphas Charusathien, who became Thanom's deputy prime minister and minister of interior, was tabbed as a tougher personality who would quickly unseat his chief and take over the government after the fashion of Phibun in the thirties and Sarit in the 1950s. But two years later Thanom was still premier, and there was no reason to expect him not to continue to retain his office.

In many respects politics and policies, especially the latter, remained much the same after Sarit's death as during his lifetime. Economic production continued to increase at a rate of 6.5 percent under the Thanom regime; savings also remained high, half as much again what they were under the government of Phibun and the Coup Group in the 1950s. Perhaps the difference in Thanom's performance since 1963 and in 1957-1958 is to be found in the fact that he inherited some very serious financial difficulties from the Phibun regime when he first served as premier, while the policies of the late Field Marshal Sarit were, for the most part, successful ones—and Thanom has merely continued these. In addition, Thanom has grown in competence with the years.

The politics of Thailand, on the other hand, have undergone some change, however slight, since Sarit's demise. For one thing, Thanom, for all his competence, is not the all-

Thailand

Whether the Communist threat to Thailand increases in the immediate future depends in large measure on the government's response. If it is no better than was that of the late President Ngo Dinh Diem in South Vietnam, the future could be bleak. Chinese Communist Foreign Minister Chen Yi stated in 1965 that "we may have a guerrilla war going in Thailand before the year is out." The year passed without such a war, but the preparations were evident. Some compared the situation to the state of affairs in South Vietnam in 1958. A large number of assassinations of rural officials, particularly in the border regions, gave particular cause for alarm to the Thai leadership in 1965; the parallel with South Vietnam a couple of years earlier was just too striking. The assassinations were partly a reflection of Thai security, however, for in such areas it is practically nonexistent. Efforts to increase the size of the provincial police by about 25 percent are underway with American help.

The year 1966 began ominously in northeastern Thailand. Thirty major incidents of terrorism took place in the first three months of the year—double the number of the last quarter of 1965. More than 50 terrorists were killed, and six times as many more captured, in the first quarter of 1966 as the Thai army moved units into the region to man joint military police-civilian command posts. Was the fight for the Thai northeast escalating? Was Thailand moving in the direction of becoming a "second Vietnam"? The nation's leaders appeared to believe that this was it—Thailand's greatest challenge since the Japanese demand to pass through the country in December 1941.

Viewed from some perspectives, Thailand is very vulnerable to the Communist challenge. From other angles, however, it would seem able to withstand the threat. Premier Thanom, for example, is giving his country extremely competent leadership. The long-forecast showdown between Thanom and Praphas has yet to come. Indeed, the two men seem to work extremely well together. Thanom, far more than Sarit before him, realizes the importance of representative government and genuinely wishes to hold early elections. The government has embarked on a vigorous program of economic development and social assistance in the long-neglected northeastern area of the country and elsewhere. The peasantry is probably among the least discontented in mainland Southeast Asia. Communist infiltration among the students is believed to be less than in most of the Southeast Asian countries.

Premier Thanom has stated that he will not play a political role when the new constitution is promulgated and elections held, unless the people demand his services. Burma's General Ne Win quit being premier once, only to return again less than two years later. Thanom might have to do the same thing, too—or Praphas. Thai civilian politicians are even fewer in number—and less experienced—than Burma's. It might be wise if their effective political role were gradually increased.

THE THAI POLITICAL PROCESS

Depending on the criteria employed to define a coup attempt, Thailand has had from a dozen to twenty-seven would-be government takeovers in the years since the revolt that toppled the absolute monarchy in 1932. Only four of these have been successful (excluding the late Premier Sarit's ouster of his personally selected protege Thanom in 1958, truly a coup against himself). Since Sarit's second takeover of October 1958, however, Thai politics have been fairly stable. Thanom, for example, did not come to power by a military takeover; he succeeded to Sarit's office both because he was deputy premier and because he was widely known to be the handpicked heir-apparent of Sarit. The years since Sarit's second coup may seem comparatively few in number by the standards of some political systems, but they represent an unparalleled accomplishment in the Thai context. On the other hand, many of the coup attempts through the years have stood virtually no chance of success and accordingly have caused hardly a political ripple when they have occurred.

This having been said, the fact remains that it is two decades now since a Thai premier came to office by virtue of election. The Coup Group seized power in 1947, and that was the end of Thailand's brief flirtation with representative government. The almost exclusive means to political predominance in Thailand during the last quarter of a century has been military force. Phibun and Sarit, the two chief figures who dominated these years, both came to power by this means. It can in fact be said that, based on past behavior, a military career is the route to high office, power, and wealth. For high office brings with it wealth in Thailand, as the late Marshal Sarit so lavishly revealed.

During the greater part of the post-1932 period Thailand's leaders have been of two types: those who had a strong following of loyal military supporters, which was basically their means to power in the first place, and those who survived because there was no one who could successfully challenge them at the moment. Phibun came to power in 1938 because of his army support, which was to a major extent personal; his return to office in 1948 was partly a reflection of such strength, but it existed in a much lesser amount than previously and ebbed proportionately as both the army and national police increased in size with the attendant growth in supporters for army chief Sarit and police head Phao. Sarit clearly gained his strength from his personal following within the armed forces. Thanom, on the other hand, continues to hold office today in part because Praphas, whose hold over sections of the armed forces is doubtful, feels unable to move against him. Phibun survived as long as he did in 1948-1957 because Sarit and Phao cancelled out one another.

The military strongman—and both Sarit and Phibun were

this in their heyday and even Thanom today—has come to play the role he has in Thai politics because of the underdeveloped nature of the Thai political system. Thailand has never evolved effective political parties or modern interest groups, such as trade unions. Thai politics are still very much elitist, with the number of real participants comparatively few in number. This is not to say that there are not real interests with a stake in public policy decisions in Thailand. These there surely are, but they are of a different sort from those to be found in North America or Western Europe or even the Philippines and Malaysia. Thai interests tend to be of two sorts primarily: those identified with the economic holdings of different members of the ruling group and those associated with the traditional activities of the different sectors of the bureaucracy. The Thai civil service makes strong demands on the policy arm of government for support of particular goals, and these are generally successful —if they do not run counter to the claims of the political-military leadership—because of the absence of competing demands from outside the governmental structure.

It is probably not accurate to say that there have not been any other interests; rather the situation is that such interests have not been effectively or strongly enough expressed, so that they have not drawn sufficient support from the leadership group. This has been particularly true in the past of the demands from the poor and underdeveloped northeastern part of the country and the peninsular Malay minority. The demands of the northeast are being heard today not because the system has improved but because the leadership group is running scared in light of the known subversive threat in that part of the land.

The absence of competing foci of power accounts for persisting executive dominance over the legislature through the years. Legislatures have generally declined in importance in the developing countries in recent years, but in Thailand's case the parliament never was important. The fact is that the military has dominated the executive for the greater part of a quarter of a century now, and there has been little that civilian legislators—and military elements have also held more than their share of legislative seats—could do about it.

That the Thai have not come up with an adequate formula for changing governments is a definite weakness of the system. The fact that Thanom succeeded Sarit peacefully should not be taken to mean that the system has finally found an answer to this problem; it has not done so. The new constitution, when promulgated, will not be an answer in itself either. All the past coups took place within the framework of existing constitutions. It has not been the coups themselves that have been the source of instability, however, but rather the jockeying for power that preceded them, such as the contest between Sarit and Phao between 1950 and 1957.

Change of one kind is immediately imminent in all probability. That is, it is only a matter of time until the new constitution is unveiled, unless Premier Thanom is ousted from office or there is a marked deterioration in the internal security situation. This constitution will permit the holding of the first elections in more than eight years. The type of political alignment that emerges from such a vote could be decisive in determining the degree of the future popularization of Thai politics.

Constitutional change, however, will not in itself amount to much if it is not accompanied by changes in the kind of personnel who participate in politics in Thailand. The last decade has seen a tremendous expansion in the numbers of younger men who have gone into careers other than the military or the bureaucracy, such as banking or other businesses. These men represent some of the better educated and more intelligent elements in the population. They also reflect important, if emergent, economic interests—part of the new Thailand that Sarit sought to develop. These men could constitute the nucleus of a new power factor in Thai politics.

There is also restlessness in the land caused in part by the dissatisfaction of growing numbers of young men and women who graduate from the universities and find themselves disgusted with the behavior, including the greedy habits, of their nation's leaders. The present Thai political system, altered though it may have been by Sarit and Thanom, came into being in a quite different age in Thailand's political evolution. It is somewhat of an anachronism today. It seems stable enough on the surface, and it may never be overthrown by revolutionary means. But it will probably be changed, hopefully peacefully.

POLITICS AND ECONOMICS

Politics and economics are interrelated in at least two ways in Thailand. The first and most obvious of these is the manner in which in the past the top Thai political leaders, who have also been the country's major military figures, have served as directors of key economic enterprises and operated economic monopolies—authorized by the state—for their own profit. The exposure of the immense personal fortune amassed by the late Premier Sarit (in excess of $25,000,000) has done much to call attention to Thailand's perennial problem of political profit at the public expense. Sarit's successor, Thanom, has tried to crack down on corruption, symbolically resigning his own post as chairman of the Golden Peninsula Development Company, bidder for important government projects. But such corruption has performed an important function in Thai politics over the years and cannot easily be eliminated. It has not only been an incentive for men to seek high position but a chief means by which they have rewarded those who have helped them to advance. Thanom seems to have made some progress in his efforts, but the job ahead is still a big one. The high living of the political-military leaders of the country, moreover, cannot help but increasingly arouse the general population of the country as it becomes aware of the dimensions of the difference in living standards of the elite and itself.

This problem, however, is more easily correctable than another. This is the race between population increase and economic growth. Thailand has been traditionally pictured as a pleasant, happy-go-lucky country where everybody has enough to eat, this being offered as a partial explanation for the alleged Thai lack of interest in politics. The country has been called "underpopulated"—which may have been so once upon a time in terms of past popular expectations but certainly is not true today. The natural rate of population increase in Thailand is 3 percent a year, which means that there could be as many as 45,000,000 Thai by the mid-1980s as contrasted with the present 25,000,000. Almost half of these will be under 15 years of age. The big question is whether economic growth and per capita income in particular can grow sufficiently to keep pace with the mounting expectations of the Thai peasant, who probably will know more rather than less in the future about how his rulers live.

This is not to say that Thai economic growth has not been impressive. Thailand's is a booming economy and presents a marked—and happy—contrast to the likes of Indonesia and Burma. National income, which increased at an average rate of 5.3 percent in the decade of the fifties, has more recently grown to nearly 7 percent a year. The relative importance of agriculture in the gross national product, the sum of all goods and services produced in the nation, declined, however, from about 50 percent to roughly one-third between 1951 and 1963. The rate of growth of the agricultural sector, not surprisingly, has been a modest 3 percent in recent years, a circumstance which takes its importance from the fact that four out of five Thai are farmers and are increasingly the objective of subversive efforts as Thailand's

Communists seemingly shift the emphasis of their agitation (after the pattern of both China and Vietnam) away from the city to the countryside. This is what gives the present economic situation in Thailand its tremendous political importance.

The government under both Sarit and Thanom has tried to deal effectively with the problem. The second phase of the National Economic Development Plan commenced in 1964, a phase that is to carry the nation through 1966. The biggest growth was expected to be in transportation and communications, where planned expansion was pegged at a high 10 percent a year. This will provide the vital infrastructure that will allow free enterprise and peasant initiative to supplement the already considerable development efforts of the government. The 1966 budget was the biggest in Thailand's history—16 percent above 1965. Almost one-third of the increase went to the ministry of national development; education expenditures rose 14 percent. Even more important, the government has set up special committees to deal with the problem of economic development in the poorer border regions. There are committees dealing especially with the development needs of the north, northeast, and south—headed, respectively, by Premier Thanom himself, Minister of Interior Praphas, and Thailand's extremely able Foreign Minister Thanat Khoman, who may also be a political figure to watch domestically in the years ahead.

MINORITIES AND NATIONAL INTEGRATION

Several countries in Southeast Asia today became nations politically in the sense of having national governments and gaining international recognition before they were nations socially. That is to say, their inhabitants did not think of themselves primarily as a single people—such as Burmese or Indonesians. This is not so on the whole for Thailand, where approximately 85 percent of the country's population are Thai ethnically, representing a blend of the original Thai stock of southwest China and the peoples the migrating Thai encountered as they moved southward into their present location. The Thai largely inhabit the heartland of the country and may possibly regard themselves more as Thai today than ever before.

Thailand's minority problems are primarily the Chinese, and the peoples living in the border regions. The largest single minority is the Chinese, who number about three million in the country as a whole and perhaps as many as one million in Bangkok, making the Thai capital city second only to predominantly Chinese Singapore as a Chinese-populated urban area in Southeast Asia today. Industrious and clannish, the Chinese have cornered major areas of Thai economic life despite government efforts to restrict their role in this respect. Immigration quotas have been in effect since 1948 in order to prevent the arrival of further Chinese, and Chinese children are required to attend public schools in order to learn the Thai language and develop a feeling of loyalty to Thailand.

The rise to power of the Chinese Communists in Peking in 1949 naturally stimulated Thai fears respecting the dangers to the state inherent in the presence of such a sizable minority which sought to retain its separate identity and which could not help but be angered by the efforts of former Premier Phibun in particular to curtail its economic activities. The Thai drive against the Chinese was the country's variation of the antiforeignism that expressed itself in Burma and Indonesia in wholesale nationalization of foreign economic holdings. Thailand was never a European colony, and so there was never the dominance of a single Western power over its economy. The Chinese were the functional equivalent of the European who kept the indigenous people from reaping the full benefits from their own country. The fears of the middle 1950s that Peking was increasing its control over Thailand's Chinese seem to have subsided in recent years. In Bangkok in particular there has been a rather large degree of assimilation, as witnessed by intermarriage, Chinese taking Thai names, and such. For the time being, the problem would not seem to be as serious as it was once thought to be. Potentially, however, it remains every bit as much a problem as ever. A minority of 3,000,000 in a population of 25,000,000 persons could be most threatening if Peking were to embark on a determined drive to exploit the maximum advantage out of this circumstance in its efforts to enlarge its influence in Southeast Asia.

The second largest minority in Thailand are the peninsular Malays, who number about 800,000. The four southernmost Thai provinces adjacent to Malaysia have large Malay majorities. These Malays speak Malay primarily and are Moslems rather than Buddhists like the majority Thai. They represent the legacy of past Thai imperialist efforts at the expense of the then weak Malay sultanates to Thailand's south. There is a sense of separatism—and a feeling of neglect—among Thailand's Malays, but this has not so far been politically important. But it could become so.

Another cause of anxiety to Thailand's leadership—and, like the Chinese, a source of Communist exploitation—are the approximately 40,000 Vietnamese refugees who inhabit the Thai side of the Mekong River which separates the country from neighboring Laos. Residents of Thailand since 1946, when they fled from the French who were then reoccupying Vietnam after the defeat of the Japanese, they are overwhelmingly Communist in their political orientation. Some of these Vietnamese even today display photographs of North Vietnamese Communist leader Ho Chi Minh in their homes. Similarly oriented are the previously mentioned leftbank Lao.

The Chinese are in many ways the most assimilated of these minorities; least so are the Vietnamese and the Lao. The Malays are a big question mark. As long as such

Thailand

minorities remain unassimilated, Thailand faces serious potential trouble and is resultingly a less strong nation.

THAILAND AND OTHER SOLDIER REGIMES

Thailand has a military-dominated government, and so has neighboring Burma and many of the other new states that have come to independence since the Second World War. Since these various countries are ruled by soldiers (or the military as a major influential political force), it is tempting to think of them as being similar. There are those, for example, who will say that the main difference between Thailand and Burma is 25 years—that is, that the Thai military came to power in the late thirties while Burma's soldiers did not take over their country's government until the 1960s. Nothing could be further from the truth.

Thailand's and Burma's are both modernizing regimes; this much is true. But Thailand's military government has long been much more like the soldier-dictators who dominated Latin American politics for so long. Neither Sarit nor Phibun could be likened to a Nasser or an Ayub Khan or a Ne Win. Both sought personal fortune as a result of their privileged political position, and the retinues of both were dominated by men who had strong vested interests in the perpetuation of major dimensions of the status quo (and were at best advocates of very much controlled change). The government of Burma, on the other hand, is a revolutionary regime dedicated specifically to overturning the existing order, as Nasser has tried to do in the United Arab Republic and Attaturk attempted in Turkey a generation ago. Admittedly Sarit showed strong reformist tendencies after his second coup of October 1958—and his immediately preceding close brush with death (probably a major reason for his subsequent political zeal). But even a reformed Sarit lined his pockets as no Thai leader had done previously. The old order is changing in Thailand, perhaps fairly quickly, but Thai soldiers still constitute a traditional military elite rather than modern military revolutionaries of the Burmese or Egyptian sort.

There is another very important difference between the Thai and Burmese situations. Burma's army ultimately came to represent, if not a near monopoly of the modern skills present in that country, at least the dominant modern-oriented sector of the elite—possibly as much so in the realm of attitudes as in any other respect. This is not the case in Thailand. The great bulk of the modernizers are to be found outside the military. Most of the top soldiers came up through the ranks the old-fashioned hard way—as did both Sarit and Thanom. In this sense French-trained Phibun was a much more formally educated person than either of his successors. Thanom, for all his present good manners and apparent idealism, profited considerably from his military position before he assumed national prominence—most believe as a result of his share of the opium trade when he was commander in the northeastern region.

This is not to say that Thailand's soldiers are not qualified. Phibun let things drift and in general made more than a moderate mess of things in his second premiership, but both Sarit and Thanom did many things very well indeed. Many young men seek careers in the armed forces in Thailand, in fact, because they see this as a near-exclusive means to power, wealth, and status. The army will maintain a strong hold on the Thai state as long as this continues to be the case. And this will be the case as long as a military career is regarded as something more than professional soldiering.

FOREIGN RELATIONS

Thailand has had unquestionably one of Asia's most successful foreign policies in modern times—much more so than those of such more generously endowed states as Japan or

China. Thailand, after all, was the only Southeast Asian country to escape conquest by the colonial Europeans in the heyday of Western imperialism. This was partly the result of Anglo-French rivalry but also the consequence of the extremely shrewd conduct of Thailand's external relations under the great monarch Chulalongkorn. Some will say that Thailand blundered in the 1930s when it sided with an expansionist Japan that ultimately threatened invasion if the Phibun government in 1941 would not allow it use of Thai soil for attacks against Malaya and Burma. Thai freedom during the Second World War was limited by the Japanese presence in the country, but it was far greater freedom than any other Southeast Asian country knew. The Thai emerged from the Second World War, moreover, with only modest damage compared to the great destruction wrought both in Burma and, even more so, in the Philippines. An American foreign policy that resulted in Pearl Harbor or its British counterpart that lost Burma and Malaya does not appear more competent than the Thai approach to Japan that attained a far higher percentage of the country's foreign policy objectives. And surely Thailand had no obligation, moral or otherwise, to the defense of European colonialism in Southeast Asia.

The late Premier Phibun has often been criticized for his crass imitation of the Japanese and his superficial modernization efforts of the late 1930s—and probably justifiably so. At the same time, Phibun was the chief architect of the policy that saved Thailand from the destructive potentiality of the Far Eastern phase of the Second World War. And he guided his country into alliance with the powerful and protective United States, so recently Japan's enemy, after the war. Both policies appear to have been the best of the possible alternatives open to Thailand at the time. In both cases Phibun served his countrymen well and acted courageously.

Thailand's identification with Japan prior to and during

the Second World War placed the burden on the Thai to fashion a new pattern of relations with the other powers when peace came. Strongly anti-Chinese, the Bangkok government nonetheless recognized Nationalist China after the war as a price of admission to membership in the United Nations. Likewise, the Thai government repealed an anti-Communist law of the early 1930s to win the support of the Soviet Union but was not forced to extend diplomatic recognition to Moscow in order to join the U.N. Territory seized from neighboring Burma, Malaya, Cambodia, and Laos was returned as part of the penalty for siding with the defeated power, Japan, in the late war. Admitted to the United Nations in 1946, the Thai immediately became one of the world body's strongest supporters. Thailand sent troops to Korea in 1950 to serve under the U.N. banner in the struggle to repel Communist aggression and has kept a small contingent there since that time. Thailand was also a member of the League of Nations before the war and so has a history of involvement in international organization.

Thai support of the U.N. was part of a broader policy of opposing aggression, particularly Communist aggression, wherever it occurred. The rise to power of the Chinese Communists in Peking in 1949 thoroughly frightened the Phibun regime. Thailand was a willing recipient of American foreign aid, accordingly, inaugurated the following year. The Thai also sought a regional military defense treaty but were thwarted until the Manila Pact was signed in 1954, bringing together the Philippines, Pakistan, Australia, New Zealand, the United States, Britain, and France, as well as the Thai, in the Southeast Asian Treaty Organization. The Thai wanted SEATO to be much stronger than it turned out to be, with provisions for automatic response in case of aggression and large-scale economic aid. The bigger powers, including the United States, were opposed to these, and so SEATO started life fairly modestly. A headquarters organization was established in Bangkok, however, and it has grown

Thailand 313

through the years. Pote Sarasin, a member of the present Thanom cabinet, was its first secretary general.

Thailand expected much from SEATO and was unquestionably disappointed. The Thai saw SEATO primarily as a vehicle for keeping Communism as far as possible from their frontiers. There never was any serious thought given to invocation of the Manila Pact to assist the anti-Communists in the Vietnamese civil war, but when the struggle between the Communists and their adversaries took a marked turn for the worse in Laos in the early 1960s, Thailand desperately wanted SEATO to respond to the situation. SEATO declined to do so for a number of reasons, not least of which were the opposition of the major non-Asian powers and the fear of the anti-Communist Laotians that such intervention might be a prelude to some sort of Thai domination. Whatever the reasons, however, the Thai were disappointed, and there was talk—but only talk—of a review of the main guidelines of Thai foreign policy. Foreign Minister Thanat visited Washington in 1962, and he and Secretary of State Dean Rusk agreed that the obligations of the Manila Pact were bilateral as well as collective—that is, that the United States was bound to come to Thailand's defense even if none of the other SEATO states did so. Subsequently, American forces were dispatched to northeastern Thailand as a show of strength in connection with the violations by the Communist Pathet Lao of the precarious cease-fire in Laos across the Mekong River. The Thai were suspicious of even this American action, however. When the Thai really wanted intervention in 1961, and President Kennedy seemed to pledge it, no such international action took place. In 1962, when there was much less of a threat, American forces were landed in Thailand—in part probably because Washington knew that they would never be used. More than a few official Thai scratched their heads and wondered. The SEATO voting formula, which had previously required unanimity, was also subsequently changed, allowing any five nations to act, provided none of the remaining three cast a veto. Any move so voted is not technically a SEATO action and is not binding on the nonsupporting members.

Thailand today is probably less interested in regional selective security, which has proved so difficult to achieve, than it is in the closest possible working relationship with the United States commensurate with its dignity and independence. The Thai, who were never anybody's colony, want American help, but they want to retain the right to reject American advice if they so desire. Between 1950 and 1964 American aid to Thailand totalled $836.5 million —about five-eighths of this military assistance. United States economic help to Thailand has averaged about $25,000,000 annually in recent years—in addition to $43,000,000 a year for Thailand's armed forces. But in 1965 economic aid alone rose to nearly forty million dollars a year. This is a fairly high level of support, and the Thai appreciate it. On the other hand, the Thai have always felt neglected in terms of the per capita level of American aid compared to that received by some other countries which have given less support to American foreign policy. Another measure of the Thai-American partnership is the increasing number of United States servicemen stationed in the country—more than 20,000 in mid-1966—and the use of airfields in Thailand for raids on the Ho Chi Minh Trail (from North to South Vietnam) and other targets in the Vietnamese war.

Thailand seeks alliance with the United States today as part of the same balance of power approach that characterized its efforts to play off British and French in the late nineteenth and early twentieth centuries and its close identification with Japan in the 1930s. Thailand's armed forces of not more than 130,000 men cannot by themselves defend the country against major invasion. Rightly or wrongly, the Thai identified the United States at the start of the fifties as the power most likely to predominate in the Far East. Thailand was fairly content with this appraisal for a while, when there seemed to be little doubt about its soundness, but more recently both the Sarit and Thanom governments have seemed to fear that perhaps the United States was fighting a losing battle in Southeast Asia. An American withdrawal from South Vietnam under practically any circumstances now imaginable would result in a major drop in Thai faith in the reliability of the United States as an ally. Many Thai have openly expressed the thought that while they are of Asia and of necessity must confront directly the problems of that continent, the United States is not an Asian nation and could—if it wanted to do so—retreat across the Pacific.

There is at least one major reason why Thailand is unlikely to give serious thought to a major revision of its foreign policy in the foreseeable future, however. This is Communist China. Thai disappointment with SEATO resulted from the fact that they joined that regional body to keep communism from their front door, but the Communists took over half of Laos and SEATO did nothing about it. Given the Thai fear of communism and of its vigorous Asian proponent, China, there would seem to be nothing to be gained from any policy change. While an argument might be made for a Cambodian-style neutralist foreign policy, this would be particularly repulsive to the Thai in view of the strained relations in recent years between Bangkok and Phnom Penh. One thing that can be safely predicted is that Thailand will definitely not take its foreign policy lead from Prince Norodom Sihanouk. Indicative of Thailand's continued hostility to Communist China is its persisting opposition to the seating of Peking in the United Nations. Bangkok continues to exchange diplomatic representatives with Nationalist China, although relations between the two countries are more correct than cordial, and early recognition of Peking is unthinkable—except within the context of a major change of American foreign policy in this respect. Thailand appears to fear such a change from time to time.

Thai relations with other Afro-Asian states vary considerably. Never having been a colony, the Thai have never been marked by the xenophobic sort of hatred of the European that has characterized the likes of Indonesia's Sukarno or Ghana's Kwame Nkrumah. Thailand is also basically a capitalist country, and it is out of step with most of Afro-Asia in this regard. The Thai find their main friends in Asia accordingly in such states as Japan, the Philippines, and Malaysia. Indeed, Thailand strongly supported efforts to bring about regional economic cooperation through the Association for Southeast Asia, in which it shared membership with the Filipinos and Malay, in the early 1960s. But ASA foundered on the Malayan-Filipino controversy over inclusion of Sabah (formerly British North Borneo), also claimed by the Philippines, in the new state of Malaysia when it was formed in 1963. Thailand warmly greeted efforts to revive ASA in 1966 and even proposed its enlargement. When Indonesia proclaimed its policy of military "confrontation" against Malaysia in 1963, the Thai sought, unsuccessfully, to mediate differences between the two states. Relations with Burma have remained correct, but Thai-Cambodian relations have been strained for a number of years. One reason was the incompatibility of the two countries' leaders, Sarit of Thailand and Sihanouk of Cambodia, but there were other more basic causes, not least of which was Phnom Penh's policy of playing up to Peking as a means of insuring China's favor in the future. The Thai approach to Peking is almost directly the opposite.

The reason why Thailand follows a foreign policy so different from those of so many other of the underdeveloped countries of Asia and Africa is mainly to be found in a complex of historical and related factors. One of the most important considerations underlying Thai foreign policy is unquestionably the nation's experience in the conduct of its own foreign relations. The fact is that most of the new states began independence with practically no experience in international relations. Thailand, on the other hand, is very much experienced, with all that means in terms of personal knowledge of how states interact and traditional guidelines which help give direction to contemporary activity on the foreign scene. Thailand, moreover, has already made some of the mistakes the other emerging countries are now making and so does not have to make them again.

Thailand's prior experience in foreign affairs has given the Thai confidence—a confidence which neither the Cambodians nor the Burmese, both of whom seek to retain their independence through accommodating Peking, do not possess. Thailand has taken risks before—back in the days of Anglo-French rivalry in mainland Southeast Asia and when Japan was beginning to expand throughout the Far East. The Burmese and the Cambodians are frightened; so, too, are the Thai, but they can live with fear in a way that their neighbors seem unable to do.

Because Thailand was never a European colony, the Thai do not have the same suspicion of the United States as the main Western power today that some of the former imperial possessions have. This gives the Thai an alternative which some of the new states are unwilling to recognize: alliance with the United States and the camp of largely democratic nations with which it is associated.

Finally, Thailand lacks various of the internal determinants to either adventurism or extreme caution that many of the less effectively nationally integrated states possess. It does not need a foreign enemy to hold the country together as some Indonesians seem to believe is necessary. Despite its less than fully assimilated minorities, it has never had ethnic rebellions after the fashion of the Burmese experience. Far more than either of these two countries, moreover, Thailand has seriously pursued policies of rapid and rational economic development these last several years. Even in the years of economic and financial bungling under Phibun, Thailand was still receiving American aid, much of which did great good, and it had even then a thriving private sector. In short,

Thailand seems more genuinely concerned with economic development—and is willing to do the things necessary to achieve such development—than many of the other developing lands. Its particular foreign policy seems to allow it to do this—one reason why it will probably be continued.

WHITHER THAILAND?

If Thailand were to lose its independence to the Chinese or even conceivably to a Communist North Vietnam (which would previously have absorbed Laos and Cambodia), it would mean that a nation which had been able to hold the Western colonial powers at bay had not been able to do the same thing with respect to Communist imperialism. In the earlier period, Thailand played off the British and the French. Today, despite the fact that it is one of America's firmest allies, Thailand is in effect using the United States as a means of preventing its absorption by Chinese Communism. Whether Thailand remains free or not depends very much on the United States. If the Americans let the Thai down, Thai diplomacy, skilled though it may be, will have an infinitely more difficult time.

On the other hand, there is little that the United States can do if Thailand is not able to hold its own against the Communist threat internally. There is in Thailand's case, as in the case of all states, an intimate connection between the internal and the external. If Thailand's Chinese, Malays, or other minorities—or other definable groups, such as intellectuals, urban workers, or peasants—become alienated from the regime, the burden on the United States as the assisting external power may well become an impossible one. This is why it is so important that Thailand's government, whether soldier-led or not, develop a meaningful relationship with the people over whom it rules.

CHAPTER 10

INTERNATIONAL RELATIONS OF SOUTHEAST ASIA

THE INTERNATIONAL RELATIONS of the Southeast Asian countries had inevitably to change with the coming of independence. Only Thailand was master of its own foreign affairs during the long years of Western-dominated Southeast Asian international relations, and even the Thai had to deal with the European masters of neighboring lands rather than with other Southeast Asians. For the Philippines, ruled first by Spaniards and then Americans, the ending of the colonial period marked the first time in nearly four hundred years that it had been able to conduct its relations with other peoples. Centuries also had lapsed since Indonesia had directed its own external affairs. The era of alien control of their foreign relations had not been so long for Burmese, Malaysians, Vietnamese, Cambodians, or Laotians, but in their eyes it had been long enough. The advent of independence meant that the Southeast Asian countries would need to develop new patterns of relations both with their neighbors and with other nations of the world—including their former colonial rulers.

The past twenty years have been largely concerned with their pursuit of altered and advantageous relations with other nations. The task has not been easy for several reasons.

For one thing, the new leaders of the recently dependent Southeast Asian lands were almost totally inexperienced in the difficult art of foreign-policy determination and implementation. It is no accident that Thailand has had probably the most successful foreign policy of the various Southeast Asian states in the years since the Second World War. The Thai managed to maintain their independence during the years of expanding British, French, and Japanese colonialism partly because of the diplomatic skill of their leaders. The resulting experience and self-confidence have served Thailand well in more recent years and partly explain why there has been less domination to date by influences emanating from Communist China than in any of the other five mainland Southeast Asian lands.

Inexperience in foreign affairs is not the only legacy of Southeast Asia. The long years of European rule effectively isolated the various peoples from one another. They were neighbors geographically but strangers in many important ways. Even the educated elite in the Southeast Asian countries know very little about the lands adjacent to their own nation—a fraction of what they know about their former colonial rulers and such present and past major powers as the United States and the United Kingdom. The result has frequently been suspicion and misunderstanding. The state of their economic development, moreover—another consequence of the former colonial condition—has served to limit trade among the Southeast Asian countries. The fact that all of these lands are primary producers and need to buy many consumer goods and most of their capital equipment from the more industrially developed countries has meant that trade among themselves is comparatively small.

Readjustment of relations with other nations has taken place, some times painfully, despite these twin legacies of inexperience and isolation. Two trends seem especially evident in the resulting pattern of associations with adjacent and more distant lands. One of these is the movement away

International Relations

from political intimacy with one or more Western nations. Three countries (Indonesia, Burma, and Cambodia) and half of another one (the Communist-ruled northern portion of divided Vietnam) have expressed differing types of hostility to one or more Western nations—and this to an increasing extent—in the years since the collapse of colonial rule. Since the Dutch, British, and French wholly directed the foreign relations of these lands only a quarter of a century ago, this has meant a major change in the pattern of Southeast Asia's international relations. Although the Philippines and Malaysia remain very close to their former American and British rulers, only never-colonial Thailand seems to have a more intimate relationship with a Western power (the United States) than it possessed in the European era. South Vietnam's military dependence upon the United States has increased markedly between 1960 and 1966, but American influence never has equaled that of the French in their heyday and there are many indications of Vietnamese opposition to such influence despite the scope and importance of American aid. All factors considered, there has been a sharp decline in Western influence in Southeast Asia since the Second World War, particularly in the half-decade, 1960-1966.

The other trend is no less important. It is the also steady movement in the direction of greater interaction (not necessarily closer cooperation) among the several Southeast Asian countries and between each of them and the major Asian and Pacific states of China, India, Japan, and Australia. Increasingly, foreign policies are being shaped, as surely they must be, with major attention focused upon the interests and intentions of the countries in, and geographically closest to, Southeast Asia. This was the state of affairs that existed when the expanding Europeans intruded upon the area, and it is altogether natural that the exit of the Europeans and the fairly sharp decline in their power and prestige should be followed by what can be considered the reestablishment of normal relations among the Southeast Asian peoples and their neighbors. But normal relations do not necessarily mean cordial or peaceful relations.

The decline in Western influence and the accompanying growth in importance of China and other Asian-Pacific powers has tended to obscure a third development of more long-range importance. This is the increasing integration of Southeast Asia into the growing world community of nations. Developments like Indonesia's departure from the United Nations in 1965 notwithstanding, Southeast Asia has steadily moved in the direction of greater dependence upon world political, economic, and military forces. The world as a whole has never been more important to Southeast Asia—or Southeast Asia to the world.

SELF-IMAGES AND WORLD VIEWS

The self-images apparently possessed by the several Southeast Asian states—and their views of the world within whose confines they must function—vary considerably. Indonesia and the Philippines present vivid examples of such differences. Sukarno's Indonesia always appeared to see itself as a power of much greater importance than any of its neighbors. This, in fact, was probably a major cause of its lack of interest in closer regional relations. President Sukarno simply did not regard the other Southeast Asian countries as equals. He sought, rather, the company of the Nehrus, the Maos, and the Nassers in preference to the Nus, the Sarits and the Macapagals. Today Indonesia considers itself to be the chief hope for the protection of Southeast Asia against both the old-style colonialists and a resurgent China (which is regarded as friend or foe, depending on circumstances), a nation capable militarily of taking on the British over Malaysia, and a country whose friendship is to be so valued that it could openly flout the mediatory efforts of the Philippines and Thailand (as well as Japan and the United States) in the Malaysian crisis.

Indonesia's flattering and frequently exaggerated self-assessment was a factor in Sukarno's decision in 1965 to quit the United Nations. There was a time when Indonesia thought that it needed the U.N. as a forum to magnify its voice in world politics. In 1965, however, it was apparently willing to forego its former position of influence within the Afro-Asian group of nations at the U.N. in favor either of self-imposed isolation or of the much less numerous company of the "new emerging forces"—that is, those recently emancipated former colonies who regard revolutionary techniques as appropriate to today's complex task of seeking peace and progress among nations.

The Philippines appeared to differ markedly on the surface from Indonesia. Whereas the Indonesians appeared cocky (as they boasted, for example, of an early atomic weapons capability), the Filipinos worried aloud about their fate if ever deserted by their military protector, the United States. Philippine military leaders openly admitted that their country could not defend itself without outside help. Philippine politicians sought to expand their country's contracts abroad, pursuing new patterns of relations with all nations except the Communists. The Philippines valued greatly its U.N. membership, was a SEATO partner, helped to found the once-promising Association of Southeast Asia, and seriously considered South Korea's proposals for a new East Asian security pact in 1965. The Philippine self-image and world view were thus in sharp contrast to those of Indonesia.

The self-images and world views of the other Southeast Asian states are not quite like those of Indonesia or the Philippines. Burma and Cambodia, like Indonesia, have shown diminished faith in the U.N. and have a narrower range of contacts than a decade ago. Burma, however, has assumed an extreme isolationist policy which has no parallel elsewhere in Southeast Asia, while Cambodia clearly has accepted the inevitability of Chinese domination of the area. The Burmese and the Cambodians display much less confidence now than formerly in their ability to influence other states; Indonesia and Malaysia show a self-confidence perhaps unwarranted by the objective circumstances of their situations. Both Thailand and the Philippines seek survival in partnership with larger powers—Burma in the limitation of involvement with bigger states of both camps. The Communist orientation of North Vietnam and its related efforts to change the status quo contrast sharply with the anti-Communist policies (and associated defense of the status quo) of Thailand, Malaysia, and the Philippines.

SOUTHEAST ASIA AND WORLD CONFLICTS

The attitudes and actions of the several Southeast Asian countries toward world conflicts also contrast sharply and are frequently factors in the rumpled relations between countries of the region. The Philippines, Thailand, and Malaysia have pursued anti-Communist foreign policies through the years and clearly regard both China and the Soviet Union as major threats to their future survival as free states. South Vietnam has also followed a strongly anti-Communist foreign policy, but this may have been a function primarily of its internal struggle between Communists and anti-Communists.

The only Communist country in Southeast Asia during the past decade has been North Vietnam, which sent high-level delegates to the 1966 Soviet party congress despite Peking's boycott of the session. There can be no doubt, however, that domination of the Laotian government by the insurgent Pathet Lao would be followed by a world foreign policy hardly different from that pursued by the North Vietnamese. Indonesia was by no means a Communist country when Sukarno was its largely unchallenged leader, but the long-time nationalist figure steadily moved his government closer to a Peking-like foreign policy in the first half of the 1960s, raising the question of how to differentiate between Communist and non-Communist states if they follow the same foreign policy approach. It remains to be seen how much of an alteration will finally take place in Indonesia's foreign policy as a result of increasing army dominance of the Djakarta government in the wake of the abortive Communist coup of October 1, 1965. First signs were suggestive of significant, if gradual, alterations—such as Foreign Minister Adam Malik's assertion in March 1966 that Indonesia would return to the United Nations and would seek to improve relations with the United States.

The mainland countries of Burma and Cambodia still pursue avowedly neutralist foreign policies. Such approaches, however, are becoming increasingly difficult to sustain, primarily as a result of China's continuing movement toward great-power status. Burma and Cambodia survive as independent states in part as a consequence of China's present contentment with their growing estrangement from the United States. There is probably no country as genuinely neutral in Southeast Asia today as were Indonesia, Burma, and Cambodia a decade ago. This fact suggests that the neutralist approach may not be a feasible one in the kind of strategic situation that has developed in recent years.

With the world now in transition, it is not clear what patterns of antagonisms will dominate the decade ahead. The cold war is by no means wholly a thing of history; the American-Soviet struggle for influence, for example, continues in Indonesia. But the split between the Chinese and the Russians, the increasing importance of the Afro-Asian nations in general, and the possibility of greater cooperation among the more revolutionary "new emerging forces" led by Peking suggest an increasingly multidimensional strategic situation. Despite the fact that they are important factors in some key aspects of this changing situation, the Southeast Asian states may retain an even greater amount of the old cold-war attitudes and policies in some instances today than the onetime chief protagonists in that struggle—possibly for reasons of inertia.

THE POWERS AND SOUTHEAST ASIA

The major powers, both of Asia and the world, have always been interested in Southeast Asia because of its resources and its strategic location. Although the various political units of this part of the world fought more or less continuously among themselves before the coming of the Europeans (and are today engaged in war—both cold and hot), no Southeast Asian state has ever sought to rule lands outside the area. This was probably a result of the technological level of their societies and of the inability of the more imperialistically oriented Southeast Asian governments of the past even to embrace most of their own region. Whatever the reasons, however, Southeast Asia has been much invaded through the centuries but its constituent countries have never been the conquerors of other lands beyond the area.

The heyday of European domination of the international relations of Southeast Asia was clearly the first three decades of the present century—that is, up to the 1930s. Never before had Southeast Asia's relations with outsiders—or the relations of the several Southeast Asian lands with their neighbors—been more under the control of foreigners. This control continued through the thirties but was increasingly challenged by an ever stronger Japan. In the first half of the 1940s Japan succeeded both in completely vanquishing the several Western colonial rulers of Southeast Asia and in subsequently losing control of an area over which it had been the sole ruler, however briefly.

Japan's defeat was followed by the surge to independence of the several onetime European colonies of Southeast Asia. Although independence included indigenous direction of the foreign policies of the new nations of Southeast Asia, it by no means meant an early departure of the Western countries from involvement in the international relations of the area. Indeed, the first decade after the Second World War was characterized as much by changes in relative importance of the interested Western countries as by any decline in European interest and influence *per se*.

The British gave up only Burma in the decade 1945-1955 while retaining control of Malaya, northern Borneo, and Singapore (with its important naval base). Even in Burma, moreover, British influence was not immediately eclipsed, and as it declined, the United States became the foreign power which probably most influenced Burma during the first decade after independence. Similarly, the French were forced to retire from Vietnam, Laos, and Cambodia, but the vacuum created by the sharp diminution in their influence was fairly rapidly filled by the Americans (except, of course, for North Vietnam). The United States granted independence to the Philippines but retained important military bases and was clearly the Filipinos' closest foreign ally. Even in Indonesia, Western influence, primarily American, was probably as important as any other foreign factor in the years immediately following independence. The formation of the Southeast Asia Treaty Organization, the inauguration of large American economic and military aid programs, and the establishment of fairly sizable Western embassies testify to both interest and influence.

The fact that both Burma and Indonesia were actively pursuing neutralist foreign policies by the end of this period should not be interpreted to mean that other powers had supplanted the Western countries as the most involved outsiders in the international relations of the Southeast Asian states. The foreign policies of Burma and Indonesia were largely reflections of their natural nationalist desire for full freedom—including freedom not to commit themselves to the cause of nations to whom they believed they owed little —as well as of declining European power to enforce dependence in international politics. The worldwide end of the colonial era, moreover, brought with it a drastic revision of previously prevalent attitudes concerning the moral acceptability of domination of the weak by the strong.

Western influence, though it clearly declined in the first decade after independence, remained strong nonetheless. Particularly did the United States increase its influence in the area during this period. The general decline in Western influence, however, probably impressed many persons more than it should have. It was difficult to escape comparing their complete domination so few years earlier with the postwar need to win the cooperation of these same Southeast Asian countries. But considering the distance of both Europe and America from Southeast Asia as well as the animosities born of the long era of colonial submission, it was surprising that Western influence remained as great as it did even during these transitional years.

The second half of the 1950s marked the beginning of the emergence of other external forces as potentially dominant ones in Southeast Asia. Soviet aid in the form of credits to some Southeast Asian countries—Indonesia, Burma, and Cambodia—started in the midfifties. Soviet trade with Burma and Indonesia also developed as a factor of strategic significance after the death of Stalin and the new look in the foreign policies of the U.S.S.R. under Nikita Khrushchev. During the same period China commenced its attempt to exert a larger influence upon the countries of Southeast Asia. Peking's active participation in the 1954 Geneva Conference on Vietnam, Laos, and Cambodia was followed by Chinese efforts to woo other Asians at the 1955 Bandung Conference in Indonesia and diplomatic visits by Premier Chou En-lai to several Southeast Asian countries in 1956. China sought in the middle 1950s to expand its trade with its southern neighbors, even anti-Communist Thailand. The later years of the decade also saw the beginning of Chinese economic aid to Southeast Asia, Cambodia being the first recipient.

If Communist influence increased in Southeast Asia during these years, so also did that of other powers—including the most powerful of the Western nations, the United States.

American influence mounted markedly in at least four of the mainland Southeast Asian countries during this period: South Vietnam, Thailand, Laos, and Cambodia. Although Japan did not assume political importance in these years (a possible reflection of memories of its recent aggression in the region), its economic involvement increased rapidly. India's influence was probably as great in Southeast Asia during the second half of the 1950s as at any time since independence. Australia, increasingly aware of both the strategic and economic importance of Southeast Asia to its survival, not only joined SEATO in 1954 but also greatly expanded its diplomatic ties with the area and stepped up both aid and trade with the region. Although French influence in the area steadily declined in the late 1950s, that of Britain remained fairly constant. Other states also increased their influence on particular countries or in specific fields, such as trade, but none of these probably could be regarded as exercising major influence; Yugoslavia, Israel, and West Germany were the most active of these other lands.

One effect of this growing diversity of interested foreign powers was to increase the opportunities for maneuverability on the part of the still weak Southeast Asian countries in their responses to outside influences. Although no country in Southeast Asia except North Vietnam could be called Communist in terms of its international orientation during this period, Communist influence did increase and lessen the dependence of several states on the West. Cambodia became markedly more neutral during these years, and the August 1960 coup changed a strongly pro-Western Laotian foreign policy to one of neutralism. Adherents of the neutralist approach even appeared and were frequently quite vocal in both the Philippines and Thailand. Burmese and Indonesian neutralism, however, remained more or less constant, perhaps reaching its height during these years. The responses of the Southeast Asian nations to external pressures were, on the whole, quite normal ones. They may have seemed less than normal to some, however, because of the gross abnormality of the situation during the first half of the century.

The late fifties, then, represented a transition period in the evolving postcolonial international relations of the several states of Southeast Asia. The first decade after independence had been marked, more or less, by a continuation of the old pattern of Western dominance (altered in form but far less so in fact than many realized at the time). The subsequent half decade was a brief transitional interlude between the immediate postwar period and the era now in existence and still forming—that of a *marked* decline in Western influence.

The deep and quickly expanding involvement of the United States in Vietnam suggests a growing American participation in the international relations of Southeast Asia, but this is quite misleading. In many other respects American influence is rapidly declining, while that of no other Western power is increasing. American influence in Burma today is practically nil. The first half of the 1960s saw a steady and fairly sharp drop in American influence in Indonesia, capped in 1965 by the suspension of American aid, vigorous anti-American demonstrations, and the termination of the United States Information Service and Peace Corps operations in the country. Although official Indonesian hostility to the United States mellowed considerably following the apparent reduction in President Sukarno's power in March 1966, this was at best probably a first step toward a return to genuine Indonesian neutralism. The American ambassador to Cambodia had to leave the country in 1964 because his credentials were not accepted by Prince Norodom Sihanouk, and relations between the two countries were subsequently suspended at Cambodia's initiative. Proferred American loan assistance to Malaysia, badly in need of foreign help to hold off Indonesian efforts to crush it, was rejected, allegedly because it was not extended on generous enough terms. In

International Relations

the usually friendly Philippines there was a marked increase of agitation in 1965 for termination of economic privileges allowed Americans, and some Filipinos even urged the end of United States military bases in the country. While American involvement in Vietnam increased, it is open to question whether it was accompanied by an advance in American influence. Only in Laos did the approach of the middle 1960s seem to see even a modest increase in American influence, while the United States position in Thailand remained fairly steady.

The decline in American (or Western) influence was paralleled in most cases by an increase in the influence of one or the other of the two major Communist powers, primarily China. China's military moves against India in late 1962 had the effect of frightening some of the Southeast Asian states into greater subservience to Peking rather than of encouraging closer relations with China's chief adversary, the United States. Indonesia and Cambodia seemed to be moving rapidly in the direction of becoming *de facto* allies of Communist China in the first half of the 1960s. Indonesian-Chinese ties largely mirrored the two countries' increasingly similar revolutionary approaches to international politics—both in terms of ends and means. President Sukarno continued to proclaim Indonesia's adherence to the "axis" of China, North Korea, North Vietnam, Cambodia, and itself even after the unsuccessful pro-Communist coup attempt of October 1, 1965, but the subsequent decline in Sukarno's power and China's termination of its economic assistance indicated that important changes were taking place in Indonesia's relations with the Communist Chinese. Cambodia, on the other hand, appeared to be moving closer to Peking—largely out of fears of Thailand and Vietnam (mainly of historic origin) and because of its calculation that China would be the dominant influence in Southeast Asia in the future. Despite the fact that the leftist orientation of its internal policies were second only to those of North Vietnam,

Burma remained remarkedly true to its proclaimed neutralist position through these years. The continuing conflicts in both South Vietnam and Laos could both be resolved in favor of the Communists, though this is by no means assured (particularly in the case of Laos).

The decline in Western influence and the increase in China's position in Southeast Asia represent a historical process still being acted out. That is, it presumably will continue at least a little longer until some new, more stable pattern of international relations involving Southeast Asia will have been established. Neither the United States nor the United Nations under existing circumstances can prevent the ultimate dominance of Southeast Asia by the Chinese. Effective cooperation among the Southeast Asian states might limit the opportunities for China's influence to be felt—as might genuine partnerships between states of the region and outsiders (such as the Philippines and the United States) or policies both strengthening the United Nations and a country's identification with the U.N.'s main proclaimed purposes (which is actually the opposite of the effect of Indonesia's withdrawal move in 1965). Even so, however, geography and China's potential power and intentions remain important likely determinants of the future relationship between the world's most populous nation and its less formidable southern neighbors.

History suggests that China's future position could be a very strong one. Traditionally the Chinese have exercised suzerainty over much of Southeast Asia, and it is significant that no strong power ever arose in the region when there was also a strong China. On at least two occasions in the past, moreover, new regimes in China have meant trouble for the states along China's southern border. Such was the case when the Mongols came to power and also in the early years of Ming rule. China's Communist complexion clearly increases the threat to Southeast Asia, but it did not create the threat. If Chiang Kai-shek had won the struggle for control of the

Chinese mainland and had subsequently consolidated his regime, there is every reason to believe that Southeast Asia would also be confronted by a major Chinese challenge from him today.

If Western influence is indeed declining in Southeast Asia and probably will continue to do so for some time to come (and if it is also true that the vacuum left by the decline in European power in the area has yet to be filled), it is difficult to see how Chinese influence can be prevented from growing —perhaps gradually and possibly even peacefully. This point, however, seems to be missed by many, although not, significantly, by Cambodia's Prince Norodom Sihanouk or Indonesia's longtime President Sukarno. Cambodia is apparently endeavoring to be China's friend in order to assure its continued independence. Indonesia has made a bid for dominance in the area itself, possibly partly to serve as a counterweight to Peking. Either of these two policies may be more sensible than a standstill attitude toward revision of SEATO, seemingly endless American aid to the Saigon government (which is no longer the same as "South Vietnam"), or Burma's faith that China will ultimately respect its genuine neutrality.

There may in fact be more than one way to maintain the independence of the several Southeast Asian states. On the other hand, there may be conditions under which it is impossible to do so. Unfortunately, only limited progress has been made over the past two decades in bringing the various countries of the area closer together in new patterns of military, economic, political, and social cooperation. The process could accelerate, of course, as the need to cooperate becomes more apparent, but there is little immediate likelihood of this happening. The consequent power vacuum thus remains highly attractive to various outsiders.

Southeast Asia has not yet fallen under the dominance of any single power or group of powers—North Vietnam again excepted. This is largely a result of the diversity of nations interested in the area's future. By playing off the powers against one another, the several Southeast Asian nations might indeed retain their freedom—as did Thailand in the past. On the other hand, various powers could once again agree on a division of the area. Dominance of a single power, the possible consequence of the present circumstances of declining Western and increasing Chinese influence, could also expose the area to a future of renewed dependency.

CONFLICTS WITHIN THE REGION

There has been a steady increase in the extent of conflict among the several countries of Southeast Asia since independence. The once widely shared myth of Asians that only Europeans started wars seems to have been thoroughly exposed by the events of recent years. The level of intraregional tensions in Southeast Asia is higher today than at any time since the end of colonial rule. Unlike the imperial rivalries of yesteryear, which tended to focus on particular parts of the area at any given moment, the situation today is one of growing hostilities in various portions of the region involving several states.

Unlike Europe over the last several centuries, however, the rivalries have yet to crystallize into definable sets of powers posed against one another. Some of the states have aligned themselves with countries outside the region—Thailand and the Philippines with the United States, Malaysia with Britain, and North Vietnam with China and the Soviet Union, for example—but the countries of Southeast Asia have yet to form alliances among themselves directed against their neighbors within the area. It may not be long, however, before they do so.

The longest running war in the area has been that between the Communist north and the non-Communist south of divided Vietnam. This is in reality a continuation of the former eight-year Communist-colonial war between

International Relations

the Ho Chi Minh-led Viet Minh and the French (1946-1954). That war was ended by the 1954 Geneva Agreements on Vietnam, Laos, and Cambodia, but the conflict between the challenging Communists and their adversaries, the successors to the French in South Vietnam, has persisted since that time, even though it did not reach the proportions of a major guerrilla war until the early 1960s. In a sense the Vietnamese war is a civil one, pitting against one another two rival indigenous regimes determined to fill the vacuum created by departed French authority. At the same time, however, North and South Vietnam are recognized as sovereign independent states by a large number of countries, though no nation has recognized both Vietnams diplomatically.

The Vietnamese war had become one of the most pressing problems in Asia by the middle of the 1960s as a consequence of the commitment of China, the U.S.S.R., and the other Communist countries to the side of the Hanoi government, while the United States and 29 other non-Communist countries were in various ways aiding the Saigon regime. There were, in fact, 255,000 American military personnel in South Vietnam by the middle of 1966, most of them fighting alongside the anti-Communist Vietnamese. Some feared that a direct American-Chinese confrontation might result from the conflict.

It was not only South Vietnam that North Vietnam threatened during the first half of the sixties. The Hanoi government also gave strong support to the Communist Pathet Lao guerrillas in adjacent Laos and used Laotian territory for the movement of men and supplies into South Vietnam. Laos was supposed to have been neutralized as a result of the 1954 Geneva Conference on Indochina, but the neutralization failed to take, in part because of external interference and in part because of an irreconcilable gap between the chief opposed political factions in the country. Another Geneva Conference in 1961-1962 tried again to neutralize Laos, but once more unsuccessfully. The indigenous Communists, aided by fighting elements from North Vietnam as well as by other assistance from the Hanoi government, resumed their attacks only a little more than six months after the 1962 Geneva Agreement was initialed. North Vietnam was clearly making a bid for incorporation of all of what used to be French Indochina.

Cambodia was another object of Hanoi's imperialist aspirations. North Vietnam was fully occupied with wars in both South Vietnam and Laos, however, and did not directly threaten Cambodia through the mid-1960s. Indeed, the Cambodians were much more frightened, at least openly, by what they regarded as South Vietnamese and Thai designs on their territory. But there was no doubt that Cambodia's astute ruler, Prince Norodom Sihanouk, realized that a united Communist Vietnam would be even more of a threat to his country's survival than a currently weak and besieged South Vietnam. Sihanouk also knew that their failure so far fully to absorb Laos meant that the Communists did not yet share a frontier with Cambodia. When they did, however, the situation could be different. This is why Cambodia sought the protection of Communist China as a counterweight against an expansionist North Vietnam.

Cambodia has not been engaged in any kind of war with South Vietnam and Thailand, even of a modest guerrilla sort, but there has been a variation of the larger world's cold war raging continuously between the Cambodians and these two neighbors. The Thai may well have offended Cambodia (meaning really Sihanouk) in various ways through the years, but they have also come to terms with two other traditional enemies, Burma and Malaya (now Malaysia). Relations have steadily improved for several years between Thailand and both the Burmese and the Malayans—which raises the question of why the Cambodians should find it so difficult to make their peace with the Thai when the Burmese, who also follow a quite different policy from the Bangkok government, found it possible to do so.

It is deceptive to explain Thai-Cambodian differences simply in terms of past personal animosities between Cambodian Prince Sihanouk and the late Thai leader Marshal Sarit Thanarat. Similarly, the conflict between Malaysia and Indonesia was also sometimes inadequately explained as growing out of the clash of personalities between Malaysian Premier Tengku Abdul Rahman and Indonesian President Sukarno. The differences were really between the elites that governed the two countries and not just between their leading members. Moreover, there were important differences in the national interests of Malaysia and Indonesia as perceived by the ruling elites of these two lands as well as such obvious opportunities for conflict as rival aspirations to alter imposed colonial boundaries, a problem throughout the area.

Indonesia's attempt to "crush Malaysia," as Sukarno put it, was an effort to assert Indonesian ascendency initially over insular Southeast Asia but subsequently over the rest of the region. The fact that the core area of Malaysia was an ethnically Malay (or Indonesian) land has also meant that widely heralded Malayan economic accomplishments since independence posed a problem for Indonesia in the sense of providing a point of potential attraction for dissatisfied elements in the Indonesian islands outside Java (and perhaps on Java, too). Malaysia, moreover, pursued economic and foreign policies that made it suspect in the eyes of the increasingly pro-Communist and anti-Western Sukarno, who apparently could not accept the notion of a partnership of equals between East and West or the idea of a nonsocialist economy that was not exploitative. Most important of all, however, Malaysia included Sarawak and Sabah, territories perhaps sought for early incorporation by Indonesia which occupies the remaining two-thirds of the island of Borneo.

The emergence of General Suharto as Indonesia's apparent new strongman following the abortive Communist coup of October 1, 1965, was accompanied by signs that the Djakarta government might be moderating its anti-Malaysian activities. Guerrilla warfare had not accomplished its purpose; Indonesia, in fact, had been hurt more by its own policies than Malaysia. There was talk in Djakarta of "peaceful confrontation instead of the physical confrontation of war," as one newspaper close to General Suharto put it. But how to back down? This was a problem. Moreover, the forces that encouraged confrontation were still very much alive. They were submerged for the time being, but they could very easily come to the surface again.

The Philippines, which hoped for increased economic cooperation with Malaya between 1959 and 1963, also split with the Kuala Lumpur government over incorporation of Sabah into Malaysia. The Filipinos seemed to side with the Indonesians in their opposition to Malaysia until Sukarno started landing Indonesian nationals on the Malay Peninsula itself, never territory in dispute between the old Malaya and Indonesia. Fear of a much larger Indonesia, which has always gripped the Philippines to a degree, seemed to grow in 1964 and subsequently as the Filipinos groped for a way to reconcile their differences with Malaysia without too much loss of political or international face.

The fact that the Southeast Asian countries have been known so far less for cooperation than for fighting among themselves is a major tragedy. As so often has been the case in the past, this has made the area vulnerable once again to external exploitation of divisions within the region. The amount of cooperation that has been attempted is indeed surprising given the extent of ideological differences and traditional animosities among these countries.

There is, however, the possibility of important structural changes in the pattern of relations among the several states of Southeast Asia. Indonesia recognized North Vietnam in August 1964 partly to establish the basis for working cooperation with the revolutionary Hanoi regime within the larger framework of what President Sukarno called the "new

International Relations

emerging forces." There is evidence that Ho Chi Minh's government convinced the Indonesians that it needed an early victory against the American-assisted South Vietnamese and a Hanoi-Djakarta axis as a means of counterbalancing Peking's influence in the Indochinese Peninsula. This may or may not be a genuine bid for a Communist Vietnamese foreign policy partially independent of China, but the consequences of a possible alliance between Hanoi and one or more other Southeast Asian governments cannot be ignored. A Djakarta-Hanoi axis would have tended to isolate the Philippines and increase the pressure on Malaysia.

A few years ago it appeared that a Kuala Lumpur-Bangkok-Manila pact was shaping up as a possible political product of the embryonic Association of Southeast Asia, ostensibly designed for economic and social cooperation. Likewise, the short-lived Maphilindo consultative grouping, launched as a result of the Manila Conference of the heads of state of the Philippines, Indonesia, and Malaya in August 1963, also seemed—for however brief a period—a hopeful sign of future regional cooperation.

Such cooperation would appear to be a major means of future survival of the independent states of Southeast Asia. But it also seems premature to expect its emergence.

SOUTHEAST ASIAN REGIONALISM

Few indeed were the political figures who thought of Southeast Asia in regional terms before the Second World War. The predominant point of political action was national freedom from colonial control, and there was little thought of the subsequent pattern of relations among the would-be nations of Southeast Asia. Except in the Philippines, the hour of liberation was probably deemed still quite distant. Manuel Quezon, president of the Philippine Commonwealth in the prewar years, did suggest a "pan-Malay union" of British Malaya, the Dutch East Indies (Indonesia), and the

Philippines, but the proposal went largely unnoticed. The Indonesian Communist Tan Malaka formulated a future "Aslia" linking Australia and Southeast Asia, but this also amounted to nothing. Hardly a form of regionalism was independent Thailand's irredentist designs against French-colonized Cambodia. The behavior of Thai Premier Phibun Songkhram's government suggested that independent Southeast Asian states might turn out to be more interested in traditional-style national territorial aggrandizement than any kind of union of equals—a forecast rather faithfully realized by events of the postcolonial years.

The Second World War strongly stimulated regional feeling in Southeast Asia. The creation of the Allies' Southeast Asia Command under Admiral Lord Louis Mountbatten in 1943 popularized the concept of the area as an interrelated whole. The Japanese occupation further encouraged awareness of the area as a single unit in world politics, this being the first time the region had ever known one common ruler. Moreover, Japan played a prominent part in the encouragement of regional political consciousness by introducing various Southeast Asian nationalist leaders to one another. President José P. Laurel of the Philippines, Prime Minister Ba Maw of Burma, and Prince Wan Waithayakon of Thailand, representing Premier Phibun, attended the Assembly of Greater East Asiatic Nations held in Tokyo in November 1943. This was the first meeting of three such prominent Southeast Asian political leaders.

Several plans for closer political collaboration among the peoples of Southeast Asia were proposed by indigenous leaders in the years which followed the Second World War. Probably the main reason why none of these ever succeeded was the widespread nationalist preoccupation with winning independence or, if it had already been won, with defending and implementing it. An unofficial Southeast Asia League was formed in Bangkok in September 1947, but this was in fact a front organization for the Vietnamese Communists and included among its activities gunrunning in support of the Ho Chi Minh-led guerrilla fighters against the French. Prince Souphanouvong, later to lead the Communist Pathet Lao insurgents in neighboring Laos, was an active member of the Southeast Asia League, as were several prominent Thai, including former Premier Pridi Banomyong and Prime Minister Thamrong Nawasawat. The League was proscribed when Phibun returned to power shortly after its formation.

Although nothing immediately came of their proposals, several other Southeast Asian political leaders advanced ambitious plans for closer regional relations after the war. One of these was General Aung San, leader of Burma's independence-seeking Anti-Fascist People's Freedom League. In October 1945, at a moment when he had apparently lost hope that British gratitude for his guerrilla assistance against Japan would result in the grant of freedom to Burma, Aung San called for an Asian "Potsdam Conference" to "plan a united campaign to achieve freedom within the shortest possible time." In January 1947, expanding this idea in a broadcast in New Delhi, he forecast the formation of an Asian Commonwealth which would constitute a united Asian front "against imperialistic rule." In explanation Aung San said, "While India should be one entity and China another, Southeast Asia as a whole should form an entity—then, finally, we should come together in a bigger union with the participation of other parts of Asia as well." The subsequent April the Burmese leader again called for regional cooperation, this time urging the formation of a Southeast Asian economic union consisting of Burma, Indonesia, Thailand, Malaya, and Indochina (Vietnam, Laos, and Cambodia). Burma's apparent interest in such regional cooperation ended, however, with the tragic assassination of Aung San in July 1947.

Even more interested in regional relations during these years was the political leadership of Burma's neighbor to the east, Thailand. On July 1, 1947, Thai Premier Thamrong

Nawasawat announced that Thailand and France would jointly sponsor the formation of a Pan Southeast Asian Union, which would include, to begin with, Thailand, Cambodia, Laos, and Vietnam and would later be expanded to embrace other states. The union would concern itself primarily, according to Thamrong, with regional plans for the joint development of irrigation, fisheries, communications, and other such resources of the area. The would-be association was never formed, however, for the Thai political opposition charged the Thamrong administration with subservience to the French and caused abandonment of the plan. Former Premier Pridi, then still the power behind the throne in Thai politics and a longtime advocate of closer regional cooperation in Southeast Asia, was a chief architect of the proposed Pan Southeast Asian Union.

Phibun Songkhram, who became premier again in April 1948 following the military coup of the previous November, seemed more genuinely interested in regional cooperation than in his first premiership (1937-1944). Marshal Phibun invited Burma, the Philippines, and India for talks in Bangkok in October 1949 on political and economic matters in Southeast Asia, but no conference was ever held because of the lack of enthusiastic response from the invited states. Thailand also expressed its interest during these years in a Southeast Asian defense pact.

The Philippines, the first of the former Western colonies to gain recognition of its independence after the Second World War, was probably the country most consistently concerned with the question of an area accord during the first postwar decade. Although some other Asians regarded the Philippines as a transpacific extension of the United States politically, the paradox is that the Philippine political leadership of these years was probably more genuinely concerned for the fate of the rest of Southeast Asia than its counterparts anywhere else in the area. The leading architect of the Philippines' efforts to draw the nations of this part of the world nearer to each other was General Carlos P. Romulo. Following the New Delhi Conference of 1949, called by India to support Indonesia's bid for independence, Romulo began working for an anti-Communist South and Southeast Asian bloc, which he hoped would include India, Pakistan, Ceylon, Australia, and New Zealand as well as the countries of Southeast Asia. Many of these nations did not wish to align themselves with either side in the raging cold war between the United States and the Soviet Union, and so nothing much resulted from the Baguio Conference convened by the Philippines in 1950. Elpidio Quirino, the Philippines' president during these years, also advocated various other types of organized cooperation between his country and different combinations of its neighbors, but to no immediate avail.

The 1950 Baguio Conference, the Franco-Thai-proposed Pan Southeast Asian Union of 1947, and the unofficial and suspicious Southeast Asia League of the same year were as close as some of the Southeast Asian states came to any kind of organized and indigenously sponsored area cooperation during the immediate postwar years. British-organized cooperation to facilitate movement of rice and other badly needed commodities soon after the war represented a largely unrecognized major contribution to the rehabilitation of the region, but most of the countries of the area were then still colonies and this particular pattern of collaboration did not survive the revival of agricultural production and the restoration of more regular trading arrangements. Most of the other proposals for some other limited sort of cooperation were similarly short-lived. Ho Chi Minh, the leader of the Communist-captured nationalist movement in Vietnam, sent a message to newly proclaimed Indonesian President Sukarno in 1945, in the wake of Japan's defeat, asking the Indonesians to join with the Vietnamese in a declaration of purpose in their common struggle against colonialism as well as to participate in the formation of a preparatory commission to organize appropriate machinery for future cooperation among the Southeast Asian countries. Indonesia was not apparently interested in Ho's proposal, and nothing accordingly followed.

Indonesia's lack of interest in institutionalized cooperation among the several Southeast Asian states was probably the chief obstacle to regional collaboration in this part of the world during these years. Foreign Minister Mohammed Rum declared in 1951 that his country had no intention of associating itself with any alignment inconsistent with its foreign policy of "active neutrality," and there was virtually no departure from this approach in the years which followed.

There were several suggestions for different types of pacts coming from countries outside the region in the first decade of the postwar period. The British and the French in particular were desirous of organized defense cooperation—including American participation—to help them fight their Chinese Communist and nationalist-Communist wars in Malaya and Vietnam, respectively. The United States was not interested, however, being then engaged in a major war in Korea. Both the Philippines and Thailand espoused the cause of a regional defense organization at various times, but their security needs appeared to be partly met by the United States-Philippines mutual defense agreement of 1951 and the inauguration of American military aid to Thailand in 1950.

The end of the Korean War in 1953 and the related subsequent increase of Communist pressure in Vietnam, which partly accounted for the partition of the country in 1954, changed the strategic situation in Southeast Asia. The United States proposed a regional defense pact to check Communist expansion beyond the northern portion of divided Vietnam, and the Filipinos and the Thai, both of whom shared the American fear of future Communist aggression elsewhere in the area, strongly endorsed the American move. Five other nations (Pakistan, Australia, New Zealand, Britain, and France) also signed the Manila

International Relations 345

Pact, the selective security agreement which resulted from a September 1954 conference in the Philippines. Each signatory to the Manila Treaty recognized that an armed attack against any of them "in the treaty area" would "endanger its own peace and safety" and agreed to "act to meet the common danger in accordance with its constitutional processes." There were mixed feelings concerning the establishment of centralized institutional arrangements to carry out the purposes of the alliance, but coordinating machinery was subsequently established and came to be known as the Southeast Asian Treaty Organization.

SEATO, which has contributed considerably to the military preparedness of most of its members to fight a war in Southeast Asia (if necessary) and has probably served as a deterrent to certain types of war as a result, is both an area defense organization and simultaneously not really a regional pact. The Manila Treaty quite specifically defined the area of application of the pact: SEATO is surely an area accord, resultingly, in terms of being "for" Southeast Asia. Only two of its eight members, on the other hand, are "of" Southeast Asia (the Philippines and Thailand), although at least two others are very close neighbors of the region (Pakistan and Australia). South Vietnam, Cambodia, and Laos might also have joined SEATO at the start if they had not been prevented from doing so by the terms of the 1954 Geneva Agreements which ended the eight-year Franco-Vietnamese war. There is even the likelihood that the latter two lands might not have developed their subsequent neutralist positions in international affairs if they had been exposed to the continuous consultative processes of the alliance. The other eligible members within Southeast Asia, Indonesia and Burma, had already assumed their neutralist postures at the time of the Manila Conference, while Malaya had yet to gain its independence.

Although SEATO did not subsequently expand its membership and may not have fulfilled all the expectations of its

Asian members in particular, it unquestionably did contribute to the further popularization of the idea of Southeast Asia as an integral unit or region in world politics. SEATO, indeed, may have led directly to the formation of still another regional association for Southeast Asia seven years later—the Association for Southeast Asia. Two of the three founding members of ASA, the Philippines and Thailand, appear to have increased their inclination to cooperate in a meaningful manner with other states as a result of their experience as members of SEATO. The third partner in ASA, which was launched in mid-1961, was Malaya, which had been an indirect participant in SEATO as a consequence of its close bilateral defense relationship with alliance member Britain. ASA grew out of talks between Malayan Premier Tengku Abdul Rahman and Philippine President Carlos P. Garcia in early 1959, although it must also be said to have had roots in earlier Philippine and Thai efforts to fashion closer relations among the several Southeast Asian states. There is some evidence to suggest that the Philippines and Malaya first sought to establish a Pan-Malay Union among the three Southeast Asian states of predominantly Malay ethnic stock—Malaya, the Philippines, and Indonesia—but Indonesia clearly wanted neither such a Pan-Malay Union, as it may have been proposed, nor ASA. Other states apparently seriously considered association with ASA (Burma and Cambodia, for example) but decided not to join.

The avowed purpose of ASA was economic and social cooperation among its three member states. They did, indeed, consider a number of possible joint projects, and they caucused and voted as a bloc at the Colombo Plan meeting which immediately followed the formation of the association. Political motivations probably also underlay ASA, however. It was not coincidental that the new union linked three of the most anti-Communist and private enterprise-oriented countries in Southeast Asia. The Filipinos and

International Relations

the Thai were clearly disappointed in the level of economic cooperation which had been developed within SEATO, moreover, while the Malayan leadership hoped that ASA would provide one of several means whereby its economic diversification might be hastened. Like SEATO, ASA had to show results before others would join it, and this it was prevented from doing by the subsequent quarrel between Malaya and the Philippines over the former's enlargement to include Singapore, Sarawak, and Sabah as the new state of Malaysia in 1963. What had seemed to some to be such a promising association foundered—at least temporarily—as a result of the clash of rival national political interests. Efforts were made to revive ASA in 1966—following the election of a new Philippine President (Ferdinand E. Marcos) and his efforts to resume close relations with Malaysia. Much of the momentum, however, may have been lost by this time.

The political differences between Manila and Kuala Lumpur over Malaysia's formation as well as those between Malaysia and Indonesia seemed briefly to be leading toward new procedures of consultation among the three countries involved in 1963. The heads of state of these nations agreed in Manila in August 1963 to cooperate in matters of security, economic development, and social and cultural affairs within a loose consultative arrangement to be called Maphilindo. The three countries pledged themselves to use Maphilindo, formed from the first few letters of their names, for the purpose of "frequent and regular consultations at all levels." The Philippine, Indonesian, and Malayan leaders also agreed to ask the United Nations secretary general to determine the willingness of the peoples of Sarawak and Sabah to participate in Malaysia, but the Indonesians in particular were not satisfied with the results. Maphilindo accordingly never got off the ground. At the June 1966 Bangkok peace talks, however, Indonesian Foreign Minister Adam Malik discussed new efforts toward regional cooperation among the four ASA-

Maphilindo states, Indonesia, Malaysia, the Philippines, and Thailand. Indonesia's change of government could also mean a change in its attitude on this question.

Twenty years after the end of the Second World War, only SEATO stood as any kind of functioning regional cooperative association in Southeast Asia, and even SEATO had only two Southeast Asian members. One of the latter, Thailand, was also cooperating with Laos, Cambodia, and South Vietnam in the technical task of surveying the lower Mekong River for its further utilization for irrigation, power, and other purposes. But this cooperation concerned none of the participants as much as their conflicts with their adversaries —mainly themselves.

NATIONALISM AND NATION BUILDING

The developing pattern of intra-regional relations in Southeast Asia has gone through three fairly distinct stages. The first of these periods was the initial half-decade after the Second World War when most of the Southeast Asian countries either obtained their independence or were vigorously struggling to free themselves from foreign rule. Although nobody ever seemed to wish to second anybody else's proposal for closer regional collaboration, almost everybody had his own plan. The sentimental unity of feeling created by the common experience of colonial rule was, no doubt, the basis of most if not all of these plans. With the attainment of independence, however, this unity began to wane. Nationalism commenced to display its inherent divisive tendencies. This, probably more than any other single factor, explains the apparently lessening appeal which regional cooperation had for many of the leaders and peoples of Southeast Asia in the 1950s. Closer collaboration would have lessened the freedom of action of the new national states— and freedom of action they wished to maintain above all things.

A regional defense association was created during the second stage (roughly, the 1950s)—SEATO. But SEATO was born and shaped largely as a consequence of American initiative, only two Southeast Asia states ever joined it, and it was conspicuously alone as an organization for area association during these years. Yet SEATO did foreshadow a new trend appearing in the first half of the 1960s. This was the growing awareness on the part of some of the Southeast Asia states that they were not by themselves or in their present form able to discharge many of the functions, such as defense and economic development, historically associated with the nation state. ASA was formed largely because its three founding members seemed to believe that there were important things they might do collectively which they could not do individually. Likewise, the Philippines, Indonesia, and Malaya appeared to be establishing Maphilindo in 1963 as the only method whereby various political questions beyond the control of any one of these countries individually could be resolved to their mutual if partial satisfaction. The expansion of Malaya in 1963 to include Singapore, Sarawak, and Sabah as the new state of Malaysia could even be considered as a unique variant of this trend.

The major difference between the proposals for regional cooperation advanced in the late 1940s and those of the early 1960s was probably the fact that the earlier plans were rooted mainly in sentimental considerations, while ASA, Maphilindo, and even Malaysia (like SEATO before them) were attempts to cope with problems that the nations involved could not otherwise solve. Even more national failures may be necessary before regional cooperation appears sufficiently attractive to have a real chance of success. Indonesia, one of the least interested of the Southeast Asian states in intra-area collaboration through the years, seemed suddenly, if briefly, to alter its attitude at the time of the August 1963 Manila Conference and the establishment of Maphilindo. Subsequently, the Indonesians returned to more traditional methods of obtaining national objectives, the unilateral employment of force in this instance, in their attempt to force the dismemberment of the new and neighboring state of Malaysia. Indonesia has so far failed in this effort, however, and one result could be renewed interest in some variant of the Maphilindo approach.

There can be little doubt that newly triumphant nationalism has been the single most important political factor in the area since the end of the Second World War. And the primary objective of this nationalism has been political, economic, and social freedom—independence in all ways possible from the peoples of other lands. Nationalism has glorified a particular people and the territory they occupy (or formerly occupied or might occupy in the future!). It has also emphasized the differences among men rather than the characteristics and problems that unite them. If it is true that ever larger numbers of men and women are identifying themselves with the national idea with each passing year in Southeast Asia, it is likely that effective regional cooperation, let alone genuine integration of the present nation states, will prove even more difficult in the years ahead than it has so far been.

Nation building has been a problem from the perspective of meaningful regional cooperation for a quite different set of reasons. None of the Southeast Asian states are today anywhere nearly as integrated nationally as are most of the Western European countries or such other nations as Japan or the United States. The nation concept has been severely strained by the persisting rebellions of ethnic minorities in Burma, for example, or Chinese-Malay antagonisms in Malaysia (not to mention the war between the Communists and the anti-Communists in Vietnam). There is thus reason to doubt that such states still lacking internal integration are yet at a stage of development appropriate to international integration. Similarly, the existence of seemingly endless

International Relations

internal problems associated with nation building has tended, not at all unnaturally, to preoccupy many political leaders with domestic questions and has caused them to look inward.

Possibly the chief difference between the persisting obstacles of nationalism and nation building is the fact that regional cooperation may become more difficult as nationalism sinks its roots deeper in a society, while successful efforts in the multisided task of nation building could provide some release from the present level of preoccupation with this labor.

PAN-ASIANISM

Another reason why various Southeast Asian political leaders have shown little interest in regional collaboration at different times has been the attraction of broader cooperation on an Asiawide basis. The idea of an all-Asian grouping goes back well beyond the postwar period. It can be traced to such earlier endeavors as the Russian-convened Congress of the Nations of the Orient at Baku in 1920, the Nagasaki Pan-Asiatic Conference of 1926, and the 1934 Pan-Asiatic Labor Conference held in Ceylon, among other events, its past sponsors including such distinguished Asians as the late Jawaharlal Nehru.

Several proposals for closer political relations among the several Asian states were put forward after the Second World War. The unofficial Asian Relations Conference in New Delhi in March-April 1947, in fact, was hailed by many as the beginning of the establishment of some kind of Asian union. All of the Southeast Asian countries were represented among the thirty-one states sending delegates to the conference, but the unity of the many prominent Asians attending the Delhi meeting was limited to an almost unanimous anti-European sentiment, moral support for the liberation struggles in those Asian lands not yet independent, and a belief in the possibility of Asian neutrality in any future world war. The representatives of the Southeast Asian countries seemed very much concerned in their speeches that integration within any Asiawide bloc would be at the expense of some of their newly won political independence.

Among those who met for the first time in New Delhi at the 1947 Asian Relations Conference were the leaders of the socialist movements of India, Indonesia, and Burma. They agreed on the need to form a South Asian socialist international organization, but circumstances prevented any action toward this end for several years. In March 1952, however, representatives of the Socialist parties of these three countries met in Rangoon, together with observers from the right and left wings of the Japanese Social Democrats, and plans were laid for the Rangoon Socialist Conference of 1953, expanded from a South Asian to an all-Asian conference "because the problems to be solved are Asiawide." Delegations from Malaya, Pakistan, Israel, and Egypt attended the 1953 Rangoon Conference, and there were observers from other lands —but no representation at all from such countries as China, Vietnam, Thailand, the Philippines, Cambodia, or Laos. An Organization of Asian Socialist Parties was established which comprised a conference (which was to meet every other year), a bureau (which met twice annually), and a permanent secretariat (located in Rangoon). The Organization of Asian Socialist Parties in fact lasted for several years, and its conferences and bureau meetings were useful in encouraging international contacts. The fact that few of the member national parties were in power in their countries was a major reason for the organization's ultimate demise.

On only one occasion prior to 1955 did the several Asian governments participate in an all-Asia conference. The occasion was the Indian-convened Conference on Indonesia in January 1949 following the second Dutch "police action" of December 1948 against the nationalist revolutionaries in the former Netherlands colony. Nineteen states (including Australia and New Zealand) attended this conference, which was called by Indian Prime Minister Nehru at the suggestion of Burmese Premier U Nu. The conference, which called upon the United Nations Security Council to arrange for the transfer of power by the Dutch over Indonesia by January 1, 1950, was generally regarded as having played a part in the ending of the Dutch-Indonesian war later in the year.

The several suggestions for an Asian union were paralleled in the postwar years by a number of proposals for a Pacific pact which would have included the United States as well as various East Asian countries. President Elpidio Quirino of the Philippines, Nationalist China's Chiang Kai-shek, and South Korean President Syngman Rhee were the chief advocates of such an association, which was never formed, in part because the latter two leaders were widely regarded as unrepresentative of contemporary Asia. The idea of such a military pact has persisted, however, and was again pursued with some intensity by the South Korean government of President Chung Hi Park in 1964 and 1965.

There has been even less interest among the Southeast Asian countries through the years in an Asian common market than in an all-Asian or pan-Pacific selective security organization. The United Nations Economic Commission for Asia and the Far East has brought representatives of practically all the governments of Asia together and has rendered various services, but it has not supplanted the activities of ordinary national governments in any way. An important reason why the Southeast Asian lands have not been enthusiastic about a pan-Asian economic community has been their fear that such a relationship with much more industrialized Japan in particular would doom them to continuance as underdeveloped primary producers. This, above all, they do not want. Japan has sought in various ways to encourage more structured economic relations but has not been successful. Regular trade relations may be creating such a *de facto* relationship, however.

SOUTH ASIAN COOPERATION

Cooperation was also proposed in the postwar years among the states of South Asia, which is generally defined to include India, Pakistan, and Ceylon as well as Southeast Asia. In January 1949 S.W.R.D. Bandaranaike, leader of the Ceylonese delegation to the Indonesian Conference in New Delhi and later prime minister of Ceylon, proposed closer economic and political cooperation among India, Pakistan, Burma, Indonesia, and Ceylon. Nothing came of the proposal at the time, and it was not until April 1954 that leaders of these five states met together ostensibly for talks about mutual relations. Sir John Kotelawala, then Ceylon's premier, convened the meeting and called upon these countries to unite in a "joint endeavor" to become an effective force in the preservation of world peace. Sir John expressed the hope that the premiers of the five lands would frequently come together for consultations along the lines of the meetings of the Commonwealth prime ministers. So preoccupied were the five premiers with matters related to the Geneva Conference on Indochina then in session, and so divided in their views about some of them, that they ignored the main reason for the calling of the meeting in the first place. However, the Colombo Powers, as the five states came to be called, did gain at least temporary recognition as a significant bloc in world politics.

The premiers of the five Colombo Powers met again in Bogor, Indonesia, in December 1954 and authorized Indonesia, one of their number, to invite various Asian and African nations to a conference at Bandung in April 1955. The chief historical significance of the Colombo Powers, who long ago ceased meeting as a bloc, was probably the impetus which these five countries provided to the developing trend toward broader Afro-Asian cooperation. As for effective cooperation among themselves, this was quite short lived.

International Relations 355

By 1965, a decade after Sir John Kotelawala first called the Colombo Powers together in Ceylon's capital city, the five states were probably more divided than they had ever been and were hardly a force for peace. Indonesia, indeed, had all but declared war against neighboring Malaysia, while India and Pakistan were engaged in major hostilities over disputed Kashmir. Indonesia and India had drifted apart, not the least as a result of Indian support of Malaysia, and the Indonesians had unilaterally renamed the Indian Ocean "the Indonesian Ocean." Burma and India followed increasingly divergent policies toward China, the late Prime Minister Nehru and his successor, Lal Bahador Shastri, who died in office in 1966, blaming the Burmese for aiding Peking by reaching a border settlement that seemed to influence adversely New Delhi's position in its frontier quarrel with Communist China.

Although lasting political cooperation has yet to establish itself among the several states of South as well as Southeast Asia, economic cooperation has steadily grown among these lands and the more highly industrialized of the British Commonwealth countries, together with Japan and the United States, in the form of the Colombo Plan, which originated at a meeting of the Commonwealth foreign ministers in the capital city of Ceylon in January 1950. The twenty-two members of the Colombo Plan agreed in November 1964 to extend this particular pattern of cooperation through 1971, a reflection of its worth in the eyes of the participant countries. The objective of the Colombo Plan is "to raise the standard of living by accelerating the pace and widening the scope of economic development in the countries of South and Southeast Asia by a cooperative approach to their problems with special emphasis on the production of food." The members of the Colombo Plan today include Afghanistan, Australia, Bhutan, Burma, Canada, Cambodia, Ceylon, India, Indonesia, Japan, Laos, Malaysia, the Maldive

Islands, Nepal, New Zealand, Pakistan, the Philippines, Singapore, South Korea, South Vietnam, Thailand, the United Kingdom, and the United States.

BANDUNG AND AFTER

Delegates from twenty-nine Afro-Asian nations, only sixteen of which were then United Nations members, attended the April 1955 Bandung Conference. They agreed to condemn colonialism, and they endorsed Indian Premier Nehru's proposal that the testing of nuclear weapons be suspended. As was to be expected, they strongly championed the cause of peace, and they also backed Indonesia's claims to Dutch-held West New Guinea, supported Yemen's pretensions to the British protectorate of Aden, and generally applauded the cause of the Arab peoples of the Middle East, whether fighting for independence against the French in Morocco or Tunisia or seeking redress of the grievances of the Palestine refugees.

If they concerned themselves with Aden, however, they ignored the problem of divided Korea completely. And although they talked of the difficulties in partitioned Vietnam, they did not do or say anything which brought any nearer a solution of these difficulties. In short, their discussions were conspicuous for their concern with matters over which they had little direct control, as in the case of nuclear weapons, or which represented grievances against nations not in attendance at the conference—for example, the Dutch in West New Guinea, the French in North Africa, the British in Aden, and the Israelis and the problem of the Arab refugees. A pattern only too obvious at the April 1954 meeting of the Colombo Powers was being repeated—the less the assembled nations could do about a given problem, the louder they talked about it.

It was not, however, the fact that the Asian community failed to shoulder its responsibilities which was the most significant thing about the Bandung Conference. It was rather that there was no real Asian community to begin with, except on a superficial sentimental level. Asia at Bandung spoke with three voices, in addition to several species of whispers. Loudest of the three voices at the outset of the conference was that of those nations friendly to the West: the Philippines, Thailand, Pakistan, Iran, Iraq, and Turkey. They condemned Communism as the new imperialism and strongly defended their alliances with the West. Ranged against them was the soft-spoken Chinese Communist Chou En-lai, who endeavored to convince his conference colleagues of Peking's peaceful intentions. Finally, there were the neutralists, comprising most of the countries participating in the conference. The neutralists, led by Burma's U Nu and Indonesia's Ali Sastroamidjojo as well as Indian Premier Nehru, apparently hoped that cold-war alignments could be forgotten amid the triumphant unity of pan-Asian sentiments. They could not have been more wrong. The impact of the cold war pervaded almost all aspects of the Bandung meeting. There were the pro-Western countries, the Communists, and the neutralists—and they succeeded in reaching no more agreement among themselves than these forces were then accomplishing in the world at large.

If Asia or Afro-Asia did not present a united front at Bandung, the 1955 conference did serve to herald the increasing importance of these nations in international politics. The Bandung meeting was part of a new phenomenon that had already exposed itself in the caucusing and cooperation of the newly independent Asian and African countries at the United Nations and in the establishment of an Anti-Colonial Bureau by the Asian Socialist Organization to help the nationalist movements of Africa in their fight for freedom from foreign rule. The countries of Afro-Asia reached new heights of international prominence and influence in the first half of the 1960s, both within the U.N. and outside it, but growing differences among the nations of Asia and Africa became increasingly evident as the decade passed its midpoint. The two most populous lands, China and India, were deadly enemies. Indonesia and Malaysia dispatched rival delegations to Africa to woo supporters for their respective positions in their "confrontation" crisis. And Algeria, scheduled site for a "second Bandung" conference in 1965, experienced a military coup d'etat on the eve of the meeting's scheduled convocation in March, forcing a postponement until November because of the domestic situation in the host country.

The November 1965 Algiers Afro-Asian conference failed to materialize, however. The reason was the extent of the divisions among the nations of Asia and Africa. The Chinese and the Indonesians in particular had sought to separate the former colonial lands of these two immense continents into progressive and procolonial categories—which only served to increase the differences among nations already badly divided among themselves as long ago as the "first Bandung." There were many who predicted, accordingly, that there would never again be an Afro-Asian meeting in any way reflective of all, or most, of the main currents of political thought in the twin continents.

A most important Southeast Asian country, Indonesia, host to the 1955 Bandung Conference, was a leading participant in the developing differences among the nations of Asia. Indonesia, together with the other Southeast Asian neutralist countries, Burma and Cambodia, played a prime part in the first conference of nonaligned nations in the Yugoslav capital of Belgrade in 1961. This meeting, in which host President Tito and Indian and Egyptian leaders Nehru and Nasser also took part, was an attempt to bring together the professed peace-loving nations of the world who stood outside the alliance structures of the opposed Western and Communist camps. At the second meeting of these states in Cairo in late 1964 Indonesia took an especially hard, nonpeaceful line—reflective perhaps of its growing affinity with

International Relations

Communist China—concerning the necessary use of force to complete the anticolonial struggle. The Indonesians were clearly seeking endorsement of their forceful stand against the new state of Malaysia in Southeast Asia. The Indonesian action almost split the conference, and Indonesia suffered a stinging diplomatic defeat.

Indonesia's position and actions were consistent with the espousal by President Sukarno of the bipolarization of the world into the camps of the "new emerging forces" and the "old established forces" (and their alleged lackeys, of which Malaysia, not surprisingly, was said to be a prime species). Sukarno's decision to depart the U.N. in early 1965 was accompanied by widespread fear that other nations might ultimately follow Indonesia's lead and possibly form a rival international organization of the so-called "new emerging forces." It was feared that Indonesia, China, North Vietnam, North Korea, and perhaps Cambodia or Cuba might provide the nucleus for such a body.

Indonesia's decision to quit the United Nations and the specter of "rival U.N.'s" provided a quite unintended reminder of the peaceful protestations of Bandung a decade earlier. Indonesia itself had mounted a small-scale but growing war against adjacent Malaysia. China, which had opposed nuclear testing along with the other Bandung countries in 1955, exploded an atomic device in 1964. The divisions so evident at Bandung had grown. A new kind of bipolarization seemed to be taking place—pitting not Communist against non-Communist or even Afro-Asian against European but rather the "revolutionary-minded" (like China and Indonesia) against allegedly more conservative forces (such as Malaysia, the United States, India, and possibly even the U.S.S.R.).

CHAPTER 11

AMERICAN POLICY IN SOUTHEAST ASIA

AMERICAN ECONOMIC interest in Southeast Asia was slight on the eve of the Second World War despite the fact that the United States acquired sovereignty over the Philippines as long ago as 1899. Senator Albert Beveridge predicted at the turn of the century that Americans would swarm to the islands and that American capital would flow to the new dependency in an ever-swelling stream, but this did not happen. The total amount of American investments in the region was estimated in 1941 to be $325,000,000—only about 2 percent of total American foreign investments at the time —and it is no more than that today. Even the value of American trade with the Philippines had an artificial significance, based as it was on a 100 percent preferential tariff policy which caused three-fourths of the exports of the Philippines to be channeled to the United States.

As a great industrial and military power, however, the United States has been forced to include in its foreign policy a continually increasing consideration of Southeast Asia as an important source of strategic materials. This region produces nearly two-thirds of the world's tin and over four-fifths of its natural rubber. While its output of oil is not large in terms of total world production, it is nevertheless of great

American Policy

strategic significance because so little oil is produced elsewhere in South or East Asia. The loss of the other important products of the region—bauxite, tungsten, iron ore, tea, sugar, coffee, spices, abaca, copra, and coconut oil—would only be inconvenient for the West, but to allow free access to them to Communist countries would greatly strengthen the latter's economic and political power. Burma, Thailand, and South Vietnam, for example, in normal times produce great quantities of rice, a staple food important to all Asian countries.

The physical and demographic dimensions of Southeast Asia also must command the attention of a nation with world responsibilities. Covering some 1,650,000 square miles spread over a large portion of the globe and containing a population of about 200,000,000, Southeast Asia is a region to be reckoned with. Half continental and half peninsular, it lies astride the great trade routes of the Eastern world, whose strategic importance became strikingly apparent in the Second World War. Once in Vietnam, it became clear that Japan was in a position to overrun Southeast Asia almost at will and to threaten Australia and India. Today the Communist foothold in Vietnam, backed by the power of adjoining China, creates a situation much more alarming than 1941. China's striking power is more limited than that of wartime Japan, but it possesses certain advantages that Japan lacked—a contiguous position and 12,000,000 of its people scattered throughout the region providing a bridgehead for infiltration and subversion. Moreover, although China has not yet attained great naval or air power nor become highly industrialized, as was Japan, the world has watched with grave concern the explosion by China of the nuclear bomb.

OBSTACLES FACING AMERICAN DIPLOMACY

As Southeast Asia has moved inexorably toward the center of the world stage and become the focus of American concern, the enormous difficulties United States diplomacy faces in dealing with the region become more painfully obvious. Besides the physical barriers of distance, the cultural barriers of language and a basically different philosophy of life, the United States, despite its long tradition of anticolonial sentiment, has come to be identified in the Asian mind with the great colonial powers of the West who dominated the region for centuries. Coupled with these is the reluctance of the American people and their Congress to engage in matters abroad unless an immediate and open military threat is directed at the United States.

Although American sentiment has traditionally been anticolonial, Americans still do not appreciate fully the frenetic and often violent quality of the emotions aroused by the term among peoples only recently freed after two centuries of dependence. In the struggle for independence there developed a feeling against all the nations of the West, and the United States, partly because of its relations with the Philippines, has come to be included not only in the anti-Western feeling but also in the hostility toward imperialism —the latter emotion cultivated assiduously and effectively by Communist propaganda. And when the poverty which prevails among almost all Asian peoples is contrasted with the opulence of American and other foreign nationals in Southeast Asia, it becomes easy for the Asian to blame first colonialism, next the West, and then, by extension, the United States for his deep and continuing social problems.

There is evident among the peoples of the region a cultural reaction to Western penetration. One sign is the revival of Buddhism in Burma and Thailand and the irreconcilable Darul Islam movement in Indonesia, which sought to establish by violence a theocratic Islamic state. The collision of Western with Eastern culture has had an extremely disturbing effect on the minds and feelings of many Southeast Asians, not only arousing hostility toward Westerners but also creating tensions among groups within the countries. Overriding this deep cultural cleavage is the clash of the

American Policy

essentially Western ideologies of communism and democracy, ideologies which have won adherents but which also have aroused resentment as being unsuitable to the Asian temperament.

Another complicating factor for American diplomacy is the presence of large alien population groups: between ten and twelve million Chinese, a million or more Indians, a few hundred thousand Europeans, and a scattering of Arabs. These groups constitute disturbing social forces because they control a disproportionately large part of the economic life of the region, they are not easily assimilated, and they are, for the most part, nationals of large and powerful neighboring countries. Nearly every country in the region has passed legislation discriminating against these alien elements in order to help their indigenous nationals improve their economic position.

But it is extreme poverty which, as always, is the breeding ground for discontent and hostility. With a total population about 15 percent greater than that of the United States, its combined national income is only 3 percent as large. In 1963 the American per capita income was $2,449; for some Southeast Asian states, it was as low as one-fiftieth that amount. There are areas, such as Java, central Luzon, and the Red River delta, where the population pressure is intense. The last-named area has a "nutritional density" of 500 persons per square mile of cultivated rice land, and wherever the population pressure is so severe, there almost invariably is grave social and political unrest.

It is wholly understandable that people living under these conditions should ascribe their poverty to foreign exploitation. The comparison between prosperous foreign enterprises and numerous affluent aliens within their own poverty-stricken society seems to point to but one conclusion. And Marxism offers a persuasive remedy, which nationalist leaders find useful in arousing resentment against foreign domination. In contrast with the nationalist revolutions in the

West, which were middle-class movements, those in Southeast Asia (with the exception of the Philippines) are headed by intellectual proletarians. The result is a strong socialistic inclination in all of these countries, the phenomenon of weak governments attempting vast socialist programs. In view of the political and administrative inexperience of these peoples, it is surprising that the results have not been even more disastrous. Though their leaders have learned and unlearned a great deal about economics, suspicion of foreign capital is still strong. The political leaders of the Southeast Asian countries regard their economies as "colonial," and they are determined to give them a "national" character in as short a time as possible. This accounts in large part for their socialistic fervor as well as the desire to acquire foreign-owned properties. Also sharpening the suspicion of foreigners is the fact that the economic life of these countries is heavily dependent on the export of a few commodities, which places them at the mercy of the world market. In the 1950s rice constituted 76 percent in value of the total exports of Burma, and in the other countries of the region the percentages of chief exports were as follows: Indonesia—rubber, 38, petroleum, 25, tin, 7, and copra, 6; the Philippines—copra, 31, and sugar, 26; Thailand—rice, 33, and tin, 21, and Malaya—rubber, 60, and tin, 23.

But why, Americans often ask, are not Asians repelled by the cruelties of Communism? They forget that Asians are not instinctively repelled by cruelty and suffering because they have lived so long in the midst of malignant poverty and disease. Many of them have experienced nothing but suffering and have lived with it all their days. They are inured to it. Moreover, their religions tend not to make them as sensitive to suffering as do the teachings of Christianity. Furthermore, Communist doctrine promises such an attractive future for Southeast Asians that they are prepared to overlook some of the cruelties in practice. Communism can point to Lenin's theory of imperialism as a simple explanation of the causes of the plight of the colonial peoples. Poverty can be conquered, says Communism, through a planned economy, and Marxist political techniques adapted for underdeveloped peoples.[1] Moreover, Communist belief in the inevitability of a proletarian victory seems to have a strong attraction for the Asian mind, which has always been absorbed with the idea of fate.

The peoples of Southeast Asia were led by their nationalist leaders to believe that with independence their living conditions would immediately improve. This has not happened; in some countries there has been serious deterioration. Indonesia, with half of the population of the region, finds its level of living considerably below that of 1938. Ironically, however, school attendance, and especially college enrollments, have boomed, pouring large numbers of intellectuals into a market which can absorb very few of them. It is not surprising, therefore, to find young intellectuals turning in frustration to dictatorship and totalitarianism as the only solutions to their difficult problems.

Finally it must be pointed out that there is little cultural unity to be found in Southeast Asia. Nearly every country has significant minorities, both religious and ethnic. In Malaysia, where the native Moslem has become a minority in his own country, the divisions are sharp. Much time must pass before the various communities of Malaysia can be merged into a nation. Developments in Indonesia indicate rather clearly that the Dutch over three centuries failed to mold the peoples of the myriad islands into a real unity. It is much the same regionally. The population of one state is predominantly Christian; that of another, Moslem; that of several, Buddhist; and Malaysia has no majority for any one faith. Because they were ruled for long periods by different powers, these countries have been drawn in different directions culturally. The absence of political and cultural unifi-

[1] Max Mark, "Nationalism versus Communism in Southeast Asia," *Southwestern Social Science Quarterly*, XXXIII (1952), 135-47.

cation aided the Western powers in establishing their control originally, and today the diversity remains in aggravated form. The colonial administrations have been replaced by weak, independent states, the economy of much of the region has deteriorated, the work of well-trained, experienced colonial officials and able foreign entrepreneurs has been taken over by untrained, inexperienced natives. Social and civil unrest, insurrection and armed strife, and political ineptitude have rendered the region exceedingly vulnerable to direct and indirect Communist aggression. Even if there were no threat of external aggression, the situation would be acute, for in several of these countries the forces of disintegration are strong. With their societies open to Communist infiltration and subversion, the situation is very serious. The region is utterly lacking in the economic and military power with which to defend itself, and, what is worse from the Western point of view, it frequently seems to lack the will to defend itself.

DEVELOPMENT OF AMERICAN POLICY

Although the United States had been involved in Southeast Asia since it acquired sovereignty over the Philippines, pledged itself to defend the islands, and imported considerable quantities of tin and rubber from the region, official interest in the area before Pearl Harbor was comparatively modest. In 1940, when the Japanese occupied French Indochina and put pressure on the Dutch to make economic concessions in Indonesia, the United States became aroused enough to give the countries with responsibilities in the region some diplomatic support in resisting Japan's demands. Little has yet been made public about American diplomacy with respect to the region during the Second World War. It is well known that President Roosevelt held strongly anti-colonial views and that he was especially critical of French policy in Indochina. Of the Dutch he was not so critical.

American Policy

The Netherlands Indies, exclusive of Sumatra, was included under General Douglas MacArthur's Southwest Pacific Area command. Dutch New Guinea became a base for the next leap northward, but Moratai (in the northern Moluccas) and Tarakan and Balikpapan, the oil ports on the east coast of Borneo, were the only other parts of the Netherlands Indies recaptured by the forces of this command. Immediately after the Borneo campaign, General MacArthur had proposed to move on to Java "and restore the Dutch Government under Van Mook, which would have rapidly brought law and order there as it had done in New Guinea." This plan for a further thrust into Java was, according to General MacArthur, "for some reason never understood, peremptorily called off and forbidden from Washington, in spite of my insistence of its complete success with little loss." MacArthur further declared that the cancellation of this movement "was one of the grave mistakes of the war and ultimately resulted in the chaotic conditions which followed in that part of Indonesia. It completely violated the basic principle of American foreign policy to support the orderly development of dependent areas toward self-government."[2]

Though the reasons for this action by Washington have not been revealed, some seem quite obvious. It may be adequately, if not wholly, explained by the need of all available forces for an early move on Japan proper. Shortly before the capitulation of Japan, the Netherlands Indies was shifted from General MacArthur's area to that of Admiral Mountbatten. Washington might have felt that it had a large enough area of responsibility in the Philippines, China, and Japan. Also, in the background there may have been a reluctance, and even fear, of becoming involved in restoring the former colonial governments in these territories. As it was, the United States did not escape all embarrassment in Indonesia or in Indochina—or even in the Philippines. It

[2] Charles A. Willoughby and John Chamberlain, *MacArthur: 1941-51* (New York 1954), 275.

was caught in an awkward position. It could ill afford to alienate the Dutch and the French, whose cooperation was needed in Europe, yet it wished to win the good will of the nationalist movements in Southeast Asia and to use its influence to end colonialism wherever it had outlived its usefulness. In Indochina the situation was desperate; the war there seemingly could not be won either with or without the French.

From 1948 on, the United States government became increasingly concerned about Communist activity in Southeast Asia. In early 1950 Secretary of State Dean Acheson declared that the countries of that region "find themselves in the path of a main thrust of Soviet subversion and expansion," but he was nevertheless unfavorably disposed toward the idea of an Asian defense pact. Acheson also warned against the obsession with military considerations in seeking solutions to Asian problems. American policy toward the region must recognize the revulsion of Asian peoples "against the acceptance of misery and poverty as the normal condition of life" and "revulsion against foreign domination." He declared that the basic interests of Americans and Asians were the same, that the United States stood ready to help the peoples of Asia to improve their social and economic conditions, but that American assistance could be effective only when it was the "missing component in a situation which might otherwise be solved." But Acheson also implied that, except for the Philippines, Southeast Asia was not regarded as an area so vital to the security of the United States that it would fight to defend it, except in fulfillment of its obligations as a member of the United Nations.

When in January 1950 Communist China and Soviet Russia recognized the Communist Ho Chi Minh's rebel regime in Vietnam, the United States very shortly thereafter announced its recognition of non-Communist Vietnam, Cambodia, and Laos. A few days later the Export-Import Bank granted Indonesia a $100,000,000 loan. It was clearly evident

American Policy

that a new and more active American policy was rapidly taking form. On February 16, Secretary Acheson made a fighting speech on "total diplomacy" in which he declared that the only way to deal with Russia was "to create situations of strength." A special economic mission was subsequently sent to Southeast Asia, followed by a military survey group. Military and economic aid began to flow to Southeast Asia in increasingly large quantities. For the fiscal year 1954 the total United States aid to Indochina alone was over $800,000,000, nearly all of it, however, for arms and military supplies. Substantial amounts also went to Thailand and the Philippines. On August 30, 1951, the United States and the Philippines signed a mutual defense treaty, and on September 1 the United States, New Zealand, and Australia formed the A.N.Z.U.S. pact.

THE 1954 GENEVA CONFERENCE

The crisis which developed in Indochina in the spring of 1954 was painful both for the American people and for the Eisenhower administration. In the 1952 election campaign the Republicans had flayed the Roosevelt and Truman administrations for the loss of China to the Communists and for getting the United States into a war in Korea which American forces (under the conditions imposed on them) could not win and which threatened to go on forever. Moreover, the Eisenhower administration, in cutting military expenditures, had reduced the armed forces, including American troops abroad. Having taken credit for ending the war in Korea, the administration could hardly justify entering upon another and similar adventure in Indochina. But the loss of Indochina to the Communists would also be embarrassing in view of the furor the Republicans had made over the American diplomatic disaster in China. Moreover, the United States had become deeply involved in the war in Indochina. By early 1954 the United States was bearing about 80 percent of the cost of the military operations in that unhappy territory.

Secretary Dulles was determined not to lose any more territory to the Communists, but American financial and defense policies tended in a more cautious direction, and the secretary of state himself had promised that the United States would not again become bogged down in local wars. Caught in the vortex of contradictory policies and forces, Dulles in desperation proclaimed his "instant, massive retaliation" threat. This outburst was understandable under the circumstances, but its effects were bad. It frightened and alienated the friends of the United States and provided its enemies with propaganda. When the military situation steadily worsened and the French at long last decided to get out of the war in Indochina at once, the Eisenhower administration apparently seriously considered the idea of sending American troops into the conflict. Vice President Richard M. Nixon on April 6, 1954, in an off-the-record, off-the-cuff speech, declared that, if the French withdrew from the fight, the United States would have to dispatch forces to Indochina. As the leader of the free world, the United States could not afford a further retreat in Asia, he said. Dulles' replies to the press, when questioned about the issue, were equivocal. The president kept his balance. He repeatedly pointed out the seriousness of the situation, but he made direct participation by American troops in the war conditional upon Allied support and the approval of congress. The decisive factor, however, seems to have been the opposition, on military grounds, of General Matthew Ridgeway, army chief of staff.

The Allied support which President Eisenhower deemed vital for direct American involvement in the Vietnamese war proved unobtainable. Secretary Dulles flew to Europe, where he publicly appealed for a "united action" policy to stop Communist aggression in Indochina, and suffered a major rebuff. The British wished to give the upcoming Geneva Conference an opportunity to bring about a peace-

American Policy 371

ful settlement and, supported by public opinion both at home and in the Commonwealth countries, rejected the Dulles overtures for joint military action. The French, once so anxious to involve the Americans in the fighting in Indochina, now also refused to endorse the Dulles policy. There was indeed widespread fear in Europe that the American secretary of state wished to scuttle the Geneva Conference on Indochina, but he clearly sought only to strengthen the anti-Communist position in order to get a more favorable settlement. Publicly disturbed by the British and French reactions, Dulles returned to Washington, and the Geneva Conference proceeded without active American participation.

Though the United States was not an active participant at Geneva, American military strength and American sentiment had much to do with the final settlement. The Communists did not dare to press their demands too far, lest they drive France into the arms of the United States and arouse America to largescale intervention. The Geneva agreements meant in effect the practical withdrawal of France from Indochina, the withdrawal of the Communist Viet Minh forces from Cambodia and Laos, the temporary division of Vietnam at about the seventeenth parallel, and a plebiscite in two years to determine the future status of the whole of Vietnam.

American diplomacy unquestionably suffered a defeat in Indochina in 1954. An internationally legitimatized new Communist state came into being—possessed of some of the most important mineral resources in all Southeast Asia, a most strategic location, and an industrious population of more than 15,500,000 persons. The plebiscite scheduled for July 1956 was not held, chiefly because of the refusal of the South Vietnamese government of Ngo Dinh Diem, supported by the United States, to cooperate in holding it. Vietnam thus joined Germany and Korea as divided countries, victims of the titanic struggle between Communism and the free world for the strategic areas of the globe.

In a press statement of July 23, Dulles declared that the

"important thing from now on is not to mourn the past but to seize the opportunity to prevent the loss in North Vietnam from leading to the extension of Communism throughout Southeast Asia and the Pacific Southwest." He stated that there were two lessons which the free nations should learn from experience: namely, "that resistance to Communism needs popular support, and this in turn means that the people should feel that they are defending their own national institutions" and "that arrangements for collective defense need to be made in advance of aggression, not after it is under way."

THE FORMATION OF SEATO

The United States proceeded without delay to call a conference which it hoped would draft a security plan for Southeast Asia to prevent further Communist expansion in that region. On September 8, 1954, eight countries signed a Southeast Asian Collective Defense Treaty in Manila. In seeking to create "a dependable barrier to further Communist expansion" in Southeast Asia in 1954, Secretary Dulles took on a formidable task. He had to find a formula for the defense of the region which would win the acquiescence, if not the enthusiasm, of France, Britain, Australia, New Zealand, Cambodia, Laos, Vietnam, Pakistan, India, and the several neutralist countries of Southeast Asia as well as the various factions of the United States congress. The difficulties encountered at Manila reveal many of the problems which American diplomacy continues to confront in Southeast Asia.

If SEATO was to be effective psychologically and militarily, it needed the support of a large number of Asian states. Suspicion of the West was strong, however, and the slogans of "Asia for the Asians" and "the peace of Asia should be maintained by Asians" had a compelling appeal. Unfortunately, the attempt to enlist Asian states in the movement

American Policy 373

and to give it an Asian character was not successful. The idea of the defense treaty originated in the West, was advocated chiefly by the United States, and received the support of only three Asian states, namely, Pakistan and Thailand, which were already receiving military assistance from the United States, and the Philippines, which was regarded by many Asians as an American satellite. The three Indochinese states might have joined at the time if the terms of the Geneva truce agreement had not precluded it, but Cambodia and Laos subsequently turned neutralist in their foreign policies. There was little about SEATO, accordingly, which was truly Asian. Whatever power the pact had necessarily came from the Western members, primarily the United States.

The treaty could not be given a broader Asian base for a number of reasons. The American policy of not extending recognition to Communist China and of continuing to recognize the Chiang Kai-shek regime as the government of China (while the British, among others, adopted the opposite policy) made it impossible to include either Nationalist or Red China. Moreover, the inclusion of Formosa would dispel any hope of ever getting India, Burma, or Indonesia to join. To avoid these difficulties, Hong Kong and Formosa were excluded from the area of applicability of the treaty. Japan could not be included as a member either, for all the countries of Southeast Asia still profoundly distrusted her, and Burma, Indonesia and the Philippines were wrangling with her over reparations. The result was a small and weak Asian base for the pact.

There was also the problem which no American Secretary of State can ever forget when he is negotiating a treaty, namely, that of getting an international agreement which will be acceptable to two-thirds of the membership of the United States senate. To insure approval by the senate and to avoid becoming involved in any war between India and Pakistan, Secretary Dulles wished to have the treaty assert specifically that it was directed against Communist aggression. The inclusion of such a statement would have alienated neutralist India and several of the Southeast Asian states beyond any hope of future adherence to the pact. Britain opposed it. As a compromise, it was agreed that the United States could attach a memorandum to the treaty expressing its own views.[3] It was probably also out of similar considerations that the obligations of the defense treaty were made not automatic, as in NATO, but merely consultative, though vulnerable states like Thailand and the Philippines strongly pleaded for the former.

Under the terms of the treaty, the signatories undertook, "separately and jointly, by means of continuous and effective self-help and mutual aid" to "maintain and develop their individual and collective capacity to resist armed attack and to prevent and counter subversive activities directed from without against their territorial integrity and political stability" (Art. II). They further undertook to "strengthen their free institutions and to cooperate with one another in the further development of economic measures, including technical assistance, designed both to promote economic progress and social well-being and to further the individual and collective efforts of governments towards these ends" (Art. III).

From a military point of view, Article IV constituted the heart of the treaty. In case of aggression by means of armed attack in Southeast Asia against any of the parties, each signatory agreed to meet "the common danger in accordance with its constitutional processes." By separate protocol the states and territories of Cambodia, Laos, and non-Communist Vietnam were designated as falling within the scope of the treaty, though they were not parties to it. However, no

---

[3] The statement of "understanding" of the United States attached to the treaty was to the effect that, in case of an armed attack which is not a Communist attack "in the treaty area against any of the Parties or against any State or territory which the Parties by unanimous agreement may hereinafter designate," the United States was under no obligation to act under the terms of the treaty. The reservation applied only to Article IV, paragraph 1.

American Policy

action would be taken on the territory of any of these states except "at the invitation or with the consent of the government concerned." The delegates to the Manila Conference knew that the chief threat to the region might not be direct attack but infiltration and subversion. They therefore further agreed that if the territorial integrity or political independence of the parties in the treaty area or the three states of Indochina "is threatened in any way other than by armed attack or is affected or threatened by any fact or situation which might endanger the peace of the area, the Parties shall immediately consult in order to agree on the measures which should be taken for the common defense." Since the treaty was so definitely consultative in character, a council so organized as to be able to meet at any time was provided for in Article V.

The territory covered by SEATO has not increased but shrunk. Malaya was removed from SEATO's operation when it became independent in 1957 and did not join the organization. Singapore, Sarawak and Sabah, also formerly British-ruled, underwent a like change when they became members of the Federation of Malaysia in 1963 (Singapore becoming independent by itself in 1965 and talking dangerously about the possibility of a Soviet naval base on its soil if Britain ever abandoned its defense responsibilities towards Malaysia or itself to the United States). Laos ceased to be a protocol state with the Geneva Agreements of 1962. Cambodia, while technically still covered by the protocol, has quite specifically spurned its promised protection. Conceivably Prince Norodom Sihanouk might still call upon SEATO for protection should Communist China or North Vietnam invade his country, but it is not likely that Cambodia would be taken over in this fashion.

Not only has the territory to which SEATO applies diminished, but actual support of the organization has also declined. Pakistan's rapprochement with China has affected the former's attitude toward the organization, while France's interest in SEATO and support of the alliance has become minimal. While India has become less critical of SEATO since its boundary difficulties with China, there is nothing to indicate that India's basic policy toward the security pact has changed or will change. On the other hand, the critical developments in Southeast Asia undoubtedly have increased the interest of Australia and New Zealand in SEATO. In the present dangerous situation in Southeast Asia SEATO is rarely mentioned, nor has the United States or any other member called on it for help.

REORIENTATION OF AMERICAN POLICY

United States policy in Southeast Asia began to undergo a change in 1956. A number of factors may account for the shift. The United States government was undoubtedly influenced by the "new look" in Russian foreign policy which followed the Geneva "Summit" Conference of July 1955. The Soviet shift involved more than a change of manner from growling to purring; it was accompanied by an announcement of a willingness to provide technical assistance and agricultural and industrial equipment to underdeveloped countries. When Russian leaders Bulganin and Khrushchev visited India in late 1955, they paid Burma the high compliment of including it in their itinerary. This was followed by an agreement to provide technical assistance and equipment in exchange for Burma's surplus rice, which was not readily finding a market. The U.S.S.R. also offered, as a gift, to build and equip an industrial institute. In September of the same year Djakarta announced an agreement between the Soviet and Indonesian governments whereby the former would extend the latter a credit of $100,000,000 at an interest rate of $2\frac{1}{2}$ percent and with repayment in 12 years.

The United States sought to counter this Soviet diplomatic and economic offensive. In March 1956, Secretary Dulles visited several Asian countries following a SEATO conference in Karachi. Indonesia seems to have been selected for special treatment on this trip. The anti-colonial theme, so dear to President Sukarno and most Indonesians, was played up very effectively (though stretched a bit). Shortly after his departure Dulles cabled President Sukarno, "You are grappling with the same problems that our own nation faced nearly two hundred years ago and which are still a vivid part of our tradition. I believe that only those who have gone through the process of transformation from being a colony can understand the problems that are involved. You and we have had a common experience which we can share with a special sense of fellowship." On behalf of President Eisenhower Dulles invited Sukarno to visit the United States.

The American government seemed to be groping for a new attitude toward neutralism. President Eisenhower at a press conference on June 6, 1956, declared that military alliances were not always an advantage and involved a risk for the country entering them. The same evening Vice President Nixon in a speech expressed essentially the same views, adding that uncommitted nations wanted time for economic development and "are not going to be frightened into alliances with the West by military power, nor can their allegiance be purchased by dollars." Reactions by America's allies to the president's statement apparently were fast and strong, for the White House issued an immediate explanatory statement. President Eisenhower did not believe that association for mutual security with the United States would involve any country in added danger, but, on the contrary, would provide increased security. In disparaging military alliances, the president meant only to disparage alliances with "great powers which have shown an aggressive disposition," meaning Communist countries. A few days later, Secretary Dulles declared neutrality to be immoral. Vice President Nixon visited the Philippines and some of the countries of South and Southeast Asia in July. In speeches and statements in Manila and Karachi he was back on the old theme of the immorality of neutralism and warned against trade agreements with the Soviet bloc.

It is evident that a change of attitude, at least, had taken place in Washington, however poorly government spokesmen explained this change. The right of neutrality was recognized, and aid was promised to countries even if they did not align themselves with the West. Instead of stressing the military dimension of defense, the United States began to emphasize the need for economic and social progress in the underdeveloped countries.

NEW AND PERSISTING PROBLEMS

The change in orientation in American foreign policy gained the United States very little. And it is open to serious question whether the change would have significantly altered the situation if it had occurred earlier. The fact is that important changes were taking place within Southeast Asia, sometimes in response to internal factors and sometimes as a result of external stimulation. The kind of foreign policy pursued by the United States probably would not have headed them off. The fact that such changes occurred, moreover, cannot be taken to indicate the failure of United States foreign policies. There are limits to what one nation, even a big and powerful one, can do to advance its interests and restrict the behavior of states halfway around the world.

The American objective was to contain the Communists, particularly China, as far as Southeast Asia was concerned, and to assist the nations of the latter region to become strong and stable so as to be able to survive in a much more troubled world than their nationalist leaders had anticipated en route to independence. Ideally, this meant democratic governments pursuing progressive economic and social policies and

American Policy

cooperating directly or indirectly with the United States and like-minded nations.

But this was not to be—for at least four reasons. First of all, the goal of democratic governments, as was apparent by the late 1950s and early sixties, was not a realistic one for most of the countries of Southeast Asia. Indonesian President Sukarno had proclaimed his aim of establishing "guided democracy" and the soldiers had taken over in Burma (only to return power to the civilians in 1960 and seize it anew in 1962). Thailand, a firm American ally, remained nonetheless army-run, while the military came to dominate the government in South Vietnam after Ngo Dinh Diem's ouster and murder in 1963. The tri-cornered struggle for power in Laos and Cambodian Prince Sihanouk's messiah-like self-image likewise made democracy most improbable for either of these formerly French-governed lands in the foreseeable future. Only the Philippines, Malaysia, and Singapore (which split away from Malaysia in 1965) seemed destined for democratic government.

Similarly, few of the Southeast Asian governments were willing seriously to seek rational solutions to their pressing economic problems. Others were unable to do so—sometimes for reasons not of their own choosing (including the limited legacy of economic development left them by the departed colonial powers). Indonesia, for example, abandoned a hopeful opportunity to stabilize its currency and begin a genuine assault on its enormous economic difficulties in favor of large expenditures of money, energy and time in an attempt to destroy newly proclaimed Malaysia. The Philippines, perhaps Southeast Asia's most stable state politically, seemed far more interested in spending its limited resources in endless political campaigning and the importation of American-manufactured luxury goods than in tightening its belt and registering economic progress sufficient to offset its exceptionally high birth-rate. Economic development was limited in Burma whether under U Nu (1948-1958), General Ne Win (1958-1960), Nu again (1960-1962), or a returned Ne Win (since 1962). And deterioration of economic conditions was a major consequence of the civil wars in both South Vietnam and Laos.

The assault of the Communists also came in a manner most difficult for the United States to counter. Vietnamese Communists who had been left behind in the south contrary to the terms of the 1954 Geneva settlement stepped up their guerrilla activity after 1959 and were joined by "invaders" from north of the seventeenth parallel. It was much easier to obtain agreement among the powers at the 1961-1962 Geneva Conference on Laos than to bring together the three warring Laotian factions—especially the Communists. Many believed that the growing pro-Communist orientation of Indonesia's Sukarno in the first half of the 1960s was a reflection of the increasing importance of the Indonesian Communist party, allegedly the largest outside the Sino-Soviet complex of countries.

Finally, countries close to China eagerly sought to make some kind of peace with Peking—usually for different and mixed reasons. Cambodia, fearful of Thailand and South (and potentially North) Vietnam, openly desired the protection of Communist China against these two traditional adjacent adversaries. The American ambassador in Rangoon rarely saw the Burmese premier, but the latter welcomed visiting Chinese statesmen and himself traveled to Peking in pursuit of good relations with Burma's giant neighbor. Indonesia and China came to cooperate to such an extent by the middle 1960s that Sukarno openly spoke of a Djakarta-Peking axis.

American willingness to accept neutralism as a reasonable species of foreign policy could accomplish little in such circumstances. The United States, accordingly, seemed subsequently to respond to the problems of Southeast Asia in a

American Policy

necessarily improvised and case-by-case fashion. Sometimes the response was military, other times diplomatic. A tough posture often was assumed, but the political cheek was also turned—again and again during the stewardship of Ambassador Howard P. Jones in Indonesia.

The degree to which American action (and related success or failure) was dependent on frequently uncontrolled circumstances is suggested by the contrasting expectations of American policy-makers concerning the quite different problems of Laos and Malaysia. The United States openly encouraged the Laotian government in the half-decade 1955-1960 to abandon the neutralist course set for it at Geneva in 1954. The result was a fragmentation of the country, initially pitting "neutralist" and Communist against a pro-American faction. The latter clearly was incapable of coping with the situation, and utlimately acquiesced in a return to a neutral foreign policy and a coalition government joining the three quarreling political groups. The United States agreed to the 1962 Laotian settlement because there was no acceptable alternative; the pro-U.S. faction could not win by itself, and the United States did not regard Laos as important enough to engage in a strength-sapping war there. The frank American expectation was that the Communists would soon come to control Laos by peaceful political means. But this was not to be. The neutralists, who were genuine nationalists, soon recognized the Communist Pathet Lao for what they were (handmaidens of Ho Chi Minh's North Vietnamese) and joined ranks with the conservatives. American military and other aid was solicited, and, four years after Geneva, Laos was still not in Communist hands—nor was it any longer likely that it would go Communist at an early date. The pessimism of the immediate post-Geneva period had shown itself to be falsely rooted. There was at least temporarily enough non-Communist strength to hold Laos, and the United States ably exploited the situation.

Expectations also failed of fulfillment respecting Malaysia, but these had been hopeful ones. When Malaya, Singapore, Sarawak and Sabah formed the state of Malaysia in 1963, Americans and others of similar orientation acclaimed the move (though not too loudly for fear of seeming to provide evidence for Peking's claim that the new nation was yet another "Western lackey"). The United States hoped that establishment of the new anti-Communist state would help to bring stability to Southeast Asia. But such was not to be. For a number of reasons, the Sukarno government adopted a policy of "confrontation" towards Malaysia, a policy clearly designed to encourage the dismemberment of the new state. Indonesia obviously hoped to pry away the northern Borneo territories of Sarawak and Sabah (and to join them to itself) and began a major guerrilla warfare towards this end. The United States as well as other countries (Thailand, Japan, and Cambodia) sought a solution to the Indonesian-Malaysian controversy but to no avail. Sarawak and Sabah were still members of the Malaysian federation after three years of confrontation, but Singapore broke away from the political partnership in mid-1965. The United States, unlike Laos, had hoped for much from Malaysia but received little. It gave both military and financial aid to Malaysia, which was being even more extensively assisted by the British, but more it probably could not do. No one, for example, even remotely suggested that it engage in any kind of military action on Malaysia's side against Indonesia, particularly in view of growing U. S. involvement in Vietnam.

Indonesia, largest by far of the Southeast Asian states, posed a particular problem for the United States. Try as it might through the years, the United States could not win the friendship of the Sukarno government. And there are those who will claim that the Americans humiliated themselves—and so lost face in the eyes of many Asian nations—by so trying. The United States played an important role

American Policy

in support of Indonesian independence in the late 1940s, and was the most important third-nation in the negotiations that led to the transfer of Western New Guinea from Dutch to Indonesian hands in 1962-1963. The American gave large amounts of economic assistance to the Indonesians and sought in different ways to encourage the Djakarta government to remedy its troubled economic situation. The long-time American ambassador, dean of the diplomatic corps in Djakarta for a number of years, was subjected (or subjected himself) to growing humiliation as he sought to maintain contact with his alleged personal friend President Sukarno, who rewarded him with increasingly vehement denunciations of the United States (sometimes delivered from the platform on which the ambassador was seated.). By late 1965, the United States had been forced to abandon its information services, withdraw Peace Corps personnel, and contract its aid program to extremely modest proportions. Private American groups—oil firms, foundations, and such—also found their activities curtailed or concluded.

The United States saw Indonesia moving in a steadily more pro-Communist direction, but what could it do? It had tried to be understanding of Indonesia's particular problems and gained nothing for its efforts. There were obviously few sanctions that could be applied to a country whose most frightening political transgression was its growing attachment to Peking and its allies—especially when that country was deliberately ridding itself of the few remaining links between the United States and itself.

United States policy in Indonesia seems to have been dominated by a determination to keep an American presence in the country, regardless of the cost to its national dignity, apparently on the assumption that it would lend encouragement to the forces of moderation and democracy. However, the effect of the policy may have been the reverse. The presence of the American ambassador on the platform with

Sukarno when the latter made his highly political speeches may have led some Indonesians to conclude either that their president had the tacit support of the United States or that Sukarno was so powerful that he could defy and publicly affront the world's greatest power. In neither case was there any encouragement to those who wanted to check Sukarno and reverse his disastrous policies. The help given to Sukarno to get West Irian on his own terms by a display of force encouraged him to turn on Malaysia with the same militant tactics, while it alienated the Dutch and embarrassed the Australian government.

Whether a tougher United States policy would have brought about a political change in Indonesia earlier it is difficult to say, but it seems obvious that little was gained by the supine attitude. Sukarno stayed on, the economy of the country was ruinously gutted and the Communists steadily acquired greater influence.

There are few grounds for optimism in Indonesia. The army apparently cannot afford to dismiss Sukarno and it is by no means certain that it can control him. Ridiculous as it may seem, Sukarnoism is so widely and fervently accepted by the masses that even the new regime must at least pay lip service to it. The economic conditions have become so bad that only a virtual genius employing extremely heroic measures could put the country on the road back to recovery. The army cannot perform economic miracles. Under the circumstances, there is no guarantee that Communism will not come back as a strong force. It recovered from previous setbacks.

By the standards of the Indonesian imbroglio, most of the rest of the problems faced by the United States in Southeast Asia seemed simple—in character if not of solution. Cambodia's Prince Sihanouk spurned American aid, refused to receive a United States ambassador, and took the first step in what became a break in diplomatic relations between the

American Policy

two countries. But Sihanouk did not endorse the Communists at home, nor did he have many of these in his country. His foreign policy, moreover, made a lot of sense, and his annoyance with the United States was more than a little justified. Likewise Burma could not be called pro-Communist; rather, the Ne Win government was seeking an accommodation with Peking that would permit Burma's survival as an independent nation. The United States was finding that it could take its chief ally in the region—the Philippines—less and less for granted, but it was adjusting fairly rapidly to the new situation. Thailand posed no major problems for the United States during this period.

It was Vietnam, however, that posed the biggest problem during these years. And it was Vietnam that so absorbed American attention that the legitimate grievances and problems of other nearby states—for example, Cambodia—received far less sympathy than they merited.

UNITED STATES POSITION IN VIETNAM

The basic problem in Asia as seen by the United States is China. Because of its location, its area, and the size and quality of its population, China is the predominant power of Asia. Recognizing this, the United States anchored its immediate postwar policy on a strong, friendly China. The United States obtained for China great power status in world politics with permanent membership in the Security Council of the United Nations. As one of the Big Five, it enjoyed the veto power in that body. China did become strong but unfortunately also extremely unfriendly to the United States. Worse still, it became militantly Communist. Hence American policy had to be reversed.

President Lyndon B. Johnson has been pressed to state clearly what American policy in Vietnam is and what its objectives are. It would seem to be obvious that the United States became involved in Indochina primarily to contain Communist China.[4] Evidence of this includes the American statement of "understanding" attached to the SEATO agreement restricting the United States' obligation under Article IV to Communist attacks. On February 17, 1965, President Johnson declared, "As I have said so many, many times and other presidents ahead of me have said, our purpose and our objective there is clear. That purpose and objective is to join in the defense and protection of the freedom of a brave people who are under attack that is controlled and that is directed from outside their country." In a news conference on July 29, 1965, the president declared that "this . . . war . . . is guided by North Vietnam and it is spurred by Communist China. Its goal is to conquer the South, to defeat American power, and to extend the Asiatic dominion of Communism." The United States' goals he declared to be, first, "to convince the Communists that we cannot be defeated by force of arms or by superior power," and, secondly, "once the Communists know, as we know, that a violent solution is impossible, then a peaceful solution is inevitable. We are ready now, as we have always been, to move from the battlefield to the conference table." As 1965 ended and a new year dawned, President Johnson had embarked on a major diplomatic offensive to bring North

[4] This position is strongly asserted in a report by a mission headed by Senator Mansfield: "This report does not deal with U.S.-Communist Chinese relations. Yet these relations are the basic factor in our present deep involvement in Southeast Asia. It was the hostility of China in Korea which first projected the United States in depth—via aid programs—into Indochina. It is Chinese hostility which evokes the continued flow of the bulk of U.S. aid and other activity into Southeast Asia. It is Chinese hostility which underlies the U.S. treaty commitment to SEATO. In short, we are involved in Southeast Asia preponderantly because of the implications of a Chinese hostility to the whole structure of our own security in the Pacific—a hostility which at this time is of unfathomable depth and uncertain duration." *Vietnam and Southeast Asia, Report of Senator Mike Mansfield, Senator J. Caleb Boggs, Senator Claiborne Pell, and Senator Benjamin A. Smith to the Committee on Foreign Relations, United States Senate, 1963.*

American Policy

Vietnam to the conference table and so end the escalating war in Vietnam.

The American position in Vietnam has not lacked weaknesses, however. Its validity demands that the war being waged in Vietnam is international, that there is a foreign invasion as well as a civil war. While Communist China and the Soviet Union have given material assistance to North Vietnam, it has not been claimed that they have sent armed forces to participate in the hostilities. It is true that North Vietnam is deeply involved, that it supplies the Vietcong with military supplies and men. Until recently the United States military representatives declared that only about 20 percent of the men and equipment came from the north, but lately the amount of aid from Hanoi has been emphasized. But is participation by the North Vietnamese sufficient to make it an international war? If it is assumed that the Vietnamese people, north and south, constitute a nation (by no means a wild assumption), then what we are dealing with in Vietnam is a civil war, a struggle between rival contenders for political control of a unified Vietnamese state. The plebiscite agreed upon by the 1954 Geneva Conference might have settled the problem, but South Vietnam's President Ngo Dinh Diem refused, possibly wisely at the time, to hold the referendum. In any case, both North and South Vietnamese presumably desire political unification, but the former want this unification only under a Communist regime, while to the latter this is unacceptable.

Even if the right of the South Vietnamese to political independence is assumed, the American position is not wholly free of difficulties. The United States justifies its military aid to South Vietnam on the grounds that it is giving this help in response to an appeal by its legitimate government. The Diem government (after it had been in office for some time) received popular endorsement, however manipulated, but not one in the parade of governments since has had even remotely an authentic democratic base. The United States has been very critical of puppet governments in Communist satellite countries, but its own position in South Vietnam in this respect falls considerably short of the democratic ideal. As early as 1954, Senator Mike Mansfield, in a report[5] of a study mission to Indochina, suggested that, in the event that the Diem government fell, the United States should "consider an immediate suspension" of all aid to Vietnam, "except that of a humanitarian nature, preliminary to a complete reappraisal of our present policies in Free Vietnam." He regarded it as improbable that substitute governments would be the kind of regimes which would be generally supported by the Vietnamese people. Nor was "it likely to be a government capable of sustaining a free and independent Vietnam generally without foreign support."

However regrettable the government's lack of a popular mandate may be, it is quite another thing to expect meaningful elections under the present disturbed conditions. Yet South Vietnam's Premier Air Marshal Cao Ky has promised elections to a constituent assembly in 1966 and to a legislature in 1967. While it is true that the problems of Vietnam cannot be solved by military measures alone, little political improvement is possible so long as Vietnam remains a battlefield. Much the same thing can be said about improving economic and social conditions. What the United States has done in this respect is truly impressive. President Johnson summarized the record in an address in Washington on May 13, 1965. Since 1954 the United States has spent more than $2 billion in economic aid for the 13 million people of South Vietnam. Much has been done in increasing food production, improving health, extending educational facilities, providing housing, and developing industry. The United States has also provided leadership for a Southeast Asian economic development project. Unfortunately, however,

[5] *Report on Indochina*, October 15, 1954. Printed for the use of the Senate Committee on Foreign Relations.

American Policy

progress is difficult amidst the ravages of war, and many of the advances have been nullified.

Although the conditions for American-style democratic elections clearly do not exist in South Vietnam, reconciliation of the opposed internal political factions—including the insurgent Vietcong—would appear to be imperative. The planned 1966 and 1967 voting may well be an important step in this direction. A political response is necessary to a political problem—and a Vietnamese response to a Vietnamese problem. At the same time, however, it would be most unwise to expect the Communists to lay down their arms at an early date, and some American military help may be needed for a long time to come (as British assistance was required in the insurgency situation in Malaya in the 1950s).

Until 1965 the United States said pointedly that American military men were in Vietnam only as advisers to the South Vietnamese government and armed forces. But even as "advisers" they became increasingly involved in the mounting hostilities. As the role of the American soldier changed, the United States was forced to admit more substantial U.S. participation in the war. Even as late as June 1965, however, a White House statement asserted that the primary mission of the American troops was to secure and safeguard important military installations like air bases. U.S. forces, it was stated, had the related mission of patrol and security activity in and near the areas so safeguarded. If help were "requested by appropriate Vietnamese commanders, General Westmoreland (United States military commander in South Vietnam) also has authority within the assigned mission to employ these troops in support of Vietnamese forces faced with aggressive attack when other effective reserves are not available and when, in his judgement, the general military situation requires it."

The degree of the war's escalation in 1965 can be partly measured by the fact that, as 1966 dawned, a combined American-Australian military operation—of sizable proportions—was mounted without Vietnamese participation (and without Vietnamese knowledge until the very last moment). American bombing raids against North Vietnam had been inaugurated in February and, when suspended in late 1965 as part of President Johnson's peace offensive, had not apparently moved the Ho Chi Minh regime any closer to the conference table. The number of American fighting men in Vietnam had increased tenfold in 1965—from about 20,000 to nearly 200,000 and to more than 255,000 by mid-1966—exclusive of personnel on naval vessels in and near Vietnamese waters (or the crews flying bombing raids from Thailand, Guam and other locations). Communist control of South Vietnamese territory nonetheless expanded during the period of this major American buildup to a point where only 10 percent of the territory nominally governed by the Saigon regime was under its effective jurisdiction. There were reports that the size of the American military forces in Vietnam would be nearly doubled before 1967.

The present dimensions—and promised buildup—in American forces in Vietnam raises serious questions concerning the propriety of the American response to the problem at hand. The French were unable to defeat a political movement by military means in Vietnam. What reason is there to believe that more American soldiers will accomplish the feat? The answer, of course, is that there is no reason at all for such a belief. And there is also no reason to believe that the American government by mid-1966 had any illusions in this respect. The problem remained, however, of how to end the war. The United States response seemed to be a steadily increased military pressure on Hanoi to make it realize how costly prolongation of the conflict could be. The pressure was lessened with the suspension of American bombing raids as 1965 gave way to 1966 and President Johnson dispatched peace emissaries literally to the four corners of the globe to see if there was any evidence that the North Vietnamese were any more ready to negotiate a settlement than they had previously seemed to be. Various nations and leaders were urged to press upon the North Vietnamese (and their allies) America's determination to push the war if the Communists would not negotiate.

The United States was not the only nation giving aid to South Vietnam, however. Twenty-nine other countries were contributing non-combat aid, three had sent troops, and another was planning in late 1965 to do so. Australia, New Zealand and South Korea had contributed combat forces, and the Philippines was preparing to do so in 1966 in anticipation of approval by its congress. But all of the aid by these countries came to only a small fraction of the contribution by the United States which in 1965 amounted to $6 billion a year, including all the costs of supporting the huge American military contingent in Vietnam.

It is not likely that the United States will get substantial assistance from others. Britain carries a heavy load in the region in the aid it is giving Malaysia to repel Indonesian confrontation. The British Labor government is supporting American policy in Vietnam, but this policy is unpopular with the left-wing of the party. Nor can any help be expected from France. Of all the former colonial powers in the region, France has most completely withdrawn from Southeast Asia. The French withdrawal occurred under such tragic conditions that it would be strange if it had left no emotional scars. President de Gaulle gave some evidence of this ten years later at a news conference. He indicated bitterness at the supplanting of French by American influence in Vietnam. When the French withdrew, "the Americans arrived, bringing their aid, their policy and their authority." He continued with sharp comments on the American policy: "The United States, in fact, considered itself as being invested throughout the world with the burden of defense against communism. Since South Vietnam was running the risk of it, as the regime established in the north was aimed at imposing itself there, Washington wanted to put this state in a position to protect itself. It can be added, without any intention of being derogatory, that their conviction of fulfilling a sort of vocation, the aversion which they had to any colonial work which had not been theirs, and finally the natural desire in such a powerful people to ensure themselves of new positions, determined the Americans to take our place in Indochina."

General de Gaulle gave a version of the late President Diem's difficulties which differs markedly from American views, official or otherwise. Diem had placed himself in the "orbit of Washington," particularly in the fields of defense, economy and administration, and, when this policy became more and more unpopular, he tried to disentangle himself from it, "while the Americans began to have their doubts about him." "Then a military *putsch* removed the President and gave him a successor. After that a new *putsch* invested another one, the latter closely linked with the war action which the United States is supporting, staffing, financing, and arming."

This is a harsh and unfair interpretation of American motives and policy in Indochina, but it contains enough truth to hurt. De Gaulle urges a return to the 1954 conference, the neutralization of Cambodia, Laos and Vietnam, and the organization of an "impartial control." "No other road can be visualized which can lead to peace in Southeast Asia." But the French president lays down a practical condition without which the plan would be ineffective. France, China, the Soviet Union, and the United States must be "effectively resolved to be involved there no longer." Is not this too much to expect of China? If the arrangement could work, an important by-product from de Gaulle's point of view would be the enhancement of French influence in the region as the old cultural ties reasserted themselves.

It would be better in every way if an Asian country or countries could fill the power vacuum in Southeast Asia.

Indonesia under Sukarno was ambitious to do this, but if it had succeeded in this effort, the situation might have been worse than ever from the free world's point of view. Prime Minister Tengku Abdul Rahman of Malaysia looks to Japan to give leadership to the countries which are "sincerely Asian at heart." Japan has accepted the obligation to pay over a billion dollars in reparations to the countries of Southeast Asia and has committed itself for another $800,000,000 for a program of economic cooperation. The Japanese government supports American policy in Indochina, though cautiously. But the Japanese people are still in a pacifist mood, and it is not likely that a government will soon come to power that could lead the country to play a major role in power politics. Moreover, bitter memories of the Japanese occupation are still too vivid in the minds of the peoples of Southeast Asia for them to accept leadership from this country. However, Japanese leaders are increasingly concerned about Japan's role in Asia. When Foreign Minister Etsusaburo Shiina was asked whether Japan and Communist China would eventually compete for the leadership of Asia, he answered that "the competition had already begun. . . . Communist China is implementing her efforts to lead on the basis of Communism, Japan on the basis of democracy and liberalism."

India, the second most populous country in Asia and the world, is not likely to enter the competition for leadership in Asia. The partition of the subcontinent has caused the Indians to concern themselves increasingly with neighboring Pakistan, once itself part of British India, which has armed itself specifically in response to the propinquity of a bigger India and which dispatched guerrilla elements into the Indian-ruled portion of divided Kashmir in 1965, setting off fairly large-scale hostilities. Persisting Chinese efforts to seize territory regarded by India as its own, coupled with the state of the Indian economy and the fairly large distance between India and most of Southeast Asia, make it highly improbable that the government of the late Pandit Nehru's successors will play a role in the region comparable to that of China, America, or Japan. Even Nehru's India took a modest view of its responsibilities as chairman of the International Control Commissions set up to supervise the 1954 Geneva agreements for Vietnam, Laos, and Cambodia.

The alternatives confronting the United States in Vietnam are several, and some of these are probably less unpalatable than they once appeared to many Americans. The option of withdrawal, of course, is out of the question. It would be a signal to America's allies throughout the world that the United States would abandon them when the going became rough, an image Washington cannot allow. It is equally unlikely that the United States will be forced out of Vietnam militarily—that is, the Americans have more than enough military capability to establish themselves almost perpetually along the eastern coastal area of South Vietnam. The collapse of the governing apparatus of the state of South Vietnam, on the other hand, is a different matter. Similarly, it is not at all inconceivable that a future Saigon government might ask the U.S. to withdraw. Ambassador Henry Cabot Lodge reportedly told a senate committee that he would not acquiesce in such a demand, but President Johnson denied this. It is difficult to see how we could avoid departing from Vietnam if all the Vietnamese with even limited credentials for representing their nation wished us to go.

American policy at present can best be described as a holding operation. The United States is endeavoring to convince the Communists that they cannot win and must negotiate. The holding action has been in operation for a fairly long period now, however, and it could last much longer. This would presumably mean continuing American preoccupation with Vietnam, partly because it is as big a problem as it is—to the exclusion of sufficient attention to many of the other actual or potentially pressing problems of Southeast Asia. A holding operation of this sort makes sense only if the time bought is wisely used. The American citizen is justified in asking whether this has in fact been the case to date.

The most likely ultimate outcome is some kind of negotiated settlement. Total victory by either side is hardly possible. The question so far, however, has partly concerned the problem of which participants in the conflict should be the negotiators. The Americans have opposed negotiations with the Vietcong. Yet the Vietcong have been the heart of the opposition to the Saigon government. Secretary of State Dean Rusk, however, has said that Hanoi could include the Vietcong within any negotiating delegation it might form.

The United States has been concerned mainly with whether Vietnam, united or divided, comes to have a Communist form of government in the south as well as the north. This is understandable, but should the U.S. be so preoccupied with the political coloration of any country's ruling regime? Should not its concern be more with Vietnam's foreign relations than its internal politics? An America that can live with Yugoslavia and Poland could probably coexist with a Communist South Vietnam, if that were all that were involved. The aim should surely be that of preventing such a Communist state from absorbing adjacent Laos and Cambodia and possibly other nations. This task is in many ways simpler than the one the United States has so far set for itself—the determination of the internal political character of South Vietnam. Simpler in a relative sense, it should be added, but not easy and not necessarily within the power of the United States alone.

Much of the support the Americans have received from other powers in Vietnam has been symbolic. This has political value internationally, but it has not appreciably added to the solution of the Vietnamese problem. What is needed is genuine help and, preferably, Asian help, help of the most broadly based international sort, and help either of an impartial or balanced sort. One approach might be a control commission composed of all the other Southeast Asian countries or, possibly, the totality of the Asian lands. The former alternative would have the advantage of involving the various other Southeast Asian nations—some of whom would be grappling with the problem of defending the region (as contrasted with only themselves) for the first time. An all-Asia control body could not help but include Communist China. But would this be evil in itself? Why is it that Americans fear that the Communists in general and the Chinese in particular necessarily influence others more than they are themselves influenced? Either arrangement could still be backstopped by American military power as well as resort to the authority of the United Nations.

The lesson of Vietnam is a several-sided one. For some, it echoes Secretary Acheson's assertion of 15 years ago that the United States can provide only the missing component, that the will to do something must be present in a people for American help to make a difference. For others, it raises serious questions concerning the ability of an outside power to influence the internal political composition of another country. For still others, it suggests limits to the power of the United States—the political as contrasted with the military power (which, as has often been said, is meaningless except as directed towards obtainable political ends).

This does not mean that the United States has been defeated in Vietnam, or that it will lose. Its staying power as revealed to date is tremendous. It has adapted with surprising skill to changing circumstances. The ultimate Vietnamese solution will bear the mark of the American presence in South Vietnam. And it will probably be more in the interest of the United States than if we had stayed out. That may be all we can hope for.

ARMS AND AID

The drive against Western foreign rule has been practically won throughout most of Southeast Asia; the reestablishment of Western colonialism is unthinkable and impossible. But the peoples of the region have not yet succeeded in establishing strong and efficient—or democratic—governments. Their societies are far from healthy. There is disillusionment, discontent, dissension, corruption, governmental weakness, and inefficiency. These conditions facilitate the penetration of the government by the Communists, who themselves work hard to help create weakness and disorder and then take over as the restorers of order. This happened in China and in North Vietnam, and the big question is whether these Communist successes are going to be repeated in other countries of the region. The discussion of the question of how much the West and the colonial powers have contributed to producing the present situation is no longer profitable. It is necessary to deal with the situation as it is.

It is clear that the advance of Communism in Southeast Asia cannot be checked by military means alone. But the military problem had become so acute by 1954 that it had to be given priority over the economic one with the formation of SEATO. It was even more acute in Vietnam in 1966. Unless the line is held militarily, the West cannot assist the governments of these countries in working out the solution of their economic and social problems. The chief danger, however, is not direct attack but infiltration and subversion, with Moscow and Peking using local Chinese and indigenous persons to spearhead the troublemaking. It has been Vietnamese who are either Communists or support the Communists who have challenged the successive Saigon governments—not Chinese invaders ("volunteers" they were called in Korea!). Likewise, the Communist threat in Malaysia and now-separated Singapore has come from local Chinese whose loyalty lay with Peking or Mao rather than the existing government arrangements and the values and society they represented.

At SEATO's start, Thailand and the Philippines desired treaty forces to be stationed in the area, but the United States would not agree. The Americans wished neither permanent forces nor bases in the area as part of the SEATO commitment, although they maintained both in the Philippines as a consequence of their bilateral military relationship with their onetime colony. A prime problem facing the SEATO powers—and especially the United States as the country with the largest forces available—was that of determining whether to incur the risk of precipitating a global war, with the possibility of atomic warfare, by an attack on China in case of overt aggression by Peking or aggression by another state, say North Vietnam, backed by China. The world—not only Asians—might be shocked at the bombing of China in retaliation for infiltration and subversion in one of the countries of Southeast Asia, it was felt in Washington.[6] A decade later, however—in the middle 1960s—the United States apparently felt less strongly in this respect as it showered Communist North Vietnam with bombing attacks, some very close to the Chinese border. But still China itself remained untouched. The possibility persisted, accordingly, that due to such considerations the great military striking power of the United States might be rendered immobile and thus not deter infiltration and subversion—or even aggression. If China reached the conclusion that the danger of American retaliation against its own soil was not great, it would surely be tempted to risk more local thrusts. It would seem that the only alternative, then, to a war with Communist China, whether supported by Russia or not, would be to become involved again in a local war with

[6] General Maxwell D. Taylor, then army chief of staff (and later American ambassador to Vietnam), expressed the view before the Senate armed services subcommittee that "small wars" are more possible "now that mutual deterrence of atomic weapons has lessened the likelihood of general war." See *New York Times*, July 27, 1956.

American Policy 399

conventional weapons like that of Korea. This also was not a pleasant alternative—as the United States realized as it assumed more and more of an actual combat role in Vietnam halfway through the 1960s.

Southeast Asia is not going to be saved from Communism unless its peoples and governments have the desire and the will to be saved. This will at the moment does not seem to be strong in some lands. But even desire and will are not sufficient; a nation must have the capability to defend itself from Communism, both internally and externally. The region must be capable of defending itself.

The economic aspect of the problem was succinctly put by a former Indonesian ambassador to the United States, who said: "The future development of the political as well as the economic stability of the world obviously cannot rest on a solid basis when so significant a part of the world as Southeast Asia remains unstable, uneasy, and a source of increasing social discontent. The significance of the danger inherent in the failure of economic developments in Southeast Asia to keep pace with those in other parts of the world has not been fully appreciated by the West. The emphasis of the Western powers has been on achieving a military balance of power. They have neglected the even more basic problem of the balance of power with respect to Southeast Asia. The danger stems from a number of factors. First is a psychological one—the achievement of substantial progress in Communist countries cannot fail to exercise powerful attraction on underdeveloped countries whose rate of progress has not been so rapid. In the second place, a nation which has no sound economic base is vulnerable both politically and militarily because it cannot retain the loyalty of its population when it does not satisfy their basic needs and their aspirations for the future. The consequence of this economic imbalance is to create pressures which may tend to attract underdeveloped countries to a system which, in a similar stage of development, has apparently succeeded in some degree in meeting the problems which they have not begun to solve."[7]

How prophetic these words, spoken in 1954, seemed a dozen years later in the case of the ambassador's own country, Indonesia.

Southeast Asia does not have the capital to finance its economic development, however; its per capita income is so low that little saving or capital accumulation is possible. Capital must come from the outside, which would seem to offer an opportunity to Americans and the United States government to join in fruitful cooperation with these countries, which so badly need technical and economic assistance; the problem is that they are often afraid of it. They fear a return of "colonialism." By "colonialism" they do not mean merely political subordination of their country to another; they mean dependence upon Western countries in any form, whether political, economic, or cultural. As a result of the many years of agitation against what their political leaders called exploitation by foreign capitalists, they have come to regard all capitalism as a hidden form of colonialism. They regard their economies as colonial because they are highly dependent upon the sale of a limited range of export commodities to a few highly industrialized countries. They regard their low standard of living as a phase of colonialism.

Because of these sentiments, governments of several Southeast Asian countries are loath to invite private foreign capital investments. And government aid, to be acceptable, must be without strings attached. It will be recalled that an Indonesian government fell in 1952 after having signed an agreement for economic aid from the United States in the amount of only $8,000,000, because the agreement contained a mild clause linking Indonesia with the free world. During the early years of the Indonesian republic the Americans contributed loans and grants in the amount of $200,000,000; in

[7] Ambassador Mukarto Notowidigdo speaking before the American Indonesian Chamber of Commerce in New York, January 14, 1954.

1964, however, President Sukarno told the United States, "To hell with your aid," and American assistance was subsequently discontinued. Burma had been the first Southeast Asian country to terminate American economic aid in 1953—because we supported Chinese Nationalist guerrillas on Burmese soil near the Chinese border. Aid was later resumed on a modest level. The Philippines and Thailand, members of SEATO, and Laos and South Vietnam receive large amounts of assistance, but Cambodia demanded an end to American aid in 1965. In the Cambodian election campaign of 1955, Prince Norodom Sihanouk was charged by his opponents with having sold his kingdom to the United States in a secret treaty granting the latter military bases in Cambodia. Sihanouk nonetheless won a resounding victory, but since then he has taken a neutralist line and, most recently, an outright hostile position towards the United States. Malaysia, greatly aided by Britain, has never received more than modest economic assistance from America.

SUMMARY AND PROSPECTS

It would be very short-sighted not to recognize the possibility—the very real possibility—that the 200,000,000 people of Southeast Asia could be lost to the Communist group of countries in the years or decades that lie ahead. This would be a loss which would come near to tilting the balance of power against the free nations in Asia. The United States as the leader of the community of free countries must do all that it can to prevent this from happening, not simply out of national pride or out of a desire to win a victory over a rival or an enemy, as some Americans appear to think, but because of the consequences this loss would bring to Asia, America, and the world.

This is not to say that Southeast Asia is indispensable to the survival of a free America—that, pursuing a style of logic comparable to the indefensible "domino theory," American security will be immediately and drastically threatened by new gains by the Communists in Southeast Asia (or even the establishment of Communist governments in all of the Southeast Asian countries). The United States will survive such eventualities, but it will survive in a different kind of world. The American government played the major role in establishing the United Nations, a body that represents the attempted international institutionalization of our political values, because it recognized the interdependence of man and the necessity to cooperate towards solving the world's problems instead of fighting over them. Aid was given to Western Europe and subsequently to Southeast Asia and other areas in the same spirit. America clearly has obligations towards the world at large, and Southeast Asia is part of that world. These obligations cannot be abandoned.

At the same time it must be recognized that the United States is only one of more than 125 nations which exist in the world today. The immediate postwar years, the years of alleged bipolarity between the Americans and the Russians, left many persons in the United States, including some of the country's leaders, with the belief that their republic could decisively influence events in all of the far corners of the globe. Americans are today discovering that there may be limits even to their power and influence. The fact is that the United States has still not been able to accomplish what it started out to do back in the 1950s in Vietnam when it became the political champion of the late President Ngo Dinh Diem. The United States attempted to help establish a particular kind of political order in South Vietnam, and almost each year since then has seen this goal more distant. Likewise, we failed to make Laos the kind of "anti-Communist bastion" envisioned by Secretary of State Dulles.

Years of wooing President Sukarno in Indonesia proved immediately fruitless. But was the effort wasted in the long run? When the Communists made their move in Indonesia on October 1, 1965, and the anti-Communists responded with vigor, perhaps the United States was fortunate in having so little influence in the country and such low-level representation. We were not accordingly tempted to help our friends. The Indonesians righted their system by themselves, something perhaps which only they could do. And yet surely America played a role in the whole affair, however indirectly. That is to say, some Indonesians knew that if they could ever make a change in their system, they could subsequently count on economic and other kinds of help from the United States.

There is a parallel here with America's Second World War relations with Thailand that ought not be overlooked. The Thai declared war on the United States in December 1941, but we wisely refused to acknowledge that act. The Thai people were our friends, we said; we could not make war against them. This made it infinitely easier to resume friendship with the Bangkok government with Japan's defeat and the end of World War II. There was, in short, an American interest and concern to keep alive the hopes of those Thai during the years of estrangement who sympathized with the kind of world we sought. Similarly, there were Indonesians during the years of Sukarno's drift in the direction of pro-Communism who were encouraged by the American presence in the Philippines, Thailand and other countries in Southeast Asia. Americans in the early postwar years of new-found world leadership were a less than ideally patient people in international politics. They still leave much to be desired in this respect, but they are improving. Even in Vietnam today there is not the same kind of impatience that the Korean stalemate provoked. The one thing the United States probably is not going to do in South Vietnam is to quit and get out.

The lesson of the Indonesian situation, however, is that there are beneficial things that can happen without American interference that might be impossible in the event of such intervention. That is to say, the tide of history is by no means running against the United States and the values it represents. The Communists postulate a wave of the future that is on their side—and some of their loudest adversaries in the United States seem to delight in proclaiming the number of "free peoples" who have allegedly "fallen to Communism since the start of World War II." The fact of the matter is that probably more people are freer today politically and in other respects—relatively speaking—than at any time in the world's history. The United States, in short, can afford to wait—it cannot afford to panic. In a very real sense America panicked into its present involvement in Vietnam, a degree of involvement that is probably no less regretted by Secretaries McNamara and Rusk than most other Americans.

There is another lesson to be learned from recent experiences. And this is that there are limits to American power in that part of the world. We cannot control the shape of events in all the countries of the area, and there is no reason why we should expect to do so. This is not the same, however, as saying that we have failed in Southeast Asia and that we ought to give up altogether trying to influence what happens in the region. To be sure, the situation from the point of view of American objectives has not improved since peace seemed to come to Indochina in 1954. Cambodia and Burma have governments that are more distant than ever from Washington—more influenced than ever by Peking. The war goes badly in Vietnam, and Laos and Cambodia seem more threatened than they were a decade ago. There are some bright spots, however, such as the seeming drift away from Communism in Indonesia since late 1965, but the dust has really yet to settle in that country—and it may be premature to state that a new beginning is at hand in that most important of Southeast Asian nations. Surely the surprising thing is not the limits to American influence in this highly volatile part of the world but the degree to which the American presence is in fact felt—particularly in the

American Policy

Philippines, Thailand, Malaysia, Laos, and certainly Vietnam. Southeast Asia is a half a world away from the United States—and is still imperfectly understood by even the most informed Americans—and yet no other power has had so much impact upon the region in the last two decades.

Ours is a world of change unparalleled in human history, a fact which might well cause many persons to fail to keep pace with it. In a curious way America's hopes have tended in the opposite direction. We have anticipated political stability, democracy, economic development, and, last but by no means least, friendship for ourselves—when we really had no reason realistically to expect any of these things. We hoped, and we too quickly believed that we had failed when our frequently unrealistic hopes did not materialize, and the world continued at its own headlong pace.

Mohammad Hatta, Indonesia's first vice president and one of the earliest political figures to break with Sukarno, stated shortly after that break that what most new nations needed before anything else was stability. A government needed to exist before that government could be liberalized. It probably is not necessary that such a government be elected in classic democratic fashion—Cambodia's Norodom Sihanouk is a very popular dictator as is the Vietnamese Communist Ho Chi Minh. The United Arab Republic's Nasser and Pakistan's Ayub Khan are other popular leaders who could hardly be considered as democratic leaders. Yet they are popular—in a way in which South Vietnam's Ngo Dinh Diem was never popular and Nguyen Cao Ky is not popular today. And this is, more than anything else, an internal matter, a matter a people must be able to handle for themselves—something which a foreigner can almost never do for them. The fact is that President Diem relied too heavily on the Americans, not enough on other Vienamese, to retain himself in power. General Phoumi Nosavan, onetime chief hope of the Central Intelligence Agency in Laos, failed to succeed for the same reason; CIA and his Thai uncle, Field Marshal Sarit, favored him, but few Laotians did. The sooner the United States abandons its self-appointed role as kingmaker in Southeast Asia, the better it will be for the leaders and peoples of the area and the United States itself.

This is not to say that the United States should not seek to help the countries of Southeast Asia—if they wish help!—politically and in other ways. Kingmaking is one thing—helping a recognized national leader discharge his responsibilities quite another. The United States has extended considerable technical assistance in the public administration field—little in the area of political leadership. There are several reasons for this. For one thing, techniques of political leadership usually arise out of a particular culture and are not easily transferable. Also some political leaders appear to be good political leaders (as contrasted, say, with being good administrators or good problem-solvers) when they really are not—for example, Sukarno of Indonesia or Burma's U Nu. Finally, helping a leader to lead involves a foreign country in a truly sensitive area, and, quite frankly, probably only the late President Ramon Magsaysay ever really sought our help in this respect. But there is no reason why we should not try to help, if our aid is asked, in this regard—so long as we realize that basically the problem of political leadership is a domestic one.

American economic aid has probably proved its worth in several respects—and in several settings—in Southeast Asia. Thailand is probably the most outstanding example of what foreign economic help can do for a country. Much also was done for South Vietnam in the second half of the 1950s—so much in fact that this was one of the contributing factors in the new Communist resort to insurrection. There is danger, however, that Southeast Asians and Americans, too, will become discouraged with the slow progress in economic development, especially in the early stages. Great gains cannot be expected at once, or even very soon, from economic or technical aid. Once the groundwork has been laid, however, and particularly once attitudes have undergone change, innovations will come easier, and there may be progress. Whether there actually will be enough progress is another matter. Population growth runs as high as 3 percent a year in the area, and it is not assurred that industrialization and other dimensions of development can outstrip this growth rate—especially when the population growth is already underway and economic development is only now beginning.

The basic American problem in dealing with Southeast Asia, however, may be one of communication. In the immediate postwar years the nationalist leaders of Southeast Asia sorely sought American help in their anti-colonial struggles against the Dutch and the French in particular. We did not hear their cries or, if we did, we chose to ignore them. For their part, these leaders—and some of the very same leaders are still around (like Sukarno and Ho Chi Minh)—did not, and probably could not, understand why we failed to seek their friendship through support of their efforts to throw off the chains of colonialism. The story has been in a sense reenacted again and again through the years. We have rarely been able to communicate to various leaders why we were doing what we were doing, and they have been no more successful in conveying their aspirations and intentions to us.

This was in part caused by a mutual lack of understanding. It also reflected an absence of enough competent politicians and other government personnel in this country genuinely interested in Southeast Asia—as other Americans understood, and were interested in, Britain or Germany or Japan. It is open to serious question, for example, how well President Johnson and Secretary McNamara today understand the problem that is Vietnam. Sukarno was always an enigma to most American leaders, for one thing. The fact is that

America is not well stocked with talent when it comes to leaders and administrators qualified to deal intelligently with Southeast Asia. Our present ambassador to South Vietnam, Henry Cabot Lodge, greeted the March 1966 compromise to hold elections in that country with the observation that voting was always "fixed" in this part of the world and dominated by politics by assassination. This was the kind of patronizing statement that only too many Americans have made through the years—and a statement that lacked factual justification. How can the United States deal intelligently with problems like the Vietnamese elections under such circumstances?

It must be said, however, that our leaders have frequently shown great insight into the problems of Southeast Asia and that some of our overseas representatives are of the highest quality, but the insight has been insufficient and too many mediocrities represent us in that part of the world. This in part accounts for our frequent lack of policy towards particular Southeast Asian countries or situations. Who can say what our policy was towards South Vietnam in 1964? Did we envisage the buildup in American fighting men that took place the very next year in that country? Was it part of a plan? Or did we blunder into Vietnam without really thinking through the consequences? And, if we did, why did this happen?

This is not to assert that all recent events have by any means been to the disadvantage of the United States in Southeast Asia. We are effectively helping Thailand, Laos and the Philippines, and Vietnam has not yet fallen to the Communists. There have been victories as well as defeats —some of them earned, others gratuitous. But this is the way international politics works. No one wins all the battles. But the informed and intelligent player wins more often than he loses. This, in all probability, is the most the United States can hope for. Southeast Asia, after all, is in China's immediate backyard—and many forces are abroad in the area which we do not yet understand. We have probably more than held our own to date in the area, and we probably will be able to continue to do so in the future. The diplomatic problems facing the United States in Southeast Asia are admittedly difficult, but they are not hopeless.

CHAPTER 12

CHANGE IN THE MAKING

FROM ANY REFLECTION upon contemporary Southeast Asia there emerges one central realization—that of the changing face of this ancient and important region of the globe. The changes, however, are not merely superficial or technological; there are deep and fundamental changes in the aspirations and goals evolving out of the conflict between the cultures of East and West in the minds of Asian peoples. These changes are finding expression in the economies and in both the international and internal political systems of the new nations. Of special interest and concern are the changes which this new situation in Southeast Asia is bringing to the rest of the world.

NATIONAL AND INTERNATIONAL POLITICS

International relations has traditionally concerned principally the relations among the several states of the European continent. The United States is a comparative newcomer to the system—and Japan an even more recent addition. The United States and Japan, indeed, qualified for participation in the system by virtue of their economic, technological and military development along the lines of the senior members among the European countries, who accepted the newcomers, however reluctantly, when they became convinced that the two new powers deserved a place in the traditional elite group. Some of the members of the system were bigger and stronger than others, but they were all comparatively stable nation-states of roughly the same technical attainment.

This was not the case with the Southeast Asian states when they joined the international system, nor is it true of them today. The Philippines and Cambodia possibly excepted, all the countries of this key area of contemporary world politics lack the stability of their counterparts in Europe and North America. Rebellions of various dimensions keep Vietnam, Laos and Burma continually unsettled. Major unassimilated minorities plague both Malaysia and Thailand. Sprawling Indonesia has been the site of politically inspired violence almost from its inception. The Philippines and Cambodia are externally threatened, a fact which counterbalances the stability provided by their relative domestic tranquillity.

The international relations of the Southeast Asian countries are naturally affected by these internal political circumstances. Instability and violence within cannot help but produce disturbed patterns of international relations—both among the countries of the region and with other countries of the world.

Malaysia is a case in point. Malaysia came into being in its present form through basically internal reasons—the numerical relationships among its diverse ethnic groups. A foreign policy of expansion—the absorption of Sarawak and Sabah (as well as Singapore)—was formulated as a means of achieving racial balance. Indonesia's counter-policy of confrontation had roots in the unstable balance of power between the Army and Communists within the country as well as in the need to find occupation for a growing military establishment that might otherwise become a threat to the ruling political elite. President Sukarno also obviously was impressed by the former Malaya's greater prosperity and did not wish to see this rival grow to larger proportions.

Likewise, Laos represented a vulnerable target in the eyes of Vietnam's aggressive Communists in the early 1950s, when they invaded the country to establish the satellite Pathet Lao movement in the northeastern corner of the land—even before they had won their war against the colonial French. Subsequently, North Vietnamese support for the Communist cause in Laos increased. Today well over half of the country is in the hands of the Pathet Lao, a circumstance brought about in large measure by the internal weaknesses of the Laotian nation, which represented a vacuum that could not help but attract Ho Chi Minh and his associates. When Hanoi's physical support of the Laotian Communists was reduced in 1965, this was a reflection of the increasing absorption of the North Vietnamese regime with the civil war in the south and of its reduced capability to aid the Pathet Lao because of American bombing raids north of the seventeenth parallel.

The latter circumstance shows the reciprocal nature of the relationship. External events in a nation's existence almost always have internal consequences. But this is particularly true of nations that are not stable domestically and are fearful of the effects of developments beyond their frontiers upon the goals and interests of their ruling elite. Thailand is by no means the least stable of the Southeast Asian countries, but Thai political development has clearly been influenced not only by the civil war in neighboring Laos but also by the bigger conflict in Vietnam, the allegedly pro-Communist drift in Cambodia's foreign policy, and even the attraction of a strong Malaysia for the Malay minority in its southern provinces. Recently escalated efforts to increase the benefits accruing to the inhabitants of the northeastern part of the nation are reflective of the Thai leadership's fear that their land is next on the Communists' list of countries to be conquered. An already completed constitution is being held back partly because of fears born of this external challenge. The soldiers may stay in power in Thailand because the foreign threat creates a rationale for their continuation.

The failure of the Thai government to promulgate a new constitution and in general to liberalize politics may increase internal dissatisfaction and make the country more vulnerable to foreign pressure. The relationship between the internal and the external must be viewed in terms of such a constantly adjusting equilibrium; changes on either side of the equation can throw the relationship off balance and necessitate adjustment. The realities of the situation may not always be immediately realized, and there will be miscalculations. But it is likely that a balance will be struck in time.

The two most important political faces of Southeast Asia, it will thus be seen, cannot be considered as autonomous. Moreover—and this is what complicates attempts to anticipate future developments in the area—they are constantly changing. Indonesia, for example, underwent major political change in late 1965, when its once-powerful Communist party, previously influential in the ranks of President Sukarno's government, suddenly found itself on the political defensive, its members hunted like criminals by soldiers and citizenry alike. General Ne Win's 1962 *coup d'etat* made Burma, formerly one of the most promising would-be democracies in Southeast Asia, a most rigorously run dictatorship literally overnight. This same swiftness of change can also be perceived in the external politics of the Southeast Asian states. In the late 1950s Laos was touted by Secretary of State Dulles as "an anti-Communist bastion"; in the early 1960s President Kennedy was forced to recognize it as a neutral country. Singapore joined Malaysia in 1963 to combat Communism but strongly attacked the United States two years later and even threatened to offer the U.S.S.R. a naval base on the island.

The internal political instability of the Southeast Asian

states is clearly a source of uncertainty in the international relations of the area. This uncertainty is compounded by the rapidity of political (if not economic) change in most of the countries.

SOUTHEAST ASIA IN WORLD POLITICS

Southeast Asia is of growing importance in worldwide international relations or, stated differently, its constituent countries are increasingly active participants in the global political system. In this worldwide system there are other "new states" which are weak internally, too, and often lack the capability to do many of the things they wish to do in domestic and international affairs. These various new additions to the system—the recently independent lands of Asia and Africa and most of the countries of the Middle East and some of those in Latin America—account for well over half the participants in world politics. This means that a majority of the states which interact in worldwide international relations probably contribute greater instability than strength to the system.

The practical consequences of this circumstance are twofold. In the first place, the older powers are constantly prevented from obtaining various of their goals in international politics in part because of the element of increased unpredictability introduced by the inability of the leaders of the new states to control either their domestic or foreign affairs as adequately as have the European nations. Southeast Asia and the other new states are thus a more or less constant source of international instability. This weakens the system—and the benefits, including protection, which the Southeast Asian countries might expect to draw from their participation in it. Secondly, the weakness of the Southeast Asian lands makes them more than ordinarily sensitive to various pressures emanating from other parts of the world. Proposals for an Asian common market, for

Change in the Making

example, have generally fallen on deaf ears in Southeast Asia because of the fear that membership in such an association with Japan could not help but result in a subordinate position for the less industrialized countries—that is, themselves.

From the point of view of the policy-maker in Washington or London this situation has both advantages and disadvantages. Unfortunately, only too many commentators are more inclined to stress the disadvantages than the ways in which the advantages might be exploited. If it is true that the weaknesses of the several Southeast Asian states make them particularly vulnerable to subversion by the Communists or others, it is also true that this same sensitivity to external influence increases the likelihood that attempts by outsiders to help these countries modernize their political, economic and other social systems will succeed. It would be a tragedy if the Communists were able to exploit this circumstance and the free nations were not able to do so.

This raises the question of the relative importance of indigenous and foreign influences upon political development as evidenced by the experiences of the countries of Southeast Asia. If political development is construed in terms of a capacity to govern and a sensitivity to the popular will, however determined, it will be seen from the previous chapters that the evolution of the Southeast Asian countries since independence has been much more influenced by historical factors and re-emergent traditional influences than by the policies of outside powers or even the general impact of worldwide economic forces. To be sure, the United States has so far prevented South Vietnam from falling to the Hanoi-directed Communists, but its influence in Vietnam is generally regarded as inferior to that of these same Communists. The political development of Indonesia, Thailand and Burma also appears to have been primarily influenced by indigenous rather than foreign factors—their political development, that is, not their public policies. British tutelage of the Malayans (now the Malaysians) for independence is probably the most clear-cut example of decisive influence on a country's internal political development in the past twenty years. The Philippines, however, was much influenced by prewar American efforts to plant democratic roots in the colony.

This is not to suggest that the Southeast Asian countries are not subject to influence—and manipulation—by outsiders. It must be said, however, that the United States in particular may be too impatient in expecting early results from its efforts to help others. In Vietnam, for example, Communism is imported; so, too, is the nationalism on which it thrives. The modernization which is the goal of all the leadership elites in Southeast Asia is a process also changing along lines suggested by the experiences of other nations. Southeast Asia, greatly affected socially by Western colonial rule, will continue to undergo alteration under the continuing—perhaps increasing—impact of worldwide forces. But this change is not visible from month to month—not always from decade to decade. The region is nonetheless still changing as a result of its collision with the Americans, the Chinese, the Russians, the British, and others—and may change more in the years that lie ahead.

THE PATTERN OF POLITICAL DEVELOPMENT

The political development of the countries of Southeast Asia since the end of colonial rule has emphasized three trends.

Probably the most conspicuous of these has been the movement away from democratic political forms. Burma, Indonesia and Cambodia have all practically abandoned democratic government—as have Laos and South Vietnam as a consequence of the Vietcong assault. Establishment of a Communist state in North Vietnam was also a setback for democracy. Nor has democracy made any headway in Thailand.

Change in the Making   417

Only the Philippines, Malaysia and Singapore remain democracies two decades after the end of the Second World War. At the same time, however, it should be noted that a very definite popularization of politics has taken place in most of the Southeast Asian lands. The ordinary man seems to count for more politically today than ever before in every Southeast Asian country except Burma. In Vietnam, neither part of which is a democracy, it is the peasant in the rice-field who holds the key to success—or failure—for the Vietcong and the Saigon soldiers. Politics has become more mass politics than formerly, even in the immediate postcolonial years when democracy was so much in vogue.

The Southeast Asian nations have also probably increased their capacity to govern themselves during the last two decades. The mismanagement of major areas of public affairs may seem to imply the contrary, but judgments derived from observation of such mismanagement usually unfavorably evaluate the Southeast Asian governments in terms of the Western model. Looking at their own rate of progress since the early years of independence, however, reveals that most of the Southeast Asian states are doing a much better job today than ever before.

The third accomplishment of the Southeast Asian states since independence relates to problem-solution. Problems still abound in Southeast Asia, and these seem to be more numerous only because of our increasing awareness. The problem of national integration is not being everywhere solved—certainly not in Burma—but progress has been registered in various countries, not least in Indonesia (which President Sukarno held together despite all his other shortcomings). Malaysia, Thailand, the Philippines and Cambodia have all made significant gains in economic development. And education is almost everywhere being expanded.

Most important of all in this respect, increasing numbers of Southeast Asians are coming to think in terms of problem-solving. If this tendency develops, then Southeast Asia may be on the verge of a new era as its several national elites seek to lead their countries to modernity and prosperity.

THE PATH AHEAD

There are tensions in Southeast Asia—within countries and between them—and such tensions can be expected periodically to result in violence, usually of a short-lived nature, as has been the case in the past. On the whole, however, internal circumstances seem to suggest a future in which at least modest—and probably adequate—progress is possible in the economic and social as well as political fields.

Whether Southeast Asia will have an opportunity to experience such a future, however, remains to be seen. For what happens in Southeast Asia is produced in part by the impact of the outside world as well as of local forces. And the outside world is once again intruding upon Southeast Asia. Whatever the motivations underlying the actions of the United States, the American government is clearly attempting to play a major role in shaping the political character of South Vietnam both today and tomorrow. Likewise, there are those who believe that China cannot allow its North Vietnamese ally to be defeated or to make political concessions that would weaken the Communist political position in the strategic southeastern corner of Asia. In short, it may be that external factors will be more decisive in the next twenty years than they have been during the last two decades in determining the development of the nations of Southeast Asia. The countries of Southeast Asia—or some of them—may have all the ingredients of sucessful political growth and stabilization, but whether these factors are allowed free play is something only the future can reveal.

Tomorrow's Southeast Asia could be China's Southeast Asia, although this would more likely come about through the efforts of Peking's southern neighbors to avoid provocation of the Chinese than through classic colonization. The free world, on the other hand, may succeed in its efforts to help the countries of Southeast Asia toward development and stability—and so head off the Communist challenge.

In all probability, however, whatever happens in Southeast Asia will represent some kind of accommodation between outside intrusion and the setting upon which it impinges. This means that tomorrow's Burma will remain Burmese—even as it was in British times. And Indonesia will remain Indonesian, and Cambodia will continue to be Cambodian. For change will not mean total acceptance of foreign values, as too many persons in both of the world's main political camps seem to believe. Nor does it necessarily mean progress, although the signs are hopeful. It means rather alteration and accommodation, and these are indeed taking place in Southeast Asia. The best evidence is the fact that the Southeast Asia of the middle 1960s is not the Southeast Asia of the middle 1940s or even of the middle 1950s—and the difference by the middle 1970s will likely be much more striking. In this respect Southeast Asia surely displays a changing face. Whether for the better—or the worse—remains to be seen.

BIBLIOGRAPHICAL NOTE

THE TWENTY-FIVE YEARS since the Second World War have seen a continuous expansion in the literature about Southeast Asia, especially its political development and problems. No attempt will be made here to provide a definitive survey of this literature, but the more important works will be cited. This should assist the reader who wishes to inquire further about the lands of Southeast Asia and how they came to be what they are today politically. This bibliography will also indicate the many studies upon which the authors have drawn in writing this book.

GENERAL

Probably the best general history of Southeast Asia is John F. Cady, *Southeast Asia: Its Historical Development* (New York, McGraw-Hill, 1964). A briefer and also authoritative work is Brian Harrison, *Southeast Asia: A Short History* (New York, St. Martin's Press, 1954). An outstanding text dealing with contemporary politics is George McT. Kahin (ed.), *Governments and Politics of Southeast Asia,* 2nd ed. (Ithaca, Cornell University Press, 1964). A shorter and topical overview of the region is offered by Richard Butwell, *Southeast Asia Today and Tomorrow,* 2nd ed. (New York, Praeger, 1964). Other good books that treat the area as a whole include Willard A. Hanna, *Eight Nation Makers: Southeast Asia's Charismatic Statesmen* (New

York, St. Martin's Press, 1964); Lennox A. Mills, *Southeast Asia: Illusion and Reality in Politics and Economics* (Minneapolis, University of Minnesota Press, 1964); Robert C. Bone, *Contemporary Southeast Asia* (New York, Random House, 1962); Tillman Durdin, *Southeast Asia* (New York, Atheneum, 1966); Saul Rose (ed.), *Politics in Southern Asia* (New York, St. Martin's Press, 1963); and Amry Vandenbosch and Richard Butwell, *Southeast Asia among the World Powers* (Lexington, University of Kentucky Press, 1957). Two especially recommended more general works which treat Southeast Asia among other areas are Michael Brecher, *The New States of Asia* (London, Oxford University Press, 1963), and John J. Johnson (ed.), *The Role of the Military in Underdeveloped Countries* (Princeton, Princeton University Press, 1962).

INDONESIA

For a scholarly and detailed introduction to this sprawling and complex land, see Ruth T. McVey (ed.), *Indonesia* (New York, Taplinger, 1963). The most authoritative treatment of postcolonial Indonesian politics is Herbert Feith, *Decline of Constitutional Democracy in Indonesia* (Ithaca, Cornell University Press, 1962). The policy of "confrontation" and its consequences are excellently treated in Arnold C. Brackman, *Southeast Asia's Second Front* (New York, Praeger, 1966). A brief but outstanding history is J. D. Legge, *Indonesia* (Englewood Cliffs, Prentice Hall, 1964). A well-written, penetrating journalist's survey is Bruce Grant, *Indonesia* (New York, Cambridge University Press, 1964). A revealing, highly popular book is *Soekarno: An Autobiography*, as told to Cindy Adams (New York, Bobbs-Merrill, 1965). Indonesian Communism is superbly treated by Ruth T. McVey, *The Rise of Indonesian Communism* (Ithaca, Cornell University Press, 1965). A fine history by a ranking Dutch scholar is H. M. Vlekke, *Nusantara: A History of the East Indian Archipelago* (Cambridge, Harvard University Press, 1943). For an excellent perspective of Indonesian Islam during the Second World War years, see Harry J. Benda, *The Crescent and the Rising Sun* (The Hague and Bandung, Van Hoeve, 1956). Prewar political developments are treated in Amry Vandenbosch, *The Dutch East Indies*, 3rd ed. (Berkeley, University of California Press, 1942). The best treatment of the independence struggle is George McT. Kahin, *Nationalism and Revolution in Indonesia* (Ithaca, Cornell University Press, 1952).

MALAYSIA

A good introduction to Malaysia is provided by Wang Gungwu (ed.), *Malaysia: A Survey* (New York, Praeger, 1964). The establishment of the new state in 1963 is excellently described in Willard A. Hanna, *The Formation of Malaysia* (New York, American Universities Field Service, 1964). Also recommended is T. E. Smith, *The Background to Malaysia* (London, Oxford University Press, 1963). A good work by a Malaysian scholar is K. J. Ratnam, *Communalism and the Political Process in Malaya* (Kuala Lumpur, University of Malaya Press, 1965). Among the other good works on Malaysia are Victor Purcell, *Malaysia* (New York, Walker, 1965); J. M. Gullick, *Malaya* (New York, Praeger, 1963); K. G. Tregonning, *Malaysia* (Vancouver, Publications Centre, University of British Columbia, 1965); Robert O. Tilman, *Bureaucratic Transition in Malaya* (Durham, Duke University Press, 1964); T. H. Silcock and E. K. Fisk (eds.), *The Political Economy of Independent Malaya* (Berkeley, University of California Press, 1963); and Lucian W. Pye, *Guerrilla Communism in Malaya* (Princeton, Princeton University Press, 1956).

THE PHILIPPINES

The prize-winning history *Between Two Empires: The Ordeal of the Philippines, 1929-1946* (New Haven, Yale University Press, 1965) provides an excellent introduction to the country. Also outstanding are George E. Taylor, *The Philippines and the United States: Problems of Partnership* (New York, Praeger, 1964), and O. D. Corpuz, *The Philippines* (Englewood Cliffs, Prentice-Hall, 1965). The best survey of the Philippine political process is Jean Grossholtz, *Politics in the Philippines* (Boston, Little Brown, 1964). A perceptive work by an outstanding Filipino political scientist is Remigio E. Agpalo, *The Political Process and the Nationalization of the Retail Trade in the Philippines* (Quezon City, University of the Philippines, 1962). Hartzell Spence, *For Every Tear a Victory* (New York, McGraw-Hill, 1964) is a readable campaign biography of Philippine President Ferdinand E. Marcos. The outstanding economic study is Frank Golay, *The Philippines: A Study in National Economic Development* (Ithaca, Cornell University Press, 1961). A particularly perceptive political study is Mary R. Hollnsteiner, *The Dynamics of Power in a Philippine Municipality* (Quezon City, University of the Philippines, 1963). By far the best and most comprehensive prewar study is Joseph Ralston Hayden's *The Philippines: A Study in National Development* (New York, Macmillan, 1942). A useful survey of postcolonial political development is Robert Aura Smith, *Philippine Freedom, 1946-1958* (New York, Columbia University Press, 1958). A good economic geography is Robert E. Huke, *Shadows on the Land* (Manila, Bookmark, 1963).

VIETNAM

The best introduction to the complicated postwar events in Vietnam is probably Bernard B. Fall, *The Two Vietnams*, rev. ed. (New York, Praeger, 1964). Fall has also collected various of his writings in an excellent anthology called *Viet-Nam Witness 1953-66* (New York, Praeger, 1966). An unusually illuminating work translated from the French is Jean Lacouture, *Viet-Nam: Between Two Truces* (New York, Random House, 1966). Still another especially competent study is Donald Lancaster, *The Emancipation of French Indochina* (London, Oxford University Press, 1961). A good but now somewhat dated paperback is Robert Scigliano, *South Vietnam: Nation under Stress* (Boston, Houghton Mifflin, 1963). Two outstanding paperback collections of articles and documents are Marcus G. Raskin and Bernard B. Fall (eds.), *The Viet-Nam Reader* (New York, Vintage, 1965), and Marvin E. Gettleman (ed.), *Viet Nam: History, Documents and Opinions on a Major World Crisis* (New York, Fawcett, 1965). P. J. Honey has written a good book on North Vietnam titled *Communism in North Vietnam* (Cambridge, M.I.T. Press, 1963) and edited another, *North Vietnam Today* (New York, Praeger, 1962). Another worthwhile study of "the other Vietnam" is Hoang Van Chi, *From Colonialism to Communism: A Case History of North Vietnam* (New York, Praeger, 1964). An excellent survey of the period leading up to the 1954 Geneva Accords is Ellen J. Hammer, *The Struggle for Indochina* (Stanford, Stanford University Press, 1954). The late Ngo Dinh Diem, a central figure in post-1954 Vietnamese politics, is the subject of Anthony Bouscaren's biography, *Diem of Vietnam* (Pittsburgh, Duquesne University Press, 1965). Two recent books by outstanding journalists who have covered different aspects of Vietnamese politics are David Halberstam, *The Making of a Quagmire* (New York, Random House, 1965), and James Cameron, *Here Is Your Enemy (James Cameron's Complete Report from North Vietnam)*

(New York, Holt, Rinehart and Winston, 1966). Halberstam won a Pulitzer Prize for his reporting from Vietnam for the New York *Times;* Cameron visited Communist North Vietnam in 1965.

LAOS

The literature on Laos, so little known to the outside world until very recently and so involved in both intraregional and broader international political competition, is comparatively scanty. The most useful study is Arthur J. Dommen, *Conflict in Laos: The Politics of Neutralization* (New York, Praeger, 1964). A revealing book by a Laotian who has since become one of his country's top leaders is Sisouk na Champassak, *Storm over Laos* (New York, Praeger, 1961). A good, if by now somewhat dated, handbook is *Laos: Its People, Its Society, Its Culture* (New York, Taplinger, 1960). George Modelski surveys the 1961-1962 Geneva Conference on Laos in his perceptive mimeographed study *International Conference on the Settlement of the Laotian Question 1961-62* (Canberra, Department of International Relations, Australian National University, 1962). Documents dealing with Laos (as well as with Vietnam and Cambodia) at the 1954 Geneva Conference are to be found in Allan B. Cole (ed.), *Conflict in Indo-China and International Repercussions: A Documentary History, 1945-55* (Ithaca, Cornell University Press, 1956). John F. Cady treats the French conquest of Laos and the other Indochinese lands in *The Roots of French Imperialism in Eastern Asia* (Ithaca, Cornell University Press, 1954). *The Brinkman* by Desmond Meiting (Boston, Houghton Mifflin, 1964) is a novel dealing with recent political events in Laos (in which the chief participants in these events are only modestly disguised). Joel Halpern has written two excellent monographs for Yale's Southeast Asia Series (Nos. 4 and 5, 1964): *Government, Politics and Social Structure in Laos: A Study of Tradition and Innovation* and *Economy and Society of Laos—A Brief Survey*.

CAMBODIA

Cambodia, like Laos, has had only a very few books written about it. Unquestionably the best of these is Roger M. Smith's highly discerning and objective study of Prince Sihanouk's controversial posture in external affairs, *Cambodia's Foreign Policy* (Ithaca, Cornell University Press, 1965). John P. Armstrong, another unusually objective observer of Cambodia and its politics, has let the assertive Sihanouk tell his own tale in his skillfully compiled *Sihanouk Speaks* (New York, Walker, 1964). Cambodia—like Laos, Indonesia, and Thailand—is also the subject of a Human Relations Area Files handbook. It is titled *Cambodia: Its People, Its Society, Its Culture* (New York, Taplinger, 1959) and is edited by David Steinberg. A concise but valuable historical introduction is Martin F. Herz, *A Short History of Cambodia* (New York, Praeger, 1958). There are also very good chapters on Cambodia in various more general works. One of the best of these—and itself an excellent introduction to the country—is Roger Smith's contribution to Kahin's *Governments and Politics of Southeast Asia*, previously cited. Another such good brief survey is Philippe Devillers' chapter in Rose's *Politics in Southern Asia*.

BURMA

There are several good books on Burma, and their number was increasing until the Ne Win government made travel and research in Burma almost impossible. The most recent of these —and so the most up to date (as well as a perceptive book)—is Frank N. Trager, *Burma's Independence* (New York, Praeger, 1966). An excellent historical introduction is provided by John F. Cady, *A History of Modern Burma* (Ithaca, Cornell University Press, 1958). Dated but still valuable is Hugh Tinker's *The Union of Burma*, 3rd ed. (London, Oxford University Press, 1961). A widely cited and excellent study is Lucian W. Pye's *Politics, Personality and Nation Building: Burma's Search for Identity* (New Haven, Yale University Press, 1962). For a biography of Burma's ranking political leader before General Ne Win took over, see Richard Butwell, *U Nu of Burma* (Stanford, Stanford University Press, 1963). William C. Johnstone's *Burma's Foreign Policy* (Cambridge, Harvard University Press, 1963) is a fine study. Two excellent recent works are Manning Nash's *The Golden Road to Modernity: Village Life in Contemporary Burma* (New York, Wiley, 1965), and Donald E. Smith, *Religion and Politics in Burma* (Princeton, Princeton University Press, 1965). Related to the latter work in its subject matter (and also excellent) is Fred von der Mahden's *Religion and Nationalism in Southeast Asia* (Madison, University of Wisconsin Press, 1963), which also treats Indonesia and the Philippines. The best economic study is Louis J. Walinsky, *Economic Development in*

Burma, 1951-60 (New York, Twentieth Century Fund, 1962). The Burmese Maung Maung has written several books—the best of which is probably *Law and Custom in Burma and the Burmese Family* (The Hague, Martinus Nijhoff, 1963). Still a classic is the prewar *Colonial Policy and Practice* by J. S. Furnivall (New York, New York University Press, 1956), which compared colonial policy in Burma and Indonesia.

THAILAND

David A. Wilson, *Politics in Thailand* (Ithaca, Cornell University Press, 1962) is an excellent overview of the Thai political process. The Thai international position is competently examined by Donald E. Neuechterlein, *Thailand and the Struggle for Southeast Asia* (Ithaca, Cornell University Press, 1965). A good general treatment of the country is *Thailand—A Political, Social and Economic Analysis* by D. Insor (New York, Praeger, 1963). Unusually revealing studies of Thailand's Chinese have been published by G. William Skinner. These are *Chinese Society in Thailand: An Analytical History* (Ithaca, Cornell University Press, 1957) and *Leadership and Power in the Chinese Community of Thailand* (Ithaca, Cornell University Press, 1958). A good description of Thai politics in the 1930s is provided by Kenneth Perry Landon in *Siam in Transition* (Shanghai, Kelly and Walsh, 1939). *Thailand: Its People, Its Society, Its Culture*, by Wendell Blanchard and others, is the Human Relations Area Files handbook (New York, Taplinger, 1958). An excellent geographical work is Robert L. Pendleton *et al., Thailand: Aspects of Landscape and Life* (New York, Duell, Sloan & Pearce, 1962). Another good political work is Joseph L. Sutton (ed.), *Problems of Politics and Administration in Thailand* (Bloomington, Indiana University Press, 1962).

INTERNATIONAL RELATIONS

The number of studies in this field is quite limited. One such work, however—and a very recent one—is Bernard K. Gordon's *The Dimensions of Conflict in Southeast Asia* (Englewood Cliffs, Prentice-Hall, 1966). A more general study than its title suggests, and a very perceptive work, is George Modelski (ed.), *SEATO: Six Studies* (Vancouver, Publications Centre, University of British Columbia, 1962). A very valuable study is A. Doak Barnett (ed.), *Communist Strategies in Asia* (New York, Praeger,

1963). Also excellent is George Modelski (ed.), *The New Emerging Forces: Documents on the Ideology of Indonesian Foreign Policy* (Canberra, Australian National University, 1963). Many of the works cited under other sections of this bibliography deal largely—or to a great extent—with the international relations of the region and Southeast Asia's relations with the principal world powers. Especially recommended in this respect are Brecher's *The New States of Asia*, Brackman's *Second Front in Southeast Asia*, Taylor's *The Philippines and the United States*, Johnstone's and Smith's books on Burmese and Cambodian foreign policies, Fall's various works on Vietnam, and several of the titles listed under Laos. Several journals have carried good articles in this subject area through the years—particularly *Asian Survey*, *Pacific Affairs*, and *Foreign Affairs*. The latter publication has opened its pages to leading political figures—such as Cambodia's Sihanouk—to explain their country's foreign policy views.

THE UNITED STATES AND SOUTHEAST ASIA

A sound basic survey is Russell Fifield's *Southeast Asia in United States Policy* (New York, Praeger, 1963). An excellent collection of essays on the topic is William Henderson (ed.), *Southeast Asia: Problems of United States Policy* (Cambridge, M.I.T. Press, 1963). There are still comparatively few books specifically treating American relations with particular Southeast Asian countries. The best such work is Taylor's *The United States and the Philippines*. Another good volume is Frank Darling, *The United States and Thailand* (Ithaca, Cornell University Press, 1965). Two perceptive but now somewhat dated books are John D. Montgomery, *The Politics of Foreign Aid: American Experience in Southeast Asia* (New York, Praeger, 1962) and Amos A. Jordan, Jr., *Foreign Aid and the Defense of Southeast Asia* (New York, Praeger, 1962). Considerable insight into the origins of United States policies in Southeast Asia can still be obtained from John Kerry King, *Southeast Asia in Perspective* (New York, Macmillan, 1956) and Miriam S. Farley, *United States Relations with Southeast Asia*, mimeographed (New York, Institute of Pacific Relations, 1955). The August 1965 issue of the Indian journal *United Asia* was wholly devoted to American relations with Southeast Asia. The literature dealing with American policies in Southeast Asia, however, is still modest in relation to the importance the United States has recently given to the area.

INDEX

Abell, Sir Anthony, 91
Abdulgani, Ruslan, 40
Acheson, Dean, 368-369, 396
Afro-Asian bloc, 323, 325, 357-358
Aguinaldo, Emilio, 112-113
Aidit, D. N., 58
Alaungpaya, 241
Algeria, 358
Ali Sastroamidjojo, 38-42, 45, 59, 357
Alliance party (Malaysia), 84-86, 95, 102-103
Anawrahta, 241
Annam, 162-167, 201, 221
Anti-Fascist Peoples Freedom League, 245-252, 255-257, 261, 268-271, 341
ANZUS pact, 369
Asian Development Bank, 187
Asian Relations Conference, 351-352
Association of Southeast Asia (ASA), 13, 95, 154, 316, 323, 339, 346-347, 349
Aung Gyi, Brigadier, 259, 262-263
Aung San, 244-246, 249, 255, 341
Australia, 10, 198, 218, 312, 321, 329, 340, 343-345, 352-353, 355, 361, 369, 372, 376, 383, 389, 391
Ayub Khan, 294, 309, 405
Azahari, 94

Ba Maw, Dr., 245, 340
Ba Swe, 246, 249-253, 255, 257, 268-270
Bandaranaike, S.W.R.D., 354

Bandung Conference of 1955, 65, 153, 276, 328, 354, 356-359
Bao Dai, 164, 167, 175
Belgium, 49, 283
Bell Act, 129
Beveridge, Albert, 360
Borneo, 13, 22, 27, 68-69, 74, 88, 92, 93-96, 98, 106, 337, 367
Boun Oum, Prince, 208-212, 214
Britain, 10, 14, 19, 31, 49, 68-69, 71, 77-78, 88-91, 97, 99-100, 164, 172, 178, 186, 211, 236, 266, 280, 320-321, 329, 341, 343-345, 355-356, 371-375, 391, 407, 416, 419; policy towards Burma, 247, 273; policy towards Laos, 211-213, 218-219; policy towards Malaysia (Malaya), 74-77, 81-82, 83-86, 326, 346, 382, 389, 401, 416; relations with Thailand, 280, 283, 286-288, 289-290, 311-312, 314, 316, 318-319; rule in Burma, 239, 241-245, 268, 326, 419
Brooke, Sir James (Raja), 88-89
Brunei, 14, 88-89, 94, 96
Bulganin, Nikolai, 275, 376
Bunker, Ellsworth, 67
Burhanuddin Harahap, 39, 43
Burma, 5-6, 8, 10, 13-15, 18-19, 63, 109-110, 127, 198-199, 212, 281, 283-284, 286, 341, 354-355, 406-417, 419: A.F.P.F.L. split, 249-251; American aid, 249, 273-274, 401; area, 5, 240;

Burma (continued):
army, 239, 251-252, 254-262, 264 271, 273, 276-277, 279, 309-310, 379-380; army coup (1958), 240, 251-254; army coup (1962), 2, 241-242, 258-259; army government of 1958-1960, 253-254, 256, 258-259, 261-262; army government since 1962, 258-265, 268, 271, 379-380; British rule, 239, 241-245, 268; Buddhism, 239-243, 246, 250, 252, 254, 257-258, 262-263, 265-267, 271, 274, 362; Chinese minority, 240, 265, 277; Communists, 246-247, 249, 251, 260, 273; economy, 11, 240, 243, 247, 249, 254, 256, 258, 261, 263-264, 268, 270-271, 275, 305, 307, 325, 327, 329, 332, 345, 364, 369; education, 264-265, 270-271; elections of 1960, 254-255, 257, 269, 271; foreign policy, 272-278, 317, 319, 321, 323-325, 345-346, 373; independence, 244-245, 248-249, 251, 254-255, 257-259; Indian minority, 240, 243, 248, 264-265; insurgents, 239, 241, 245, 247-248, 251, 257, 259-260, 271, 273, 411; Japanese occupation, 239, 241, 245, 247, 249, 253, 311; minorities, 240, 258, 260, 271, 317, 350; nationalism, 239, 243-245, 249, 253, 263; neutralism, 273-275, 305, 307, 325, 327, 329, 332, 345, 364, 369; population, 240-241; precolonial era, 241-242, 259, 268; press, 18, 261-262; relations with Britain, 273; relations with China, 247, 271-278, 317, 333, 355, 380, 385, 404; relations with India, 273, 277; relations with Thailand, 311-312, 316, 336; relations with the United States, 249, 273-275, 326, 330, 380, 401, 404; relations with the U.S.S.R., 273-275, 277, 376; second Nu government, 255-258, 268, 271, 380; socialism, 239, 248-249, 252, 263-266, 268, 270, 352
Burma Socialist Program Party, 260, 262
"Burmese Way to Socialism", 9, 261, 263, 268
Byinnaung, 241

Cambodia, 4-5, 12, 14-15, 71, 154, 166-168, 172-174, 186, 199, 202, 210, 212, 219, 283-284, 318, 341-342, 352, 355, 359, 371-372, 374, 392, 395, 411, 416-417, 419; appeal to the United Nations (1964), 234-237; area, 220; Buddhism, 221, 235; Chinese minority, 227; Communism, 225, 227, 230, 232, 235, 237, 285; economy, 227, 229-230, 233-234; elections, 225; foreign policy, 222, 227-238, 317-318, 321, 323, 325, 345-346, 375, 382, 385, 388, 405; French rule, 162-163, 221, 281; independence, 221-223; Japanese occupation, 221; monarchy, 221-223, 225; national congress, 224; nationalism, 221; neutralism, 229-235, 325, 329, 345, 373, 401; population, 220; provisions of the 1954 Geneva Accords, 204, 228; relations with Communist China, 225, 227-229, 231-234, 238, 316-317, 323, 328, 331, 333, 336, 375, 380, 404; relations with France, 221-222, 233; relations with North Vietnam, 225, 227-228, 230, 236-237, 336, 375; relations with South Vietnam, 13, 221, 224, 226, 231-235, 330-331, 336, 380; relations with Thailand, 13, 221, 224, 226, 228, 232-233, 331, 336, 380; relations with the United States, 226, 228, 230-238, 328, 330, 368, 384-385, 401, 404; relations with the U.S.S.R., 229-231, 236-237; Viet Minh invasion (1954), 228, 371; Vietnamese minority, 221, 227
Cameron, James, 196
Canada, 172, 187, 355
Cao Dai, 175
Ceylon, 246, 269, 353, 351, 354-355
Chen Yi, 299
Chiang Kai-shek, 168, 332, 353, 373
China, 3-5, 11-12, 24, 97, 109-110, 164, 171, 240-241, 258, 284, 307, 310, 321-322, 341, 352, 355, 358, 361
China (Communist), 2, 4, 9, 70-73, 97, 105, 152-155, 161-163, 169-170, 173-174, 186-187, 191, 196, 228, 237, 306, 312, 318, 373, 375-376, 378, 380, 382, 385-387, 396-398, 408; foreign policy, 325, 328, 331-335, 358-359,

Index 431

China (Communist) (*continued*):
361, 369, 376, 386, 392-394, 396, 416;
relations with Burma, 247, 272-278,
330, 380, 385, 404; relations with
Cambodia, 225, 227, 231-234, 238,
328, 380, 404; relations with North
Vietnam, 9, 181-183, 186-187, 191,
198, 211, 368, 386-387, 418; relations with Thailand, 280, 314-315,
328, 339; support of Laotian Communists, 204, 211, 218
China (Nationalist), see Taiwan
Chinese (overseas), 10-11, 15, 361-362, 398
Chins, 240
Chou En-lai, 191, 276, 328, 357
Chulalongkorn, 283, 292, 311
Chung Hi Park, 353
Cobbold, Lord, 94
Cochin China, 162, 165-167
Colombo Plan, 276, 346, 355-356
Colombo Powers, 354-356
Czechoslovakia, 69

Darul Islam, 362
De Gaulle, Charles, 294, 391-392
Democracy, 8, 14, 18, 29, 39, 41, 45, 50-51, 82-86, 108, 120, 123, 125, 130, 138, 141, 143-145, 164, 194, 223, 226, 239, 243, 255-256, 258, 265, 268-270, 273, 282, 285-289, 291, 295, 297, 301, 363, 378-379, 383, 387, 389, 393, 397, 405, 413, 416-417
Democratic party (Cambodia), 222-223, 225
Diem, Ngo Dinh, 174-180, 181, 183, 193, 198-199, 299, 371, 379, 387, 392, 402, 405
Dien Bien Phu, 169, 171
Djuanda, 42-45
Dobama Asiayone, 244-245
Dulles, John Foster, 171-173, 370-373, 376-377, 402, 413
Durdin, Tillman, 176

Eisenhower, Dwight D., 170, 172, 369-370, 377
Elysée Agreements (1950), 168

France, 119, 173-174, 186, 219, 228, 230, 280, 285, 321, 329, 335, 344-345,

France (*continued*):
366, 368, 370-372, 375, 379, 390-392, 406; policy towards Cambodia, 221-223, 234; policy towards Laos, 211, 213-214, 218-219; relations with Thailand, 283-284, 311-312, 314; rule in Indochina, 162-168, 201, 221, 368; war against the Viet Minh, 166-167, 170-172, 198
Free Cambodians, 238
Free Laos movement, 202
Free Thai movement, 287
French Union, 165, 167, 202

Garcia, Carlos P., 135-137, 139, 141, 147, 346
Gavin, James M., General (ret.), 196
Geneva Accords (1954), 166, 170-175, 185, 192, 196-197, 200, 203-206, 210, 212-213, 219, 223, 229, 234, 236, 328, 335, 354, 369-373, 387, 392
Geneva Conference of 1961-1962, 197, 200, 211-215, 217, 335, 345, 375, 380-381
Germany, 139, 329, 371, 407
Goldberg, Arthur, 188
Green, Marshall, 72

Hamengku Buwono, Sultan of Djokjakarta, 36-38, 43-44, 58, 61-62
Hammarskjold, Dag, 70, 207-208
Harris, Louis, 197
Harrison, Francis Burton, 115-116, 119
Hatta, Mohammad, 31-32, 34, 42-44, 62, 405
Hoa Hao, 175
Ho Chi Minh, 161, 164, 166-170, 180-181, 188, 195, 198, 225, 308, 314, 338, 340, 343-344, 368, 381, 389, 405, 407, 412
Ho Chi Minh Trail, 216, 218-219
Honolulu Conference (1966), 192-193
Hukbalahaps, 126, 132-135, 146

Iglesia ni Kristo, 145
Ilocanos, 109, 139
India, 3-4, 153, 173, 186, 213, 219, 228, 233, 240, 242-246, 268, 273, 276-277, 283, 321, 325, 331, 341, 343, 352-353, 355, 358-361, 372-376, 393

Indochina, 4, 119, 164-166, 168, 170, 172, 174, 185-186, 201, 219, 228-229, 236, 283, 286, 336, 341-342, 366-369, 375, 386-387, 392, 394
Indochinese Federation, 165-167
Indochinese Peoples Conference, 237
Indonesia, 3, 5, 9-15, 18, 21-22, 73, 94-101, 109, 127, 148-149, 199, 272, 277, 286, 352-355, 365, 367, 400, 411, 415-417; army, 22, 36-40, 43, 45-47, 51, 54, 56-58, 60-63, 68, 72-73, 105, 383, 411; attempted Communist coup of 1965, 56-62, 72, 105, 325, 331, 337, 402; climate, 22; Communists, 22, 38-42, 44, 46-47, 51, 54-63, 68, 98, 337, 380, 383, 402, 404, 411, 413; "confrontation", 2, 4, 47, 67-69, 74, 80, 95-106, 154, 316, 322, 337-338, 350, 355, 358-359, 382, 391, 411; constituent assembly, 40-41, 45, 52; constitution of 1945, 45-46, 51-52; Dutch rule, 10, 24-30, 75, 114, 119, 366, 369, 383; economy, 23, 26-27, 38, 43, 47-50, 58, 59, 68, 101, 102, 105, 127, 305, 307, 364, 365, 383; education, 1, 28, 53, 55; elections of 1955, 38-41, 45; federalism, 27, 32-34, 36; foreign policy, 35-36, 51, 63-73, 104-107, 317, 319, 321-333, 337, 339, 343-350, 358, 373; "gotong rotong" parliament, 45-46; "guided democracy", 41-42, 45-48, 51, 101, 379; Japanese occupation, 30-31; national council, 41-42, 46; National Front, 45; nationalism, 30, 40, 47, 50, 54; overseas Chinese, 24, 49; Pantja Sila (Five Principles), 50-51; parliament, 37, 39, 41-42; 45; population, 5, 22, 25, 27, 31, 35, 49-50; press, 45, 55; provisional constitution, 34, 39, 52; Provisional Peoples Consultative Congress, 45, 61-62; rebellion of 1958, 43, 47-48; relations with Communist China, 38, 70-73, 105, 322, 324, 331, 333, 358-359, 380, 383; relations with North Vietnam, 338-339, 343-344; relations with the Netherlands, 36-37, 49, 63-67; relations with the United Nations, 68-71, 322-323, 325, 332, 359; relations

Indonesia (*continued*):
with the United States, 35-36, 67, 71-73, 325, 330, 367-368, 377, 382-384, 400-403; relations with the U.S.S.R., 44, 66, 70, 99, 376; religion, 24, 50-51, 54, 57; resources, 23; Round Table Agreement, 32-33, 35, 51, 63-66; socialism, 48-49, 51, 53, 54; trade, 23, 30; transportation, 26, 49; war against the Dutch, 31
International Control Commissions, 172, 207, 211, 213, 223, 394
Israel, 266, 329, 352, 356

Japan, 29, 35, 49, 102, 120, 122-126, 128, 139, 152, 154-155, 164, 201, 221, 243, 277, 280, 310, 321-322, 326, 329, 340-343, 350, 352-353, 355, 361, 382, 393-394, 407, 410, 415; occupation of Southeast Asia, 366-367, 393; relations with Thailand, 286-287, 289, 310-312, 316, 319; relations with the Philippines, 155
Java, 22, 24, 26-27, 32, 37, 40, 42, 48-49, 62, 75, 110, 363, 367
Johnson, Lyndon B., 152, 156, 161, 184, 187-190, 192, 194-195, 197, 385-386, 388, 407
Jones, Howard P., 381, 383

Kachins, 240, 257-258, 262
Kantol, Norodom, Prince, 225
Karen National Defense Organization, 260
Karens, 240, 247, 258, 260
Kennedy, John F., 177, 179, 183, 192, 212-213, 313, 413
Kennedy, Robert, 99
Kennedy, Ted, 192
Khmer Serai dissident movement (Cambodia), 226
Khrushchev, Nikita S., 275, 295, 328, 376
Kong Le, 208-210, 215
Korea, 153, 161, 164, 171-172, 174, 211, 228, 312, 344, 356, 369, 371, 386, 398-399
Korea, North, 71, 331, 359
Korea, South, 198, 276, 323, 353, 356, 392

Index 433

Kotelawala, Sir John, 354-355
Kusuma Sumantri, Iwa, 38
Kyaw Nyein, 246, 249-253, 255, 257, 268-270
Ky, Nguyen Cao, 189, 192-193, 198, 388, 405

Lao Dong party (North Vietnam), 181
Lao Issara, 202-203
Lao Thai, 201, 298, 308
Laos, 4-5, 11-15, 166-168, 172-174, 199, 220, 227-228, 237, 258, 271, 283-284, 286, 293, 298, 318, 332, 336, 341, 355, 413, 416; area, 200; army, 205-209, 215-216; Buddhism, 201; Communists, 201-202, 206, 209-211, 215, 217, 219, 380-381; Communist supply route to South Vietnam, 185-186, 216-219, 334, 352, 371-372, 374, 379, 395; economy, 201, 217-218, 380; foreign aid, 205-206, 209-210, 212-217; foreign policy, 204-211, 219, 319, 329, 345, 373, 381; French rule, 163, 201-202; insurgency, 207-213, 215-216, 219, 411; Japanese occupation, 201-202; nationalism, 201-202, 219; neutralists, 207-211, 213, 215, 217, 381; neutralization, 2, 185-186, 197, 204-208, 210, 212-215, 217, 219, 335, 381, 392, 413; North Vietnamese invasions, 202-203, 371, 412; population, 201-202; post-Geneva II developments, 197-198, 215-219; relations with China, 204, 206, 209, 211, 218; relations with France, 204, 213-214, 218; relations with North Vietnam, 204, 206-207, 209, 211, 216-217, 298; relations with Thailand, 201, 209, 213, 312-315, 348; relations with the United States, 205-213, 215-219, 331, 368, 381, 401, 405, 408; relations with the U.S.S.R., 206, 209-213; relationship to the war in Vietnam, 216, 218-219
Lapulapu, 107f, 108
Laurel, José P., 124, 130, 132, 340
Laurel, José P., Jr., 130
Laurel-Langley Agreement, 157-158
Law Yone, U, 261
Le Duan, 198

Lee Kuan Yew, 88, 91, 103
Liberal party (Philippines), 130, 134, 136-144
Lie, Trygve, 70
Lim Yew Hock, 87
Lindley, Ernest K., 176
Lodge, Henry Cabot, Jr., 189, 394, 408
Lopez, Ferdinand, 131
Luang Prabang (kingdom), 201-202
Luns, Joseph, 66-67
Luzon, 108, 111, 133, 139, 146, 363
Lyttelton, Sir Oliver, 84

Macapagal, Diosdado, 95, 99-100, 130-131, 135-142, 144, 146-147, 150, 152-154, 156, 322
MacArthur, Douglas, 126, 367
Magellan, Ferdinand, 107-108, 110
Magsaysay, Ramon, 133-138, 143-144, 226, 406
Majapahit, 24, 101
Malacca, 75-76, 82
Malik, Adam, 61-62, 71, 105-106, 325
Malayan Chinese Association, 84
Malayan Indian Association, 84-85
Malaysia, 4, 7-8, 11-15, 18-19, 71-72, 199, 277, 302, 308, 356, 359, 379, 382, 411-414, 417; British policy, 75-77, 81-86, 92-94, 119, 416; Chinese residents, 76-86, 92-93, 103, 350; communalism, 84; Communists, 77-79, 105; constitutional conference (1956), 85; citizenship, 83; economy, 77, 80-81, 101-102, 337, 364; elections of 1955, 85; elections of 1959, 86; elections of 1964, 95; "emergency", 77-79, 86-87, 344, 389; federal government, 82-86; foreign policy, 318, 323-324, 337-339, 358, 375, 411; formation, 91-95, 349, 382; Indian residents, 76-80, 82-83, 86, 92; indigenous Malays, 76-77, 79-86, 91-93, 102-103, 350; Indonesia's policy of "confrontation", 67-69, 74, 95-99, 101-106, 316, 337-339, 350, 355, 358-359, 382-383, 391, 411; Islamic religion, 76, 80, 91, 365; Japanese occupation, 77-78, 81-82; literacy, 80; Malayan Union, 81-82; "plural society", 80; population,

Malaysia *(continued)*: 79-80, 92, 103; relations with Britain, 321, 334, 346, 382; relations with Thailand, 316, 336, 339; relations with the Philippines, 74, 338-339, 346-348; relations with the United States, 381-382, 401, 405; resettlement program, 78-79; "special privileges", 85, 102; trade, 81; union with Singapore, 87, 91-93
Manahan, Manuel, 136
Manglapus, Raul S., 143
Manila Conference (1954), 153, 345, 375
Manila Treaty, 156, 312-313, 344-345, 372
Mansfield, Mike, Senator, 190, 386f, 387
Maphilindo, 13, 96-98, 153, 339, 346, 349-350
Marcos, Ferdinand E., 6, 130, 138-139, 141, 143, 347
Marshall, David, 87
Masjumi party (Indonesia), 34-36, 39-40, 45, 51
Maung, E, Dr., 273
Maung Maung, Colonel, 258
McMichael, Sir Harold, 82
McNamara, Robert S., 179, 190-191, 404, 407
McNutt, Paul V., 127
Mekong River project, 348
Mendes-France, Pierre, 228
Mindanao, 13, 108-109, 111, 133, 148
Mons, 241
Mountbatten, Lord Louis, 340, 367
Moutet, Marius, 166

Nacionalista party (Philippines), 115, 130, 132, 134-135, 137-144
Nahdatul Islam (Moslem Teachers party), 40
Nasser, Gamel Abdul, 322, 358, 405
Nasution, Abdul Haris, 57-58, 60-61, 73, 97
National Liberation Front, 195, 236-237
National Solidarity Associations (Burma), 256-257
Nationalist party (Indonesia), 34-40, 51, 56

NATO, 155-156, 374
Natsir, Mohammad, 34-35, 39, 43
Nehru, Jawaharlal, 228, 243, 322, 351, 353-354, 356, 358
Neo Lao Hak Xat, 205
Netherlands-Indonesian Union, 32, 64, 66
New Emerging Forces, 71-73, 323, 325, 338, 359
Ne Win, 18, 239-241, 245-247, 250, 252-254, 256, 258-271, 276-278, 300, 309, 380, 413
New Zealand, 312, 343, 345, 353, 355, 369, 372, 376, 391
Ngo Dinh Canh, 178
Ngo Dinh Luyen, 178
Ngo Dinh Nhu, 178, 180
Ngo Dinh Nhu, Madame, 178
Ngo Dinh Thuc, 178
Nixon, Richard M., 370, 377
North Borneo, 88-96, 99, 105, 326, 382
Nu, U, 6, 18-19, 239-242, 244-263, 265-277, 322, 353, 357, 380, 406

Onn Bin Jaafar, Dato, 82
Osmena, Sergio, 115, 117, 124-126, 130
Osmena, Sergio, Jr., 130, 140
Overbeck, Baron, 89

Pakistan, 63, 153, 246, 277, 312, 343-345, 352, 354-357, 372-373, 375, 393
Palar, L. N., 97
Pan-Asianism, 351-353, 357
"Pan-Malay Union", 339, 346
Pan Southeast Asian Union, 342-343
Pathet Lao, 13, 202-207, 209-219, 313, 324, 341, 351, 412
Paul VI, Pope, 186, 195
Pelaez, Emmanuel, 140-141, 143, 153
People's Action Party (Singapore), 87-88, 95, 102-103
People's Progressive Party (the Philippines), 143
Pham Van Dong, 181, 195, 198
Phao Sriyanon, 290-291, 295, 301, 303
Phibun Songkhram, 279, 284-291, 295-296, 301, 307, 309-311, 317, 340-342
Philippine Rehabilitation Act, 129
Philippine Trade Act, 128
Philippines, 3-15, 18-19, 30, 72, 75, 95, 106, 185, 199, 226, 230, 269, 272,

Index 435

Philippines (continued):
282, 417; agrarian unrest, 122-123, 133-135, 146-147; American rule, 107, 113-125, 133, 145, 148, 150, 244, 366, 416; area, 108; as a democracy, 143-145; attitude towards China, 324; Catholicism, 107, 111-112, 145, 148-149, 152; claim to Sabah, 98, 154, 316, 338, 347; Commonwealth period, 116-118, 120, 123, 127, 130; Communism, 126, 132-135, 146; corruption, 132-133, 136-138, 144, 147; economy, 113, 115, 120-123, 124-135, 137-141, 145-149, 156-158; education, 28, 119, 121, 134, 140; election of 1946, 126, 130; election of 1949, 132, 137; election of 1953, 134, 144; election of 1957, 135-136; election of 1961, 136-137, 141, 144; election of 1965, 130-131, 137-139, 141-143, 146-147, 153; foreign policy, 99-100, 149-159, 319, 322-324, 329, 342, 364, 374, 391, 398; independence, 115-117, 119, 123, 125-130, 137, 142-144, 146-149, 152; interest groups, 144-145; involvement in Vietnam, 152-153, 156; Japanese occupation, 120, 122-126, 130, 133, 156; land reform, 134-136, 138, 147; law and order, 125, 138, 147-148; military relations with the United States, 129, 151-152, 155-158, 330, 344-348, 368-369, 373, 398, 408; Moslem minority, 109-110, 148; nationalism, 111-114, 116, 151, 154, 157-158; opposition to Malaysia, 95, 97, 99-100; "parity", 128-130, 157-158; population, 5, 146; pre-Spanish times, 109-110; press, 18, 143; relations with Indonesia, 151, 153-154, 322, 339; relations with Japan, 155; relations with Malaysia, 74, 99-100, 153-154, 316, 338-339, 346-348; relations with Taiwan, 154-155; relations with Thailand, 153-154, 316, 339; relations with the United States, 9, 100, 126-130, 132, 151-152, 154-159, 228, 273, 321, 323, 330-331, 334, 342, 344-345, 369, 385, 401; revolt against Spain, 112, 117, 148; Spanish rule, 107-108, 110-112, 148,

Philippines (continued):
151, 242; trade relations with the United States, 117, 121-122, 126-130, 156-158, 360
Phin Chunhawan, 290
Phoui Sananikone, 206, 208
Phoumi Nosavan, 208-210, 214, 217, 405
Phumiphon Adunyadet, King, 281, 292, 295
Poland, 172, 199, 395
Portugal, 74-75, 107
Pote Sarasin, 297, 313
Praphas Charusathien, 296-297, 299-301, 306
Prawiranegara, Sjafruddin, 43-44
Pridi Banomyong, 285, 287-289, 295, 341-342
Progressive party (Philippines), 136

Quezon, Manuel, 115, 117-118, 121-122, 124-126, 130, 149-150, 339
Quinim Pholsena, 215
Quirino, Elpidio, 131-134, 137, 139, 147, 343, 353

Rahman, Tengku Abdul, 85-87, 91-93, 96-98, 103-104, 337, 346, 393
Raffles, Sir Stamford, 75
Raschid, U, 256
Razak, Abdul, 106
Recto, Claro M., Senator, 150, 153
Regional integration, 9, 13, 95-96, 312-314, 316, 320-323, 331, 333, 338, 350
Ridgeway, Matthew, 376
Rizal, José, 112
Romauldez, Daniel, 139
Romulo, Carlos P., General, 150, 343
Roosevelt, Franklin D., 116, 126, 171, 366, 369
Roxas, Gerardo, 130
Roxas, Manuel, 126, 129-131, 133-134, 141, 143, 149
Rum, Mohammed, 344
Rum-Van Royen Agreement, 32
Rusk, Dean, 189-191, 313, 395, 404

Sabah, 12, 68-69, 74, 89-90, 93-98, 104, 154, 316, 337-338, 347, 349, 375, 382, 411; absorption into Malaysia, 90,

Sabah *(continued)*:
  93-95, 98, 154; Indonesian minority, 105
Sakdalistas, 123, 133
Sangkum Reastr Niyum (Peoples Socialist Community) (Cambodia), 224-226
Sarawak, 12, 68-69, 74, 88-91, 93-96, 98, 104, 337, 347, 349, 375, 382, 411; absorption into Malaysia, 93-95, 98
Sarit Thanarat, 209, 213, 290-297, 300-301, 303-304, 306, 309-310, 315-316, 322, 337, 406
Savang Vatthana, King, 210, 212
Saw, U, 246
SEATO, 13, 93, 152-153, 156, 213-214, 228, 230, 312-315, 323, 327, 329, 333, 344-349, 372-377, 386, 397-398, 401; and Laotian crisis, 213-214, 297, 312
Sein Win, U, 261
Seni Pramoj, 287
Shans, 13, 240, 258, 260-261, 280, 286
Shastri, Lal Bahador, 355
Shiina, Etsusaburo, 393
Sihanouk, Prince Norodom, 6, 19, 221-234, 267, 315-316, 330, 333, 336-337, 375, 379, 384-385, 401, 405
Siho Lanpouthacoul, 217
Singapore, 2, 7, 10, 14-15, 18, 68, 74-75, 78-79, 81, 83, 86-88, 98, 101, 199, 347, 349, 356, 375, 382, 411, 413, 417; British policy towards, 86-87, 92-94, 104, 326; Chinese residents, 79, 86-87, 90, 102, 307; Communism, 97, 102; economy, 81, 104; elections of 1959, 88; formation of Malaysia, 93-95, 411; Indian residents, 79; internal security, 87-88; internal self-government, 87-88; Malay residents, 79, 102; ouster from Malaysia, 103-104, 379, 382; population, 79-92; referendum of 1962, 94-95; socialism, 87; trade, 102-104; union with Malaya, 87-88, 91-95
Sisavong Vong (King), 202
Sisouk na Champassak, 217
Socialist party (Burma), 249-250
Socialist party (Indonesia), 45
Souphanouvong, Prince, 202, 205, 214, 219, 341

South Asia, 352-356
Southeast Asia League, 340-341, 343
Souvanna Phouma, 205-206, 208-210, 214-219
Spain, 10, 19, 113; rule in the Philippines, 107-112, 133, 148, 242
Subandrio, 46, 54-55, 67, 96, 153
Sudjarwo, 101
Suharto, 61, 105, 337
Sukarno, 6, 19, 21-22, 31-32, 36-39, 41-48, 50-66, 68, 70-73, 95-100, 103-105, 123, 150, 153-154, 266, 316, 322-324, 330-331, 333, 337-338, 343, 359, 377-380, 382-383, 393, 401-403, 405-407, 411, 413, 417
Sukarnoism, 50-55, 57
Sukiman, 35
Sulu, Sultan of, 89, 99
Sulzberger, C. L., 191
Sumatra, 26-27, 32, 36-38, 40, 43-44, 68, 76, 367
Suramarit, Norodom, King, 224

Taft, William H., 114
Tagalogs, 109
Taiwan (Formosa) (Nationalist China), 72, 109, 154-155, 274, 312, 315, 373; irregulars in Burma, 274, 401
Tan, Cheng-lock, Sir, 84
Tan, Malaka, 340
Taruc, Luis, 133
Taylor, Maxwell D., General, 179, 183, 398f
"Thai Independence Movement", 298
Thailand, 4, 7, 13-15, 63, 72, 75, 95, 109, 153-154, 184, 189, 217, 220, 223, 238, 240, 258, 260, 272, 322, 341, 352, 356, 416; area, 284; army, 279, 284-286, 288-290, 293, 295, 297, 299-304, 309-310; attitude towards the Vietnamese war, 161, 199, 314-315, 390, 412; Buddhism, 281, 293, 308, 362; Chinese minority, 282, 284, 298, 307-308, 318; Chinese threat, 299; civil service, 301, 303; Communism, 284-285, 294, 297-300, 302, 305-306, 308, 312-315, 318; constitution-making, 294-295, 297-298; "Coup Group", 288-291, 296, 301; coup of 1932, 284-285, 293; coup of 1947, 288-290, 301, 342;

Index

Thailand (continued):
coup of 1957, 291; education, 293-295, 297, 300, 303-304, 306, 309; effects of Laotian situation, 295, 297-298, 312-315, 412; elections of 1957, 290; foreign policy, 280, 283, 286-289, 293, 297, 306, 310-321, 324, 329, 333, 341-342, 344-346, 348, 357, 373-374, 382, 398; Malay minority, 282, 284, 302, 308, 318, 412; monarchy, 279, 281, 283-286, 289, 293, 295; National Liberation Front, 298; northeast region, 295, 298-300, 302, 306, 310, 313, 412; population, 284, 295, 305, 308; press, 18, 286, 291; relations with Britain, 280, 283, 286-290, 311-312, 314, 316, 318-319; relations with Burma, 281, 286, 311-312, 316, 336, 342; relations with Cambodia, 224, 226, 228, 232-233, 281, 312, 315-316, 337, 340, 348, 380, 412; relations with China, 281, 307, 312, 314, 316, 318-319, 324, 336; relations with France, 280, 283-284, 311-312, 314, 316, 318-319, 341; relations with Laos, 201, 209, 212, 213, 281, 312, 348; relations with Japan, 286-287, 289, 299, 310-312, 316, 319; relations with Malaysia, 286, 298, 308, 312, 316, 336, 339, 412; relations with South Vietnam, 348; relations with the Philippines, 312, 316, 339, 342; relations with the United States, 280, 283, 286, 289-290, 299, 311-315, 317-318, 321, 331, 334, 344-345, 369, 373, 379, 385, 401, 403, 405-406, 408; "revolution" of 1958, 292, 294, 300, 309; ties with Shans, 281, 286; United States troops in Thailand, 213, 313-314; Vietnamese minority, 284, 298, 308

Thakin Tin, 250-251, 253, 255
Thakins, 245-246, 248
Thamrong Nawasawat, 341
Thanat Khoman, 306, 313
Thanom Kittikachon, 292, 296-304, 306, 310, 313, 315
Thant, U, 67, 96, 186, 188, 236
Than Tun, 244-245
Thi, Nguyen Chanh, 192-193

Tia Somsanith, 208
Tin Pe, Brigadier, 258, 262-263
Tito, President, 358
Tonkin, 162-163, 165
Tri Quang, Thich, 193
Truman, Harry S., 126, 131, 171, 194, 369
Truong Chinh, 198
Tuomioja, S. S., 207
Tydings-McDuffie Act, 116, 125-127

Union party (Burma), 256-257, 261, 271
United Malay National Organization, 82, 84-85
United Nations, 31, 65-67, 68-71, 86, 96-99, 101, 150, 155, 161, 186-188, 195, 201, 204, 223, 232, 312, 315, 322-323, 325, 331, 353, 355-357, 359, 368, 385, 396, 402; and Laos, 207-208, 276; Cambodian appeal (1964), 234-237; Economic Commission for Asia and the Far East, 353; involvement in the Malaysian controversy, 98-99, 347
United States, 2-3, 9, 19, 30-31, 35, 49, 55, 71, 89, 98, 100, 111-112, 130, 139, 150, 154, 182, 218, 246, 284, 311, 320, 322-323, 325, 328-329, 331, 344, 349-350, 356, 359, 416; and the 1954 Geneva Accords, 204; economic rights in the Philippines, 128-130, 155-158, 331; involvement in Vietnam, 152, 161, 170-175, 178-180, 183-199, 216, 321, 326, 329-331, 333, 335, 368-371, 382, 384-396, 399, 401-408, 415, 418; Johnson peace offensive in Vietnam, 188-190, 195, 386-387, 389-391; military aid to Laos, 206-210, 212, 215-218, 381; policies towards Laos, 205-207, 326, 329, 331, 368, 381, 401, 405, 408-409; policy in Southeast Asia, 360-409, 416; relations with Burma, 249, 273-275, 326, 330, 380, 401, 404; relations with Cambodia, 226, 228, 230-238, 326, 329-330, 368, 384-385, 401, 404; relations with Indonesia, 35-36, 67, 71-73, 325, 330, 367-368, 377, 382-384, 400-403; relations with Malaysia, 381-382, 401, 405; rela-

United States (continued):
tions with the Philippines, 126-130, 132, 151-152, 154-159, 228, 273, 321, 323, 329-331, 344-345, 360, 368-369, 373, 385, 398, 401, 403-405, 408; role in Laotian civil war (1960-1962), 209-213, 381; rule in the Philippines, 10, 107, 113-125, 145, 148, 416; servicemen in Vietnam, 161, 183-184, 188-190, 325, 327, 330, 335, 389-391; trade relations with the Philippines, 117, 121-122, 126-130, 326; troops in Thailand, 213, 313-314

Untung, Lieutenant Colonel, 56

U.S.S.R., 4, 66, 99, 169, 172, 186-187, 207, 210-211, 228, 243, 266, 285, 312, 325, 335, 359, 368-369, 375-376, 378, 380, 387, 392, 398, 402, 416; relations with Burma, 273-275, 277, 328, 376; relations with Cambodia, 229-231, 236-237, 328; relations with Indonesia, 328, 367, 376; relations with Laos, 209-213; relations with North Vietnam, 181-183, 191, 198, 368

Vietcong, 13, 162, 182-185, 191-192, 194-195, 198, 218, 232-233, 235-236, 389, 395, 416-417; use of Cambodian soil, 232-233, 235-236

Viet Minh, 164-170, 172, 174-176, 202, 228, 335, 371

Vietnam, 2-5, 11-12, 14, 18, 72, 109-110, 152, 173, 201-204, 216, 218-219, 225, 228, 237, 258, 267, 293, 306, 341-342, 370-371, 372, 395; area, 162; economy, 162-163; French colonial rule, 162-168; Japanese occupation, 160, 164, 169, 198; nationalism, 163-164, 169-170; overseas Chinese, 163-164; war (1946-1954), 166-168, 198, 284, 335, 344, 390

Vietnam, North, 4-5, 8-9, 11-14, 71, 162, 170, 174, 180-183, 186, 189-191, 198, 217, 219, 225, 237, 277, 324, 329, 331, 333, 335, 338, 352, 356, 371, 381, 387, 389, 391-392, 395, 398, 416; area, 179; direction of Vietcong, 184-185, 190, 386-387, 415; economy, 180-182; foreign policy,

Vietnam, North (continued):
181-182, 199, 321, 336, 338-339, 359; interference in Laos, 204, 216-217, 219, 298, 334, 336, 412; land reform, 181; peasant uprisings, 181; population, 173, 179, 181, 371; relations with Cambodia, 236-237, 336; relations with Communist China, 9, 181-183, 186-187, 191, 198, 324, 334, 339, 368, 386-387, 418; relations with Indonesia, 338-339, 343-344; relations with the U.S.S.R., 181-183, 191, 198, 324, 334, 368, 387; response to peace proposals, 188-189, 195-196

Vietnam, South, 4, 12-13, 63, 72, 163, 174-181, 183-186, 219-220, 227, 234, 238, 286, 298, 299, 332-333, 335, 356, 374, 384-396; area, 174, 179, 191, 198; army, 175, 177, 180, 183-186, 192-194, 379, 392; Buddhism, 178, 193-194, 267; Catholics, 174, 178, 194; Communism, 175-178, 183-186, 192, 194, 198-199, 389-390, 394-396, 398, 415, 418; economy, 174-177, 180, 192, 361, 380, 388; foreign policy, 324, 344; land reform, 176; military coup of 1963, 183-184; peace proposals, 186-190, 195, 236, 386-387, 389-391; population, 174, 179; refugees, 174, 176-177, 191-192; relations with Cambodia, 224, 226, 232-234, 331, 336, 380; war (1960s), 160-162, 179, 183-186, 189-192, 194, 196-199, 334-335, 350, 380, 386-387, 389-390, 397, 399, 403-404, 411-412

Visayans, 109, 139

Vo Nguyen Giap, 169, 198

Wan Waithayakon, Prince, 340
Westmoreland, William, General, 389
West Irian, 26-28, 34, 47, 63-68, 71
Westerling, Captain Raymond ("Turk"), 33
Wilopo, 36, 38
Wilson, Harold, 186
Wilson, Woodrow, 115-116

Young Men's Buddhist Association, 244
Yugoslavia, 276, 329, 358, 395
Yulo, José, 136

www.ingramcontent.com/pod-product-compliance
Lightning Source LLC
Chambersburg PA
CBHW021826220426
43663CB00005B/147